THE THEORY OF LEGISLATION

Introduced by
James E. Crimmins
Huron University College, Ontario

Volume 1

THOEMMES CONTINUUM

The Theory of Legislation

Introduced by **James E. Crimmins,**
Huron University College, Ontario

Printed in England by Antony Rowe Ltd, Chippenham

THE THEORY OF LEGISLATION

I

Jeremy Bentham

Translated from the French of Étienne Dumont by
Richard Hildreth

With an Introduction, Bibliography and Index by
James E. Crimmins

THOEMMES CONTINUUM

This edition published by Thoemmes Press, 2004

Thoemmes Press
11 Great George Street
Bristol BS1 5RR, England

http://www.thoemmes.com

The Theory of Legislation
2 Volumes : ISBN 1 84371 121 4

British Library Cataloguing-in-Publication Data
A CIP record of this title is available from the British Library

Publisher's Note

The Publisher has gone to great lengths to ensure the quality of this reprint but points out that some imperfections in the original book may be apparent.

This book is printed on acid-free paper, sewn, and cased in a durable cloth.

INTRODUCTION

In a recent essay Professor Philip Schofield mounted a vigorous and persuasive defence against several criticisms of the English utilitarian philosopher and political radical Jeremy Bentham (1748–1832).[1] Professor Schofield's approach involved recovering the 'historical Bentham', by revealing the intentions of the philosopher in what he actually wrote in expounding the basic propositions of his utilitarian theory. This 'historical Bentham' is delineated by Professor Schofield utilizing several of Bentham's most important philosophical writings, most notably *An Introduction to the Principles of Morals and Legislation* (1789) and writings on ontology dating from the second decade of the nineteenth century. However, there is at least one other 'historical Bentham' that needs further attention, and this is the legal philosopher who became most well-known to his contemporaries. This Bentham was not the Bentham of the *Introduction* and the writings on ontology, texts little read in the early and middle decades of the nineteenth century, but rather the Bentham of Étienne Dumont's various translated and edited texts, the most important of which are the three volumes of the *Traités de législation civile et pénale* (1802).[2] In 1840 the main parts of the *Traités de législation* were translated into English by the American Richard Hildreth and published as *The Theory of Legislation*. Hildreth published a second corrected edition in 1864, and this is the text reproduced in the present volumes. It was this version of Bentham's utilitarian moral and legal philosophy that

[1] Philip Schofield, 'Jeremy Bentham, the Principle of Utility, and Legal Positivism', *Current Legal Problems 2003*, vol. 56, ed. M.D.A. Freeman (Oxford 2003), pp.3–39. The main issues addressed by Professor Schofield turn around the criticism that Bentham committed the 'naturalistic fallacy' when stating the basic propositions of his utilitarian theory.

[2] *Traités de législation civile et pénale. Précédés de Principes généraux de Législation, et d'une Vue d'un Corps complet de Droit: terminés par un Essai sur l'influence des Tems et des Lieux relativement aux Lois. Par M. Jérémie Bentham, jurisconsulte anglois. Publiés en François par Ét. Dumont, de Genève, d'aprés les Manscrits confiés par l'Auteur*, 3 vols. (Paris 1802).

received the widest distribution in nineteenth-century Europe and the Americas.[3]

I have two objectives in this introduction. First, my aim is to explain the history of the text contained in these volumes. It is a complex story of an edition first published in French by Dumont, but based on Bentham's original writings (mainly in English, but some written in French) from twenty years before, and subsequently re-translated into English a generation after Dumont by Hildreth. Inevitably, the question of authorship arises: whose work is this, and how faithful is it to the philosophy of its originating source? It may be that a definitive answer to these questions is no longer available to us, but a review of the facts may be helpful in settling certain of its dimensions. My second objective is to explain the principal elements of Bentham's theory of civil law as it appears in these volumes. This is the only published work of Bentham's in which his theory of civil law is set forth alongside his more well-known views on penal law. Too often overlooked, an understanding of the civil law component of Bentham's legal philosophy takes us a long way towards reconstructing the 'liberal' characteristics of the utilitarian tradition, a task which has for long depended too much on the weighty presence of John Stuart Mill.[4] The tensions between utility and liberty that often exercise scholars of Mill's thought, find a potential solution in Bentham's theory of civil law. For many in the early nineteenth century, in Europe and the continents of North and South America, this was an important feature of Bentham's utilitarian philosophy as they first came to know it.

Mill famously recorded his own encounter with Dumont's volumes, his first serious study of Bentham's ideas, in his *Autobiography*:

3 This 'historical Bentham' also has a substantial presence in James E. Crimmins and Mark G. Spencer (eds), *Utilitarians and their Critics in America, 1789–1914*, 4 vols. (Bristol 2005).

4 In following this line of argument in the closing section of the introduction I am indebted to the work of Paul Kelly, esp. *Utilitarianism and Distributive Justice: Jeremy Bentham and the Civil Law* (Oxford 1990). Kelly has also mapped out the relationship between the principles of Bentham's theory of civil law and his economic theory and policy prescriptions in 'Utilitarianism and Distributive Justice: The Civil Law and the Foundations of Bentham's Economic Thought', *Utilitas*, vol. 1, no. 1 (1989), pp.62-81. The 'liberal' character of Bentham's economic thought was influenced by his reading of Adam Smith, but he disagreed with one element of Smith's theory – the placing of legal limits on interest rates attached to loans; see Bentham, *Defence of Usury* (London 1787).

> The reading of this book was an epoch in my life; one of the turning points in my mental history... The 'principle of utility' understood as Bentham understood it, and applied in the manner in which he applied it..., fell exactly into its place as the keystone which held together the detached and fragmentary component parts of my knowledge and beliefs. It gave unity to my conceptions of things. I now had opinions; a creed, a doctrine, a philosophy; in one among the best senses of the word, a religion; the inculcation and diffusion of which could be made the principal outward purpose of a life.[5]

Mill was particularly struck by the sections in which Bentham dismissed other modes of reasoning in morals and legislation,[6] and by those dealing with the 'Classification of Offences',[7] which he found 'much more clear, compact and imposing in Dumont's rendition' than in Bentham's own *Introduction*.[8] Such comments underscore the significance of the *Traités de législation* and its subsequent translation in enhancing the influence of Bentham's philosophy.

Dumont's text

In 1802, Bentham's friend, the Genevan reformer Pierre-Étienne-Louis Dumont (1759–1829), published a French redaction and translation of the utilitarian philosopher's writings on moral and legal philosophy, including a selection of hitherto unpublished manuscripts on civil law.[9] Collectively, Dumont's three volumes were titled *Traités de législation civile et pénale*, and prefaced by a 'Discours prélimi-

[5] J.S. Mill, *Autobiography*, in *The Collected Works of John Stuart Mill*, ed. J.M. Robson, *et al* (Toronto 1963– 91), I. 67–8.

[6] See the present edition, vol. I, 'Principles of Legislation', Chs. I–V, pp.4–20. Henceforth Hildreth.

[7] Hildreth, vol. II, 'Principles of the Penal Code', Chs. I–III, pp.239–46.

[8] Mill, *Autobiography*, p.69. See *An Introduction to the Principles of Morals and Legislation*, ed. J. H. Burns and H. L. A. Hart (London 1970), Ch. XVI, in *The Collected Works of Jeremy Bentham*, Gen. Eds. J. H. Burns, J. R. Dinwiddy, F. Rosen, T. P. Schofield (London and Oxford 1968 – in progress). Henceforth writings in the *Collected Works* will be indicated by (*CW*), and references to the *Introduction* will appear as *IPML* (*CW*).

[9] The extant mss. in the Bentham Papers at University College London mostly date from the 1780s, with later additions in the 1790s; see Alexander T. Milne, *Catalogue of the Manuscripts of Jeremy Bentham in the Library of University College* (1937; 2nd edn. London 1962).

naire' in which he clarified his role as an editor and translator of Bentham's original manuscripts.[10] Dumont became acquainted with Bentham in April 1788 in the circle of reformers connected to Lord Lansdowne, by whom he had been employed to tutor his second son. Their association was facilitated by their mutual friend, the law reformer Samuel Romilly, and Dumont's connection with Bentham continued until near the end of his life.[11] In 1788–9 he assisted Bentham in correcting the French versions of several essays he wrote in response to events in France.[12] Shortly after, he translated Bentham's *Panopticon; Or the Inspection-House* (1791), which was printed by order of the French National Assembly and distributed to its members.[13] In the summer of 1792 Dumont embarked upon the formidable task to produce a text which would contain Bentham's legal philosophy in a comprehensive form. Between October 1796 and April 1798 he published a series of extracts from his ongoing work on the *Traités de législation* and Bentham's *Manual of Political Economy* in the Genevan journal the *Bibliothèque Britannique*.[14] The aim of this widely-read journal was to publicise progressive English

10 See the present edition vol. 2, Appendix, 'Preliminary Discourse. By M. Dumont' (translated by John Neal). The contents of Dumont's volumes are detailed in the Comparative Table of Editions and Bibliography following this introduction.

11 On Dumont see Cyprian Blamires, 'Étienne Dumont: Genevan Apostle of Utility', *Utilitas*, vol. 2, no.1 (May 1990), pp.55–70. Blamire cites among his sources Jean Martin, *Étienne Dumont 1759–1829: L'ami de Mirabeau, le voyager, le patriote genevois* (Neuchâtel 1942), Charles Blount, 'Bentham, Dumont and Mirabeau', *University of Birmingham Historical Journal*, vol. III, no. 2 (1952), pp.153–67, J.R Dinwiddy, 'Bentham and the Early Nineteenth Century', *The Bentham Newsletter*, no.8 (1984), pp.15–33, and the Dumont archive at the Bibliothèque Publique et Universitaire in Geneva.

12 See Bentham to Samuel Romilly (2 December 1788) and Romilly to Bentham (3 December 1788), *The Correspondence of Jeremy Bentham* (*CW*), vol. 7, ed. J.R. Dinwiddy (London 1988), pp.17–19. The essays in question are contained in *Rights, Representation, and Reform: Nonsense upon Stilts and other Writings on the French Revolution* (*CW*), ed. P. Schofield, C. Pease-Watkin and C. Blamires (Oxford 2002).

13 *Panoptique, Mémoire Sur un nouveau principe pour construire des maisons d'inspection, et nommément des maisons de force; Par Jérémie Bentham. Imprimé par ordre de l'Assemblée Nationale* (Paris 1791), edited, abridged and translated from Bentham's English mss. by Dumont for the National Assembly in France, and later reprinted, with some revisions in *Traités de législation*, III. 201–72 (1–66 in 2nd edn.).

14 For the details of these publications see *The Correspondence of Jeremy Bentham* (*CW*), vol. 5, ed. A. T. Milne (London 1981), p.200n.

ideas in Europe, and it was through this medium that Dumont first introduced Bentham's utilitarian legal theory to a continental audience.[15] Following the publication of the *Traités de législation* in 1802 Dumont produced four more publications based on Bentham's writings: *Théorie des peines et des récompenses* (1811),[16] *Tactiques des assemblée législatives, suivi d'un traité des sophismes politiques* (1816),[17] *Traité des preuves judiciare* (1823),[18] and *De l'organisation judiciaire et de la codification* (1828).[19] All these texts were published in a single collected edition in 1829–30, together with French translations of a number of other writings by Bentham.[20] None of these texts was a straightforward translation by Dumont. They are commonly called 'redactions' or 'recensions', either edited from the original manuscripts or combining manuscript material with extracts from published works, substantially re-written in plainer language, and often divested of the cumbersome detail characteristic of Bentham's writing.[21] In this form Bentham's ideas reached a substantially larger audience than would have been possible without Dumont's assistance. As important as each of these texts were in popularising Bentham's philosophy, none was as significant as the *Traités de législation*.

15 Blamires, 'Étienne Dumont: Genevan Apostle of Utility', p.64.

16 *Théorie des peines et des récompense. Par M. Jérémie Bentham, jurisconsulte anglois, rédigée en Français d'aprés les manuscits. Par Et. Dumont*, 2 vols. (Londres 1811); first published in English as *Rationale of Reward* (London 1825) and *The Rationale of Punishment, by Jeremy Bentham* (London 1830), translated and edited by Richard Smith.

17 *Tactiques de assemblée legislatives, suivi d'un traité des sophismes politiques*, 2 vols., trans. E. Dumont (Geneva & Paris 1816).

18 *Traité des preuves judiciares, ouvrage extrait des manuscrits de Jérémie Bentham*, 2 vols., trans. E. Dumont (Paris 1823); first published in English as *A Treatise on Judicial Evidence, Extracted from the Manuscripts of Jeremy Bentham, Esq. by M. Dumont* (London 1825).

19 *De l'organisation judiciaire et de la codification, extraits de divers ouvrages de Jérémie Bentham, Juricsonsulte Anglois, par Ét. Dumont de Genève* (Paris 1828).

20 *Œuvres de Bentham*, 3 vols. (Bruxelles 1829–30), 2nd edn. 1832, 3rd edn. 1840; for a detailed list of contents for each edition see *A Bibliographical Catalogue of the Works of Jeremy Bentham* (Tokyo 1989), pp.3–7.

21 See Catherine Pease-Watkin, 'Bentham's Panopticon and Dumont's *Panoptique*', *Journal of Bentham Studies*, no.6 (2003), p.3: www.ucl.ac.uk:80/Bentham Project/journal/index.htm

Dumont records that three thousand copies of the work were distributed, and 'it has been frequently quoted in many official compositions relating to civil or criminal codes'.[22] Soon after publication it was translated into Russian,[23] and later into Spanish, German, and Hungarian.[24] It was sold in large numbers in Spain, Portugal, and Latin America,[25] and received considerable attention during the liberal triennium of 1820–3 in Spain,[26] including a scathing critique by José Vidal, a Dominican theologian at the University of Valencia.[27] Vidal's book contains lengthy quotations from the Spanish edition of the *Traités de législation* with a commentary.[28] Vidal charged that Bentham's assumption that each individual was the best judge of his or her own interests,[29] coupled with the principle of utility as the criterion of morals, produced

22 *The Works of Jeremy Bentham, Published under the Superintendence of his Executor, John Bowring*, 11 vols. (Edinburgh 1838–43), I. 388. Henceforth Bowring.

23 3 vols. (St Petersburg 1805–11); see *Correspondence* (*CW*), vol. 7, p.366n. Ogden relates that three hundred copies of the *Traités de législation* were imported into Russia, and a hundred copies found their way to Spain; *The Theory of Legislation, by Jeremy Bentham, edited with an introduction and notes by C. K. Ogden* (London 1931), p.xxxiii.

24 The first Spanish translation was by Ramón de Salas, at one time Professor of Civil Law at the University of Salamanca, and published in 5 vols. in Madrid 1821–2; the first German edition was produced by Friedrich Eduard Beneke in Berlin 1830; and the Hungarian translation was published in Kolozvārt 1842–4. It is thought there were also Polish and Portuguese translations; see Elie Halévy, *The Growth of Philosophic Radicalism* [*La Formation du radicalisme philosophique*] (1901–4, trans. M. Morris, 1928: Clifton, New Jersey 1972), p.530.

25 On the influence in Latin America of the *Traités de législation* and Bentham's ideas in general see Almira de Avila-Martel, 'The Influence of Bentham on the Teaching of Penal Law in Chile', Theodora L. McKennon, 'Benthamism in Santander's Colombia', and Antonio-Enrique Pérez Luño, 'Jeremy Bentham and Legal Education in the University of Salamanca during the Nineteenth Century', *The Bentham Newsletter*, no. 5 (1981), pp.22–8, 29–43, 44–54, respectively.

26 J.R. Dinwiddy, 'Early-Nineteenth-Century Reactions to Benthamism', *Transactions of the Royal Historical Society*, 5th series, vol. 34 (1984), pp.47–69, reprinted in Bhikhu Parekh (ed.), *Jeremy Bentham: Critical Assessments*, 4 vols. (London and New York 1993), I. 259. Dinwiddy's reference is Pedro Schwartz, 'La Influentia de Jeremías Bentham en Expaña', *Información Comercial Española* (September 1976), pp.39, 44, 50.

27 José Vidal, *Orígen de los errores revolucionarios de Europe, y su remedio* (Valencia 1827).

28 Dinwiddy, 'Early-Nineteenth-Century Reactions to Benthamism', p.259.

29 Hildreth, I. 63.

potentially dangerous consequences. Moreover, the statement that the decision whether to obey or not to obey laws contrary to utility rested on the calculation of the probable evils of disobedience, was an outright encouragement to revolution.[30] Elsewhere in the Spanish world the reception of Bentham's ideas was quite different. Andrés Bello, for example, used the *Traités de législation* as the basic text for the course on legislation he taught at the Colegio de Santiago in Chile.[31] Pedro Alcántra de Somellera, Professor of Civil Law at the University of Buenos Aires based his teaching on Dumont's edition, and extensively employed the Spanish translation of the work in his own writing on civil law.[32] In 1825 Francisco de Paula Santander, the Vice President of Gran Columbia, decreed that the *Traités de législation* be required reading for all law students in the new republic. On the other hand, the revolutionary 'Liberator' Simón Bolívar, after previously embracing the utilitarian principles of legislation, bowed to clerical and conservative opposition in Columbia and banned the teaching of the *Traités de législation* in March 1828, as detrimental to religion, morality and social order.[33] The text was restored to the curriculum in 1832 when Santander became president.[34]

Bentham's *Introduction to the Principles of Morals and Legislation*, the foundational text of his legal philosophy, had appeared in 1789 but, as Bentham explained in a letter to Lord Wycombe, 'the edition was very small and half of that devoured by the rats'.[35] The restricted circulation of the work ensured that it attracted little attention.

30 See Hildreth, I. 65n.

31 Dinwiddy, 'Early-Nineteenth-Century Reactions to Benthamism', p.265.

32 Pedro Alcántra de Somellera, *Principios de derecho civil* (Buenos Aires 1824); see *The Correspondence of Jeremy Bentham* (CW), vol. 11, ed. Catherine Fuller (Oxford 2000), p.145n.

33 Dinwiddy, 'Early-Nineteenth-Century Reactions to Benthamism', p.258. See also Armando Rojas, 'La Batalla de Bentham en Columbia', *Revista de Historica de América*, vol. XXIX (1950), pp.37–51.

34 As a private university, the University of Rosario, one of Columbia's oldest universities, founded in 1653, was not bound by the prohibitions on Bentham's teachings, but the University itself banned the study of Bentham, and the ban remained in force until 2002; see 'Bentham Ban Lifted' (21 February 2002): http://www.ucl.ac.uk:80/Bentham-Project/

35 Bentham to Lord Wycombe (1 March 1789), *The Correspondence of Jeremy Bentham* (CW), vol. 4, ed. A. T. Milne (London 1981), p.34.

Much of the opening section of the *Traités de législation*, titled 'Principes de législation', is based on chapters in the *Introduction*, and the first and third parts of 'Principes du Code pénal' are also derived from this source.[36] In this form the parts of the *Introduction* used by Dumont were almost certainly read more widely on both sides of the Atlantic than the book in which they first appeared.[37]

These historical and philosophical considerations make the *Traités de législation* of unquestionable importance in fathoming the nature of Bentham's philosophy as it would have appeared to the world in the first half of the nineteenth century. As one noted commentator on Bentham's philosophy put it, 'Dumont is an important component of the production of that body of thought that made Benthamism something worth bothering about. By making Bentham readable, he made Bentham read'.[38] But, how faithful to Bentham's original writings was Dumont? This is not an easily answered question.

In the opinion of the editor's of the modern edition of the *Introduction*, the various editions and translations of the *Traités de législation* 'all perpetuated the influence of a text which, however close to Bentham's mind was not Bentham's own'.[39] Dumont's own version of his role suggests that he played a substantial part in editing Bentham, but that the ideas were Bentham's alone. As he put it in the 'Preliminary Discourse' to the work, 'I beg leave to say that I have neither part nor share in the composition of these different works: they belong to the author, and to him alone'.[40] In the Advertisement to his edition of Bentham's *Théorie des peines et des recompense* Dumont wrote in relation to both this text and the *Traités de législation*: 'this cooperation on my part has had reference to the details only, and ought not to diminish the confidence of the readers; it is not my work that I present to them, it is, as faithfully as the nature of things will permit, the work of Mr. Bentham'.[41] At the same time Dumont did not wish to diminish unduly his role in bringing Bentham's writings to publication. The 'Preliminary Discourse'

36 For the details see the Comparative Table of Editions following this Introduction.

37 See *IPML* (*CW*), Introduction, p.xli.

38 Ross Harrison, *Bentham* (London and New York 1983, reprt. 1999), p.xii.

39 *IPML* (*CW*), Introduction, pp.xli–xlii.

40 The present edition, vol. 2, Appendix, 'Preliminary Discourse', p. i.

41 Bowring, I. 389.

presents the reader with a fascinating insight to the peculiar tasks he undertook in producing the *Traités de législation*:

> My work, which is of a subordinate character, has only been applied to details. It was necessary to make a choice among a great number of various readings, to suppress repetitions, to clear up some obscurities, to bring together all that belong to the same subject, and to fill up the chasms which the author had left in the heat of the composition. I have had more to retrench than to add, more to abridge than to extend. The mass of manuscripts which have passed through my hands, and which I have had to decypher and compare, is considerable. I have had much to do for the uniformity of style and in the way of correction; little or nothing for the ideas. ...
>
> The changes that I have had to make have varied according to the nature of the manuscript. When I have found several relating to the same subject, but composed at different periods and with different views, I have tried to reconcile them to each other, and so to unite them as to make but one whole. Where the author had discarded something that grew up out of the circumstances of the day, and which would not be interesting nor even intelligible now, I have not always been willing to have it utterly lost, but have rescued, as it were from the ruins, whatever was capable of being preserved. Where he had given himself up to abstractions that were too profound, or to metaphysics that were, I will not say too subtle, but too dry, I have tried to give more development to the ideas, and to render them more familiar by applications, by facts and by examples; and I have even permitted myself to scatter a few ornaments over the field of research as I proceeded. I have had to make up some entire chapters, but when I have done so, it has always been after the indications of the author and by the help of his notes; and the difficulty I have experienced when trying to supply his deficiencies would have led me back to a modest opinion of myself, even if I had been tempted astray.
>
> His *Introduction of the Principles of Morals and Legislation*, which is regarded by a small number of enlightened judges as one of those extraordinary works that form an era and a revolution in science, in spite of its philosophical merit, or peradventure because of that merit, produced little or no sensation, and continued almost unknown to the public; ... In making use of several chapters of that work for the *General Principles of Legislation*, I have tried to avoid what interfered with its success – forms that were too scientific,

> subdivisions that were too numerous, and an analysis that was too abstract. I have not translated the words; I have translated the ideas. I have made in some respects an abridgment, and in others a commentary; but in doing this, I have been guided by the counsels and indications of the author, in a preface, posterior by many years to the work itself; and I have found in his papers all the additions of any importance, that are assembled here.[42]

Clearly, Dumont's role in re-presenting Bentham's ideas was substantial. But, it should also be noted that there are parts of the *Traités de législation* in which Dumont was rather less free in his editorial work, and produced a text very close to Bentham's original manuscripts. This is most obviously the case when Bentham's original drafts were written in French, as in the instance of substantial sections of his writing on civil law. For example, the axioms of mental pathology, as they appear in the 'Principles of the Civil Code' in Dumont, are of crucial importance in Bentham's theory.[43] Ross Harrison has made a close comparison of these sections of Dumont's text with the original manuscripts and concluded that 'nearly all of what is in Dumont is in Bentham, nearly all in the same words'. In other parts of the text matters were quite different. Dumont omitted certain material and corrected and improved Bentham's French, and to some extent re-arranged the text. Nevertheless, Harrison concluded 'although Dumont's text is clearly nothing like Bentham's thought as Bentham wrote it, it is still Bentham's thought'.[44] Nor did Bentham think otherwise.

Bentham did not assist Dumont greatly in producing the work, and on occasion he appeared less than grateful for the power of good Dumont had done his reputation.[45] Beyond arranging the mass of manuscript material he gave to Dumont, Bentham studiously avoided involvement in his disciple's project.[46] When Dumont began translating Bentham's manuscripts in the summer of 1792 he soon realised

42 The present edition, vol. 2, Appendix, 'Preliminary Discourse', pp. ii–iii. The preface in question was written by Bentham in 1789; the text of *IPML* was completed and printed in 1780, to which a Concluding Note was added in 1789.

43 Hildreth, I. 102–9.

44 Harrison, *Bentham*, p.xiii.

45 Ibid., pp.xiii–xiv.

46 Bentham to Dumont (16 August 1792), *Correspondence* (*CW*), vol. 4, pp.385–6.

he needed the author's assistance to fathom the ideas he was attempting to translate into French. He beseeched Bentham:

> I want only a word or two – only a word or two – and you must conquer your repugnance. I want not finished labours, but hints. Mark the way by a few posts, and I will follow you. Your ideas are all in ready money; so I can draw on you at sight. But I must consult you; for if I suspend my labours, the interest will cool, ennui will seize me, and the devil will do the rest.[47]

Bentham was evidently reluctant to engage in work that would distract him from his chief occupation of these years – the Panopticon penitentiary scheme, a project which consumed a vast amount of his time in the first half of the 1790s.[48] Bentham felt he had reason to complain about Dumont. The original plan, he explained to the Duc de Liancourt in 1795, 'was that *Dumont* should take my half-finished manuscripts as he found them – half English, half English-French – and make what he could of them in Genevan-French, without giving me any further trouble about the matter. Instead of that, the lazy rogue comes to me with everything that he writes, and teases me to fill up every gap he has observed'.[49] Having given Dumont *carte blanche* to utilise his editorial acumen and skills as a translator, as publication approached Bentham suddenly took an interest in the volumes set to appear with his name on the title page. Shortly after receiving the proofs of the first two volumes, he wrote on four separate occasions in the second half of May 1802, in the hope that Dumont might use some of his suggestions in the 'Preliminary Discourse' at the front of the book and make corrections where possible in the text.[50] Bentham expressed the hope that the 'Preliminary Discourse' would contain

47 Dumont to Bentham (8 May 1794), *Correspondence* (CW), vol. 5, p. 33.

48 See *Correspondence* (CW), vols. 4–5, *passim*.

49 Bentham to the Duc de Liancourt (11 October 1795), *Correspondence* (CW), vol. 5, p.160.

50 Bentham to Dumont (14 May, 17 May, 18 May, and 21 May 1802), *Correspondence* (CW), vol. 7, pp.24–9, 29–38, 39–44, 44–56. The editorial notes to these letters indicate where and in what manner Dumont was able to accommodate Bentham's suggestions and corrections, some of which were held back and incorporated in the second edition of the *Traités de législation* in 1820. Over a year later Bentham was still feeding Dumont comments and corrections, presumably to be integrated into any new edition of the work; Bentham to Dumont (27 November 1803), ibid., p.252.

what is necessary 'in order to exonerate me from the responsibility attached to opinions which are not mine'.[51] He set out several minor corrections to Dumont's version of his views on the laws of inheritance, priests, property laws, pardons, insurance, and treason law, commented on Dumont's choice of terminology at points in the text, and bemoaned at length the absence of cross-referencing between the same subject-matter discussed in different parts of the text. His main problem, however, centred on Dumont's comments on English law, which he thought demonstrated an inadequate understanding and from which he wished to distance himself as far as possible:

> It is a perilous task for any Englishman who is not a Lawyer, and still more for any man who is not an Englishman, to undertake to give any sort of account of the English Law: you must take care in your Preface ['Preliminary Discourse'] to exonerate me of this part of the infamy; otherwise the gainsayers among the lawyers, that is to say all the lawyers but our particular friends, will see nothing in the whole book but the unpopular parts of it, plus those mistakes in point of existing law.[52]

Bentham well knew that not all the problems he addressed in these letters to Dumont were the fault of the editor; at times the fault could be traced to the original manuscripts, in which Bentham had not always presented his arguments in a finished form.[53] But these caveats aside, Bentham clearly appreciated Dumont's labours. 'Courage! Courage! my Prince of bold actions', he ended one letter, 'you shall not only sit on my right hand, but have a cushion for your a——e'.[54]

Once published, however, there were occasions when Bentham exhibited ambivalence in his references to the *Traités de législation*. In a letter to a friend, written soon after the series of letters he sent to Dumont in May 1802, he described it as Dumont's work,[55] and thereafter frequently called it 'Dumont's Principles'. However, the implication that Bentham wished to disown the work is doubtfully

51 Bentham to Dumont (17 May 1802), ibid., p.29.

52 Ibid., p.32. For Dumont's exoneration of Bentham see the present edition vol. 2, Appendix, 'Preliminary Discourse', p. iv.

53 Bentham to Dumont (21 May 1802), *Correspondence* (*CW*), vol. 7, p.54.

54 Bentham to Dumont (17 May 1802), ibid., p.38.

55 Bentham to George Wilson (22 May 1802), ibid., p.57.

correct. Rather, it appears to have been Bentham's way of acknowledging the commitment and time devoted by the disciple to bringing the master's ideas before the public. On the other hand, toward the end of his life, in a moment of vexation, Bentham once declared that Dumont 'does not understand a word of my meaning'.[56] Such declarations cannot be lightly dismissed, but it is clear that Bentham did not always think this way. A fairer view of the matter is conveyed in a letter to Dumont in which he wrote that 'with very few exceptions' he 'was not able to distinguish' Dumont's text from his own manuscripts.[57] Nor was Bentham reluctant to recommend the *Traités de législation* to his connections when offering his services as a codifier of law.[58] And, in a letter to Dumont dated 29 November 1821, Bentham waxed in a lyrical vein about the success of their collaboration, evoking religious imagery, as he often did when considering his place in the eyes of posterity:

> Courage! Son of my mind: we are growing young together. At what a pitch of juvenility may we not have arrived twenty years hence! Existence shaken off, we shall go on hand in hand through all future ages: doing good, diminishing pain, increasing pleasure, all the way, and all the while, as we go: all the way; – and (not to speak of the moon) our way will cover the whole earth. We shall, for we will, be despots of the moral world: Locke and Helvétius, offering incense to us every morning, both of them on their knees, Bacon and Newton I have not determined yet what to do with them. Thou wilt sit on my right hand, as we travel in a chariot of fire which the present owner (what is his name Elias?) will procure us with. Thou, on my right hand: citizen I-don't-know-who, on my left. ... We have already superseded Locke and Helvétius – taken their places in the car, and planted them in the basket. But nobody shall ever supersede us ...[59]

56 Bowring, X. 185.

57 Bentham to Dumont (28 June 1802), *Correspondence* (*CW*), vol. 7, p.60.

58 See, for example, Bentham's letters to James Madison (30 October 1811), Alexander I (January 1814), and Simon Snyder, Governor of Pennsylvania 1808–17 (14 July 1814), *The Correspondence of Jeremy Bentham* (*CW*), vol. 8, ed. ed. S. R. Conway (Oxford 1988), pp.183, 369, 390.

59 Bentham to Dumont (29 November 1821), *The Correspondence of Jeremy Bentham* (*CW*), vol. 10, ed. Stephen Conway (London 1994), pp.442–3.

These are hardly the words of a man disgruntled that he had been inadequately represented by his editor. Rather they convey Bentham's gratitude for what Dumont achieved in rendering his ideas in a form accessible to an audience he could not have hoped to reach alone.

Nevertheless, given the nature of Dumont's task it is not surprising to find differences between certain of Bentham's ideas and the manner in which Dumont rendered them. Forty years ago David Baumgardt conducted a detailed examination of the relevant texts in order to make plain the nature of Dumont's editorial work.[60] While he found the texts of 'Principes du Code civil' and 'Principes du Code pénal' to be faithful to the arguments of their originals, he discerned a number of discrepancies between the content of the introductory 'Principes de législation' and the relevant parts of *An Introduction to the Principles of Morals and Legislation*. Certain of the differences he explained in terms of Dumont's urge to popularise Bentham's ideas and make them appeal to a wider readership, while others resulted from a misunderstanding of Bentham's arguments or Dumont's desire not to cause offence.

In general, Baumgardt argued that the *Traités de législation* contained a less critical approach to the utility principle. In particular, he singled out the critique of the principles opposed to utility in Chs. II and III of the 'Principes de législation',[61] which represents 'little more than a fraction of the text of the *Introduction*',[62] and Dumont's perfunctory dismissals of the distinctions (1) between virtue and utility, and (2) between the function of the utility principle in morals and politics.[63] In addition, Dumont inexplicably reversed the logical order of the text found in the *Introduction*, discussing the classes of pleasures and pains as 'final causes' before turning to the four sanctions as 'sources of pain and pleasure'.[64] In the discussion of circumstances influencing

[60] David Baumgardt, *Bentham and the Ethics of Today, with Bentham Manuscripts Hitherto Unpublished* (New York 1966), pp.321–69; see also pp.26–8. Also, see Halévy's comparisons in *The Growth of Philosophic Radicalism*, Appendix, pp.515–21.

[61] Hildreth, I. 4–13.

[62] See *IPML* (*CW*), Ch. II, pp.17–33.

[63] Baumgardt, *Bentham and the Ethics of Today*, pp.328–9; see Hildreth, I. 16.

[64] Baumgardt, *Bentham and the Ethics of Today*, p.331; see *IPML* (*CW*), Chs. III and V, pp.34–7, 42–50, and Hildreth, I. Chs. VI–VII, pp.20–30.

sensibility we find the list of primary circumstances reduced from 32 to 15, while the list of secondary circumstances is unchanged from the *Introduction*.[65] Beginning with Ch. X of the 'Principes de législation', Dumont completely abandoned the succession of topics as they appear in the *Introduction*, omitting Bentham's analyses 'Of Human Actions in General', 'Of Intentionality', 'Of Consciousness', 'Of Motives', and 'Of Human Dispositions in General', though elements of these discussions are found in briefer form later in Dumont's text.[66] Other notable differences between Dumont's version and Bentham's originals include 'some watering down of the radicalism of Bentham's argument' that both jurisprudence and private morality are part of the same general concern with ethics, and Dumont's more conciliatory attitude towards religion.[67] Dumont did not conceal the secular character of Bentham's theory, but he toned down or omitted the more antagonistic views expressed in the *Introduction*.[68] To Baumgardt's list of differences we might turn to Harrison for one further point of contrast. Dumont's text includes repeated use of the terminology of 'moral calculation',[69] an expression (along with 'felicific calculus') which has often engaged the attention of critics of classical utilitarianism as an impractical method for both private individuals and legislators in the process of decision-making. However, though the expression is not to be found in Bentham's own writing up to this point, it is one that certainly captures his approach to the evaluation of pleasures and pains. As Harrison points out, the idea is implicit in the *Introduction*,[70] and Bentham's later use of the terminology of

65 Baumgardt, *Bentham and the Ethics of Today*, p.333; see *IPML* (*CW*), Ch. VI, pp.51–73, and Hildreth, I. Ch. IX, pp.33–48.

66 Baumgardt, *Bentham and the Ethics of Today*, p.333; see *IPML* (*CW*), Chs. VII–XI, pp.74–142. On the discrepancies between Dumont and Bentham in the description of 'motives' see Baumgardt, pp.357–9.

67 Baumgardt, *Bentham and the Ethics of Today*, p.338; see *IPML* (*CW*), Ch. XVII, pp.281–300, and Hildreth, I. Ch. XII, pp.60–6. For further remarks on the religious differences between Dumont and Bentham see Baumgardt, pp.363–4, and Halévy, *The Growth of Philosophic Radicalism*, p.520.

68 This did not save the *Traités de législation* from being listed in the Papal Index of prohibited books in March 1819; Joseph Hilgers (ed.), *Der Index der verbotenen Bücher* (Freiburg 1904), p.456.

69 Hildreth, I. 32; see also the Index in the present edition, vol. 2.

70 *IPML* (*CW*), pp.173–4.

'political arithmetic' and 'applying arithmetical calculation to the elements of happiness' in the *Codification Proposal* (1822) may well have been influenced by Dumont's earlier phrasing in the *Traités de législation*.[71]

It is fair to say that the presentation of the arguments of significant parts of the text of the *Traités de législation* was fashioned by Dumont. At the same time, it is clear that by and large Bentham was pleased with Dumont's success in publicizing his views on legislation, and once the text was published he rarely offered criticisms of it. Not much more can be said; the issue of 'authorship' is now impervious to a definitive settlement. As the editor of the journal *l'Utilitaire* wrote in 1829, after commenting on the contributions to Bentham's fame made by Dumont, the names of Bentham and Dumont 'must no more be separated than those of Kepler and Newton'.[72]

Whether we consider the *Traités de législation* a Bentham text, or a text produced in collaboration with Dumont, it does not need to be stressed that Dumont's volumes provide a detailed statement of the *utilitarian* theory of legislation. And, it was on the basis of Dumont's rendering of the theory, that Bentham came to prominence in continental Europe before the philosophical prophet was widely known in his own country. Naturally, Hildreth had no doubt of the importance of Dumont's work in disseminating Bentham's ideas: 'Fortunately for the cause of science, these materials were not left to perish; an interpreter, a compiler, a spokesman was found, [in] every way worthy of the task he assumed'.[73] Moreover, it was in Dumont's French edition that Bentham's legal philosophy first circulated and gained currency in the United States of America.[74] For example, John

71 Harrison, *Bentham*, p.139; his reference is Bowring, IV. 540. *Codification Proposal addressed to all Nations Professing Liberal Opinions*, first printed in 1822 with supplements in 1827 and 1830, included in *'Legislator of the World': Writings on Codification, Law, and Education* (CW), eds. P. Schofield and J. Harris (Oxford 1998).

72 *L'Utilitaire*, vol. I (1829), 'Discours Préliminaire', p.xxxn, quoted by Blamires, 'Étienne Dumont: Genevan Apostle of Utility', p.55.

73 Hildreth, 'Translator's Preface', I. iv.

74 Later, Bentham personally took it upon himself to distribute many of his writings in the United States through various American friends and acquaintances. For an illustration of this see James E. Crimmins, 'From an "ultra democrat" to an "ultra aristocrat": Bentham Tracts in the Adams Collection, Quincy, Massachusetts', *The Book Collector*, vol. 43, no. 2 (1994), pp.229–55.

Neal's familiarity with Dumont's text, evident in his translation of the introductory 'Principes de législation', provided him with the basis for his dissemination of Bentham's ideas in the pages of *The Yankee* (later *The Yankee and Boston Literary Gazette*) in 1828–9.[75] Edward Livingston was influenced by Bentham in drafting various codes of law for the state of Louisiana, and reported to Bentham that the *Traités de législation* 'fortified me in a design to prosecute the subject'.[76] And, it was Dumont's text that provided Hildreth with the foundational ideas of his own utilitarian disquisition on the *Theory of Morals* (1844), one of the few recognisably utilitarian texts on ethics published in the United States in the nineteenth century.[77]

Hildreth's translation

The issue of authorship is further complicated by the fact that the present volumes are a re-translation from Dumont's French into English by a third party – Richard Hildreth (1807–65) – the American historian, anti-slave propagandist, and utilitarian admirer of Bentham. In a letter to Bentham a few months after the appearance of the *Traités de législation*, Sir Frederick Eden lamented

75 See the various articles from *The Yankee* (1828–9) reproduced in Crimmins and Spencer (eds), *Utilitarians and their Critics in America, 1789–1914*, vol. 1. This collection also contains Neal's 'Chapter on Utility' from *Principles of Legislation: From the Ms. of Jeremy Bentham; Bencher of Lincoln's Inn. By M. Dumont, Member of the Representative and Sovereign Council of Geneva. Translated from the Second Corrected and Enlarged Edition* [Paris 1820]; with Notes and a Biographical Notice of Jeremy Bentham and of M. Dumont. By John Neal. (Boston 1830), pp.119–47.

76 Edward Livingston to Bentham (10 August 1829), Bowring, XI. 23. A reviewer of Livingston's *A System of Penal Law for the State of Louisiana, prepared under the authority of a law of said State* (Philadelphia 1833) argued that he 'reduced to practice what Bentham had only suggested; who, taking up the subject of law-reform where the master had left it, pursued important parts of it to a complete consummation; and who, not satisfied with the speculations of the closet, succeeded in inducing the legislative power of a magnificent state to request him to make law of that which had been before only theory'. 'Edward Livingston and his Code', *The United States Magazine and Democratic Review*, New Series, vol. I, no. I (July 1841), p.4.

77 Richard Hildreth. *Theory of Morals: An Inquiry Concerning the Law of Moral Distinctions and the Variations and Contradictions of Ethical Codes* (Boston 1844). This text is also included in Crimmins and Spencer (eds), *Utilitarians and their Critics in America.*

the absence of an English version of the work in Britain,[78] and Bentham informed him that Romilly had proposed undertaking the task, but could not make a start on it before the following year. Bentham asked Eden whether he would be prepared to translate the work, but Eden declared he was not competent.[79] A few years later Basil Montagu, the law reformer and death penalty abolitionist, was engaged upon the business, but after making some headway he never completed the translation.[80] Another of Bentham's disciples, Richard Smith, undertook to translate parts of Dumont's text for the first volume of Bowring's edition of *The Works of Jeremy Bentham*, but it enjoyed a very limited circulation at the time of its first publication in 1838.[81] It was left to Hildreth on the other side of the Atlantic to be the first to publish a stand-alone English translation of the principal parts of Dumont's text. In the course of time America came to identify Hildreth's name with that of Bentham's, where he was recognised as a 'zealous Benthamist'.[82] Hildreth re-translated into English the first two volumes of the second edition of the *Traités de législation* (1820) in the summer of 1836,[83] but it took several years to find a publisher willing to undertake the risk of publishing a lengthy work on such a dry topic by a philosopher who was still little known in America, except among a small selection of scholars and politicians.

78 Sir Frederick Morton Eden to Bentham (3 September 1802), *Correspondence* (*CW*), vol. 7, p.116. The need for an English translation was also underscored by Aaron Burr's remark to Dumont that 'he knew not four persons in America who had read the *Principes*'. Dumont to Bentham (4 September 1811), *Correspondence* (*CW*), vol. 8, p.173. There had been talk of a translation being done by Burr's daughter, Theodosius Burr Alston, but nothing came of this; *ibid.*, p.5n.

79 Bentham to Eden, (4 September 1802), and Eden to Bentham, (8 September 1802), ibid., pp.125–6, 131–2.

80 Dumont to Bentham (3 November 1807), *Correspondence* (*CW*), vol. 7, p.450. From the completed translations, Montagu published several extracts on punishment in *The Opinions of Different Authors Upon the Punishment of Death, Selected by Basil Montagu, Esq.*, 3 vols. (London 1809–13), I. 216–32.

81 For the details of Smith's translation see the Comparative Table of Editions following this introduction.

82 Thomas Low Nichols, *Forty Years of American Life, 1821–61* (New York [1937?]), p.299.

83 Richard Hildreth, *My Connection with the Atlas Newspaper* (Boston 1839), p.7.

Educated at Harvard, Hildreth trained for the law but practised only intermittently, preferring to make a career as an author.[84] His distaste for some of the doubtful practices of lawyers appears to have been influenced by his reading of Bentham on the subject.[85] A one-time candidate for the Massachusetts House of Representatives, Hildreth was a frequent contributor to the journals of the day, writing in support of temperance and against slavery, and commenting on other political and social issues. In arguing that alcohol should be banned by law, Hildreth differed from Bentham, who doubted the efficacy of direct law in such cases and preferred the more subtle mechanisms of 'indirect' legislation.[86] However, like Bentham, Hildreth was an inveterate opponent of slavery throughout his life, and published extensively in support of abolition, including the popular *The Slave: Or Memoirs of Archy Moore*, reputedly the first anti-slavery novel in the United States.[87] Like Bentham, too, Hildreth (the son of a Unitarian minister) had little time for the beliefs of organised religion, and frequently flavoured his writings with anti-clericalism. He followed Bentham

[84] Hildreth may have first encountered Bentham's legal philosophy during his study of law at Harvard in David Hoffman's popular *A Course of Legal Study; Respectfully Addressed to the Students of Law in the United States* (Baltimore 1817), later revised and expanded as *A Course of Legal Study, Addressed to Students and the Profession Generally*, 2 vols. (Baltimore 1836). Donald E. Emerson, *Richard Hildreth* (Baltimore 1946), p.91; this is how John Neal was first introduced to Bentham's legal philosophy.

[85] See Emerson, *Richard Hildreth*, pp.42–3, and 91. In his 'scrapbook' Hildreth transcribed a quote from the second of Bentham's three *Letters to Count Toreno, on the Proposed Penal Code* (1822), in which he castigated the legal profession as opponents of the public interest; the text in English is in Bowring, VIII. 501. Hildreth quoted from the French translation included in *Essais de Jérémy Bentham, sur la situation politique de l'Espagne, sur la constitution et sur le nouveau code Espagnol, sur la constitution du Portugal, etc., etc.* (Paris 1823), and later reprinted in Dumont's *Œuvres de J. Bentham*, I. 127–80.

[86] Hildreth, I. 61–2; II. 364, 376.

[87] Richard Hildreth, *The Slave: or, Memoirs of Archy Moore* (New York 1836), later reissued in an enlarged edition titled *The White Slave; A True Picture of Slave Life in America* (Boston 1852). The claim that the *Memoirs of Archy Moore* was the first American anti-slavery novel is made by Emerson, *Richard Hildreth*, p.73. See also Hildreth's *Despotism in America; or, An Inquiry into the Nature and Results of the Slave-holding System in the United States. By the author of "Archy Moore"* (Boston 1840). Bentham's position on slavery is explained in 'Principles of the Civil Code', Ch. II, Hildreth, I. 201–9.

in his 'Plea for Sunday Freedom' (addressed to John Quincy Adams).[88] Hildreth's diverse writing encompassed books on banking and currency,[89] theological controversy,[90] and a study of modern Japan.[91] The crowning work of his later life was a six-volume *History of the United States*, which went through several editions, and has received some attention in American historiography.[92] His *Theory of Morals* (1844), in which he presented an amended version of utilitarian theory,[93] and *Theory of Politics* (1853), were the first two of a projected six-volume philosophical series, intended to include essays on 'wealth', 'taste', 'knowledge', and 'education', but the series was never completed.[94] Hildreth

[88] 'A Plea for Sunday Freedom: in a Letter to John Quincy Adams, President of the late Baltimore Lord's-day Convention. By "One of the New Generation"', *Liberator*, 24 January 1845; see Emerson, *Richard Hildreth*, p.124. For Bentham's arguments against keeping the sabbath free from non-religious engagements see Hildreth, II, 378–80.

[89] Richard Hildreth, *A History of Banks: To which is added, A Demonstration of the Advantages and Necessity of Free Competition in the Business of Banking* (Boston 1837), and *Banks, Banking and Paper Currencies* (Boston 1840), a revised version of the earlier book.

[90] Richard Hildreth, *A Letter to Andrews Norton on Miracles as the Foundation of Religious Faith* (Boston 1840), a response to Norton's alumni address *On the Latest Form of Infidelity* to the Cambridge Divinity School in 1839, reprinted in Martha M. Pingel, *An American Utilitarian: Richard Hildreth as a Philosopher* (New York 1948), pp.129–52.

[91] Richard Hildreth, *Japan as It Was and Is* (Boston 1855), and *Japan and the Japanese* (Boston 1860).

[92] Richard Hildreth, *The History of the United States of America from the Discovery of the Continent to the Organization of Government under the Federal Constitution, 1497–1789*, 3 vols. (New York 1849), and *The History of the United States of America from the Adoption of the Federal Constitution to the end of the Sixteenth Congress, 1788–1821*, 3 vols. (New York 1851–2). On Hildreth as a historian see Alfred H. Kelly, 'Richard Hildreth', in William T. Hutchinson (ed.), *The Marcus W. Jernegan Essays in American Historiography* (1937; reprt. New York 1958), pp.25–42.

[93] Hildreth's utilitarianism and its differences from Bentham are discussed in David Baumgardt, 'The Forgotten Moralist: Richard Hildreth's Theory of Morals', *Ethics*, vol. 57, no.3 (April 1947), pp.191–8. Baumgardt's essay is in part a reply to the account of Bentham's utilitarian influence on Hildreth stated in Arthur M. Schlesinger, Jr., 'The Problem of Richard Hildreth', *New England Quarterly* (June 1940), pp.237–9. See also Pingel, *An American Utilitarian*, pp.11–23.

[94] The extant mss. on 'Theory of Wealth' and 'Theory of Taste' were published by Pingel, *An American Utilitarian*, pp.43–120.

planned other translations of Dumont's redactions of Bentham's writings, but none were ever published.[95] Toward the end of his life he wrote short biographies of Bentham and Dumont for the *New American Cyclopædia*,[96] in the first of which he offered the view that the general reader will find the best introduction to Bentham's system in *The Theory of Legislation*, though without identifying himself as its translator.[97]

Hildreth's declared mission was to introduce Bentham's utilitarianism to America, where his writings had been little read up to this point. In particular, he believed that the current widespread interest in legal reform in the United States would benefit enormously from the ideas expounded in *The Theory of Legislation*. In this respect, he announced in the preface to the work, 'the translator flatters himself that he will have performed a useful and acceptable service, in restoring to its native tongue the following treatise'.[98] Hildreth registered his own caution about utility as a guide in morals, while praising Bentham's use of it as the foundation for law: 'Whatever may be thought of the *Principle of Utility*, when considered as the foundation of morals, no one now-a-days will undertake to deny that it is the only safe rule of legislation'.[99] To Dumont's original text, Hildreth added no more than a handful of illustrative and explanatory footnotes, each of which is acknowledged as being inserted by the 'Translator'.[100] When C.K. Ogden published his own edition of *The Theory of Legislation* (1931), directly from the plates of Hildreth's 1864 edition, he paid the American the ultimate compliment: 'The present translation, made by an American lawyer

95 Emerson, *Richard Hildreth*, p.113.

96 [Richard Hildreth], 'Jeremy Bentham', and 'Pierre Étienne Louis Dumont', *The New American Cyclopædia: A Popular Dictionary of General Knowledge*, 16 vols. (New York 1858–63), III. 136–42, and VI. 668–70, respectively. These articles were attributed to Hildreth by Emerson, *Richard Hildreth*, p.172.

97 *The New American Cyclopædia*, III. 142.

98 Hildreth, I. ix.

99 Hildreth, I. iii.

100 This includes a lengthy note at II. 346–7, in which Hildreth employs Bentham's stipulations on the essential characteristics of punishment to argue that imprisonment is the only punishment the legislator needs.

..., has so long been a classic that it has become an almost integral part of the Benthamic canon'.[101]

There are other translations and editions of *The Theory of Legislation* to note: (1) John Neal's translation of the introductory part of Dumont's first volume, *Principles of Legislation: From the Ms. of Jeremy Bentham; Bencher of Lincoln's Inn. By M. Dumont* (1830);[102] (2) Richard Smith's *Principles of the Civil Code* and *Principles of Penal Law* in the first volume of *The Works of Jeremy Bentham* (ed. Bowring, 1838–43);[103] and Charles Milner Atkinson's *Bentham's Theory of Legislation* (1914).[104]

Neal's edition does not appear to have met with much success, though he informed Bentham that four hundred copies of the five hundred printed were sold.[105] In his 'Biographical Notice of Jeremy Bentham' Neal, who was a guest at Bentham's home in London for eighteen months in 1825–6 and who styled himself as Bentham's spokesman in America, described the English philosopher as 'the great high-priest of legislation',[106] and commented in effusive terms on Dumont's role in popularising Bentham:

> until within a very few years, the most valuable of his works were not only unknown to the great body of English every where, but actually unheard of by his next-door neighbours, and by most of the lawgivers of the British Empire. ... And this, while they were to be found in every public library of Europe, out of the author's own country – and upon the table of every statesman, jurist, or

101 *The Theory of Legislation*, ed. Ogden, p.l (for bibliographical details see above note 23). Ogden mistakenly assumed that Hildreth's translation was first published in 1864; in this error he was followed by Charles Milner Atkinson in his edition of *Bentham's Theory of Legislation, Being Principes de Législation and Traités de Législation, Civile et Pénale*, translated and edited from the French of Étienne Dumont by Charles Milner Atkinson, 2 vols. (London 1914), I. iv.

102 For complete bibliographical information see above note 75.

103 Bowring, I. 297–580.

104 For bibliographical details see above note 101.

105 John Neal to Bentham (11 March 1830), in Irving T. Richards, *Life and Works of John Neal* (unpublished thesis, Harvard University 1932), p.744, cited by Paul A, Palmer, 'Benthamism in England and America', *The American Political Science Review*, vol. 35, no.5 (Oct. 1941), p.863.

106 John Neal, 'Biographical Notice of Jeremy Bentham', in *Principles of Legislation*, p.14.

> philosopher of the continent: *this*, after nearly as many as ten thousand copies of one work in three large octavo volumes,[107] and nearly as many more of several other works by the same author, had been rescued by a foreigner from a heap of neglected manuscripts – a treasury of wisdom – store-house of wonderful thought – worked over into French, published at Paris – re-translated, and republished in four or five other languages, and circulated in chapters throughout every corner of the globe ...; and the whole being regarded everywhere, except in the immediate neighbourhood of the author, among his fellow-countrymen, or among those who speak the same language, as by far the most profound, extraordinary and useful work of the age.[108]

Despite the generally eulogistic character of Neal's appreciation of the utilitarian philosopher, Bentham seems to have had mixed feelings about his American guest. He described Neal as 'a nondescript' who was 'always cheerful and talkative', and his tendency to talk 'on every subject with equal confidence' led Bentham to comment: 'I might as well have had a rattlesnake in my house as that man'. Of Neal's *Brother Jonathan* (1842–3) Bentham opined, it 'is really the most execrable stuff that ever fell from mortal pen'.[109] Neal's primary use to Bentham, it seems, was in supplying information about American legal practice and the operations of American government.[110]

Neal's text is sometimes misdescribed as a translation of the *Traités de législation*. In fact, it contains only a fraction of that work – an English version of 'Principes de législation', which constituted Chs. I–XIII of Dumont's first volume.[111] To this he added his own 'Biographical Notice of Jeremy Bentham', a 'Chapter on Utility', a

[107] Dumont says there were three thousand copies printed of the first edition of the *Traités de législation* in 1802 (see above p. x). However, a second edition published in Paris in 1820 would have significantly added to the number of copies in circulation; for the details of these editions see the Bibliography following this Introduction.

[108] Neal, *Principles of Legislation*, pp.10–11.

[109] Bowring, XI. 555–6

[110] See Bentham, *Constitutional Code* (*CW*), vol. 1, ed. F. Rosen and J. H. Burns (London 1983), pp.xxviii, 55 note, 515 note; also Bowring, IX. 648, 656–8, 661–2.

[111] *Traités de législation*, I. 1–132 (1–140 in 1st edn.).

'Biographical Notice of M. Dumont [by J.B.]', a 'Sketch of the Life and Character of Stephen Dumont. – By J.C.L. De Sismondi', and an English translation of Dumont's 'Discourse préliminaire'.[112] Neal did not reproduce any of the material from the 'Principes du Code civil' or the 'Principes du Code pénal', which constitute the major parts of Dumont's three volumes.[113] At best Neal's text provided an appetizer for the real meat of the *Traités de législation*.

Smith must have been engaged on his edition for Bowring at roughly the same time as Hildreth conducted his own translation, since the first volume of Bowring appeared in 1838, though neither Smith nor Hildreth appears to have been aware of the work of the other. Smith's translation of the civil code sections of the *Traités de législation* follow fairly closely the originals in Dumont's edition, and the variations from Hildreth are largely differences of style. In the *Principles of Penal Law* Smith replaced the third part of Dumont's text with 'Rationale of Punishment',[114] which is identical to *Rationale of Punishment* (1830), an English translation by Smith of parts of Dumont's redaction of Bentham's manuscripts titled *Théorie des peines et des recompense*, with the addition of a selection of other unpublished manuscript material.[115] Smith omitted the introductory 'Principles of Legislation',[116] elements of which are to be found elsewhere in the Bowring edition of *The Works of Jeremy Bentham*.

112 *Neal, Principles of Legislation,* pp.1–118, 119–47, 148–57, 157–72, and 175–93 (the latter included in this edition, vol. 2, Appendix, pp. i–xv). Neal's source for the 'Sketch of the Life and Character of Stephen Dumont. – By J.C.L. De Sismondi' is an English translation of parts of Sismondi's biographical memoir of Dumont which appeared in the *Revue Encyclopedique,* and subsequently in English translation in the *Boston Advertiser* (10 February 1830); see Neal, *Principles of Legislation,* p.148n. The 'Biographical Notice [Sketch] of M. Dumont' is by Neal, but it contains a lengthy quote from Bentham (pp.151–7), presumably transcribed from conversations with Bentham by Neal during his stay with the philosopher in London in 1825–6.

113 See the Comparative Table of Editions following this Introduction.

114 *Traités de législation*, II. 'Troisième Partie. Des Peines'.

115 Bowring I. 367 n; the relevant text is at pp.390–532 and identical to Smith's edition of *The Rationale of Punishment* (see above note 16).

116 See Hildreth, I. 1–87.

Though Atkinson did not rely on Hildreth's translation, his text appears to be much the same as the American's and is arranged in an identical manner. However, there are several differences to note. There are variations in chapter headings and in the numbering of chapters between the two editions, and Atkinson has introduced text from other sources in Bentham's writings, to which he has added numerous notes. He explained his approach in the editorial introduction: 'In the present edition, where access has been had to the original writings of Bentham, or the same ideas have been found expressed in other portions of his work, the text has been based on the passages referred to rather than on the presentment of his expositor in the *Traités*, in case clearness or simplicity seemed to be favoured by the departure'.[117] Given this explanation of his approach, it is understandable why Atkinson is the only one of the editor's to stress that this is *Bentham's* theory of legislation.

Hildreth's translation received two major reviews in the American journals of the day, one of which was highly supportive and the other largely critical.[118] *The United States Magazine and Democratic Review* was one of the most important journals of its kind in America, and from 1837 to 1846 it was edited by John O'Sullivan, whose interest in utilitarianism was long standing. The anonymous reviewer (it may well have been Sullivan), provided a relatively acute and succinct account of the moral and legal theory contained in *The Theory of Legislation*. He described Bentham as 'the father of law reform, the founder of legislative science, the powerful advocate of political emancipation, and a distinguished friend of the moral advancement of the human race'.[119] Hildreth is praised for making Bentham's ideas 'more widely known to the American public ... at a time when the subject of law reform is beginning to be agitated in the legislatures of several of the States, and when the young men of the nation, as we fondly believe, are attaching themselves to sentiments of democratic freedom and

117 Atkinson, *Bentham's Theory of Legislation*, I. viii.

118 *The United States Magazine and Democratic Review*, vol. VIII, no. XXXIII (September 1840), pp. 251–71; *The North American Review*, vol. LI, no. CIX (October 1840), pp. 384–96. Both reviews are included in Crimmins and Spencer (eds), *Utilitarians and their Critics in America, 1789–1914.*

119 *The United States Magazine and Democratic Review*, vol. VIII, no. XXXIII (September 1840), p.252.

progress. … The legislator who should go forth armed with the weapons of this magazine of thought would prove an invincible champion in the cause of justice and truth'.[120] The reviewer offered certain criticisms of Bentham's moral theory, but refrained from the well-worn charge of atheism, and indeed did not mention religion at all in the review. The principal questions about which he expressed reservations were, first, whether pleasure and pain are the sole governing motives of men, and second, whether the tendency of an act to produce the greatest amount of happiness is the only reason why it is binding upon the consciences of men.[121] These reservations, however, pale alongside the reviewer's praise for the great service Bentham has performed for legislative science and political reform. The systematic manner in which he set about his analysis of existing law, the stress on the practical business of the law, his arguments for codification, and influence upon law reformers like Samuel Romilly, are all commended in the strongest language.[122] Moreover, the reviewer credits Bentham with making plain 'the true functions of government'. Unaware, it seems, of the existence of Bentham's writings advocating democratic institutions,[123] he nevertheless applauded the democratic tendencies of his ideas:

> He has stated with more clearness than any preceding writer the real objects of the civil law, and the best methods of attaining them. If he has not carried his ideas to the extent to which American statesmen are disposed to push their theories of government, he has made a near approximation to it. Indeed, the most radical of American statesmen can find much instruction in what he has uttered on this head.[124]

Reflecting on the principles of civil law stated in *The Theory of Legislation*, the reviewer summarised Bentham's recommendations to the legislator as follows:

[120] Ibid., p.256.

[121] Ibid., p.259.

[122] Ibid., pp.264–9.

[123] See esp. *The Plan of Parliamentary Reform, in the Form of a Catechism* (London 1817), Bowring, III. 433–557.

[124] Ibid., p.269.

> the single aim of the legislator should be to promote the greatest possible happiness of the community. But happiness is increased as our sufferings are lighter and fewer, and our enjoyments greater and more numerous. As the care of his enjoyments ought, however, to be left entirely to the individual, it becomes the principal duty of government to guard against pains. If it protects the rights of personal security, if it defends property, if it watches over honor, if it succors the needy, it accomplishes its main purposes. Government approaches perfection in proportion as the sacrifice of liberty on the part of the subject is diminished, and his acquisition of rights is increased.[125]

It is in this respect, according to the writer in *The United States Magazine and Democratic Review*, that Bentham contributed most to our understanding of the correct functioning of the law in relation to the individual, his liberty, property and security.

By contrast, W. Phillips struck a more critical vein of anti-Benthamism in *The North American Review*. Phillips noted that while the *Traités de législation* has had an 'immense circulation' in Europe, 'The force of his [Bentham's] ethical writings is almost spent; the principle of utility as the sole foundation and criterion of morals is about passing into the limbo of vanities'. What is of real value in Bentham's theory is its application to the science of legislation, 'a science which has come to be much more studied, and better understood, on the continent of Europe, than in either England or this country'.[126] But, according to Phillips, even this is purchased by the reader at too heavy a price, and it is only Dumont's editorial surgery that makes Bentham readable at all:

> Perhaps there was more meaning and wisdom in this scientific parade and solemn marshalling of forces, thirty years ago, when this treatise was originally written; but, at this day, it certainly appears to be mere mummery, the "uniform result" of which, to the reader, is, that Mr. Bentham cannot think and express himself with scientific simplicity, and clearness, and precision. He mistakes obscurity for profoundness. It is this scientific parade

125 Ibid.

126 *The North American Review*, vol. LI, no. CIX (October 1840), pp.385, 395.

> without definite meaning, or meaning worth expression, that renders him so insupportably tedious; insomuch that his most docile and confiding disciple, most happily endued with patience and long-suffering fortitude, cannot choose but give over, and pass by the scientific flummery, and choose out the passages where he talks with plain straightforwardness upon a practical, interesting question, where he heaves out masses of sense, with frequent felicity of phrase, illustration, and historical and classical references, though often with too bitter antipathy to creeds and hierarchies.[127]

Similar sentiments had been expressed before about the cumbersome and unreadable style of Bentham's writing and about Dumont's efforts in rendering the philosopher's ideas more readable and more palatable. But even among those well-disposed to Bentham's science of legislation, and this includes Neal and Hildreth, reservations about Bentham's moral theory were nearly always present in comments by Americans on his utilitarian philosophy.

Theory of civil law

In the path-breaking *Introduction to the Principles of Morals and Legislation* Bentham set out to delineate the component parts of utilitarian theory, with the aim of founding a comprehensive science of morals and legislation upon the principle of utility. He then considered the *Introduction* to be the foundational text of his thought, and plans for future works were intended to elucidate the practical application of the utility principle across a wide range of legal, political, and economic areas. No previous moralist could lay claim to such ambition or to the precision that Bentham brought to the task. Though he did not complete all the elements of the enormous task he had set for himself, looking back over his life's work Bentham would have been satisfied that the basic principles and concepts of his philosophy had provided the underpinnings of his entire approach to settling social issues. This approach was essentially that of a legal philosopher who looked to law as the pivotal structural determinant of the well-being of the individual

127 Ibid., p.388.

and the community. It is as a legal philosopher that Bentham is most well-known today, and this is how he viewed himself for much of his extensive career: a critical analyst of the law who would render it entirely rational in accordance with the principle of utility, and who would demonstrate the multiple ways in which properly constituted law could enhance the greatest happiness. In this respect, he envisaged the 'Pannomiom' or complete body of law supplying the functional framework for a society that facilitated individuals in achieving the greatest happiness.

It is not my intention here to spell out in detail the component elements of Bentham's utilitarian philosophy – these have been well enough described elsewhere by numerous scholars and continue to be debated in the literature on the subject.[128] The reader will find the relevant principles and concepts enunciated in the introductory part of *The Theory of Legislation*. Nor is it my intention to discuss Bentham's theory of penal law, the subject of the third part,[129] which has also received a good deal of attention in the literature on Bentham. Rather I want to highlight certain facets of the theory of civil law, the subject of the second part, since this is a topic upon which Bentham had not published anything at all prior to the appearance of the *Traités de législation*. Moreover, with the exception of Smith's translation in Bowring's edition of *The Works of Jeremy Bentham*, Bentham's theory of civil law did not exist in a published English version before Hildreth's translation of Dumont. This essential element of Bentham's general philosophy of law was read and digested by law reformers on both sides of the Atlantic in this form. It provides a compelling testimony to Bentham's early 'liberal' tendencies, and provides a vital counterpoint to the more directive and imposing theory of penal law.

In praising Bentham's science of legislation, Hildreth's American reviewers paid particular attention to the systematic presentation of his views on civil law. Also, it was the theory of civil law that particularly impressed itself on the teaching of law in the newly independent states of South America.[130] When the English jurist Sir James Fitzjames Stephen reviewed Hildreth's second edition of *The*

128 Some of these texts are listed in the Bibliography following the introduction.

129 Also the subject of much of *IPML* (*CW*), *passim*.

130 See above p. xi and note 32.

Theory of Legislation (1864) for *The Saturday Review*, he took the view that Bentham had single-handedly rescued this element of legal theory from neglect:

> The power of law over people's expectations and plans of life, and the inclination of mankind to judge of the character of the law by the way in which this power is exercised, are no doubt matters of the highest importance in legislation, and Bentham deserves great credit for having been the first writer to invest them with anything approaching to a fair share of prominence.[131]

Stephen believed it was this aspect of Hildreth's translation that made it 'one of the most influential of modern books'.[132] Likewise, in the brief introduction to the civil law part of the *Traités de législation*, Dumont had no reservations about the significance of Bentham's contribution to our understanding of this aspect of the law: 'he has made a new science of Civil Law: new and even paradoxical for those who have been bred in the opinions of the old schools; but simple, natural, and even familiar, to those who have not been bewildered by false systems'.[133] Its subject-matter deals with the basic elements of civil society: 'It treats of everything that is most interesting to men: of their security, of their property, of their mutual and daily transactions; of their domestic condition, in the relations of father, of children, of husband, and of wife. Here it is that *rights* and *obligations* spring up; for all the objects of law may be reduced, without mystery, to these two terms'.[134] The real mystery, according to Dumont, was the failure of law scholars to properly understand the inter-relationship between civil law and penal law, a relationship clearly evident in the establishment of 'rights':

[131] James Fitzjames Stephen, 'Bentham's "Theory of Legislation"', *Horæ Sabbaticæ. Reprint of articles contributed to* The Saturday Review, 3rd series (London 1892), p.215.

[132] Ibid, p.219; for Stephen the principles of the penal code were 'hardly so interesting, and … neither so original nor so profound, as those of the Civil Code'. (pp.217–18)

[133] Hildreth, I. 91.

[134] Hildreth, I. 89.

> To establish *rights*, is to grant permissions; it is to make prohibitions; it is, in one word, to create offences. To commit a private offence is to violate an obligation which we owe to an individual, – a right which he has in regard to us. To commit a public offence is to violate an obligation which we owe to the public, – a right which the public has in regard to us. Civil law, then, is only penal law viewed under another aspect. If I consider the law at the moment when it confers a right, or imposes an obligation, this is the civil point of view. If I consider the law in its sanction, in its effects as regards the violation of that right, the breaking through that obligation, that is the penal point of view.[135]

If rights and obligations are the principal concerns of the civil law, then according to what criteria should particular rights and obligations be established? In these introductory pages to the theory of the civil law, Dumont made plain Bentham's rejection of the 'fictions' of natural law and contract as the foundations of rights and obligations, and his consistent adherence to utility as the only basis upon which they should be created by law.

Bentham's position on the general objective of law is stated at the beginning of Ch. XII of the 'Principles of Legislation', where he writes that 'legislation has the same centre with morals, but it has not the same circumference', and just as morality is 'the art of directing the actions of men in such a way as to produce the greatest possible sum of good', so legislation should have 'precisely the same object'.[136] Bentham goes on to add certain caveats to this statement by indicating those areas in which legal intervention is inappropriate, even when the legislator might believe that some benefit will accrue. First, on the basis that all punishment is in its nature an evil (it threatens or delivers pain), the legislator is counselled to calculate that there is a clear and certain gain for the public in attempting to strengthen moral precepts by the application or threat of punishment. Where the evil of punishment outweighs the evil of the offence, the legislator should not intervene, since this will 'spread through society a degree of alarm more injurious than the evil intended to be prevented'. Second, the hand of the legislator

135 Ibid.

136 Hildreth I. 60.

should be stayed when there is 'the danger of overwhelming the innocent in seeking to punish the guilty'. The danger may arise from 'the difficulty of defining an offence, and giving a clear and precise idea of it'. Bentham had in mind here 'hard-heartedness, ingratitude, perfidy, and other vices', vices which should be left to the punishment of the 'popular sanction', that is the informal operations of public opinion.[137] These exceptions aside, Bentham's science of legislation has often been viewed as interventionist in character, with the only goal in the legislator's view being the aggregate happiness of the community. This interpretation of Bentham receives support from his panopticon writings and essays on the poor law, projects in which utility seemed to determine a paternalist approach to solving social questions, and could not help but be reinforced by such typical Bentham proposals as the use of tattoos to identify individuals and to track their activities as a way of ensuring public morality in the essay *Indirect Means of Preventing Offences*.[138] However, this view of Bentham's utilitarian legal philosophy is often pressed without giving adequate consideration to the writings on civil law, a point eloquently made by Paul Kelly.[139]

In *The Theory of Legislation* the 'Principles of the Civil Code' is divided into three parts. The second part deals with the distribution of property, and part three considers rights and obligations as they relate to 'private conditions', including relations between master and servant (and slaves), guardian and ward, father and child, and husband and wife. It is in the first part that the objects of the civil law are mapped out, and the principles upon which they should be based are explained.

As Stephen recognised, the essence of Bentham's civil law position is the argument that outside the area of criminal activity 'the care of his enjoyments ought to be left almost entirely to the individual',

[137] Ibid.

[138] The essay constitutes Part Fourth of 'Principles of the Penal Code' in Hildreth, II. 358–472, and the tattoo identification proposal is at pp.416–18.

[139] In *Utilitarianism and Distributive Justice* Kelly attempts a reconstruction of Bentham's utilitarianism, placing the theory of civil law at its core. My reservations about the ultimate coherence of this approach are stated in James E. Crimmins, 'Contending Interpretations of Bentham's Utilitarianism', *Canadian Journal of Political Science*, vol. 29, no. 4 (1996), pp.751–77, but I do not wish to detract from the value of Kelly's work in making us aware of the significance of the theory of civil law within the structure of Bentham's legal philosophy.

and that 'the principal function of government is to guard against pains'. From this perspective, the way for governments to protect individuals is to create and confer rights, such as the 'rights of personal security, rights of protection for honour, rights of property, rights of receiving aid in case of need'. Infringements of these rights should be regarded as offences punishable by law.[140] To this basic utilitarian structure of the civil law, Bentham added the 'subordinate ends' of utility – security, subsistence, abundance, and equality, in this order of priority – intended as a guide to the legislator in the development of policy and law. 'The more perfect enjoyment is in all these respects, the greater is the sum of social happiness: and especially of that happiness which depends upon the laws'.[141] The hierarchy of these subordinate ends is explained as follows: 'At first glance we see subsistence and security arising together to the same level; abundance and equality are manifestly of inferior importance. In fact, without security, equality could not last a day; without subsistence, abundance could not exist at all. The two first objects are life itself; the two latter, the ornaments of life. ... [And] unless the laws are made directly for security, it would be quite useless to make them for subsistence'.[142]

The priority Bentham gave to security in this analysis encompassed the liberty of the individual, which is not considered as a separate object of the law, since rightly conceived liberty is only a branch of security. Personal liberty is 'security against a certain kind of injuries which affect the person', while political liberty 'is another branch of security, – security against injuries from the ministers of government'.[143] In later life Bentham prosecuted the cause of political liberty when he advocated democracy as a mechanism to hold political representatives accountable to the people, and to check the misuse of power. In the civil law manuscripts of the 1780s (used by Dumont for the *Traités de législation*) Bentham was at pains to underscore the degree to which he associated liberty with security – security of expectations, security of property, and security against misrule. To the idea of liberty as the absence of coercion

140 Hildreth, I. 95.

141 Hildreth, I. 96.

142 Hildreth, I. 98.

143 Hildreth, I. 97.

should be added, therefore, the consideration that the coercive force of the law is needed to maintain security; both have a place in Bentham's thinking about the various relationships between the individual and the law.

At the root of Bentham's understanding of security as the principal object of law is the security of 'expectation' – the guarantee against future loss, which enables individuals to confidently plan for the future in their labour and contractual arrangements, knowing that they will not be disappointed in their legitimate expectations.[144] It is not enough to secure a person from 'actual loss'; it is also necessary 'to guarantee him, as far as possible, against future loss'.[145] Since expectation 'is a chain which unites our present existence to our future existence', the principle of security must be extended to protect our expectations: 'it requires that events, so far as they depend upon laws, should conform to the expectations which law itself has created'.[146] As Bentham explained, 'The legislator is not master of the dispositions of the human heart, he is only their interpreter and their minister. The goodness of the laws depends upon their conformity to general *expectation*. The legislator ought to be well acquainted with the progress of this expectation, in order to act in concert with it'.[147] Every attack upon such expectations 'produces a distinct and special evil, which may be called *a pain of disappointment*'.[148]

The most important of our expectations are related to property. Property is a creature of law, not an *a priori* claim rooted in natural right; without law there is no 'right' to one's possessions. The law functions both to create and protect the expectations associated with property, for 'Property is nothing but a basis of expectation; the expectation of deriving certain advantages from a thing which we are said to possess, in consequence of the relation in which we stand towards it'. The idea of property, according to this analysis, 'consists in an established expectation,' which is the persuasion that we are able to draw an advantage from our possessions. This persuasion is the work of law: 'I cannot count upon the enjoyment of that which

144 Hildreth, I. 154, 161, 177.

145 Hildreth, I. 110.

146 Hildreth, I. 111.

147 Hildreth, I. 148.

148 Hildreth, I. 111.

I regard as mine, except through the promise of the law which guarantees it to me'.[149] It would be contradictory for the law to threaten that security of expectation which it has itself created, and when the legislator does not contradict it 'he does what is essential to the happiness of society; when he disturbs it, he always produces a proportionate sum of evil'.[150] Therefore, the first duty of the law is to maintain the established distribution of property.[151]

Here we see the development of what Bentham later (in the 1820s) termed the 'disappointment-preventing principle', intended as a practical strategy to be followed by the legislator when the effect of new legislation would be to thwart an individual's legitimate expectations. Where possible, disappointment must be avoided, but where it cannot be avoided, it must be adequately compensated. This was intended as a safeguard against wide-ranging and ill-conceived plans to redistribute property, such as Bentham believed occurred in France following the Revolution. But, it was not meant as a bulwark against all reform in the distribution of property. Slavery should be abolished, Bentham thought, but not in a manner that might reduce to poverty those legally involved in the trade; compensation from public funds would make up for the disappointed expectations of legal slave traders.[152] Moreover, government could intervene to redistribute wealth on those occasions when legitimate expectations would not be thwarted, for example when a man dies leaving to his heirs a vast inheritance or if he should die without an immediate heir. On such occasions the law may intervene, albeit cautiously, 'either by limiting in certain respects the testamentary power, in order to prevent too great an accumulation of wealth in the hands of an individual; or by regulating the succession in favour of equality in cases where the deceased has left no consort, nor relation in the direct line, and has made no will'. In the latter circumstances 'equality may do what is best for all without disappointing any'.[153] Moreover, Bentham leaves

[149] Hildreth, I. 111–12.

[150] Hildreth, I. 113.

[151] Hildreth, I. 119.

[152] Hildreth, I. 122–3; also see Bentham's discussion at pp.206–8.

[153] Hildreth, I. 122. Another practical application of the principle can be seen in Bentham's plan, elaborated in *Church-of-Englandism and its Catechism Examined* (London 1818), Appendix No.IV, §2, to compensate dispossessed clergy in the event of the disestablishment of the Anglican Church (here described as the '*uti possidetis* principle'). The strategy was implemented by the

room for taxation, on the grounds that this does not constitute an attack upon security, but rather should be considered a 'defalcation', that is 'a fixed, regular, and necessary deduction, which is expected; which produces only an evil of the first order; but no danger, no alarm, no discouragement to industry'.[154] On this basis, the law could intervene to ensure that the state provides necessary services and, where other options are not available, to assist the indigent.[155] Nevertheless, the tendency of Bentham's thinking is at bottom conservative when dealing with property rights.

Once a system of property is established, the pain associated with changing it (the frustration of the desires of those who possess property) determines that security of expectations is given priority over the potential benefits to be gained by a forced re-distribution. In the same way that theft of property causes pain to the victim, so legally-sanctioned dispossession produces the same effect: 'the suffering of him who incurrs a loss is always greater than the enjoyment of him who makes a gain'.[156] Even so, according to Bentham's own analysis this cannot hold absolutely. Given the diminishing marginal utility of pleasure,[157] there must come a point when the loss to an extremely wealthy person will be outweighed by the gains to others if a portion of his wealth were dispossessed for redistribution. But to this Bentham would respond that even the smallest dispossession of property that is rightfully-owned, unless conducted in accordance with the principles stated, would be viewed as an attack on the general security of all and serve to undermine the confidence of the people that their property will be protected by the state. It was on these grounds that he opposed all general schemes for the equalization of wealth, and argued that policies to enhance equality must only be incremental, at all times respecting existing expectations, and proceeding strictly in accord with the compensatory requirements of the 'disappointment-prevention principle'.

British government when it disestablished the Irish church following the division of Ireland in 1920.

154 Hildreth, I. 124.

155 Bentham discussed the problem of indigence in Hildreth, I. 127–33.

156 *Manual of Political Economy*, in *Jeremy Bentham's Economic Writings*, 3 vols., ed. Werner Stark (London 1952–4), I. 239.

157 See Hildreth, I. 103–9.

With few exceptions Bentham's economic writings are based on the principles of his theory of civil law.[158] Delineating and protecting property rights and upholding contract law is the way for government to facilitate individuals in the pursuit of their interests in a free market, because this is the proven best way to maximise the public good. Where *laissez-faire* does not produce the best result, the legislator can act in other direct and indirect ways to produce the optimal outcome. The question, as Bentham explained in *Manual of Political Economy* (written 1793–5), 'is to know what ought and what ought not to be done by government. It is in this view, and in this view only that the knowledge of what is done and takes place without the interference of government can be of any practical use'.[159] In the later *Institute of Political Economy* (written 1801–4), he argued that past experience provided sufficient evidence to convince us that governments should not act in the economic realm as much as they often do, hence the motto 'Be quiet' and the lists of 'non-agenda' items. Where departures from this general rule are required – such as when vital subsistence goods would be priced beyond the reach of many – they become 'agenda' items for government.[160] This seems to point to a political economy that is 'liberal' in a distinctly modern sense, one in which *laissez-faire* holds general sway, the basic rules of which are maintained by government, with occasional exceptions justified on the grounds of utility (or its subordinate ends).

John Rawls, one of the most influential of modern critics of utilitarianism, was clearly not persuaded in *A Theory of Justice* (1971) that the principles of the civil law developed by Bentham made much difference to how we understand the general maximizing objective of utilitarian theory.[161] Rawls's view is implicitly based on the legislative utilitarian perspective that takes for its model the 'felicific calculus' in its relationship to law, a focus that is ill-prepared

[158] The best recent discussion of the relationship between Bentham's theory of civil law and his writings on economic questions is Paul Kelly, 'Utilitarianism and Distributive Justice: The Civil Law and the Foundations of Bentham's Economic Thought,' *Utilitas*, vol. 1, no. 1 (1989), pp. 62–81.

[159] *Manual of Political Economy*, Stark, I. 224.

[160] Stark, III. 333; see also Bentham's *Defence of a Maximum*, Stark, III. 247–302.

[161] See John Rawls, *A Theory of Justice* (Cambridge, Mass. 1971), esp. Ch. I, sec. 5. Kelly (in *Utilitarianism and Distributive Justice*) has had much to do with challenging Rawls' position, but also see the relevant chapters in Frederick Rosen, *Classical Utilitarianism from Hume to Mill* (Routledge 2003), in which he stresses the place of liberty in the utilitarian tradition.

to address questions related to the distribution of rights and goods and which, as Rawls insists, 'does not take seriously the distinction between persons'.[162] This is not to say that Rawls was incorrect in his reasoning about the defects of a utilitarian approach that concerns itself *only* with the maximization of happiness, without regard to its distribution or the inclusion of the specific individuals who constitute the relevant community. And, he may well have been right to suggest that utilitarians, at least classical utilitarians, only set forth contingent secondary or subsidiary principles as a refinement of the maximizing imperative of their theory (to produce the greatest happiness of the community). However, that Bentham was at times ambiguous about the nature of the relationship between the utility principle and other principles used to decide distributive questions, suggests there is room to construct a more 'liberal' version of his theory, one which defines the utility principle in terms of other principles, rather than these secondary principles being justified themselves solely in terms of their contribution to general utility.

In reply to Rawls, Paul Kelly has sought to exploit this opening by reconstructing Bentham's utilitarianism to argue that he intended equal rights to operate as a set of minimum guarantees, designed to enable individuals to go about their business and pursue their own happiness in ways they determine for themselves, secure in the knowledge that their legally-sanctioned rights would be protected. In line with this interpretation, Kelly believes the civil law writings show Bentham constructing a utilitarian theory of justice upon the twin foundations of the 'security-providing principle' and 'the disappointment-preventing principle', by means of which the legislator was to bring about the overall end of maximum social well-being.[163] The use of these two principles enabled Bentham to reconcile the reformist implications of his utilitarianism with an indirect strategy founded on the primacy of securing expectations. On this view, his utilitarianism embodies a theory of distributive justice, enabling him to take seriously liberal values such as liberty, equality, and independence, and a notion of law as setting the conditions within which individuals can exercise their own judgement and pursue their own self-defined

162 Rawls, *A Theory of Justice*, pp.26–7.

163 Kelly's interpretation in *Utilitarianism and Distributive Justice* is in large part based on the extant civil law mss. from the 1780s in the Bentham Papers at University College London.

interests. The maximization of well-being is achieved by extending to each agent as wide a sphere of personal inviolability as possible, in ways that are compatible with the same security for others.[164] Beyond this, in so far as social well-being depends on the provision of subsistence, this too is best secured through the provision of security of expectations, enabling each individual to secure his subsistence through productive labour. For those who are unable to provide for themselves, the legislator must guarantee the provision of the means of subsistence, since only on the basis of continued existence can interest formation and realization take place.

Whether or not we are persuaded by Kelly's interpretation of Bentham, it is worth noting that the economic ramifications of Bentham's theory of civil law, with its stress on the limited role for government and the need to uphold the rights of the people, were not likely to be lost on American readers of Hildreth's translation of Dumont. Though based on entirely different assumptions, the utilitarian argument for individual liberty, rights and security, property ownership and the rules of contract, ended in conclusions not very different from those drawn from natural law and the idea of the social contract. This may explain why this aspect of Bentham's legal philosophy proved resistant to criticism from his American readers, while the application of utilitarian principles to moral questions received far rougher treatment. Moreover, we should not be surprised to find the developing political societies of nineteenth-century Europe and the Americas paying particular attention to his civil law prescriptions as they concern property. The rights of ownership and the principles governing distribution will always be matters of immediacy in societies experiencing political upheaval, or when governments attempt large-scale political and social reform.

James E. Crimmins, *2004*
Huron University College, Ontario

[164] I present only the gist of Kelly's interpretation; the reader interested in the grounding and details of the argument should consult *Utilitarianism and Distributive Justice*.

COMPARATIVE TABLE OF EDITIONS

Dumont 1802	**Dumont, 2nd edn. 1820 (also Dumont, 3rd edn. 1830, with variations in pagination)**
Vol. 1: 'Discourse préliminaire', vi–xxxvi. Ouvrages, xxxvii. Tables des Chapitres du Tome Premier, xxxviii–xli. (1) 'Principes de législation', Chs. I–XIII, 1–140. (2) 'Vue générale d'un Corps complet de législation', 141–370.[2]	Vol. 1: 'Discourse préliminaire', v–xxxii. Ouvrages, xxxiii. Tables des Chapitres du Tome Premier, xxxv–xl. (1) 'Principes de législation', Chs. I–XIII, 1–132. (2) 'Principes du Code civil' [in three parts], 133–368.
Vol. 2: [Introduction by Dumont], v–xv, and Tables des Chapitres du Tome Second, xvi–xx. (3) 'Principes du Code civil' [in three parts] , 1–236. (4) 'Principes du Code pénal' [in four parts; quatrième partie in vol. 3] , 237–434.	Vol. 2: Tables des Chapitres du Tome Second, i–iv. (3) 'Principes du Code pénal' [in four parts], pp.1–379.
Vol. 3: Tables des Chapitres du Tome Troisième, v–viii. 'Principes du Code pénal' [cont.], 'Quatrième Partie. Des moyens indirects de prévenir Délits', 1–199. (5) 'Panoptique. Mémoire sur un nouveau principe pour construire des Maisons d'inspection, et nommément des Maisons de force', 201–72 [includes editor's introduction, 203–7].[5] (6) 'Promulgation des lois. – Promulgation des raisons des lois', 273–321. (7) 'De L'influence des tems et des lieux en matière de législation', 323–95. (8) 'Table des matières', 397–452 [summary account of the *Traités*].	Vol. 3: Table des Chapitres du Tome Troisième, v–viii. [Introduction], 1–6. (4) 'Panoptique. Mémoire sur un nouveau principe pour construire des Maisons d'inspection, et nommément des Maisons de force', 1–66. (5) 'Promulgation des lois. – Promulgation des raisons des lois', 67–112. (6) 'De L'influence des tems et des lieux en matière de législation', 113–79. (7) 'Vue générale d'un Corps complet de législation', 181–400 [includes Advertissement, 183–4]. (8) 'Table des matières'.

1 Hildreth's 1840 edn. was published in two volumes: I. 'Principles of Legislation' and 'Principles of the Civil Code'; II. 'Principles of the Penal Code'.

2 Located in tome III in the later editions of the *Traités*.

3 Edited by Richard Smith (see Bowring, X. 548 n); includes 'Appendix. Of the Levelling System' (358–64), probably based on Bentham mss.; not in Dumont or Hildreth.

Hildreth, 2nd edn. 1864 (translated from Dumont, 2nd edn. 1820)[1]	Bowring or *Collected Works* (CW) compared with Hildreth 1864 (Dumont 1820)
Translator's Preface, iii-ix [containing a translation of part of Dumont's 'Discourse préliminaire', iv-viii]. Contents, xi-xv. (1) 'Principles of Legislation', Chs. I-XIII, 1-87. (2) 'Principles of the Civil Code': 'Introduction by Dumont', 88-92. 'Part First. Objects of the Civil Law', 93-157; 'Part Second. Distribution of Property', 158-98; 'Part Third. Rights and Obligations attached to Several Private Conditions', 199-236.	(1) Chs. I-XI, 1-59 based on *IPML* (*CW*), Chs. I-VI; Ch.XII, 60-66, based on *IPML* (*CW*), Ch.XVII; no comparable published text for Ch.XIII, 66-87 [probably based on Bentham mss.; see UC c. 105]. (2) 'Principles of the Civil Code', Bowring (with variations), I. 297-358 [title-page and contents, 297-8; 'Introduction', 299-300].[3]
(3) 'Principles of the Penal Code' [title-page, 237]: 'Part First. Offences', 239-70; 'Part Second. Political Remedies against the Evil of Offences', 271-321; 'Part Third. Of Punishments', 322-57; 'Part Fourth. Indirect Means of Preventing Offences', 358-472.	(3) Part First, sections based on *IPML* (*CW*), Ch. XVI; Part Second is 'Principles of Penal Law', Part I, Bowring, I. 367-88; Part Third is partly derived from *IPML* (*CW*), Chs. XIII-XV; Part Fourth is 'Principles of Penal Law', Part III, Bowring, I. 533-80.[4]
Hildreth omits contents of Vol. 3.	(4) *Panopticon; Or, The Inspection House* (1791), Bowring, IV. 37-171. (5) Bowring, I. 155-68 [edited from Dumont, Bentham's Mss., and printed works of Bentham]. (6) Bowring, I. 169-94 [from Bentham's mss.]. (7) 'A General View of a Complete Code of Laws', Bowring, III. 155-210 [based on Dumont, Bentham mss., and other printed works by Bentham]. (8) No comparable text.

[4] 'Principles of Penal Law', Bowring I. 365–525, edited by Richard Smith (Bowring, X. 548 n). Part II (Bowring, I. 390–532) is identical to *Rationale of Punishment* (London 1830), an English translation by Smith of parts of Dumont's redaction of Bentham's mss., titled *Théorie des peines et des récompense* (Paris 1811), together with material from the original mss. (Bowring, I. 367 n). Bowring omits Dumont's introductory 'Advertisement', in which he explained his role in the production of the work; the 1830 edition does not include the appendix in Bowring (I. 525–32), 'On Death Punishment', written by Bentham in 1831.

[5] An abridged version of the text in Bowring, IV. 37–171, originally printed for distribution to the National Assembly: *Panoptique, Imprimé par ordre de l'Assemblée Nationale* (Paris 1791).

BIBLIOGRAPHY

A. Editions of the *Traités de législation* and *The Theory of Legislation*

See the Comparative Table of Editions for variations between the editions of Dumont, Hildreth, Smith (Bowring), and *IPML* (*CW*).

[Étienne Dumont], *Traités de législation civile et pénale. Précédés de Principes généraux de Législation, et d'une Vue d'un Corps complet de Droit: terminés par un Essai sur l'influence des Tems et des Lieux relativement aux Lois. Par M. Jérémie Bentham, jurisconsulte anglois. Publiés en François par Ét. Dumont, de Genève, d'aprés les Manscrits confiés par l'Auteur*, 3 tom. (Paris, Chez Bossange, Masson et Besson, 1802).

——— [second edition] *Traités de législation civile et pénale; ouvrage extrait des manuscrits de M. Jérémie Bentham, jurisconsulte anglois; par Ét. Dumont, membre du Conseil Représentatif de Genève. Seconde édition, revue, corigée et augmentée,* 3 tom. (Paris, Bossange, Père et Fils, Rey et Gravier, 1820).

——— [third edition] *Traités de législation civile et pénale; ouvrage extrait des manuscrits de M. Jérémie Bentham, jurisconsulte anglois; par Ét. Dumont, membre du Conseil Représentatif de Genève. Troisième édition, revue, corigée et augmentée,* 3 tom. (Paris, Rey et Gravier, 1830).

——— [reprint of vols. 1–2 of Dumont], 2 tom. (Londres, Taylor et Francis, 1858).

[John Neal], *Principles of Legislation: From the Ms. of Jeremy Bentham; Bencher of Lincoln's Inn. By M. Dumont, Member of the Representative and Sovereign Council of Geneva. Translated from the Second Corrected and Enlarged Edition [Paris 1820]; with Notes and a Biographical Notice of Jeremy Bentham and of M. Dumont. By John Neal.* (Boston: Wells and Lilly–Court-Street [etc.] 1830). viii, 310 pp.

Includes Preface [by Neal], pp.iii–v; Contents, pp.vii–viii; 'Biographical Notice of Jeremy Bentham' [by Neal]: Ch.I. 'His

General Character', pp.9–26; Ch.II. 'General View of his Works', pp.27–40; Ch.III. 'Familiar Anecdotes of Mr. Bentham', pp.41–55; Chs.IV–VI. ['Bentham's Reminiscences'], pp.56–118; 'Chapter on Utility' [by Neal], pp.119–47; 'Biographical Sketch of M. Dumont, of Geneva' [by Neal, including a lengthy description attributed to Bentham], pp.148–57; 'Sketch of the Life and Character of Stephen Dumont. By J. C. L. de Sismondi', pp.157–72; 'Principles of Legislation' [Neal's translation], Chs. I–XIII, 175–310. The latter includes Neal's translation of 'Preliminary Discourse. By M. Dumont' (pp.173–93), and the text which follows (Chs. I–XIII, pp.194–310) correlates with Hildreth, I, Chs. I–XIII, pp.1–87.

[Richard Hildreth], *Theory of Legislation; by Jeremy Bentham. Translated from the French of Etienne Dumont, by R. Hildreth, Author of "Banks, Banking, and Paper Currencies," "Despotism in America," "Archy Moore," &c.*, 2 vols. (Boston, Weeks, Jordan & Co., 1840).

Hildreth's translation of the corrected 2nd edn. of Dumont's text (Paris, Bossange, Père et Fils, Rey et Gravier, 1820).

——— [second edition, in one volume] (London, Trübner & Co., 1864), xv, 472 pp. [identical reprint, 1871; subsequent editions and reprints 1876, 1882, 1890, 1891, 1894, 1896, 1900, 1908, 1911].

[Richard Smith], *Principles of the Civil Code* and *Principles of Penal Law*, in *The Works of Jeremy Bentham, Published under the Superintendence of his Executor, John Bowring*, 11 vols. (Edinburgh, William Tait, 1838–43), I. 297–580.

[Charles Milner Atkinson], *Bentham's Theory of Legislation, Being Principes de Législation and Traités de Législation, Civile et Pénale*, translated and edited from the French of Étienne Dumont by Charles Milner Atkinson, 2 vols. (London, Oxford University Press, 1914).

Atkinson's translation of Dumont with additional notes, together with an introduction (I. iii–xii), and index (II. 338–62). Though the text is much the same as Hildreth's and is arranged in an identical manner, there are several differences, including variations in chapter headings and in the numbering of chapters between the two editions, and Atkinson has introduced text from other sources in Bentham's writings.

[C. K. Ogden], *The Theory of Legislation, by Jeremy Bentham, edited with an introduction and notes by C. K. Ogden* (London, Kegan Paul, Trench, Trubner & Co. Ltd., 1931). li, 555 pp.

Ogden's text is printed from the plates of Hildreth's corrected 2nd edn. 1864, together with an introduction (pp.ix–li), an appendix titled 'Bentham on Sex' (pp.473–97), notes to the text (pp.499–539), 'A Note on English Law' (pp.541–2), and two indexes (To the Body of the Work, pp.543–50, and To Notes, Introduction, and Appendix, pp.551–5).

B. Manuscripts

Bentham manuscripts at University College London (UC followed by box and page/folio No.)

Douglas G. Long, *The Manuscripts of Jeremy Bentham: A Chronological Index to the Collection in the Library of University College London*, printed by the Bentham Committee at UCL, 1982.

A. Taylor Milne, *Catalogue of the Manuscripts of Jeremy Bentham in the Library of University College* (1937; 2nd edn., London, Athlone Press, 1962).

C. Collected Works

The Works of Jeremy Bentham, Published under the Superintendence of his Executor, John Bowring, 11 vols. (Edinburgh, William Tait, 1838–43).

Jeremy Bentham's Economic Writings, 3 vols., ed. Werner Stark (London, Allen and Unwin, 1952–54).

The Collected Works of Jeremy Bentham (= *CW*), General Editors: J. H. Burns, J. R. Dinwiddy, F. Rosen, T. P. Schofield (London: Athlone Press; Oxford: Clarendon Press, 1968 –), in progress:

– *An Introduction to the Principles of Morals and Legislation*, ed. J. H. Burns and H. L. A. Hart (1970).

– *Of Laws in General*, ed. H. L. A. Hart (1970).

– *A Comment on the Commentaries and A Fragment on Government*, ed. J. H. Burns and H. L. A. Hart (1977).

– *Chrestomathia*, ed. M. J. Smith and W. H. Burston (1983).

– *Constitutional Code*, vol. i, ed. F. Rosen and J. H. Burns (1983).

– *Deontology together with A Table of the Springs of Action and the Article on Utilitarianism*, ed. A. Goldworth (1983).

– *First Principles Preparatory to Constitutional Code*, ed. P. Schofield (1989).
– *Securities against Misrule and other Constitutional Writings for Tripoli and Greece*, ed. P. Schofield (1990).
– *Official Aptitude Maximized; Expense Minimized*, ed. P. Schofield (1993).
– *Colonies, Commerce, and Constitutional Law: Rid Yourselves of Ultramaria and other Writings on Spain and Spanish America*, ed. P. Schofield (1995).
– "*Legislator of the World": Writings on Codification, Law, and Education*, eds. P. Schofield and J. Harris (1998).
– *Political Tactics*, eds. M. James, C. Blamires and C. Pease-Watkin (1999).
– *Writings on the Poor Laws*, vol. 1, ed. M. Quinn (2001).
– *Rights, Representation, and Reform: Nonsense upon Stilts and other Writings on the French Revolution*, ed. P. Schofield, C. Pease-Watkin and C. Blamires (2002).
– *The Correspondence of Jeremy Bentham*: vols. i–ii, 1752–76, 1777–80, ed. T. L. S. Sprigge (1968); vol. iii, 1781–88, ed. I. R. Christie (1971); vols. iv–v, 1788–93, 1794–97, ed. A. T. Milne (1981); vols. vi–vii, 1798–1801, 1802–8, ed. J. R. Dinwiddy (1984, 1988); vols. viii–x, 1809–16, 1817–20, 1820–21, ed. S. R. Conway (1988, 1989); vol. xi, 1822–24, ed. C. Fuller (2000).

D. Selected Secondary Sources

Almira de Avila-Martel, 'The Influence of Bentham on the Teaching of Penal Law in Chile', *The Bentham Newsletter*, no. 5 (1981), pp.22–8.
[Anon.], 'JEREMY BENTHAM', *The United States Magazine and Democratic Review*, vol. VIII, no. XXXIII (September 1840), pp. 251–71.
David Baumgardt, 'The Forgotten Moralist: Richard Hildreth's Theory of Morals', *Ethics*, vol. 57, no. 3 (April 1947), pp.191–8.
——— *Bentham and the Ethics of Today, with Bentham Manuscripts Hitherto Unpublished* (New York, Princeton University Press 1966).
Cyprian Blamires, 'Étienne Dumont: Genevan Apostle of Utility', *Utilitas*, vol. 2, no. 1 (1990), pp.55–70.
Charles Blount, 'Bentham, Dumont and Mirabeau', *University of*

Birmingham Historical Journal, vol. III, no. 2 (1952), pp.153–67.

James E. Crimmins, 'Contending Interpretations of Bentham's Utilitarianism', *Canadian Journal of Political Science*, vol. 29, no. 4 (1996), pp.751–77.

——— *On Bentham*, Wadsworth Philosophers Series (Belmont, CA: Wadsworth 2004).

——— and Mark G. Spencer (eds), *Utilitarians and their Critics in America, 1789–1914*, 4 vols. (Bristol, Thoemmes Continuum 2005).

J.R Dinwiddy, 'Bentham and the Early Nineteenth Century', *The Bentham Newsletter*, no.8 (1984), pp.15–33.

——— 'Early-Nineteenth-Century Reactions to Benthamism', *Transactions of the Royal Historical Society*, 5th series, vol. 34 (1984), pp.47–69.

——— *Bentham* (Oxford, Oxford University Press 1989).

Donald E. Emerson, *Richard Hildreth* (Baltimore, Johns Hopkins University 1946).

Elie Halévy, *The Growth of Philosophic Radicalism* [*La Formation du radicalisme philosophique*] (1901–4, trans. M. Morris, 1928: Clifton, New Jersey: Augustus M. Kelley 1972).

Ross Harrison, *Bentham* (London and New York, Routledge 1983, reprt. 1999).

Paul Kelly, 'Utilitarianism and Distributive Justice: The Civil Law and the Foundations of Bentham's Economic Thought,' *Utilitas*, vol. 1, no. 1 (1989), pp. 62–81.

——— *Utilitarianism and Distributive Justice: Jeremy Bentham and the Civil Law* (Oxford, Clarendon Press 1990).

Douglas G. Long, *Bentham on Liberty: Jeremy Bentham's Idea of Liberty in Relation to his Utilitarianism* (Toronto, University of Toronto Press 1977).

Antonio-Enrique Pérez Luño, 'Jeremy Bentham and Legal Education in the University of Salamanca during the Nineteenth Century', *The Bentham Newsletter*, no. 5 (1981), pp.44–54.

Theodora L. McKennon, 'Benthamism in Santander's Colombia', *The Bentham Newsletter*, no. 5 (1981), pp.29–43.

Bhikhu Parekh (ed.), *Jeremy Bentham: Critical Assessments*, 4 vols. (London, Routledge 1993).

[W. Phillips], '*Theory of Legislation; by* JEREMY BENTHAM. *Translated from the French of* ETIENNE DUMONT, by R.

HILDRETH, [etc.]', *The North American Review*, vol. LI, no. 109 (October 1840), pp. 384–96.

Martha M. Pingel, *An American Utilitarian: Richard Hildreth as a Philosopher* (New York, Columbia University Press 1948).

Frederick Rosen, *Classical Utilitarianism from Hume to Mill* (London, Routledge 2003).

James Fitzjames Stephens, 'Bentham's "Theory of Legislation"', *Horæ Sabbaticæ*, 3rd series (London, MacMillan 1892), pp. 210–29.

ACKNOWLEDGEMENTS

I am indebted to my student Toby Schwartz for invaluable research assistance, and to Huron University College for funding support. Also, my thanks to Professor Philip Schofield and Professor Hugo Adam Bedau for information relating to the English translation and editorial work conducted on Dumont's volumes by Richard Smith. As ever, I am particularly grateful to Johanne for fortifying me with the necessary encouragement, and for her boundless patience while I conducted the work for this project. Parts of the introduction are based on previously published work, including 'Contending Interpretations of Bentham's Utilitarianism', *Canadian Journal of Political Science*, vol. 29, no. 4 (1996), pp.751–77, and *On Bentham* (Belmont, CA: Wadsworth 2004).

J.E.C.
Huron University College
2004

THEORY

OF

LEGISLATION;

BY

JEREMY BENTHAM.

TRANSLATED FROM THE FRENCH OF ETIENNE DUMONT,

BY

R. HILDRETH.

LONDON:
TRÜBNER & CO., 60, PATERNOSTER ROW.
MDCCCLXIV.

TRANSLATOR'S PREFACE.

WHATEVER may be thought of the *Principle of Utility*, when considered as the foundation of morals, no one now-a-days will undertake to deny that it is the only safe rule of legislation.

To establish and illustrate this proposition, and to show how it ought to be, and might be carried into practice, was the aim and end of Bentham's life and writings.

Bacon derives his fame from the fact that he was the first who fully appreciated and formally laid down the proposition, now familiar to everybody, that experiment and observation are the only solid bases of the physical sciences. In the moral sciences, and especially in legislation, the principle of utility is the only certain guide; and, in the estimation of an impartial posterity, Bentham will rank with Bacon, as an original genius of the first order.

Already, upon the continent of Europe, his writings have attained the highest reputation. In England and America, though frequently spoken of, they are little read; though they are often criticised, or sneered at, by persons who have never seen them, and who are totally ignorant of their contents. This circumstance is easily explained. Bentham was born and bred in England, and spent all his life there; but his works, in any compact and collected form, exist only in French. He published many treatises in English; but for the generality of readers they have very few attractions. He was not skilful in the art of composition; he did not possess the gift of eloquence. Though endowed with a great genius for investigation, he lacked the talent of communicating his ideas. During a long life, devoted solely and assiduously to the study of jurisprudence, besides his occasional publications, he produced an immense mass of manuscripts, containing a fund of most valuable ideas, but unshaped, unarranged, and in a state quite unfit for publication. Fortunately for the cause of science, these materials were not left to perish; an interpreter, a compiler, a spokesman was found, every way worthy of the task he assumed.

Dumont, a citizen of Geneva, whom political troubles had driven from his own country, after a residence of some years at St Petersburg, where he gained a high reputation as a preacher of the Reformed Church, came to London under the patronage of the Lansdowne family, and there made Bentham's acquaintance. He became his friend and disciple, was permitted to examine and to study his manuscript treatises; and, having discovered the value of this hidden treasure, he solicited the task of arranging, condensing, filling out, compiling, and translating into the French language.

But Dumont's relation to the writings of Bentham will best be explained in his own words. "If, in labouring upon these manuscripts," he says,* "I had been able to confine myself to a mere translation, I should be more tranquil as to my success; but I am not in a position so fit to inspire me with confidence. I owe it to the public not to conceal my share in this compilation; I owe it to the author to declare, that he only yielded to the solicitations of friendship, and that he often unwillingly

* Preliminary Discourse to the first edition of the *Treatise on Legislation*.

gave up to me works unfinished, and sometimes materials unformed.

"In giving a general idea of my part in this undertaking, I begin with a declaration which ought to shield me from undeserved blame, as well as from the distress of unmerited praise. I declare that I have no share, no claim of association, in the composition of these works. They belong entirely to the author, and to him alone. The more I esteem them, the more desirous am I to disavow an honour which would be a usurpation, as contrary to the faith of friendship as it is repugnant to my personal character. This declaration, which I owe to myself, would, I know, be superfluous if all readers were philosophers. Such will themselves discover, amid all the diversity of these writings, the impress of one mind,—a unity of plan, an original genius, as analytic and profound in the general design as in the execution of the parts.

"My labour, subaltern in its kind, has been limited to details. It was necessary to make a choice among various observations upon the same subject; to suppress repetitions; to throw light upon obscurities; to bring together all that appertained to the same subject; and to fill up those gaps which, in the hurry of composition, the author had left. I have had more to retrench than to add; more to abridge than to expand. The mass of manuscripts put into my hands was considerable. I have had much to do in attaining correctness, and preserving uniformity of style; little or nothing as respects the fundamental ideas. A profusion of riches left me only the care of economy. As manager of this great fortune I have spared no pains to realize it, and put it into circulation.

"The changes I have made have varied with the manuscripts. When I have found many treatises relative to the same subject, but composed at different times and with different views, it has been necessary to reconcile them, and to incorporate them together, so as to form a perfect whole. The author perhaps had thrown aside some occasional composition, which now would not be interesting, or even intelligible. Unwilling that the whole should perish, I have stripped it, like an abandoned house, of everything worth preserving. When he has delivered himself up to abstractions too profound, to metaphysics, I do not say too subtle, but too dry, I have endeavoured to give more development to his ideas, to illustrate them by applications, by facts, by examples; and I have allowed myself to scatter, with discretion, some ornaments. I have been obliged to write out some entire chapters, but always after hints and notes of the author; and the difficulty of the task would have sufficed to bring me back to a modest estimation of myself, if at any time I had been exposed to the temptation of thinking otherwise.

"The author's *Introduction to the Principles of Morals and Legislation,* regarded by a small number of enlightened judges as one of those original productions which form an epoch and a revolution in science, in spite of its philosophical merit, and perhaps on account of that merit, produced no sensation, and remained almost unknown to the public,—though in England, more than elsewhere, a useful book may come into notice, though it does not happen to be easy and agreeable. In using many chapters of that work to form the *General Principles of Legislation,* I have endeavoured to avoid what prevented its success,—forms too scientific, sub-divisions too much multiplied, analysis too abstract. I have translated not the words, but the ideas; I have sometimes made an abridgment, and at others a commentary, I have been guided by the advice and the hints of the author, contained in a preface, written many years after the work itself; and I have found among his papers all the additions of any consequence.

"Upon considering how much this enterprise, which I thought to confine to two or three volumes, has extended by degrees, and what a vast career I have run through,* I regret that the labour had not fallen into abler hands; yet I am encouraged to applaud my perseverance, convinced as I am that otherwise these manuscripts would for a long time have remained buried in their own bulk, and that the author, always rushing forward, would never have found the leisure nor the courage to give himself up to the ungrateful labour of a general revision.

"This ardour to produce, and this indifference to publication; this perseverance in the severest labours; and this disposition to abandon his work at the moment of completion, presents a singularity which needs to be explained.

"As soon as Bentham had discovered the great divisions, the great classifications of laws, he embraced legislation as a whole, and formed the vast project of treating it in all its parts. He considered it not as composed of detached works, but as forming a single work. He had before his eyes the general chart of the science, and after that model he framed particular charts of all its departments. Hence it follows that the most striking peculiarity of his writings is their perfect correspondence. I have found the earlier ones full of references to works which were merely projected, but of which the divisions, the forms, the principal ideas, existed already in separate tables. It is thus that, having subjected all his materials to a general plan, each branch of legislation occupies its appropriate place, and none is to be found under two divisions. This order necessarily supposes an author who has for a long time considered his subject in all its relations; who masters the whole of it; and who is not influenced by a puerile impatience for renown.

"I have seen him suspend a work almost finished, and compose a new one, only to assure himself of the truth of a single proposition which seemed to be doubtful. A problem in finance

* This refers to other works of Bentham, announced by Dumont as ready for publication.

has carried him through the whole of political economy. Some questions of procedure obliged him to interrupt his principal work till he had treated of judicial organization. This preparatory labour, this labour in the mines, is immense. No one can form an idea of it except by seeing the manuscripts, the catalogues, the synoptical tables in which it is contained.

"But I am not writing a panegyric. It must be confessed that the care of arrangement and correction has few attractions for the genius of Bentham. While pushed on by a creative force he feels only the pleasure of composition; when it becomes necessary to shape, to put in order, to finish, he experiences nothing but fatigue. If a work is interrupted the evil becomes irreparable; the charm vanishes; disgust succeeds; and passion, once quenched, can only be rekindled by a new object.

"This same turn of mind has prevented him from taking any part in the compilations which I now present to the public. It was rarely that I was able to obtain any explanations, or even that aid of which I was absolutely in need. It cost him too much to suspend the actual course of his ideas, and to return again upon old tracks.

"But it is, perhaps, to this kind of difficulty that I owe my perseverance. If it had been my business only to translate, I should soon have grown wearied of a task so uniform yet so difficult; while the labour of a free compilation flatters by a kind of illusion, which lasts as long as it is useful, and vanishes when the work is done."

Among Dumont's first publications from the manuscripts of Bentham, was the treatise of which these volumes contain a translation. He afterwards brought out several other works, compiled in the same way, and from the same sources; and it is only in these compilations that we find anything like a clear and complete development of the ideas of Bentham, or a full exposition of his system of legislation.

Public attention in America is every day more and more attracted to the subject of Legal Reform; and the translator flatters himself that he will have performed a useful and acceptable service, in restoring to its native English tongue the following treatise.

It includes a vast field, never before surveyed upon any regular plan, and least of all according to such principles as Bentham has laid down. In the application of those principles he has, doubtless, made some mistakes; for mistakes are of necessity incident to a first attempt. But he has himself furnished us with the means of detecting those mistakes and of correcting them. He asks us to receive nothing on his mere authority. He subjects everything to the test of *General Utility.*

CONTENTS.

Part Second.

DISTRIBUTION OF PROPERTY.

Part Third.

RIGHTS AND OBLIGATIONS ATTACHED TO SEVERAL PRIVATE CONDITIONS.

PRINCIPLES OF THE PENAL CODE.

Part First.

Of Offences.

Part Second.

Political Remedies against the Evil of Offences.

Part Third.

OF PUNISHMENTS.

Part Fourth.

INDIRECT MEANS OF PREVENTING OFFENCES.

PRINCIPLES OF LEGISLATION.

CHAPTER I.

The Principle of Utility.

THE PUBLIC GOOD ought to be the object of the legislator; GENERAL UTILITY ought to be the foundation of his reasonings. To know the true good of the community is what constitutes the science of legislation; the art consists in finding the means to realize that good.

The principle of *utility*, vaguely announced, is seldom contradicted; it is even looked upon as a sort of common-place in politics and morals. But this almost universal assent is only apparent. The same ideas are not attached to this principle; the same value is not given to it; no uniform and logical manner of reasoning results from it.

To give it all the efficacy which it ought to have, that is, to make it the foundation of a system of reasonings, three conditions are necessary.

First,—To attach clear and precise ideas to the word *utility*, exactly the same with all who employ it.

Second,—To establish the unity and the sovereignty of this principle, by rigorously excluding every other. It is nothing to subscribe to it in general; it must be admitted without any exception.

Third,—To find the processes of a moral arithmetic by which uniform results may be arrived at.

The causes of dissent from the doctrine of utility may all be referred to two false principles, which exercise an influence, sometimes open and sometimes secret, upon the judgments of men. If these can be pointed out and excluded, the true principle will remain in purity and strength.

These three principles are like three roads which often cross each other, but of which only one leads to the wished-for destination. The traveller turns often from one into another, and loses in these wanderings more than half his time and strength. The true route is however the easiest; it has mile-stones which cannot be shifted, it has inscriptions, in a universal language, which cannot be effaced; while the two false routes have only contradictory directions in enigmatical characters. But without abusing the language of allegory, let us seek to give a clear idea of the true principle, and of its two adversaries.

Nature has placed man under the empire of *pleasure* and of *pain*. We owe to them all our ideas; we refer to them all our judgments, and all the determinations of our life. He who pretends to withdraw himself from this subjection knows not what he says. His only object is to seek pleasure and to shun pain, even at the very instant that he rejects the greatest pleasures or embraces pains the most acute. These eternal and irresistible sentiments ought to be the great study of the moralist and the legislator. The *principle of utility* subjects everything to these two motives.

Utility is an abstract term. It expresses the property or tendency of a thing to prevent some evil or to procure some good. *Evil* is pain, or the cause of pain. *Good* is pleasure, or the cause of pleasure. That which is conformable to the utility, or the interest of an individual, is what tends to augment the total sum of his happiness. That which is conformable to the utility, or the interest of a community, is what tends to augment the total sum of the happiness of the individuals that compose it.

A *principle* is a first idea, which is made the beginning or basis of a system of reasonings. To illustrate it by a sensible image, it is a fixed point to which the first link of a chain is attached. Such a principle must be clearly evident;—to illustrate and to explain it must secure its acknowledgment. Such are the axioms of mathematics; they are not proved directly; it is enough to show that they cannot be rejected without falling into absurdity.

The *logic of utility* consists in setting out, in all the operations of the judgment, from the calculation or comparison of pains and pleasures, and in not allowing the interference of any other idea.

I am a partisan of the *principle of utility* when I measure my approbation or disapprobation of a public or private act by its tendency to produce pleasure or pain; when I employ the words *just*, *unjust*, *moral*, *immoral*, *good*, *bad*, simply as collective terms including the ideas of certain pains or pleasures; it being always understood that I use the words *pain* and *pleasure* in their ordinary signification, without inventing any arbitrary definition for the sake of excluding certain pleasures or denying the existence of certain pains. In this matter we want no refinement, no metaphysics. It is not necessary to consult Plato, nor Aristotle. *Pain* and *pleasure* are what everybody feels to be such—the peasant and the prince, the unlearned as well as the philosopher.

He who adopts the *principle of utility*, esteems virtue to be a good only on account of the pleasures which result from it; he regards vice as an evil only because of the pains which it produces. Moral good is *good* only by its tendency to produce physical good. Moral evil is *evil* only by its tendency to produce physical evil; but when I say *physical*, I mean the pains and pleasures of the soul as well as the pains and pleasures of sense. I have in view man, such as he is, in his actual constitution.

If the partisan of the *principle of utility* finds in the common list of virtues an action from which there results more pain than pleasure, he does not hesitate to regard that pretended virtue as a vice; he will not suffer himself to be imposed upon by the general error; he will not lightly believe in the policy of employing false virtues to maintain the true.

If he finds in the common list of offences some indifferent action, some innocent pleasure, he will not hesitate to transport this pretended offence into the class of lawful actions; he will pity the pretended criminals, and will reserve his indignation for their persecutors.

CHAPTER II.

*The Ascetic Principle.**

This principle is exactly the rival, the antagonist of that which we have just been examining. Those who follow it have a horror of pleasures. Everything which gratifies the senses, in their view, is odious and criminal. They found morality upon privations, and virtue upon the renouncement of one's self. In one word, the reverse of the partisans of utility, they approve everything which tends to diminish enjoyment, they blame everything which tends to augment it.

This principle has been more or less followed by two classes of men, who in other respects have scarce any resemblance, and who even affect a mutual contempt. The one class are philosophers, the other, devotees. The ascetic philosophers, animated by the hope of applause, have flattered themselves with the idea of seeming to rise above humanity, by despising vulgar pleasures. They expect to be paid in reputation and in glory, for all the sacrifices which they seem to make to the severity of their maxims. The ascetic devotees are foolish people, tormented by vain terrors. Man, in their eyes, is but a degenerate being, who ought to punish himself without ceasing for the crime of being born, and never to turn off his thoughts from that gulf of eternal misery which is ready to open beneath his feet. Still, the martyrs to these absurd opinions have, like all others, a fund of hope. Independent of the worldly pleasures attached to the reputation of sanctity, these atrabilious pietists flatter themselves that every instant of voluntary pain here below will procure them an age of happiness in

* Ascetic, by its etymology, signifies *one who exercises.* It was applied to the monks, to indicate their favourite practices of devotion and penitence.

another life. Thus, even the ascetic principle reposes upon some false idea of utility. It acquired its ascendancy only through mistake.*

The devotees have carried the ascetic principle much further than the philosophers. The philosophical party has confined itself to censuring pleasures; the religious sects have turned the infliction of pain into a duty. The stoics said that pain was not an evil; the Jansenists maintained that it was actually a good. The philosophical party never reproved pleasures in the mass, but only those which it called gross and sensual, while it exalted the pleasures of sentiment and the understanding. It was rather a preference for the one class, than a total exclusion of the other. Always despised or disparaged under its true name, pleasure was received and applauded when it took the titles of *honour*, *glory*, *reputation*, *decorum*, or *self-esteem*.

Not to be accused of exaggerating the absurdity of the ascetics, I shall mention the least unreasonable origin which can be assigned to their system.

It was early perceived that the attraction of pleasure might seduce into pernicious acts; that is, acts of which the good was not equivalent to the evil. To forbid these pleasures, in consideration of their bad effects, is the object of sound morals and good laws. But the ascetics have made a mistake, for they have attacked pleasure itself; they have condemned it in general; they have made it the object of a universal prohibition, the sign of a reprobate nature; and it is only out of regard for human weakness that they have had the indulgence to grant some particular exemptions.

* This mistake consists in representing the Deity in words, as a being of infinite benevolence, yet ascribing to him prohibitions and threats which are the attributes of an implacable being, who uses his power only to satisfy his malevolence.

We might ask these ascetic theologians what life is good for, if not for the pleasures it procures us?—and what pledge we have for the goodness of God in another life, if he has forbidden the enjoyment of this?

CHAPTER III.

Section I.

The Arbitrary Principle; or the Principle of Sympathy and Antipathy.

This principle consists in approving or blaming by sentiment, without giving any other reason for the decision except the decision itself. *I love, I hate;* such is the pivot on which this principle turns. An action is judged to be good or bad, not because it is conformable, or the contrary, to the interest of those whom it affects, but because it pleases or displeases him who judges. He pronounces sovereignly; he admits no appeal; he does not think himself obliged to justify his opinion by any consideration relative to the good of society. "It is my interior persuasion; it is my intimate conviction; I feel it; sentiment consults nobody; the worse for him who does not agree with me—he is not a man, he is a monster in human shape." Such is the despotic tone of these decisions.

But, it may be asked, are there men so unreasonable as to dictate their particular sentiments as laws, and to arrogate to themselves the privilege of infallibility? What you call the *principle of sympathy and antipathy* is not a principle of reasoning; it is rather the negation, the annihilation of all principle. A true anarchy of ideas results from it; since every man having an equal right to give *his* sentiments as a universal rule, there will no longer be any common measure, no ultimate tribunal to which we can appeal.

Without doubt the absurdity of this principle is sufficiently manifest. No man, therefore, is bold enough to say openly, "I wish you to think as I do, without giving me the trouble to reason with you." Every one would revolt against a pretension so absurd. Therefore, recourse is had to diverse inventions of disguise. Despotism is veiled under some ingenious phrase. Of this the greater part of philosophical systems are a proof.

One man tells you that he has in himself something which has been given him to teach what is good and what is evil; and this he calls either his *conscience* or his *moral sense*. Then, working at his ease, he decides such a thing to be good, such another to be bad. Why? Because my moral sense tells me so; because my conscience approves or disapproves it.

Another comes and the phrase changes. It is no longer the moral sense,—it is *common sense* which tells him what is good and what is bad. This common sense is a sense, he says, which belongs to everybody; but then he takes good care in speaking of everybody to make no account of those who do not think as he does.

Another tells you that this moral sense and this common sense are but dreams; that the *understanding* determines what is good and what is bad. His understanding tells him so and so; all good and wise men have just such an understanding as he has. As to those who do not think in the same way, it is a clear proof that their understandings are defective or corrupt.

Another tells you that he has an *eternal and immutable rule of right*, which rule commands this and forbids that; then he retails to you his own particular sentiments, which you are obliged to receive as so many branches of the eternal rule of right.

You hear a multitude of professors, of jurists, of magistrates, of philosophers, who make the *law of nature* echo in your ears. They all dispute, it is true, upon every point of their system; but no matter—each one proceeds with the same confident intrepidity, and utters his opinions as so many chapters of the *law of nature*. The phrase is sometimes modified, and we find in its place, *natural right, natural equity, the rights of man*, &c.

One philosopher undertakes to build a moral system upon what he calls *truth;* according to him, the only evil in the world is lying. If you kill your father, you commit a crime, because it is a particular fashion of saying that he is not your father. Everything which this philosopher does not like, he disapproves under the pretext that it is a sort of falsehood—since it amounts to asserting that we ought to do what ought not to be done.

The most candid of these despots are those who say openly, "I am one of the elect; and God takes care to enlighten the elect as to what is good and what is evil. He reveals himself to me, and speaks by my mouth. All you who are in doubt, come and receive the oracles of God."

All these systems, and many more, are at bottom only the *arbitrary principle, the principle of sympathy and antipathy*, masked under different forms of language. The object is, to make our opinions triumph without the trouble of comparing them with the opinions of other people. These pretended principles are but the pretext and the support of despotism,—at least of that despotism of disposition which has but too much inclination to develop itself in practice whenever it can do so with impunity. The result is, that with the purest intentions a man torments himself, and becomes the scourge of his fellows. If he is of a melancholy disposition, he falls into a sullen taciturnity, and bitterly deplores the folly and the depravity of man. If he is of an irascible temper, he declaims furiously against all who do not think as he does. He becomes one of those ardent persecutors who do evil in the spirit of holiness; who blow the fires of fanaticism with that mischievous activity which the persuasion of duty always gives; and who brand with the reproach of perversity or of bad faith all who do not blindly adopt the opinions which they hold sacred.

However, it is essential to observe that the *principle of sympathy and antipathy* must often coincide with the *principle of utility*. To love what benefits us, to hate what hurts us, is a universal principle of the human heart. It thus happens that, from one end of the world to the other, acts beneficent or hurtful are regarded with the same sentiments of approbation or dislike. Morality and jurisprudence, led by this kind of instinct, have often reached the great end of utility without having a clear idea of it. But these sympathies and these antipathies are not a sure and invariable guide. Let a man refer his happiness or his misery to an imaginary cause, and he becomes subject to unfounded loves and unreasonable hates. Superstition, charlatanism, the spirit of sect and party, repose almost entirely upon blind sympathies and blind antipathies.

Incidents the most frivolous,—a difference in fashion, a slight diversity of opinion, a variety in taste, are enough to present a man to the eyes of another under the aspect of an enemy. What is history, but a collection of the absurdest animosities, the most useless persecutions? A prince conceives an antipathy against certain men who use some indifferent expressions; he calls them Arians, Protestants, Socinians, Deists. He builds scaffolds; the ministers of the altar array the executioners; the day on which the heretics perish in the flames is celebrated as a national festival. In Russia a civil war was undertaken to settle a long controversy as to the number of fingers which ought to be used in making the sign of the cross. The citizens of Rome and Constantinople were divided into implacable factions about players, charioteers, and gladiators; and to give importance to such shameful quarrels, it was pretended that the success of the *greens* or of the *blues* presaged abundance or famine, victories or reverses to the empire.

Antipathy may sometimes be found in unison with the principle of utility; but even then it is not a good basis of action. When a person through resentment prosecutes a robber before the tribunals, the action is certainly good, but the motive is dangerous. If it sometimes produces good actions, more often its fruits are fatal. The sole basis of action always surely good is the consideration of utility. Good is often done from other motives; it is never constantly done except from that consideration alone. Sympathy and antipathy must be subjected to it, to prevent them from becoming hurtful; but the principle of utility is its own regulator; it admits no other; and it is impossible to give that principle too great extension.

To sum up;—the *ascetic principle* attacks utility in front. The *principle of sympathy* neither rejects it nor admits it; it pays no attention to it; it floats at hazard between good and evil. The ascetic principle is so unreasonable, that its most senseless followers have never attempted to carry it out. The principle of sympathy and antipathy does not prevent its partisans from having recourse to the principle of utility. This last alone neither asks nor admits any exception. *Qui non sub me contra me;* that which is not under me is against me; such is its motto. According to this principle, to legislate is an affair of observation and calculation; according to the ascetics, it is an affair of fanaticism; according to the principle of sympathy and antipathy, it is a matter of humour, of imagination, of taste. The first method is adapted to philosophers; the second to monks; the third is the favourite of wits, of ordinary moralists, of men of the world, of the multitude.

Section II.

Causes of Antipathy.

Antipathy exercises so powerful an influence over morals and legislation, that it is important to investigate the principles which give birth to it.

First Cause.—*Repugnance of Sense.*—Nothing is more common than the transition from a physical to a moral antipathy, especially with feeble minds. A multitude of innocent animals suffer a continual persecution, because they have the misfortune to be thought ugly. Everything unusual has the power of exciting in us a sentiment of disgust and hatred. What is called a *monster* is only a being which differs a little from others of its kind. Hermaphrodites, whose sex is undetermined, are regarded with a sort of horror, only because they are rare.

Second Cause.—*Wounded Pride.*—He who does not adopt my opinion, indirectly declares that he has but little respect for my knowledge upon the point in dispute. Such a declaration offends my self-love, and shows me an adversary in this man, who not only testifies a degree of contempt for me, but who will propagate that contempt in proportion as his opinion triumphs over mine.

Third Cause.—*Power controlled.*—Even when our vanity does not suffer, we perceive by the difference of tastes, by the resistance of opinions, by the shock of interests, that our power is limited, that our dominion, which we desire to extend everywhere, is bounded on every side. This compulsive feeling of our own weakness is a secret pain, a germ of discontent against others.

FOURTH CAUSE.—*Confidence in the future weakened or destroyed.*—We love to believe that men are such as we imagine our happiness requires them to be. Every act on their part which tends to diminish our confidence in them, cannot but give us a secret disgust. An example of falsehood makes us see that we cannot always rely upon what they say, or what they promise; an example of absurdity inspires a general doubt as to their reason, and consequently as to their conduct. An act of caprice, or of levity, makes us conclude that we cannot rely on their affections.

FIFTH CAUSE.—*The desire of unanimity.*—Unanimity pleases us. This harmony of sentiment is the only pledge we can have, apart from our own reason, of the truth of our opinions, and of the utility of the actions founded upon those opinions. Besides, we love to dwell upon subjects to our taste; it is a source of agreeable recollections and of pleasing hopes. The conversation of persons whose taste conforms to ours, augments this fund of pleasure, by fixing our attention upon agreeable objects, and presenting them to us under new points of view.

SIXTH CAUSE.—*Envy.*—He who enjoys himself without doing harm to anybody, ought not, it would seem, to have enemies. Yet it may be said that his enjoyment impoverishes those who do not partake it.

It is a common observation, that envy acts with most force against recent advantages, while it spares older ones. Thus it is, that the word *upstart* always has an injurious acceptation. It expresses a new success; envy adds, as accessory ideas, humbling recollections and a feigned contempt.

Envy makes ascetics. The differences of age, of wealth, of circumstances, prevent all men from having equal enjoyments; but the severity of privation can reduce all to the same level. Envy inclines us towards rigid speculations in morals, as a means of reducing the amount of pleasures. It has been said,—and with reason,—that a man who should be born with an organ of pleasure, which the rest of us do not possess, would be pursued as a monster.

Such is the origin of antipathy; such is the collection of sentiments of which it is composed. To moderate its violence, let us recollect that there is no such thing as a perfect conformity even between two individuals; that if we yield to this unsociable sentiment, it will always go on increasing, and will contract more and more the circle of our good-will and of our pleasures; that, in general, our antipathies re-act against ourselves; that it is in our power to enfeeble, and even to extinguish them, by banishing from our minds the ideas of those objects by which they are excited. Fortunately, the causes of sympathy are constant and natural, while the causes of antipathy are accidental and transitory.

Moral writers may be arranged in two classes; those who labour to extirpate the venomous plants of antipathy; and those who seek to propagate them. The first class are apt to be calumniated; the others gain respect and popularity, because, under the specious veil of morals, they are in the service of vengeance and of envy. The books which attain the most speedy celebrity, are those which the demon of antipathy has dictated, such as libels, works of party, satirical memoirs, &c. *Telemachus* did not owe its brilliant success to its morality, or to the charm of its style; but to the general opinion that it contained a satire upon Louis XIV. and his Court. When Hume, in his History, wished to calm the spirit of party, and to treat the passions like a chemist who analyzes poisons, the mob of readers rose up against him; they did not like to see it proved that men were rather ignorant than wicked, and that past ages, always extolled to depreciate the present, had been far more fertile in misfortunes and crimes.

Fortunate for himself, fortunate is the writer who can give himself up to these two false principles; to him belong the field of eloquence, the employment of figures, the vehemence of style, exaggeration of expressions, and all the vulgar vocabulary of the passions. All his opinions are dogmas, eternal, immutable truths, as immoveable as God and nature. As a writer, he exercises the power of a despot, and proscribes those who do agree with him.

The partisan of the principle of utility is in a position by no means so favourable to eloquence. His means are as different as his object. He can neither dogmatize, dazzle, nor astonish. He is obliged to define all his terms, and always to employ the same word in the same sense. He consumes a long time in getting ready, in making sure of his foundation, in preparing his instruments; and he has everything to fear from that impatience which grows weary with preliminaries, and which wishes to arrive in a moment at great results. However, this slow and cautious advance is the only one which leads to the end desired; for if the power of spreading truth among the multitude belongs to eloquence, the power of discovering it appertains only to analysis.

CHAPTER IV.

Operation of these principles upon Legislation.

The principle of utility has never yet been well developed, nor well followed out by any legislator; but, as we have already mentioned, it has penetrated from time to time into laws, from its occasional alliance with the principles of sympathy and antipathy. The general ideas of vice and virtue, founded upon a confused perception of good and evil, have been sufficiently uniform in every essential point; and the early laws, without which no society can exist, have been made in conformity with these popular ideas.

The ascetic principle, though embraced with warmth by its partisans in their private conduct, has never had much direct influence upon the operations of government. On the contrary, every government has had for its system and its object the acquisition of strength and prosperity. The rulers of states have never made evil an end; they have been seduced into it by false views of greatness and power, or by private passions which have resulted in public evils. The system adopted at Sparta—a discipline which well entitles that community to be called a convent of warriors—in relation to the circumstances of that state, was necessary to its preservation, or, at least, was esteemed so by its legislator; and under that aspect, was conformable to the principle of utility. Many Christian states have permitted the establishment of monastic orders; but the vows are *supposed* to be voluntary. To torment one's self was esteemed a work of merit; to torment another against his will has been always regarded as a crime. St. Louis wore sackcloth, but he obliged none of his subjects to wear it.

The principle which has exercised the greatest influence upon governments, is that of sympathy and antipathy. In fact, we must refer to that principle all those specious objects which governments pursue, without having the general good for a single and independent aim; such as good morals, equality, liberty, justice, power, commerce, religion; objects respectable in themselves, and which ought to enter into the views of the legislator; but which too often lead him astray, because he regards them as ends, not as means. He substitutes them for public happiness, instead of making them subordinate to it.

Thus, a government, entirely occupied with wealth and commerce, looks upon society as a workshop, regards men only as productive machines, and cares little how much it torments them, provided it makes them rich. The customs, the exchanges, the stocks, absorb all its thoughts. It looks with indifference upon a multitude of evils which it might easily cure. It wishes only for a great production of the means of enjoyment, while it is constantly putting new obstacles in the way of enjoying.

Other governments esteem power and glory as the sole means of public good. Full of disdain for those states which are able to be happy in a peaceful security, they must have intrigues, negotiations, wars and conquests. They do not consider of what misfortunes this glory is composed, and how many victims these bloody triumphs require. The *éclat* of victory, the acquisition of a province, conceal from them the desolation of their country, and make them mistake the true end of government.

Many persons do not inquire if a state be well administered; if the laws protect property and persons; if the people are happy. What they require, without giving attention to anything else, is political liberty—that is, the most equal distribution which can be imagined of political power. Wherever they do not see the form of government to which they are attached, they see nothing but slaves; and if these pretended slaves are well satisfied with their condition, if they do not desire to change it, they despise and insult them. In their fanaticism they are always ready to stake all the happiness of a nation upon a civil war, for the sake of transporting power into the hands of those whom an invincible ignorance will not permit to use it, except for their own destruction.

These are examples of some of the phantasies which are substituted in politics, instead of the true search after happiness. They do not grow out of an opposition to happiness; they are the fruits of inadvertence or mistake. A small part of the plan of utility is seized upon; an exclusive attachment is evinced for that small part; in the pursuit of some particular branch of the public good, the general happiness is disregarded; it is forgotten that all these particular objects have only a relative value, and that happiness alone has a value which is intrinsic.

CHAPTER V.

Further Explanations.—Objections answered.

Some trifling objections, some little verbal difficulties, may be raised against the *principle of utility;* but no real or distinct objection can be opposed to it. In fact, how can it be contested except by reasons taken from itself? To say that it is a dangerous principle, is to say that it would be contrary to utility to consult utility.

The difficulty upon this question grows out of a kind of perversion of language. It has been customary to speak of *virtue* in opposition to *utility*. Virtue is described as the sacrifice of our interest to our duties.

To convey clear ideas upon this subject, it should be explained, that there are interests of different orders, and that different interests, in certain circumstances, are incompatible. Virtue is the sacrifice of a less interest to a greater, of a momentary to a durable, of a doubtful to a certain interest. Every idea of virtue not derived from this notion, is as obscure in conception as it is precarious in motive.

Those who, for the sake of accommodation, are willing to distinguish between politics and morals, to assign utility as the principle of the one, and justice as the foundation of the other, announce nothing but confused ideas. The only difference between politics and morals is, that one directs the operations of governments, and the other the actions of individuals; but their object is common; it is happiness. That which is politically good cannot be morally bad, unless we suppose that the rules of arithmetic, true for large numbers, are false for small ones.

While we imagine that we follow the *principle of utility*, we may nevertheless do evil. A feeble and narrow soul deceives itself by taking into consideration but a small part of evil or of good. An ardent disposition deceives itself by giving an extreme importance to a particular good, by which all consecutive evils are concealed from its sight. That which constitutes a bad man, is the habit of pleasures injurious to others; but this very habit supposes the absence of many kinds of pleasure. One ought not to hold *utility* responsible for mistakes contrary to its nature, and which it alone is able to rectify. If a man calculates badly, it is not arithmetic which is in fault; it is himself. If the charges which are alleged against Machiavel are well founded, his errors did not spring frcm having consulted the principle of utility, but from having applied it badly. This fact, the author of the *Anti-Machiavel* has clearly perceived. He refutes the *Prince* by making it appear that its maxims are fatal; and that bad faith is bad policy.

Those who, from reading Cicero's *Offices* and the Platonic moralists, have a confused notion of the *useful* as opposed to the *honest*, often quote that observation of Aristides upon the scheme which Themistocles was unwilling to disclose, except to him alone. "The project of Themistocles is *very advantageous*," said Aristides to the assembled people, "but it is *very unjust*." Here seems to be a decided opposition between the useful and the just. Not so. It is only a comparison of good and evil. *Unjust* is a term which presents the collective idea of all those evils which result from a situation in which men can no longer trust one another. Aristides might have said, "The project of Themistocles would be useful for a moment, but injurious for ages; what it would give is nothing in comparison with what it would take away." *

It is sometimes said that the *principle of utility* is only a revival of epicureanism. The ravages which that doctrine made in morals are well known. It was adopted by the most corrupt of men.

It is true that Epicurus alone of all the ancients had the merit of having known the true source of morals; but to suppose that his doctrine leads to the consequences that have been imputed to it, is to suppose that happiness may become the enemy of happiness. *Sic præsentibus utaris voluptatibus, ut futuris non noceas,* —So use present pleasures as not to lessen those which are to come. In this sentiment Seneca coincides with Epicurus; and what more can morality desire than the retrenchment of every pleasure injurious to one's self or to others? Now this is the very principle of utility.

But, it is again objected, every one makes himself the judge of his own utility, and upon this system every obligation will lose its force the moment people cease to see their interest in regarding it.

* This anecdote is not worth being cited except to clear up the sense of words. Its falsity has been proved. See Mitford's *History of Greece*. Plutarch wished to compliment the Athenians; but he would have been much embarrassed to reconcile the greater part of their history with this noble sentiment.

Every one makes himself the judge of his own utility; such is the fact, and such it ought to be; otherwise man would not be a rational agent. He who is not a judge of what is agreeable to him, is less than a child; he is an idiot. The obligation which binds men to their engagements is nothing but the perception of a superior interest, which prevails over an inferior interest. A man is bound not only by the particular utility of such or such an engagement; but when the engagement becomes onerous to one of the parties, he is still bound by the general utility of engagements; by the confidence in his word which every sensible man wishes to inspire, in order that he may be considered a man of truth, and enjoy the advantages incident to the reputation of probity. It is not the engagement itself which constitutes the obligation; for some engagements are void, and some are unlawful. Why? Because they are esteemed injurious. It is, then, the utility of a contract which gives force to it.

It is easy to reduce to a calculation of good and of evil all the acts of the most exalted virtue; and virtue is neither degraded nor weakened by being represented as an effect of reason, and being explained in a simple and intelligible manner.

If we refuse to acknowledge the principle of utility, we fall into a complete circle of sophistry. I ought to keep my promise. Why? Because my conscience bids me do it. How do you know that your conscience bids you do it? Because I have an interior feeling to that effect. Why ought you to obey your conscience? Because God is the author of my nature, and to obey my conscience is to obey God. Why ought you to obey God? Because it is my first duty. How do you know that? My conscience tells me so, &c., &c. We can never get out of this circle, which presently becomes the source of obstinate and inveterate error. For if we judge of everything by feeling, there is no means left to distinguish the dictates of an enlightened conscience from those of a blinded one. All persecutors will have the same pretence; all fanatics the same right.

If you desire to reject the principle of utility because it may be ill applied, what is there to put in its place? Where is the rule which cannot be abused? Where is this infallible guide?

Will you substitute for it some despotic principle, which orders men, like passive slaves, to act so and so, without knowing why?

Will you substitute for it some fluctuating and capricious principle, founded only upon your own intimate and particular feelings?

If so, what motives will you hold out to induce people to follow you? Shall these motives be independent of interest? In that case, if people do not agree with you, how will you reason with them,—how bring them to terms? Whither will you cite all the sects, all the systems, all the contradictions that cover the world, if not to the tribunal of a common interest?

The most obstinate opposers of the principle of utility are those who take their stand upon what they call the *religious principle.* They profess to take the will of God for the only rule of good and evil. It is the only rule, they say, which has all the requisite characters; which is infallible, universal, sovereign, and so on. I answer that the religious principle is not a distinct principle by itself; it is only a particular form of one or the other of those above described. Unless God explains himself to each individual by immediate acts and particular revelations, what is called his will can only be what we presume to be such. How does a man presume the will of God? From his own. Now his particular will is always directed by one of the three principles above described. How do you know that God forbids such and such a thing? "Because it would be prejudicial to the happiness of mankind," answers the partisan of utility. "Because it includes a gross and sensual pleasure," says the ascetic. "Because it wounds the conscience, is contrary to natural sentiments, and ought to be detested without stopping to examine it,"—such is the language of antipathy.

But revelation, it will be said, is the direct expression of the will of God. There is nothing left to be questioned or disputed. Here is a guide far preferable to human reason.

I do not answer indirectly that revelation is not universal; that even among Christian nations there are many persons who do not admit it; and that in morals and politics, some principle of reasoning is necessary, which is common to all men. But I reply that revelation is not a system of politics nor of morals; that all its precepts need to be explained, modified, and limited, one by the other; that, taken in a literal sense, they would overturn the world, annihilate self-defence, industry, commerce, reciprocal attachments; and that ecclesiastical history is an incontestable proof of the frightful evils which have resulted from religious maxims badly understood.

What a difference between the Protestant and Catholic theologians—between the moderns and the ancients! The gospel morality of Paley is not the gospel morality of Nicole. That of the Jansenists was not that of the Jesuits.

The interpreters of Scripture may be divided into three classes. The first class have the principle of utility for their rule of criticism; the second class are ascetics; the third class follows the mixed impressions of sympathy and antipathy. The first, far from excluding pleasure, quote it as a proof of the goodness of God. The ascetics are its mortal enemies; if they ever permit it, it is not for itself, but only in view of some certain necessary end. The last approve it, or condemn it, according to their fancy, without being guided by the consideration of consequences. It seems, then, that revelation is not a principle by itself; for nothing can be properly called a principle except that which needs no proof, and which serves to prove everything else.

CHAPTER VI.

The different kinds of Pleasures and Pains.

We experience without cessation a variety of sensations which do not interest us, and which glide by without fixing our attention. Thus, the greater part of the objects which are familiar to us no longer produce a sensation sufficiently vivid to cause us either pain or pleasure. These names cannot be given except to sensations which attract our attention; which make themselves noticeable in the crowd; and of which we desire the continuance or the end. These pleasurable perceptions are either simple or complex: simple, when they cannot be decomposed into others; complex, when they are composed of several simple pains or simple pleasures, or perhaps of a mixture of pleasures and pains. What determines us to regard several pleasures as a complex pleasure, and not as so many simple pleasures, is the nature of the cause which excites them. We are led to consider all the pleasures which are produced by the action of the same cause as a single pleasure. Thus a theatrical show which gratifies many of our senses at the same time by the beauty of decorations, music, company, dresses, and the action of performers, constitutes a complex pleasure.

It has cost a great labour of analysis to prepare a complete catalogue of the simple pleasures and pains. This catalogue has a dryness which will repulse many readers, for it is not the work of a writer of romance, who only seeks to please and move; it is a bill of particulars, it is the inventory of our sensations.

SECTION I.

Simple Pleasures.

1st. *Pleasures of Sense.*—Those which can be immediately referred to our organs independently of all associations, viz., the pleasures of *taste*, of *smell*, of *sight*, of *hearing*, of *touch*, especially the blessing of *health*, that happy flow of spirits, that perception of an easy and unburdensome existence, which cannot be referred to any of the senses in particular, but which appertains to all the vital functions; finally, the pleasures of *novelty*, those which we experience when new objects are applied to our senses. They do not form a separate class, but they play so conspicuous a part, that it is necessary to mention them expressly.

2nd. *Pleasures of Riches*—meaning thereby that kind of pleasure which we derive from the possession of a thing, which is a means of enjoyment or security,—a pleasure which is most lively at the moment of acquisition.

3rd. *Pleasures of Address.*—Those which result from some difficulty overcome, from some relative perfection in the handling and employ of the instruments which aid in the attainment of pleasure or utility. A person who touches a harpsichord, for example, experiences a pleasure perfectly distinct from that of hearing the same piece of music executed by another.

4th. *Pleasures of Friendship.*—Those which accompany the persuasion of possessing the good will of such and such individuals, and the right of expecting from them, in consequence, spontaneous and gratuitous services.

5th. *Pleasures of a good Reputation.*—Those which accompany the possession or acquisition of the esteem and good will of the people about us, the persons with whom we may have relations or common interests; and as a fruit of this disposition on their part, the right of expecting their voluntary and gratuitous services, should we happen to need them.

6th. *Pleasures of Power.*—Those which a man experiences who perceives in himself the means of disposing others to serve him through their hopes or their fears; that is, by the fear of some evil, or the hope of some good which he can do them.

7th. *Pleasures of Piety.*—Those which accompany the persuasion of acquiring or possessing the favour of God; and the power, in consequence, of expecting particular favours from him, either in this life or in another.

8th. *Pleasures of Benevolence.*—Pleasures which we are sensible of tasting, when we contemplate the happiness of those who love us. They may also be called *pleasures of sympathy* or *pleasures of the social affections.* Their force is more or less expansive. They have the power of concentrating themselves into a narrow circle, or of spreading over entire humanity. Benevolence extends itself to animals of which we love the species or individuals; the signs of their happiness affect us agreeably.

9th. *Pleasures of Malevolence.*—They result from the sight or the thought of pain endured by those beings who do not love us, whether men or animals. They may also be called *pleasures of the irascible passions, of antipathy, or of the anti-social affections.*

10th. When we apply our mental faculties to the acquisition of new ideas, and discover, or think we discover, interesting truths in the moral or physical sciences, the pleasure which we experience may be called the *pleasure of knowledge.* The transport of joy which Archimedes felt at the solution of a difficult problem, is easily understood by all those who have applied themselves to abstract studies.

11th. When we have tasted such or such a pleasure, and in certain cases even, when we have suffered such or such a pain, we love to retrace them exactly in the precise order of all their circumstances. These are the *pleasures of memory.* They are as varied as the recollections in which they originate.

12th. But sometimes memory suggests certain pleasures, which we arrange in a different order, according to our desires; and to which we join the most agreeable circumstances we have noticed, either in our own life or in that of others. These are *pleasures of the imagination.* The painter who copies after nature, represents the operations of memory; he who selects groups here and there, and arranges them to suit himself, represents the workings of the imagination. New ideas in the arts and sciences, and all discoveries which interest our curiosity, contribute to the pleasures of the imagination, which sees in these discoveries an extension of its field of enjoyments.

13th. The idea of a future pleasure, joined to the expectation of presently enjoying it, constitutes the *pleasure of hope.*

14th. *Pleasures of Association.*—An object may be unable to give any pleasure in itself; but if it is connected in the mind with some other object which is agreeable, it participates in the charm of that object. Thus the different incidents of a game of chance, when we play for nothing, derive their interest from an association with the pleasure of gaining.

15th. Lastly, there are pleasures founded upon pains. When one has suffered, the cessation or diminution of the pain is itself a pleasure, and often a very lively one. These may be called *pleasures of relief*, or *of deliverance*. They are as various as our pains.

Such are the materials of all our enjoyments. They unite, combine, and modify each other in a thousand ways, so that it requires some little attention and experience to discover, in a complex pleasure, all the simple pleasures which are its elements.

The delight which a country landscape gives, is composed of different pleasures—pleasures of the senses, of the imagination, and of sympathy. The variety of objects and their various colours, the flowers, the trees, the intermixture of light and shade, gratify the sight; the ear is soothed by the song of birds, the murmur of fountains, and the gentle rustling which the wind makes among the leaves; the air, embalmed with the perfume of fresh vegetation, wafts agreeable odours; while its elastic purity makes the circulation more rapid and exercise more agreeable. Imagination and benevolence unite to embellish the scene, by presenting ideas of wealth, of abundance, of fertility. The innocence and happiness of the birds, the flocks, and the domestic animals, furnish an agreeable contrast to the recollection of the fatigues and agitations of human life. We transfer to the inhabitants of the country all the pleasures with which the novelty of these objects inspires us. Finally, a sentiment of gratitude to that eternal Being, whom we regard as the author of all these benefits, augments our confidence and our admiration.

Section II.

Simple Pains.

1st. *Pains of Privation.*—These correspond to all the pleasures whose absence excites a sentiment of chagrin. They exist in three principal modifications. *First,* if we desire a certain pleasure, but have more fear of wanting it than hope of obtaining it, the pain that results may be called *pain of desire,* or *of unsatisfied desire.* *Second,* if we have had strong hopes of enjoying the pleasure in question, but these hopes have suddenly failed, this privation is a *pain of disappointment.* *Third,* if we have enjoyed a good, or, what amounts to the same thing, if we have counted strongly upon its possession, and then lose it, the sentiment which this loss produces is called *regret.* That languor of soul described by the word *ennui* is a pain of privation which cannot be referred to any particular object, but to the absence of every agreeable sensation.

2nd. *Pains of Sense.*—There are nine kinds: those of *hunger* and *thirst;* those of *taste,* of *smell,* of *touch,* produced by the application of substances which excite disagreeable sensations; those of *hearing* and *sight,* produced by sounds or images which offend those organs, independently of association; *excess of cold or heat,*—unless these pains ought to be referred to the sense of touch; *diseases* of all kinds; finally, *fatigue,* whether of mind or body.

3rd. *Pains of Mal-address.*—Those which are sometimes experienced in fruitless attempts or laborious efforts to apply to their different uses the various kinds of tools or instruments, whether of pleasure or pain.

4th. *Pains of Enmity.*—Those which a man feels when he believes himself an object of malevolence on the part of certain individuals, and apprehends that he may be exposed in consequence to experience the practical effects of their hatred.

5th. *Pains of a Bad Reputation.*—Those which a man feels when he believes himself actually an object of the malevolence or contempt of the world which surrounds him, or exposed to become so. They may also be called *pains of dishonour,* or *pains of the popular sanction.*

6th. *Pains of Piety.*—They result from the fear of having offended the Supreme Being, and of incurring his chastisements, either in this life or in the life to come. If they are thought to be well founded, they are called *religious fears,*—if ill founded, they are denominated *superstitious fears.*

7th. *Pains of Benevolence.*—These are the pains which we

experience at the sight or thought of the suffering whether of men or animals. The emotions of pity make us weep at the miseries of others, as well as at our own. They may also be called *pains of sympathy, pains of the social affections.*

8th. *Pains of Malevolence.*—These are the pains we experience at reflecting on the happiness of those we hate. They may also be called *pains of antipathy, pains of the anti-social affections.*

9th, 10th, and 11th. The *pains of memory,* of the *imagination,* and of *fear,* are the exact reverse and counterpart of the pleasures of corresponding names.

The labour of preparing this catalogue of pleasures and pains is dry, but its utility is great. The whole system of morals, the whole system of legislation, rests upon a single basis, and that basis is, the *knowledge of pains and pleasures.* It is the only foundation of clear ideas upon those subjects. When we speak of vices and virtues, of actions innocent or criminal, of a system remuneratory or penal, what is it that we speak of? Of pains and pleasures, and of nothing else. A reason in morals or politics, which cannot be translated by the simple words *pain* or *pleasure,* is an obscure and sophistical reason, from which nothing can be concluded.

You wish, for example, to study the subject of offences,—that great object which directs all legislation. This study, at bottom, will be nothing but a comparison, a calculation, of pains and pleasures. You consider the *criminality* or the *evil* of certain actions, —that is, the pains which result from them to such and such individuals; the *motive* of the delinquent,—that is, the expectation of pleasure which led him to commit the action in question; the *advantage* of the offence,—that is, the acquisition of pleasure which has resulted from it; the *legal punishment* which ought to be inflicted,—that is, what pain the guilty person ought to undergo. It thus appears that the theory of pains and pleasures is the sole foundation of all knowledge upon the subject of legislation.

The more these two catalogues are examined, the more matter for reflection they will be found to contain.

It is obvious at once, that pleasures and pains may be divided into two classes: *pleasures and pains which relate to others;—pleasures and pains purely personal.* Those of benevolence and of malevolence compose the first class; all the rest belong to the second.

It is worthy of observation that many kinds of pleasure exist without having corresponding pains. 1st. *Pleasures of novelty.* The sight of new objects is a source of pleasures, while the simple absence of new objects is not felt as a pain. 2nd. *Pleasures of love.* The want of them is not attended with positive pain, except when there is disappointment. Some temperaments may suffer from this want, but in general continence is in the power of every one, and is very far from being a state of pain. 3rd. *Pleasures of riches and of acquisitions;* they have no corresponding pains except where there is disappointment. To acquire is always agreeable; simple non-acquisition is not felt as a pain. 4th. It is the same with the *pleasures of power.* Their possession is a good; their mere absence is not an evil; it is only felt as an evil by reason of some particular circumstance, such as privation or disappointment.

CHAPTER VII.

Pains and Pleasures considered as Sanctions.

The will cannot be influenced except by motives; but when we speak of *motives,* we speak of *pleasures* or *pains.* A being whom we could not affect either by painful or pleasurable emotions would be completely independent of us.

The pain or pleasure which is attached to a law form what is called its sanction. The laws of one state are not laws in another, because they have no sanction there, no obligatory force.

Pleasures and pains may be distinguished into four classes:

1st. Physical.
2nd. Moral.
3rd. Political.
4th. Religious.

Consequently, when we come to consider pains and pleasures under the character of punishments and rewards, attached to certain rules of conduct, we may distinguish four sanctions.

1st. Those pleasures and pains which may be expected in the ordinary course of nature, acting by itself, without human intervention, compose the *natural or physical sanction.*

2nd. The pleasures or pains which may be expected from the action of our fellow-men, in virtue of their friendship or hatred, of their esteem or their contempt—in one word, of their spontaneous disposition towards us, compose the *moral sanction;* or it may be called the *popular sanction, sanction of public opinion, sanction of honour, sanction of the pains and pleasures of sympathy.*

3rd. The pleasures or pains which may be expected from the action of the magistrate, in virtue of the laws, compose the *political sanction;* it may also be called the *legal sanction.*

4th. The pleasures or pains which may be expected in virtue of the threats or promises of religion, compose the *religious sanction.*

A man's house is destroyed by fire. Is it in consequence of his imprudence?—It is a pain of the natural sanction. Is it by the sentence of a judge?—It is a pain of the political sanction. Is it by the malice of his neighbours?—It is a pain of the popular sanction. Is it supposed to be the immediate act of an offended Divinity?—In such a case it would be a pain of the religious sanction, or, vulgarly speaking, a judgment of God.

It is evident from this example that the same sort of pains belong to all the sanctions. The only difference is in the circumstances which produce them.

This classification will be very useful in the course of this work. It is an easy and uniform nomenclature, absolutely necessary to distinguish and describe the different kinds of moral powers, those intellectual levers which constitute the machinery of the human heart.

These four sanctions do not act upon all men in the same manner, nor with the same degree of force. They are sometimes rivals, sometimes allies, and sometimes enemies. When they agree, they operate with an irresistible power; when they are in opposition, they mutually enfeeble each other; when they are rivals, they produce uncertainties and contradictions in the conduct of men.

Four bodies of laws may be imagined, corresponding to these four sanctions. The highest point of perfection would be reached if these four codes constituted but one. This perfection, however, is as yet far distant, though it may not be impossible to attain it. But the legislator ought always to recollect that he can operate directly only by means of the political sanction. The three others must necessarily be its rivals or its allies, its antagonists or its ministers. If he neglects them in his calculations, he will be deceived in his results; but if he makes them subservient to his views, he will gain an immense power. There is no chance of uniting them, except under the standard of utility.

The natural sanction is the only one which always acts; the only one which works of itself; the only one which is unchangeable in its principal characteristics. It insensibly draws all the others to it, corrects their deviations, and produces whatever uniformity there is in the sentiments and the judgments of men.

The popular sanction and the religious sanction are more variable, more dependent upon human caprices. Of the two, the popular sanction is more equal, more steady, and more constantly in accordance with the principle of utility. The force of the religious sanction is more unequal, more apt to change with times and individuals, more subject to dangerous deviations. It grows weak by repose, but revives by opposition.

In some respects the political sanction has the advantage of both. It acts upon all men with a more equal force; it is clearer and more precise in its precepts; it is surer and more exemplary in its operations; finally, it is more susceptible of being carried to perfection. Its progress has an immediate influence upon the progress of the other two; but it embraces only actions of a certain kind; it has not a sufficient hold upon the private conduct of individuals; it cannot proceed except upon proofs which it is often impossible to obtain; and secrecy, force, or stratagem are able to escape it. It thus appears, from considering what each of these sanctions can effect, and what they cannot, that neither ought to be rejected, but that all should be employed and directed towards the same end. They are like magnets, of which the virtue is destroyed when they are presented to each other by their contrary poles, while their power is doubled when they are united by the poles which correspond.

It may be observed, in passing, that the systems which have most divided men have been founded upon an exclusive preference given to one or the other of these sanctions. Each has had its partisans, who have wished to exalt it above the others. Each has had its enemies, who have sought to degrade it by showing its weak side, exposing its errors, and developing all the evils which have resulted from it, without making any mention of its good effects. Such is the true theory of all those paradoxes which elevate nature against society, politics against religion, religion against nature and government, and so on.

Each of these sanctions is susceptible of error, that is to say, of some applications contrary to the principle of utility. But by applying the nomenclature above explained, it is easy to indicate by a single word the seat of the evil. Thus, for example, the reproach which after the punishment of a criminal falls upon an innocent family is an error of the popular sanction. The offence of usury, that is, of receiving interest above the legal interest, is an error of the political sanction. Heresy and magic are errors of the religious sanction. Certain sympathies and antipathies are errors of the natural sanction. The first germ of mistake exists in some single sanction, whence it commonly spreads into the others. It is necessary, in all these cases, to discover the origin of the evil before we can select or apply the remedy.

CHAPTER VIII.

The measure of Pleasures and Pains.

The sole object of the legislator is to increase pleasures and to prevent pains; and for this purpose he ought to be well acquainted with their respective values. As pleasures and pains are the only instruments which he employs, he ought carefully to study their power.

If we examine the *value* of a pleasure, considered in itself, and in relation to a single individual, we shall find that it depends upon four circumstances,—

1st. *Its intensity.*
2nd. *Its duration.*
3rd. *Its certainty.*
4th. *Its proximity.*

The value of a pain depends upon the same circumstances.

But it is not enough to examine the value of pleasures and pains as if they were isolated and independent. Pains and pleasures may have other pains and pleasures as their consequences. Therefore, if we wish to calculate the *tendency* of an act from which there results an immediate pain or pleasure, we must take two additional circumstances into the account, viz.—

5th. *Its productiveness.*
6th. *Its purity.*

A *productive pleasure* is one which is likely to be followed by other pleasures of the same kind.

A *productive pain* is one which is likely to be followed by other pains of the same kind.

A *pure pleasure* is one which is not likely to produce pains.

A *pure pain* is one which is not likely to produce pleasures.

When the calculation is to be made in relation to a collection of individuals, yet another element is necessary,—

7th. *Its extent.*

That is, the number of persons who are likely to find themselves affected by this pain or pleasure.

When we wish to value an action, we must follow in detail all the operations above indicated. These are the elements of moral calculation; and legislation thus becomes a matter of arithmetic. The *evil* produced is the outgo, the *good* which results is the income. The rules of this calculation are like those of any other. This is a slow method, but a sure one; while what is called sentiment is a prompt estimate, but apt to be deceptive. It is not necessary to recommence this calculation upon every occasion. When one has become familiar with the process; when he has acquired that justness of estimate which results from it; he can compare the sum of good and of evil with so much promptitude as scarcely to be conscious of the steps of the calculation. It is thus that we perform many arithmetical calculations almost without knowing it. The analytical method, in all its details, becomes essential, only when some new or complicated matter arises; when it is necessary to clear up some disputed point, or to demonstrate a truth to those who are yet unacquainted with it.

This theory of moral calculation, though never clearly explained, has always been followed in practice; at least, in every case where men have had clear ideas of their interest. What is it, for example, that makes up the value of a landed estate? Is it not the amount of pleasure to be derived from it? and does not this value vary according to the length of time for which the estate is to be enjoyed; according to the nearness or the distance of the moment when the possession is to begin; according to the certainty or uncertainty of its being retained?

Errors, whether in legislation or the moral conduct of men, may be always accounted for by a mistake, a forgetfulness, or a false estimate of some one of these elements, in the calculation of good and evil.

CHAPTER IX.

Section I.

Circumstances which affect Sensibility.

All causes of pleasure do not give the same pleasure to all; all causes of pain do not always produce the same pain. It is in this that *difference of sensibility* consists. This difference is in degree, or in kind: in degree, when the impression of a given cause upon many individuals is uniform, but unequal; in kind, when the same cause produces opposite sensations in different individuals.

This difference of sensibility depends upon certain circumstances which influence the physical or moral condition of individuals, and which, being changed, produce a corresponding change in their feelings. This is an experimental fact. Things do not affect us in the same manner in sickness and in health, in plenty and in poverty, in infancy and old age. But a view so general is not sufficient; it is necessary to go deeper into the human heart. Lyonet wrote a quarto volume upon the anatomy of the caterpillar; morals are in need of an investigator as patient and philosophical. I have not courage to imitate Lyonet. I shall think it sufficient if I open a new point of view—if I suggest a surer method to those who wish to pursue this subject.

1st. The foundation of the whole is *temperament*, or the original constitution. By this word I understand that radical and primitive disposition which attends us from our birth, and which depends upon physical organization, and the nature of the soul.

But although this radical constitution is the basis of all the rest, this basis lies so concealed that it is very difficult to get at it, so as to distinguish those varieties of sensibility which it produces from those which belong to other causes.

It is the business of the physiologist to distinguish these temperaments; to follow out their mixtures; and to trace their effects. But these grounds are as yet too little known to justify the moralist or legislator in founding anything upon them.

2nd. *Health.*—We can hardly define it except negatively. It is the absence of all sensation of pain or uneasiness of which the first seat can be referred to some part of the body. As to sensibility in general, it is to be observed, that, when sick, we are less sensible to the causes of pleasure, and more so to those of pain.

3rd. *Strength.*—Though connected with health, this is a separate circumstance; since a man may be feeble compared with the average of men, and yet not be an invalid. The degree of strength may be measured exactly enough by the weight one can lift, or in other ways. *Feebleness* is sometimes a negative term, signifying the absence of strength; sometimes a relative term, signifying that such an individual is not so strong as such another, with whom he is compared.

4th. *Corporal Imperfections.*—I mean some remarkable deformity; the want of some limb or some faculty which other men enjoy. Its particular effects upon sensibility depend upon the kind of imperfection. Its general effect is, to diminish more or less agreeable impressions, and to aggravate those which are painful.

5th. *The degree of Knowledge.*—That is, the amount of ideas which an individual possesses of a nature calculated to exercise an influence upon his happiness, or that of others. The man of knowledge is he who possesses many of these important ideas; the ignorant, he who has but few, and those few of minor importance.

6th. *Strength of the Intellectual Faculties.*—That is, the degree of facility in recalling ideas already acquired, or in acquiring new ones. Different qualities of mind may be referred to this head, such as exactness of memory, capacity of attention, clearness of discernment, vivacity of imagination, &c.

7th. *Firmness of Soul.*—This quality is attributed to a man when he is less affected by immediate pleasures or pains, than by great pleasures or great pains, which are distant or uncertain. Turenne lacked firmness of soul when he was prevailed upon by the prayers of a woman to betray a state secret. The young Lacedæmonians, who suffered themselves to be scourged to death before the altar of Diana, without uttering a single cry, proved that the fear of shame and the hope of glory had more influence over them than present pain of the most piercing kind.

8th. *Perseverance.*—This circumstance relates to the *length* of time during which a given motive acts upon the will with a continuous force. We say of a man that he wants perseverance when the motive which makes him act loses all its force without the happening of any external event, or the occurrence of any reason which ought to weaken it; or when he is susceptible of yielding by turns to a great variety of motives. It is thus that children are delighted with playthings, yet soon grow tired of them.

9th. *The bent of Inclination.*—The ideas we have previously formed of a pleasure or a pain, have a great influence upon the manner in which we are affected, when we come to experience that pleasure or that pain. The effect does not always answer the expectation, though it commonly does so. The pleasure which results from the possession of a woman is not to be measured by her beauty, but by the passion of her lover. The inclinations of a man being known, we can calculate with tolerable certainty the pleasure or the pain which a given event will cause him.*

10th. *Notions of Honour.*—By *honour* is meant that sensibility to pains and pleasures, which springs from the opinion of other men; that is, from their esteem or their contempt. The ideas of honour vary much with nations and with individuals; so that it becomes necessary to distinguish, in the first place, the force of this motive, in the second place, its direction.

11th. *Notions of Religion.*—It is well known to what a degree the entire system of sensibility may be affected by religious ideas. It is at the birth of a religion that its greatest effects appear. Mild nations have become bloody; pusillanimous nations have grown bold; slaves have regained their freedom;

* The four following circumstances are only sub-divisions of this head; they are passions—that is, inclinations, considered in reference to certain given pleasures and pains.

and savages have submitted to the yoke of civilization. There is not any cause which has produced such sudden and extraordinary effects upon mankind. There is also an astonishing diversity in the particular bias which religion gives to individuals.

12th. *Sentiments of Sympathy.*—I call *sympathy* that disposition which makes us find pleasure in the happiness of others, and compels us to share their pains. When this disposition extends to a single individual only, it is called *friendship;* when it acts in relation to persons in pain, it is called *pity* or *compassion;* if it embraces an entire class of individuals, it constitutes what is called *esprit de corps,* or *party spirit;* if it embraces a whole nation, it is *public spirit* or *patriotism;* if it extends to all men, it is *humanity.*

But the kind of sympathy which plays the greatest part in common life is that which binds the affections to certain fixed individuals, such as parents, children, a husband, a wife, an intimate friend. Its general effect is to augment the sensibility, whether to pains or pleasures. The individual acquires more extension; he ceases to be solitary; he becomes collective. We see ourselves, so to speak, doubled in those we love; and it is by no means impossible to love ourselves better in these others than in our actual self; and to be less sensible to the events which concern us, by reason of their immediate effect upon ourselves, than on account of their operation upon those connected with us; to feel, for example, that the most bitter part of an affliction is the pain it will cause our friends, and that the greatest charm of personal success is the pleasure we shall take in their joy. Such is the operation of sympathy. These sentiments received and paid back, increase by communication. They may be compared to mirrors, so arranged as mutually to transmit the rays of light, collect them in a common focus, and produce an increase of heat by their reciprocal reflections. The force of these sympathies is one of the reasons which has made legislators prefer married men to bachelors, and fathers of a family to those who have no children. The law has more power over those who expose a greater surface to its operations. Such men, through an interest in the happiness of those who are to succeed them, look to the future as well as the present; while men who have not the same ties are satisfied with a transitory possession.

With regard to the sympathy which the paternal relation produces, it may be sometimes observed to act independently of any affection. The honour acquired by the father extends to the son; the disgrace of the son spreads back to the father. The members of a family, although disunited by interest and inclination, have a common sensibility for all that appertains to the honour of each.

13th. *Antipathies.*—These are the reverse of those expansive and affectionate sentiments, of which we have been speaking. It is fortunate that the sources of sympathy are constant and natural; they are found everywhere, at all times, and under all circumstances; while antipathies are accidental, and of course transitory. They vary according to times, places, events, and persons; and they have nothing fixed nor determinate. Still, these two principles sometimes coalesce and act together. Humanity makes us hate the inhuman; friendship renders us hostile to the adversaries of our friends; and antipathy itself becomes a cause of union between two persons who have a common enemy.

14th. *Folly, or Disorder of Mind.*—Imperfections of mind may be reduced to ignorance, feebleness, irritability, and inconstancy. What is called *folly* is an extraordinary degree of imperfection, as striking to all the world as the most obvious corporal defect. It not only produces all the imperfections above mentioned, and carries them to excess; but, in addition, it gives an absurd and dangerous turn to the inclinations.

The sensibility of a maniac becomes extreme upon a certain point, while in other respects it is quite benumbed. He seems to have an excessive distrust, a hurtful malignity, a cessation of every sentiment of benevolence; he has no respect for himself nor for others; he braves all decorum and propriety; he is not insensible to fear, nor to good treatment—he yields to firmness at the same time that mildness makes him tractable; but he has hardly any regard for the future, and can only be acted upon by immediate means.

15th. *Pecuniary Circumstances.*—They consist of the sum total of *means*, compared with the sum total of *wants*. Means comprise, 1st, property, that which is possessed independently of labour; 2nd, the profits of labour; 3rd, the pecuniary aids which we may expect from our relations and friends.

Wants depend upon four circumstances: 1st. Habits of expense. What is beyond these habits is superfluity, what is within them is privation. The greater part of our desires exist only in the recollection of some past enjoyment. 2nd. The persons with whose support we are charged, either by the laws or by opinion, children, poor relations, old servants. 3rd. Unexpected wants. A given sum may have a much greater value at one moment than another; if it is needed, for instance, for an important lawsuit, or for a journey upon which the fate of a family depends. 4th. Expectations of a profit, of an inheritance, &c. It is evident that the hopes of fortune, in proportion to their force, are true wants; and that their loss may affect us almost as much as that of a property already in possession.

Section II.

Secondary Circumstances which affect Sensibility.

Authors who have wished to account for differences of sensibility have ascribed them to circumstances of which no mention has yet been made, viz , sex, age, rank, education, habitual occupations, climate, race, government, religion—circumstances all very apparent, very easy to observe, and very convenient for explaining the different phenomena of sensibility. Still, they are but secondary circumstances; I mean that in themselves they are not reasons, but must be explained by the circumstances described in the first section, which are here represented and combined; each secondary circumstance containing in itself many primary circumstances. As a matter of convenience, we speak of the influence of sex upon sensibility; including in that single phrase all the primary circumstances of strength, knowledge, firmness of soul, perseverance, ideas of honour, sentiments of sympathy, &c. Do we speak of the influence of rank?—We mean by it a certain assemblage of primary circumstances, such as the degree of knowledge, ideas of honour, connections of family, habitual occupations, pecuniary circumstances. It is the same with all the others. Each of these secondary circumstances may be translated by a certain number of the primary. This distinction, though essential, has not yet been analyzed. Let us pass to a more particular examination.

1st. *Sex.*—The sensibility of women seems to be greater than that of men. Their health is more delicate. They are generally inferior in strength of body, knowledge, the intellectual faculties, and firmness of soul. Their moral and religious sensibility is more lively; sympathies and antipathies have a greater empire over them. The honour of a woman consists more in modesty and chastity; that of man in probity and courage. The religion of a woman more easily deviates towards superstition; that is, towards minute observances. Her affections for her own children are stronger during their whole life, and especially during their early youth. Women are more compassionate for those whose sufferings they see; and the very pains they take to relieve them form a new bond of attachment. But their benevolence is locked up in a narrower circle, and is less governed by the principle of utility. It is rare that they embrace in their affections the well-being of their country, much less that of mankind; and the interest which they take in a party depends almost always upon some private sympathy. There enters into all their attachments and antipathies more of caprice and imagination; while men have more regard to personal interests or public utility. Their habitual amusements are more quiet and sedentary. On the whole, woman is better fitted for the family, and man for matters out of doors. The domestic economy is best placed in the hands of the women; the principal management of affairs in those of the men.

2nd. *Age.*—Each period of life acts differently upon sensibility; but it is extremely difficult to state particulars, since the limits of the different ages vary with individuals, and, in fact, are arbitrary with regard to all. In considering infancy, adolescence, youth, maturity, decline, and decrepitude as divisions of human life, we can only speak of them vaguely, and in general terms. The different imperfections of mind, which we have mentioned, are so striking in infancy, that it needs a vigilant and constant protection. The affections of adolescence and early youth are prompt and lively, but are seldom governed by the principle of prudence. The legislator is obliged to protect this age from the errors into which the want of experience or the vivacity of the passions are apt to lead it. As to decrepitude, in many respects it is only a return to the imperfections of infancy.

3rd. *Rank.*—This circumstance depends so much for its effects upon the political constitution of states, that it is almost impossible to announce any proposition with respect to it which is universally true. In general it may be said that the amount of sensibility is greater in the upper ranks than in the lower; the ideas of honour in particular are more predominant.

4th. *Education.*—Health, strength, robustness, may be referred to *physical education;* to *intellectual education* belong the amount of knowledge, its kind, and, to a certain degree, firmness of soul, and perseverance; to *moral education* appertain the bent of the inclinations, the ideas of honour and religion, the sentiments of sympathy, &c. To education in general may be referred the habitual occupations, amusements, attachments, habits of expense, and pecuniary resources. But when we speak of education, we ought not to forget that its influence in all these respects is so modified, either by a concurrence of external circumstances or by natural disposition, that it is often impossible to calculate its effects.

5th. *Habitual occupations,* whether of profit or of amusement and choice. They influence all the other causes—health, strength, knowledge, inclinations, ideas of honour, sympathies, antipathies, fortune, &c. Thus we see common traits of character in certain professions, especially in those which constitute a class or condition, such as ecclesiastics, soldiers, sailors, lawyers, magistrates, &c.

6th. *Climate.*—Formerly too much was attributed to this cause; it has since been underrated. What renders this examination difficult, is the circumstance that a comparison of nation with nation can only be made as to some great facts, which may be explained in different ways. It seems to be proved that in warm climates men are less strong, less robust; they have less need to labour, because the earth is more fertile; they are more inclined to the pleasures of love, a passion which in those latitudes manifests itself earlier, and with more ardour. All their sensibilities are quicker; their imagination is more lively; their spirit is more prompt, but less vigorous and less persevering. Their habitual occupations announce more of indolence than of activity. They have probably at their birth a physical organization less vigorous, and a temperament of soul less firm and less constant.

7th. *Race.*—A negro born in France or England is in many respects a different being from a child of the French or English race. A Spanish child born in Mexico or Peru at the hour of its birth is very different from a Mexican or Peruvian child. The race may perhaps have an influence upon that natural disposition, which serves as a foundation for all the rest. Afterwards it operates much more sensibly upon the moral and religious bias, upon the sympathies and antipathies.

8th. *Government.*—This circumstance exercises an influence of the same sort with that of education. The magistrate may be considered as a national instructor; and under a vigilant and attentive government the particular preceptor, even the father himself, is but a deputy, a substitute for the magistrate, with this difference, that the authority of the father has its limit, while that of the magistrate extends through the whole life.

The influence of this cause is immense; it extends to almost everything; in fact, it embraces everything except temperament, race, and climate; for even health may depend upon it in many respects, so far as relates to regulations of police, the abundance of provisions, and the removal of apparent causes of disease. The method of education, the plan followed in the disposal of offices, and the scheme of rewards and punishments, will determine in a great measure the physical and moral qualities of a nation.

Under a government well constituted, or only well administered, though with a bad constitution, it will be seen that men are generally more governed by honour, and that honour is placed in actions more conformed to public utility. Religious sensibility will be more exempt from fanaticism and intolerance, more free from superstition and servile reverence. A common sentiment of patriotism springs up. Men perceive the existence of a national interest. Enfeebled factions will see ancient rallying signs losing their power. The popular affection will be rather directed towards the magistrate than towards the heads of a party, and towards the whole country rather than towards anything else. Private revenge will neither be protracted, nor will it spread through society; the national taste will be directed towards useful expenses, such as voyages of discovery, the perfecting of agriculture, improvements in the sciences, and the embellishment of the country. There will be perceptible, even in the productions of human genius, a general disposition to discuss with calmness important questions of public good.

9th. *Religious Profession.*—We may derive from this source pretty clear indications with respect to religious sensibility, sympathy, antipathy, and the ideas of honour and virtue. In certain cases we may even judge of the intelligence, the strength or weakness of mind, and the disposition of an individual from the sect to which he belongs. I admit that it is common to profess in public, from motives of convenience or good breeding, religious opinions which are not very sincerely entertained. But in these cases the influence of religious profession, though weakened, is not destroyed. Early habits, the ties of society, the power of example, continue to operate even after the principle upon which they are founded ceases to exist.

The man who at heart has ceased to be a Jew, a Quaker, an

Anabaptist, a Calvinist, or a Lutheran, will still be apt to retain a partiality for those of the denomination to which he nominally belongs, and a corresponding antipathy for those of every other.

Section III.

Practical application of this Theory.

We cannot calculate the motion of a vessel without knowing the circumstances which influence her sailing, such as the force of the wind, the resistance of the water, the model of the hull, the weight of the lading, &c. In like manner we cannot operate with any certainty upon a question of legislation without considering all the circumstances which affect the sensibility.

I confine myself here to what concerns the penal code. In all its parts a scrupulous attention to this diversity of circumstances is necessary.

1st. *To ascertain the Evil of an Offence.*—The same nominal offence is not in fact the same real offence, when the sensibility of the injured individual is not the same. An action, for example, might be a serious insult to a woman, which to a man would be wholly indifferent. A corporal injury, which, if done to an invalid, would put his life in danger, would be of little comparative consequence to a man in full health. An imputation which might ruin the honour or the fortune of one individual might do no harm to another.

2nd. *To give a proper Satisfaction to the Individual injured.*—Where the sensibility is different, the same nominal satisfaction is not the same real satisfaction. A pecuniary satisfaction for an affront might be agreeable or offensive, according to the rank of the person affronted, according to his fortune, or according to prevailing prejudices. Am I insulted?—my pardon, publicly asked, would be a sufficient satisfaction on the part of my superior, or my equal; but not so on the part of my inferior.

3rd. *To estimate the force of Punishments and their Impression upon Delinquents.*—When the sensibility is essentially different, the same nominal punishment is not the same real punishment. Exile is not the same thing to a young man and to an old man; to a bachelor and to the father of a family; to an artisan who has no means of subsistence out of his country, and to a rich man who would only find himself obliged to change the scene of his pleasures. Imprisonment would not be an equal punishment for a man and for a woman, for an invalid and for a person in health; for a rich man whose family would not suffer in his absence, and for one who lives only by his labour, and who would leave his children in distress.

4th. *To transplant a Law from one Country to another.*—The same verbal law would not be the same real law, if the sensibility of the two nations was essentially different. A law on which depends the happiness of European families, transported into Asia, would become the scourge of society. Women in Europe are accustomed to enjoy liberty, and even a sort of domestic empire; women in Asia are prepared by their education for the imprisonment of the seraglio, and even for servitude. Marriage is not a contract of the same kind in Europe and in the East; and, if it were submitted to the same laws, the unhappiness of all parties would certainly ensue.

The same punishments, it is said, *for the same offences.* This adage has an appearance of justice and impartiality which seduces the superficial observer. To give it a reasonable sense, we must determine beforehand what is meant by the same punishments and the same offences. An inflexible law, a law which should regard neither age, nor fortune, nor rank, nor education, nor the moral and religious prejudices of individuals, would be doubly vicious, at once inefficacious and tyrannical. Too severe for one, too indulgent for another; always failing through excess or deficiency; under the appearance of equality, it conceals an inequality the most monstrous.

When a man of great wealth, and another of a moderate condition, are condemned in the same fine, is the punishment the same? Do they suffer the same evil? Is not the manifest inequality of this treatment rendered yet more odious by its delusive equality? And does not the law fail in its object; since the one may lose all his resources of living, while the other pays, and walks off in triumph? Let a robust youth and a weak old man be both condemned to wear irons for the same number of years—a reasoner skilful in obscuring the most evident truths might undertake to prove the equality of this punishment; but the people, who are little given to sophistry, the people, faithful to nature and to sentiment, would feel an internal murmuring of spirit at the sight of such injustice; and their indignation, changing its object, would pass from the criminal to the judge, and from the judge to the legislator.

There are some specious objections which I do not wish to dissemble. "How is it possible to take account of all the circumstances which influence the sensibility? How can we appreciate internal and secret dispositions, such as strength of mind, knowledge, inclinations, sympathies? How can we measure these different qualities? The father of a family, in the treatment of his children, may consult these interior dispositions, these diversities of character; but a public instructor, though charged with but a limited number of pupils, cannot do it. A legislator, who has a numerous people in view, is obliged to confine himself still more to general laws; and he is bound to take care how he increases their complication by descending into particulars. If he leaves to the judges the right of varying the application of the laws according to the infinite diversity of circumstances and characters, there will be nothing to restrain them from the most arbitrary judgments. Under pretext of observing the true spirit of the legislator, the judges will make the laws an instrument of caprice or antipathy."

To all this, there needs less an answer than an explanation; for it is rather an objection than a decisive attack. The principle is not denied, but its application is thought to be impossible.

1st. I allow that the greater part of these differences in sensibility cannot be appreciated; that it would be impossible to prove their existence in individual cases, or to measure their strength and degree. But, happily, these interior and secret dispositions have certain outward and manifest indications. These are the secondary circumstances above enumerated, viz., *sex, age, rank, race, climate, government, education, religious profession*;—palpable and evident circumstances, which represent interior dispositions.

Thus the legislator is aided as to the most difficult point. He need not trouble himself with metaphysical or moral qualities; he may confine himself to circumstances that are obvious. For example, he directs a given punishment to be modified, not in proportion to the sensibility of the criminal, his perseverance, his strength of mind, his knowledge, &c., but according to sex or age. It is true that presumptions drawn from these circumstances are liable to error. A child of fifteen *may* have more knowledge than a man of thirty; an individual woman may have more courage or less modesty than an individual man; but these presumptions are in general just enough for the avoidance of tyrannical laws, and will be sufficient to gain for the legislator the suffrages of opinion.

2nd. These secondary circumstances are not only easy to seize, but they are few in number, and they form general classes. They furnish grounds of justification, of extenuation, or of aggravation. Thus the difficulty disappears, and simplicity pervades the whole.

3rd. In this there is nothing arbitrary. It is not the judge, it is the law which modifies such and such a punishment, according to the sex, the age, the religious profession. As to other circumstances of which the examination must be absolutely left to the judge, as the *more* or *less* of derangement of mind, the *more* or *less* of strength, the *more* or *less* of fortune, the legislator, who cannot decide upon individual cases, will direct the tribunals by general rules, and will leave them a certain latitude in order that they may proportion their judgment to the particular nature of the circumstances.

What is here recommended is not a utopian idea. There has scarcely been a legislator so barbarous or so stupid, as entirely to neglect the circumstances which influence sensibility. A more or less confused feeling of them has guided the establishment of civil and political rights; and more or less of regard to these circumstances has always been shown in the institution of punishments. Hence the differences which have been admitted in the case of women, children, freemen, slaves, soldiers, priests, &c.

Droco seems to have been the only penal legislator who rejected all these considerations. In his view all crimes were equal, because they were all violations of the law. He condemned all delinquents to death, without distinction. He confounded, he overturned all principles of human sensibility. His horrible work endured but a short time; nor is it probable that his laws were ever literally followed. Without falling into this extreme, how many faults of the same kind have been committed? I should never finish were I to cite examples. It is notorious that there have been sovereigns who have preferred to lose provinces, and to make blood flow in streams, rather than humour a particular sensibility, rather than tolerate a custom indifferent in itself, rather than respect an ancient prejudice in favour of a certain dress, or a certain form of prayer.

A prince of our times,* active, enlightened, and animated by the desire of glory, and a wish to promote the happiness of his subjects, undertook to reform everything in his territories; and, in so doing, excited all to oppose him. On the eve of his death, recalling all the vexations he had experienced, he wished it to be inscribed upon his tomb, that he had been unfortunate in all his enterprises. It would have been well to add, for the instruction of posterity, that he had never known how to respect and to humour the prejudices, the inclinations, the sensibilities of men.

When a legislator studies the human heart, when he makes provision for the different degrees, the different kinds of sensibility, by exceptions, limitations, and mitigations, these temperaments of power charm us as a paternal condescension. It is the foundation of that approval which we give to the laws, under the names, a little vague it is true, of humanity, equity, adaptation, moderation, wisdom.

* Joseph II. of Austria.

We may here discover a striking analogy between the art of the legislator and that of the physician. A catalogue of circumstances which influence sensibility, is alike necessary to these two sciences. That which distinguishes the physician from the empiric, is an attention to everything which constitutes the particular state of the individual. But it is especially in maladies of the soul, in those where the moral nature is affected, and where it is necessary to surmount injurious habits and to form new ones, that it is necessary to study everything which influences the disposition of the patient. A single error here may change all the results, so that what were intended as remedies, may prove to be aggravations.

CHAPTER X.

Analysis of Political Good and Evil.—How they are diffused through Society.

It is with government as with medicine; its only business is the choice of evils. Every law is an evil, for every law is an infraction of liberty. Government, I repeat it, has but the choice of evils. In making that choice, what ought to be the object of the legislator? He ought to be certain of two things: 1st, that in every case the acts which he undertakes to prevent are really evils; and, 2nd, that these evils are greater than those which he employs to prevent them.

He has then two things to note—the evil of the offence, and the evil of the law; the evil of the malady, and the evil of the remedy.

An evil seldom comes alone. A portion of evil can hardly fall upon an individual, without spreading on every side, as from a centre. As it spreads, it takes different forms. We see an evil of one kind coming out of an evil of another kind; we even see evil coming out of good, and good out of evil. It is important to know and to distinguish all these kinds of evil, for in this the very essence of legislation consists. But, happily, these modifications are few in number, and their differences are strongly marked. Three principal distinctions, and two sub-divisions, will be enough to solve the most difficult problems.

Evil of the first order.
Evil of the second order.
Evil of the third order.
Primitive Evil—Derivative Evil.
Immediate Evil—Consequential Evil.
Extended Evil—Divided Evil.
Permanent Evil—Evanescent Evil.

These are the only new terms which it will be necessary to employ to express the variety of forms which evil may take.

The evil resulting from a bad action may be divided into two principal parts:—1st, That which falls immediately upon such and such assignable individuals, I call *evil of the first order;* 2nd, That which takes its origin in the first, and spreads through the entire community, or among an indefinite number of non-assignable individuals, I call *evil of the second order.*

Evil of the first order may be distinguished into two branches, viz., 1st, the *primitive evil,* which is peculiar to the individual injured, to the first sufferer—the person, for example, who is beaten or robbed; 2nd, the *derivative evil,* that which falls upon certain assignable individuals, as a consequence of the primitive evil, by reason of some relation between them and the first sufferer, whether it be a relation of personal interest or merely of sympathy.

Evil of the second order may also be distinguished into two branches: 1st, *alarm;* 2nd, *danger.* Alarm is a positive pain, a pain of apprehension, the apprehension of suffering the same evil which we see has already fallen upon another. Danger is the probability that a primitive evil will produce other evils of the same kind.

These two branches of evil are closely connected, yet they are so distinct as to be capable of a separate existence. There may be alarm where there is no danger, there may be danger where there is no alarm. We may be frightened at a conspiracy purely imaginary; we may remain secure in the midst of a conspiracy ready to break out. But, commonly, alarm and danger go together, as natural effects of the same cause. The evil that has happened makes us anticipate other evils of the same kind, by rendering them probable. The evil that has happened produces danger; danger produces alarm. A bad action is dangerous as an example; it prepares the way for other bad actions—1st, By suggesting the idea of their commission; 2nd, By augmenting the force of temptation.

Let us follow the train of thought which may pass in the mind of an individual when he hears of a successful robbery. Perhaps he did not know of this means of subsistence, or never thought of it. Example acts upon him like instruction, and gives him the first idea of resorting to the same expedient. He sees that the thing is possible, provided it be well managed; and, executed by another, it appears to him less difficult and less perilous than it really is. Example is a track which guides him along where he never would have dared to be the first explorer. Such an example has yet another effect upon him, not less remarkable. It weakens the strength of the motives which restrain him. The fear of the laws loses a part of its force so long as the culprit remains unpunished; the fear of shame diminishes in the same degree, because he sees accomplices who afford him an assurance against the misery of being utterly despised. This is so true, that wherever robberies are frequent and unpunished, they are as little a matter of shame as any other means of acquisition. The early Greeks had no scruples about them; they are gloried in by the Arabs of the present day.

Let us apply this theory. You have been beaten, wounded, insulted, and robbed. The amount of your personal sufferings, so far as they relate to you alone, forms the *primitive* evil. But you have friends, and sympathy makes them share your pains. You have a wife, children, parents; a part of the indignity which you have suffered, of the affront to which you have been subjected, falls upon them. You have creditors, and the loss you have experienced obliges them to wait. All these persons suffer a less or greater evil, *derivative* from yours; and these two portions of evil, yours and theirs, compose together the *evil of the first order.*

But this is not all. The news of the robbery, with all its circumstances, spreads from mouth to mouth. An idea of *danger* springs up, and *alarm* along with it. This alarm is greater or less, according to what is known of the character of the robbers, of the personal injuries they have inflicted, of their means and their number; according as we are near the place or distant from it; according to our strength and courage; according to our peculiar circumstances, such as travelling alone, or with a family, carrying little money with us, or being intrusted with valuable effects. This danger and alarm constitute the *evil of the second order.*

If the evil which has been done to you is of a nature to spread of itself—for example, if you have been defamed by an imputation which envelops a class of individuals more or less numerous, it is no longer an evil simply private, it becomes an *extended* evil. It is augmented in proportion to the number of those who participate in it.

If the money of which you were robbed did not belong to you, but to a society, or to the State, the loss would be a *divided* evil. This case differs from the former in the important circumstance, that here, the evil is diminished in proportion to the number among whom it is shared.

If, in consequence of the wound you have received, you suffer an additional evil distinct from the first, such as the abandonment of a lucrative business, the loss of a marriage, or the failure to obtain a profitable situation, that is a *consequential* evil. A *permanent* evil is that which, once done, cannot be remedied, such as an irreparable personal injury, an amputation, death, &c. An *evanescent* evil is that which may pass away altogether, such as a wound which may be healed, or a loss which may be entirely made up.

These distinctions, though partly new, are far from being useless subtilties. It is only by their means that we can appreciate the difference of malignity in different offences, and regulate accordingly the proportion of punishment.

This analysis will furnish us a moral *criterion*, a means of decomposing human actions, as we decompose the mixed metals, in order to discover their intrinsic value, and their precise quantity of alloy.

If among bad actions, or those reputed to be so, there are some which cause no alarm, what a difference between these actions and those which do cause it! The primitive evil affects but a single individual; the derivative evil can extend only to a small number; but the evil of the second order may embrace the whole of society. Let a fanatic commit an assassination on account of what he calls heresy, and the evil of the second order, especially the alarm, may exceed many million times the evil of the first order.

There is a great class of offences of which the entire evil consists in danger. I refer to those actions which, without injuring any particular individual, are injurious to society at large. Let us take, for an example, an offence against justice. The bad conduct of a judge, of an accuser, or a witness, causes a criminal to be acquitted. Here is doubtless an evil, for here is a danger; the danger that impunity will harden the offender, and excite him to the commission of new crimes; the danger of encouraging other offenders by the example and the success of the first. Still, it is probable that this danger, great as it is, will escape the attention of the public, and that those who by the habit of reflection are capable of perceiving it, will not derive from it any alarm. They do not fear to see it realized upon anybody.

But the importance of these distinctions can only be perceived in their development. We shall presently see a particular application of them.

If we carry our views still further, we shall discover another evil, which may result from an offence. When the alarm reaches a certain point, and lasts a long time, the effect is not limited to the passive faculties of man; it extends to his active faculties; it deadens them; it throws them into a state of torpor and decrepitude. Thus, when vexations and depredations have become habitual, the discouraged labourer only works to save himself from starvation; he seeks in idleness the only consolation which his misfortunes allow; industry fails with hope, and brambles gain possession of the most fertile fields. This branch of evil is the *evil of the third order.*

Whether an evil happens by human agency, or whether it results from an event purely physical, all these distinctions are equally applicable.

Happily, this power of propagation and of diffusion does not appertain to evil only. Good has the same prerogatives. Follow an analogous division, and you will see coming out of a good action, a *good of the first order*, divisible into primitive and derivative; and a *good of the second order,* which produces a certain degree of confidence and security.

The *good of the third order* is manifested in that energy, that gaiety of heart, that ardour of action, which remuneratory motives alone inspire. Man, animated by this sentiment of joy, finds in himself a strength which he did not suspect.

The propagation of good is less rapid and less sensible than that of evil. The seed of good is not so productive in hopes as the seed of evil is fruitful in alarms. But this difference is abundantly made up, for good is a necessary result of natural causes which operate always; while evil is produced only by accident, and at intervals.

Society is so constituted that, in labouring for our particular good, we labour also for the good of the whole. We cannot augment our own means of enjoyment without augmenting also the means of others. Two nations, like two individuals, grow rich by a mutual commerce; and all exchange is founded upon reciprocal advantages.

It is fortunate also that the effects of evil are not always evil. They often assume the contrary quality. Thus, juridical punishments applied to offences, although they produce an evil of the first order, are not generally regarded as evils, because they produce a good of the second order. They produce alarm and danger, —but for whom? Only for a class of evil-doers, who are voluntary sufferers. Let them obey the laws, and they will be exposed neither to danger nor alarm.

We should never be able to subjugate, however imperfectly, the vast empire of evil, had we not learned the method of combating one evil by another. It has been necessary to enlist auxiliaries among pains, to oppose other pains which attack us on every side. So, in the art of curing pains of another sort, poisons well applied have proved to be remedies.

CHAPTER XI.

Reasons for erecting certain Acts into Offences.

We have made an analysis of evil. That analysis shows us that there are acts from which there results more of evil than of good. It is acts of this nature, or at least acts reputed to be such, that legislators have prohibited. A prohibited act is what we call an *offence.* To cause these prohibitions to be respected, it is necessary to establish *punishments.*

But is it necessary to erect certain acts into offences? or, in other words, is it necessary to subject them to legal punishments?

What a question! Is not all the world agreed on this matter? Why seek to prove a truth universally acknowledged, and so firmly rooted in the minds of men?

Doubtless, all the world is agreed upon this matter. But on what is their agreement founded? Ask his reasons of every man who assents, and you will see a strange diversity of sentiments and principles; and that not only among the people, but among philosophers. Will it be a waste of time to seek out some uniform basis of consent upon a subject so important?

The agreement which actually exists is only founded upon prejudices, which vary according to times and places, customs and opinions. I have always been told that such an action is a crime, and I think that it is so; such is the guide of the people, and even of legislators. But, if usage has erected innocent actions into crimes; if it has made trifling offences to be considered as grave ones, and grave ones as trifling; if it has varied everywhere, it is plain that usage ought to be subjected to some rule, and ought not to be taken as a rule itself. Let us appeal, then, to the principle of utility. It will confirm the decrees of prejudice when they are just; it will annul them when they are wrong.

I suppose myself a stranger to all the common appellations of vice and virtue. I am called upon to consider human actions only with relation to their good or bad effects. I open two accounts; I pass to the account of pure profit all the pleasures, I pass to the account of loss all the pains. I faithfully weigh the interests of all parties. The man whom prejudice brands as vicious, and he whom it extols as virtuous, are, for the moment, equal in my eyes. I wish to judge prejudice itself; to weigh all actions in a new balance, in order to form a catalogue of those which ought to be permitted, and of those which ought to be forbidden. This operation, which appears at first so complicated, is rendered easy by the distinction between evils of the first, second, and third orders.

Am I to examine an act which attacks the security of an individual? I compare all the pleasure, or, in other words, all the profit, which results to the author of the act, with all the evil, or all the loss, which results to the party injured. I see at once that the evil of the first order surpasses the good of the first order. But I do not stop there. The action under consideration produces throughout society danger and alarm. The evil which at first was only individual spreads everywhere, under the form of fear. The pleasure resulting from the action belongs solely to the actor; the pain reaches a thousand—ten thousand—all. This disproportion, already prodigious, appears infinite upon passing to the evil of the third order, and considering that, if the act in question is not suppressed, there will result from it a universal and durable discouragement, a cessation of labour, and, at last, the dissolution of society.

I will now run through the strongest of our desires, those whose satisfaction is accompanied with the greatest pleasures; and we shall see that, when brought about at the expense of security, their gratification is much more fertile in evil than in good.

I. In the first place let us consider the passion of *hatred.*

This is the most fruitful cause of assaults upon the honour and the person. I have conceived, no matter why, an enmity against you. Passion bewilders me. I insult you; I humble you; I wound you. The sight of your pain makes me experience, at least for a time, a feeling of pleasure. But, even for that time, can it be believed that the pleasure which I taste is equivalent to the pain you suffer? If every atom of your pain separately painted itself in my soul, is it probable that each corresponding atom of my pleasure would appear to have an equal intensity? In fact, only some scattering atoms of your pain present themselves to my troubled and disordered imagination. For you, none is lost; for me, the greater part is completely thrown away. But this pleasure, such as it is, soon betrays its natural impurity. Humanity, a principle not to be entirely quenched, even in the most savage souls, wakes up a secret remorse. Fears of every kind, the fear of vengeance on your part, or on the part of those connected with you; fear of public disapprobation; and, if any sparks of religion are left to me, religious fears;—fears of all kinds come to trouble my security and to disturb my triumph. Passion has died away, the pleasure of its gratification vanishes, and an inward reproach succeeds. But on your side the pain still continues, and may have a long duration. This is the case, even with trifling wounds, which time may cicatrize. How will it be when the injury is incurable in its nature?—when limbs have been maimed, features disfigured, or faculties destroyed? Weigh the evils—their intensity, their duration, their consequences; measure them under all their dimensions, and you will see that in every sense the pleasure is inferior to the pain.

Let us now pass to the effects of the second order. The news of your misfortune instils the poison of fear into every soul. Every man who has an enemy, or who may have an enemy, contemplates with terror what the passion of hate may inspire. Among feeble beings, who have so much to dispute about, and so many causes of mutual envy, among whom a thousand little rivalries excite as many causeless hostilities, the spirit of revenge holds forth a succession of endless evils.

Thus, every act of cruelty produced by a passion, the principle of which exists in every heart, and from which everybody is exposed to suffer, creates an alarm, which will continue until the punishment of the culprit has transferred the danger to the side of injustice, and of cruel enmity. This alarm is a suffering common to all; and there is another suffering resulting from it, which we ought not to forget,—that pain of sympathy felt by generous hearts at the sight of such aggressions.

II. If we examine the actions which may spring from that imperious motive, that desire to which nature has intrusted the perpetuation of the species, we shall see that, when it attacks the security of the person, or of the domestic condition, the good which results from its gratification cannot be compared to the evil it produces.

I speak here only of that attack which manifestly compromits the security of the person, viz., ravishment. It is useless by a gross and puerile pleasantry to deny the existence of this crime, or to diminish the horror of it. Whatever may be said, it is certain that women the most prodigal of their favours do not love to have them snatched by a brutal fury. But, in this case, the greatness of the alarm renders all discussion of the primitive evil unnecessary. However it may be of the actual offence, the possible offence will always be an object of terror. The more universal the desire which gives rise to this offence, the greater and more violent is the alarm. In times when the laws have not had sufficient power to repress it, when manners have not been sufficiently regulated to brand it, it produced acts of vengeance of which history has preserved the recollection. Whole nations have interested themselves in the quarrel; and hatreds originating in this source have been transmitted from fathers to their children. It is possible that the close confinement of women, unknown among the Greeks in the time of Homer, owes its origin to an epoch of troubles and revolutions, when the feebleness of the laws had multiplied disorders of this kind, and spread a general terror.

III. With respect to the motive of *cupidity*,—if we compare the pleasure of acquiring by a violation of another's rights with the pain which such a proceeding occasions, they will not prove to be equivalents. It is true there are cases in which, if we confine ourselves to the effects of the first order, the good will have an incontestable preponderance over the evil. Were the offence considered only under this point of view, it would not be easy to assign any good reasons to justify the rigour of the laws. Everything depends upon the evil of the second order; it is this which gives to such actions the character of crime, and which makes punishment necessary. Let us take, for example, the physical desire of satisfying hunger. Let a beggar, pressed by hunger, steal from a rich man's house a loaf, which perhaps saves him from starving,—can it be possible to compare the good which the thief acquires for himself, with the evil which the rich man suffers? The same is true of less striking examples. Let a man pillage the public treasury; he enriches himself and impoverishes nobody. The wrong which he does to individuals is reduced to impalpable parts. It is not on account of the evil of the first order that it is necessary to erect these actions into offences, but on account of the evil of the second order.

If the pleasure which attends the satisfaction of such powerful desires as hatred, the sexual appetite, and hunger, when that satisfaction runs counter to the interests of others, is not equal to the pain which it causes, the disproportion will appear much greater, as respects motives less active and strong.

The desire of self-preservation is the only one beside which seems to demand a separate examination.

If the question relates to an evil which the laws themselves seek to impose upon an individual, this can only be for some very pressing reason, such as the necessity of carrying into execution punishments ordained by the tribunals, punishments without which there would be no security and no government. Now, if the desire of escaping an evil of this sort be gratified, the law, to the same extent, will be rendered inefficient. It appears, then, that the evil resulting from this satisfaction is that which results from the inefficiency of the laws, or, what amounts to the same thing, from the non-existence of laws. But the evil which results from the non-existence of laws is, in fact, an assemblage of all the different evils which the laws are established to prevent; that is to say, of all the evils which men are liable to experience on the part of other men. It is true that a single triumph over the laws, obtained in this way by an individual, is not sufficient to shake the whole system; nevertheless, every example of this kind is a symptom of weakness, a step towards destruction. There results, then, from it an evil of the second order, an alarm, at least a danger; and, if the laws connive at this evasion, they will do it in contradiction to their own aim. In order to escape one evil, they will admit another, much more than its equivalent.

There remains the case in which an individual repels an evil to which the laws have not chosen to subject him. If they have not chosen to subject him to it, they do not wish him to submit to it. To repel this evil is itself a good. It is possible that, in making efforts to preserve himself from it, the individual in question may do an evil more than equivalent to this good. Is the evil he does in his own defence confined to what is necessary for that object, or does it go beyond? What is the proportion of the evil which he does to the evil he avoids? Is it equal, greater, or less? Would the evil he has avoided have been susceptible of compensation if, instead of defending himself by a method so costly, he had preferred to submit to it for a time? These are questions of fact, which the law ought to take into consideration, before establishing in detail the regulations of self-defence. It is a subject which belongs to that part of the penal code which treats of the means of justification or extenuation in regard to offences committed. It is sufficient to observe here that in all these cases, though there is, in fact, an evil of the first order, yet all the evil which an individual may do in self-defence produces no alarm and no danger. Other men have nothing to fear, unless they first commence an illegal attack.

CHAPTER XII.

The Limits which separate Morals from Legislation.

MORALITY in general is the art of directing the actions of men in such a way as to produce the greatest possible sum of good.

Legislation ought to have precisely the same object.

But although these two arts, or rather sciences, have the same end, they differ greatly in extent. All actions, whether public or private, fall under the jurisdiction of morals. It is a guide which leads the individual, as it were, by the hand through all the details of his life, all his relations with his fellows. Legislation cannot do this; and, if it could, it ought not to exercise a continual interference and dictation over the conduct of men.

Morality commands each individual to do all that is advantageous to the community, his own personal advantage included. But there are many acts useful to the community which legislation ought not to command. There are also many injurious actions which it ought not to forbid, although morality does so. In a word, legislation has the same centre with morals, but it has not the same circumference.

There are two reasons for this difference: 1st. Legislation can have no direct influence upon the conduct of men, except by punishments. Now these punishments are so many evils, which are not justifiable except so far as there results from them a greater sum of good. But, in many cases in which we might desire to strengthen a moral precept by a punishment, the evil of the punishment would be greater than the evil of the offence. The means necessary to carry the law into execution would be of a nature to spread through society a degree of alarm more injurious than the evil intended to be prevented.

2nd. Legislation is often arrested by the danger of overwhelming the innocent in seeking to punish the guilty. Whence comes this danger? From the difficulty of defining an offence, and giving a clear and precise idea of it. For example, hard-heartedness, ingratitude, perfidy, and other vices which the popular sanction punishes, cannot come under the power of the law, unless they are defined as exactly as theft, homicide, or perjury.

But, the better to distinguish the true limits of morals and legislation, it will be well to refer to the common classification of moral duties.

Private morality regulates the actions of men, either in that part of their conduct in which they alone are interested, or in that which may affect the interests of others. The actions which affect a man's individual interest compose a class called, perhaps improperly, *duties to ourselves;* and the quality or disposition manifested in the accomplishment of those duties receives the name of *prudence.* That part of conduct which relates to others composes a class of actions called *duties to others.* Now there are two ways of consulting the happiness of others: the one negative, abstaining from diminishing it; the other positive, labouring to augment it. The first constitutes *probity;* the second is *beneficence.*

Morality upon these three points needs the aid of the law; but not in the same degree, nor in the same manner.

I. The rules of prudence are almost always sufficient of themselves. If a man fails in what regards his particular private interest, it is not his will which is in fault, it is his understanding. If he does wrong, it can only be through mistake. The fear of hurting himself is a motive of repression sufficiently strong; it would be useless to add to it the fear of an artificial pain.

Does any one object, that facts show the contrary? That excesses of play, those of intemperance, the illicit intercourse between the sexes, attended so often by the greatest dangers, are enough to prove that individuals have not always sufficient prudence to abstain from what hurts them?

Confining myself to a general reply, I answer, in the first place, that, in the greater part of these cases, punishment would be so easily eluded, that it would be inefficacious; secondly, that the evil produced by the penal law would be much beyond the evil of the offence.

Suppose, for example, that a legislator should feel himself authorized to undertake the extirpation of drunkenness and fornication by direct laws. He would have to begin by a multitude of regulations. The first inconvenience would therefore be a complexity of laws. The easier it is to conceal these vices, the more necessary it would be to resort to severity of punishment, in order to destroy by the terror of examples the constantly recurring hope of impunity. This excessive rigour of laws forms a second inconvenience not less grave than the first. The difficulty of procuring proofs would be such, that it would be necessary to encourage informers, and to entertain an army of spies. This necessity forms a third inconvenience, greater than either of the others. Let us compare the results of good and evil. Offences of this nature, if that name can be properly given to imprudences, produce no alarm; but the pretended remedy would spread a universal terror; innocent or guilty, every one would fear for himself or his connexions; suspicions and accusations would render society dangerous; we should fly from it; we should involve ourselves in mystery and concealment; we should shun all the disclosures of confidence. Instead of suppressing one vice, the laws would produce other vices, new and more dangerous.

It is true that example may render certain excesses contagious; and that an evil which would be almost imperceptible, if it acted only upon a small number of individuals, may become important by its extent. All that the legislator can do in reference to offences of this kind is, to submit them to some slight punishment in cases of scandalous notoriety. This will be sufficient to give them a taint of illegality, which will excite the popular sanction against them.

It is in cases of this kind that legislators have governed too much. Instead of trusting to the prudence of individuals, they have treated them like children, or slaves. They have suffered themselves to be carried away by the same passion which has influenced the founders of religious orders, who, to signalize their authority, and through a littleness of spirit, have held their subjects in the most abject dependence, and have traced for them, day by day, and moment by moment, their occupations, their food, their rising up, their lying down, and all the petty details of their life. There are celebrated codes, in which are found a multitude of clogs of this sort; there are useless restraints upon marriage; punishments decreed against celibacy; sumptuary laws regulating the fashion of dress, the expense of festivals, the furniture of houses, and the ornaments of women; there are numberless details about aliments permitted or forbidden; about ablutions of such or such a kind; about the purifications which health or cleanliness require; and a thousand similar puerilities, which add, to all the inconvenience of useless restraint, that of besotting the people, by covering these absurdities with a veil of mystery, to disguise their folly.

Yet more unhappy are the States in which it is attempted to maintain by penal laws a uniformity of religious opinions. The choice of their religion ought to be referred entirely to the prudence of individuals. If they are persuaded that their eternal happiness depends upon a certain form of worship or a certain belief, what can a legislator oppose to an interest so great? It is not necessary to insist upon this truth—it is generally acknowledged; but, in tracing the boundaries of legislation, I cannot forget those which it is the most important not to overstep.

As a general rule, the greatest possible latitude should be left to individuals, in all cases in which they can injure none but themselves, for they are the best judges of their own interests. If they deceive themselves, it is to be supposed that the moment they discover their error they will alter their conduct. The power of the law need interfere only to prevent them from injuring each other. It is there that restraint is necessary; it is there that the application of punishments is truly useful, because the rigour exercised upon an individual becomes in such a case the security of all.

II. It is true that there is a natural connection between prudence and probity; for our own interest, well understood, will never leave us without motives to abstain from injuring our fellows.

Let us stop a moment at this point. I say that, independently of religion and the laws, we always have some natural motives—that is, motives derived from our own interest for consulting the happiness of others. 1st. The motive of pure benevolence, a sweet and calm sentiment which we delight to experience, and which inspires us with a repugnance to be the cause of suffering. 2nd. The motives of private affection, which exercise their empire in domestic life, and within the particular circle of our intimacies. 3rd. The desire of good repute, and the fear of blame. This is a sort of calculation of trade. It is paying, to have credit; speaking truth, to obtain confidence; serving, to be served. It is thus we must understand that saying of a wit, *that, if there were no such thing as honesty, it would be a good speculation to invent it, as a means of making one's fortune.*

A man enlightened as to his own interest will not indulge himself in a secret offence through fear of contracting a shameful habit, which sooner or later will betray him; and because the having secrets to conceal from the prying curiosity of mankind leaves in the heart a sediment of disquiet, which corrupts every pleasure. All he can acquire at the expense of security cannot make up for the loss of that; and, if he desires a good reputation, the best guarantee he can have for it is his own esteem.

But, in order that an individual should perceive this connection between the interests of others and his own, he needs an enlightened spirit and a heart free from seductive passions. The greater part of men have neither sufficient light, sufficient strength of mind, nor sufficient moral sensibility to place their honesty above the aid of the laws. The legislator must supply the feebleness of this natural interest by adding to it an artificial interest, more steady and more easily perceived.

More yet. In many cases morality derives its existence from the law; that is, to decide whether the action is morally good or bad, it is necessary to know whether the laws permit or forbid it. It is so of what concerns property. A manner of selling or acquiring, esteemed dishonest in one country, would be irreproachable in another. It is the same with offences against the state. The state exists only by law, and it is impossible to say what conduct in this behalf morality requires of us before knowing what the legislator has decreed. There are countries where it is an offence to enlist into the service of a foreign power, and others in which such a service is lawful and honourable.*

III. As to beneficience some distinctions are necessary. The law may be extended to general objects, such as the care of the poor; but, for details, it is necessary to depend upon private morality. Beneficence has its mysteries, and loves best to employ itself upon evils so unforeseen or so secret that the law cannot reach them. Besides, it is to individual free-will that benevolence owes its energy. If the same acts were commanded, they would no longer be benefits, they would lose their attraction and their essence. It is morality, and especially religion, which here form the necessary complement to legislation, and the sweetest tie of humanity.

However, instead of having done too much in this respect, legislators have not done enough. They ought to erect into an offence the refusal or the omission of a service of humanity when it would be easy to render it, and when some distinct ill clearly results from the refusal; such, for example, as abandoning a wounded man in a solitary road without seeking any assistance for him; not giving information to a man who is ignorantly meddling with poisons; not reaching out the hand to one who has fallen into a ditch from which he cannot extricate himself; in these, and other similar cases, could any fault be found with a punishment, exposing the delinquent to a certain degree of shame,

* Here we touch upon one of the most difficult of questions. If the law is not what it ought to be; if it openly combats the principle of utility; ought we to obey it? Ought we to violate it? Ought we to remain neuter between the law which commands an evil, and morality which forbids it? The solution of this question involves considerations both of prudence and benevolence. We ought to examine if it is more dangerous to violate the law than to obey it; we ought to consider whether the probable evils of obedience are less or greater than the probable evils of disobedience.

or subjecting him to a pecuniary responsibility for the evil which he might have prevented?

I will add, that legislation might be extended further than it is in relation to the interests of the inferior animals. I do not approve the laws of the Hindus on this subject. There are good reasons why animals should serve for the nourishment of man, and for destroying those which incommode us. We are the better for it, and they are not the worse; for they have not, as we have, long and cruel anticipations of the future; and the death which they receive at our hands may always be rendered less painful than that which awaits them in the inevitable course of nature. But what can be said to justify the useless torments they are made to suffer; the cruel caprices which are exercised upon them? Among the many reasons which might be given for making criminal such gratuitous cruelties, I confine myself to that which relates to my subject. It is a means of cultivating a general sentiment of benevolence, and of rendering men more mild; or at least of preventing that brutal depravity, which, after fleshing itself upon animals, presently demands human suffering to satiate its appetite.*

CHAPTER XIII.

False Methods of Reasoning on the Subject of Legislation.

It has been the object of this introduction to give a clear idea of the principle of utility, and of the method of reasoning conformable to that principle. There results from it a legislative logic, which can be summed up in a few words. What is it to offer a *good reason* with respect to a law? It is to allege the good or evil which the law tends to produce: so much good, so many arguments in its favour; so much evil, so many arguments against it; remembering all the time that good and evil are nothing else than pleasure and pain.

* See *Barrow's Voyage to the Cape of Good Hope*, for the cruelties of the Dutch settlers toward their cattle and their slaves.

What is it to offer a *false reason?* It is the alleging for or against a law something else than its good or evil effects.

Nothing can be more simple, yet nothing is more new. It is not the principle of utility which is new; on the contrary, that principle is necessarily as old as the human race. All the truth there is in morality, all the good there is in the laws, emanate from it; but utility has often been followed by instinct, while it has been combatted by argument. If in books of legislation it throws out some sparks here and there, they are quickly extinguished in the surrounding smoke. BECCARIA is the only writer who deserves to be noted as an exception; yet even in his work there is some reasoning drawn from false sources.

It is upwards of two thousand years since Aristotle undertook to form, under the title of *Sophisms*, a complete catalogue of the different kinds of false reasoning. This catalogue, improved by the information which so long an interval might furnish, would here have its place and its use. But such an undertaking would carry me too far. I shall be content with presenting some heads of error on the subject of legislation. By means of such a contrast, the principle of utility will be put into a clearer light.

1. *Antiquity is not a Reason.*

The antiquity of a law may create a prejudice in its favour; but in itself, it is not a reason. If the law in question has contributed to the public good, the older it is, the easier it will be to enumerate its good effects, and to prove its utility by a direct process.

2. *The Authority of Religion is not a Reason.*

Of late, this method of reasoning has gone much out of fashion, but till recently its use was very extensive. The work of Algernon Sidney is full of citations from the *Old Testament;* and he finds there the foundation of a system of Democracy, as Bossuet had found the principles of absolute power. Sidney wished to combat the partisans of divine right and passive obedience with their own weapons.

If we suppose that a law emanates from the Deity, we suppose that it emanates from supreme wisdom, and supreme bounty.

Such a law, then, can only have for its object the most eminent utility; and this utility, put into a clear light, will always be an ample justification of the law.

3. *Reproach of Innovation is not a Reason.*

To reject innovation is to reject progress: in what condition should we be, if that principle had been always followed? All which exists has had a beginning; all which is established has been innovation. Those very persons who approve a law to-day because it is ancient, would have opposed it as new when it was first introduced.

4. *An Arbitrary Definition is not a Reason.*

Nothing is more common, among jurists and political writers, than to base their reasonings, and even to write long works, upon a foundation of purely arbitrary definitions. This artifice consists in taking a word in a particular sense, foreign from its common usage; in employing that word as no one ever employed it before; and in puzzling the reader by an appearance of profoundness and of mystery.

Montesquieu himself has fallen into this fault in the very beginning of his work. Wishing to give a definition of law, he proceeds from metaphor to metaphor; he brings together the most discordant objects—the Divinity, the material world, superior intelligences, beasts and men. We learn, at last, that *laws are relations; and eternal relations.* Thus the definition is more obscure than the thing to be defined. The word *law*, in its proper sense, excites in every mind a tolerably clear idea, the word *relation* excites no idea at all. The word *law*, in its figurative sense, produces nothing but equivocations; and Montesquieu, who ought to have dissipated the darkness, has only increased it.

It is the character of a false definition, that it can only be employed in a particular way. That author, a little further on (ch. iii.), gives another definition. *Law in general*, he says, *is human reason, in so far as it governs all the people of the earth.* These terms are more familiar; but no clear idea results from them. Is it the fact, that so many laws, contradictory, ferocious, or absurd, and in a perpetual state of change, are always *human reason?* It would seem that reason, so far from being the law, is often in opposition to it.

This first chapter of Montesquieu has given occasion to an abundance of nonsense. The brain has been racked in search of metaphysical mysteries, where none in fact exist. Even Beccaria has suffered himself to be carried away by this obscure notion of *relations.* To interrogate a man in order to know whether he is innocent or guilty, is to force him, he tells us, to accuse himself. To this procedure he objects; and why? because, as he says, it is *to confound all relations.** But what does that mean? To enjoy, to suffer, to cause enjoyment, to cause suffering: those are expressions which I understand; but to follow relations and to confound relations, is what I do not understand at all. These abstract terms do not excite any idea in my mind; they do not awaken any sentiment. I am absolutely indifferent about *relations;—pleasures* and *pains* are what interest me.

Rousseau has not been satisfied with the definition of Montesquieu. He has given his own, which he announces as a great discovery. *Law,* he says, *is the expression of the general will.* There are, then, no laws except where the people have spoken in a body. There is no law except in an absolute democracy. Rousseau has suppressed, by this supreme decree, all existing laws; and at the same time he has deprived of the possibility of existence all those which are likely to be made hereafter,—the legislation of the republic of San Marino alone excepted.

5. *Metaphors are not Reasons.*

I mean either metaphor properly so called, or allegory, used at first for illustration or ornament, but afterwards made the basis of an argument.

Blackstone, so great an enemy of all reform, that he has gone so far as to find fault with the introduction of the English language into the reports of cases decided by the courts, has neglected

* Beccaria, ch. xii.

no means of inspiring his readers with the same prejudice. He represents the law* as a castle, as a fortress, which cannot be altered without being weakened. I allow that he does not advance this metaphor as an argument; but why does he employ it? To gain possession of the imagination; to prejudice his readers against every idea of reform; to excite in them an artificial fear of all innovation in the laws. There remains in the mind a false image, which produces the same effect with false reasoning. He ought to have recollected that this allegory might be employed against himself. When they see the law turned into a castle, is it not natural for ruined suitors to represent it as a castle inhabited by robbers?

A man's house, say the English, is his castle. This poetical expression is certainly no reason; for if a man's house be his castle by night, why not by day? If it is an inviolable asylum for the owner, why is it not so for every person whom he chooses to receive there? The course of justice is sometimes interrupted in England by this puerile notion of liberty. Criminals seem to be looked upon like foxes; they are suffered to have their burrows, in order to increase the sports of the chase.

A church in Catholic countries is the *House of God*. This metaphor has served to establish asylums for criminals. It would be a mark of disrespect for the Divinity to seize by force those who had taken refuge in his house.

The balance of trade has produced a multitude of reasonings founded upon metaphor. It has been imagined that in the course of mutual commerce nations rose and sank like the scales of a balance loaded with unequal weights; people have been terribly alarmed at what appeared to them a want of equilibrium; for it has been supposed that what one nation gained the other must lose, as if a weight had been transferred from one scale to the other.

The word *mother-country* has produced a great number of prejudices and false reasonings in all questions concerning colonies

* 3 Comm. ch. xvii.

and the parent state. Duties have been imposed upon colonies, and they have been accused of offences, founded solely upon the metaphor of their filial dependence.

6. *A Fiction is not a Reason.*

I understand by fiction an assumed fact notoriously false, upon which one reasons as if it were true.

The celebrated Cocceiji, the compiler of the *Code Frederic*, furnishes an example of this kind of reasoning on the subject of last wills. After a deal of circumlocution about the natural right, he decides that the legislator ought to grant to individuals the power of making a will. Why? *Because the heir and the deceased are one and the same person, and consequently the heir ought to continue to enjoy the property of the deceased.* (*Code Fred.* part ii. l. 110, p. 156.) He offers, it is true, some arguments which involve, to a small extent, the principle of utility; but that is in the preface. The serious reason, the judicial reason, is the identity of the living and the dead!

The English lawyers, to justify the confiscation of property in certain cases, have employed a style of reasoning not unlike that of the chancellor of the great Frederic. They have imagined a *corruption of blood* which arrests the course of legal succession. A man has been capitally punished for the crime of high treason; his innocent son is not only deprived of his father's goods, but he cannot even inherit from his grandfather, because the channel by which the goods ought to pass has been corrupted. This fiction of a sort of political original sin serves as a foundation to all this point of law. But why stop there? If in fact the father's blood is corrupted, why not destroy the vile offspring of corruption? Why not execute the son at the same time with the father?

Blackstone, in the seventh chapter of his first book, in speaking of the royal authority, has given himself up to all the puerility of fiction. The king, he tells us, is everywhere present; he can do no wrong; he is immortal.

These ridiculous paradoxes, the fruits of servility, so far from furnishing just ideas of the prerogatives of royalty, only serve to dazzle, to mislead, and to give to reality itself an air of fable and of prodigy. But these fictions are not mere sparkles of imagination. He makes them the foundation of many reasonings. He employs them to explain certain royal prerogatives, which might be justified by very good arguments, without perceiving how much the best cause is injured by attempting to prop it up by falsehoods. *The judges*, he tells us, *are mirrors, in which the image of the king is reflected.* What puerility! Is it not exposing to ridicule the very objects which he designs to render the most respectable?

But there are fictions more bold and more important, which have played a great part in politics, and which have produced celebrated works: these are *contracts.*

The *Leviathan* of Hobbes, a work now-a-days but little known, and detested through prejudice and at second-hand as a defence of despotism, is an attempt to base all political society upon a pretended contract between the people and the sovereign. The people by this contract have renounced their natural liberty, which produced nothing but evil; and have deposited all power in the hands of the prince. All opposing wills have been united in his, or rather annihilated by it. That which he *wills* is taken to be the will of all his subjects. When David brought about the destruction of Uriah, he acted in that matter with Uriah's consent, for Uriah had consented to all that David might command. The prince, according to this system, might sin against God, but he could not sin against man, because all his actions proceeded from the general consent. It was impossible to entertain the idea of resisting him, because such an idea implied the contradiction of resisting one's self.

Locke, whose name is as dear to the friends of liberty as that of Hobbes is odious, has also fixed the basis of government upon a contract. He agrees that there is a contract between the prince and the people; but according to him the prince takes an engagement to govern according to the laws, and for the public good; while the people, on their side, take an engagement of obedience so long as the prince remains faithful to the conditions in virtue of which he receives the crown.

Rousseau rejects with indignation the idea of this bilateral contract between the prince and the people. He has imagined a *social contract*, by which all are bound to all, and which is the only legitimate basis of government. Society exists only by virtue of this free convention of associates.

These three systems—so directly opposed—agree, however, in beginning the theory of politics with a fiction, for these three contracts are equally fictitious. They exist only in the imagination of their authors. Not only we find no trace of them in history, but everywhere we discover proofs to the contrary.

The contract of Hobbes is a manifest falsehood. Despotism has everywhere been the result of violence and of false religious ideas. If a people can be found which by a public act has surrendered up the supreme authority to its chief, it is not true that, in so doing, that people submitted itself to all the caprices, however strange or cruel, of its sovereign. The singular act of the Danish people in 1660 includes essential clauses which limit the supreme power.

The *social contract* of Rousseau has not been judged so severely, because men are not difficult about the logic of a system which establishes that which they best love—liberty and equality. But where has this universal convention been formed? What are its clauses? In what language is it written? Why has it always been unknown? Upon coming out of the forests, upon renouncing savage life, what tribe has possessed those great ideas of morals and politics upon which this primitive convention is built?

The contract of Locke is more specious, because, in fact, there are some monarchies in which the sovereign takes certain engagements upon his accession to the throne; and accepts certain conditions upon the part of the nation he is to govern.

However, even this contract is but a fiction. The essence of a contract consists in the free consent of the parties interested. It supposes that all the objects of the engagement are specified and known. Now if the prince is free, at his accession, to accept or to refuse, are the people equally so? Can a few vague acclamations be counted as an act of individual and universal assent? Can this contract bind that multitude of individuals who never heard of it, who have never been called to sanction it, and who could not have refused their consent without endangering their fortunes and their lives?

Besides, in the greater part of monarchies, this pretended contract has not even the appearance of reality. We do not see even the shadow of an engagement between the prince and the people.

It is not necessary to make the happiness of the human race dependent on a fiction. It is not necessary to erect the social pyramid upon a foundation of sand, or upon a clay which slips from beneath it. Let us leave such trifling to children; men ought to speak the language of truth and reason.

The true political tie is the immense interest which men have in maintaining a government. Without a government there can be no security, no domestic enjoyments, no property, no industry. It is in this fact that we ought to seek the basis and the reason of all governments, whatever may be their origin and their form; it is by comparing them with their object that we can reason with solidity upon their rights and their obligations, without having recourse to pretended contracts which can only serve to produce interminable disputes.

7. *Fancy is not a Reason.*

Nothing is more common than to say, *reason decides, eternal reason orders*, &c. But what is this reason? If it is not a distinct view of good or evil, it is mere fancy; it is a despotism, which announces nothing but the interior persuasion of him who speaks. Let us see upon what foundation a distinguished jurist has sought to establish the paternal authority. A man of ordinary good sense would not see much difficulty in that question; but your learned men find a mystery everywhere.

"The right of a father over his children," says Cocceiji, "is founded in reason;—for, 1st, Children are born in a house, of which the father is the master; 2nd, They are born in a family of which he is the chief; 3rd, They are of his seed, and a part of his body." These are the reasons from which he concludes, among other things, that a man of forty ought not to marry without the consent of a father, who in the course of nature must by that time be in his dotage. What there is common to these three reasons is, that none of them has any relation to the interests of the parties. The author consults neither the welfare of father nor that of the children.

The right of a father is an improper phrase. The question is not of an unlimited, nor of an indivisible right. There are many kinds of rights which may be granted or refused to a father, each for particular reasons.

The first reason which Cocceiji alleges is founded upon a fact which is true only by accident. Let a traveller have children who are born at a tavern, on board a vessel, or in the house of a friend, such a father would lack this first basis of paternal authority. According to this reasoning, the children of a domestic, and those of a soldier, ought not to be subject to their fathers' commands, but to those of the person in whose house they are born.

If the second reason has any determinate sense, it is only a repetition of the first. Is the child of a man who lives in his father's house, or in the house of an elder brother, or a patron, born in a family of which his father is the chief?

The third reason is as futile as it is indecent. "The child is born of the seed of his father, and is a part of his body." If this is the foundation of the right, it ought to put the power of the mother far above that of the father.

And here we may remark an essential difference between false principles and the true one. The principle of utility, applying itself only to the interests of the parties, bends to circumstances, and accommodates itself to every case. False principles, being founded upon things which have nothing to do with individual interests, would be inflexible if they were consistent. Such is the character of this pretended right founded upon birth. The son naturally belongs to the father, because the matter of which the son is formed once circulated in the father's veins. No matter how unhappy he renders his son;—it is impossible to annihilate his right, because we cannot make his son cease to be his son. The corn of which your body is made formerly grew in my field; how is it that you are not my slave?

8. *Antipathy and Sympathy are not Reasons.*

Reasoning by antipathy is most common upon subjects connected with penal law; for we have antipathies against actions reputed to be crimes; antipathies against individuals reputed to be criminals; antipathies against the ministers of justice; antipathies against such and such punishments. This false principle has reigned like a tyrant throughout this vast province of law. Beccaria first dared openly to attack it. His arms were of celestial temper; but if he did much towards destroying the usurper, he did very little towards the establishment of a new and more equitable rule.

It is the principle of antipathy which leads us to speak of offences as *deserving* punishment. It is the corresponding principle of sympathy which leads us to speak of certain actions as *meriting* reward. This word *merit* can only lead to passion and to error. It is *effects*, good or bad, which we ought alone to consider.

But when I say that *antipathies and sympathies are no reason,* I mean those of the legislator; for the antipathies and sympathies of the people may be reasons, and very powerful ones. However odd or pernicious a religion, a law, a custom may be, it is of no consequence, so long as the people are attached to it. The strength of their prejudice is the measure of the indulgence which should be granted to it. To take away an enjoyment or a hope, chimerical though it may be, is to do the same injury as if we took away a real hope, a real enjoyment. In such a case the pain of a single individual becomes, by sympathy, the pain of all. Thence results a crowd of evils; antipathy against a law which wounds the general prejudice; antipathy against the whole code of that law is a part; antipathy against the government which carries the laws into execution; a disposition not to aid in their execution; a disposition secretly to oppose it; a disposition to oppose it openly and by force; a disposition to destroy a government which sets itself in opposition to the popular will—all the evils produced by those offences, which, in a collective shape, form that sad compound called *rebellion* or *civil war*—all the evils produced by the punishments which are resorted to as a means of putting a stop to those offences. Such is the succession of fatal consequences which are always ready to arise from fancies and prejudices violently opposed. The legislator ought to yield to the violence of a current which carries away everything that obstructs it. But let us observe, that in such a case, the fancies themselves are not the reason that determines the legislator; his reason is the evils which threaten to grow out of an opposition to those fancies.

But ought the legislator to be a slave to the fancies of those whom he governs? No. Between an imprudent opposition and a servile compliance there is a middle path, honourable and safe. It is to combat these fancies with the only arms that can conquer them—example and instruction. He must enlighten the people, he must address himself to the public reason; he must give time for error to be unmasked. Sound reasons, clearly set forth, are of necessity stronger than false ones. But the legislator ought not to show himself too openly in these instructions, for fear of compromitting himself with the public ignorance. Indirect means will better answer his end.

It is to be observed, however, that too much deference for prejudices is a more common fault than the contrary excess. The best projects of laws are for ever stumbling against this common objection,—"Prejudice is opposed to it; the people will be offended!" But how is that known? How has public opinion been consulted? What is its organ? Have the whole people but one uniform notion on the subject? Have all the individuals of the community the same sentiments, including perhaps nine out of ten, who never heard the subject spoken of? Besides, if the people are in error, are they compelled always to remain so? Will not an influx of light dissipate the darkness which produces error? Can we expect the people to possess sound knowledge, while it is yet unattained by their legislators, by those who are regarded as the wise men of the land? Have there not been examples of other nations who have come out of a similar ignorance, and where triumphs have been achieved over the same obstacles?

After all, popular prejudice serves oftener as a pretext than as a motive. It is a convenient cover for the weakness of statesmen. The ignorance of the people is the favourite argument of pusillanimity and of indolence; while the real motives are prejudices from which the legislators themselves have not been able to get free. The name of the people is falsely used to justify their leaders.

9. *Begging the Question is not a Reason.*

The *petitio principii*, or begging the question, is one of the sophisms which is noted by Aristotle; but it is a Proteus which conceals itself artfully, and is reproduced under a thousand forms.

Begging the question, or rather assuming the question, consists in making use of the very proposition in dispute, as though it were already proved.

This false procedure insinuates itself into morals and legislation, under the disguise of *sentimental* or *impassioned* terms; that is, terms which, beside their principal sense, carry with them an accessory idea of praise or blame. *Neuter* terms are those which simply express the thing in question, without any attending presumption of good or evil; without introducing any foreign idea of blame or approbation.

Now it is to be observed that an impassioned term envelops a proposition not expressed, but understood, which always accompanies its employment, though in general unperceived by those who employ it. This concealed proposition implies either blame or praise; but the implication is always vague and undetermined.

Do I desire to connect an idea of utility with a term which

commonly conveys an accessory idea of blame? I shall seem to advance a paradox, and to contradict myself. For example, should I say that such a piece of *luxury* is a good thing? The proposition astonishes those who are accustomed to attach to this word *luxury* a sentiment of disapprobation.

How shall I be able to examine this particular point without awakening a dangerous association? I must have recourse to a neuter word; I must say, for example, *such a manner of spending one's revenue* is good. This turn of expression runs counter to no prejudice, and permits an impartial examination of the object in question. When Helvetius advanced the idea that all actions have *interest* for their motive, the public cried out against his doctrine without stopping to understand it. Why? Because the word *interest* has an odious sense; a common acceptation, in which it seems to exclude every motive of pure attachment and of benevolence.

How many reasonings upon political subjects are founded upon nothing but impassioned terms! People suppose they are giving a reason for a law, when they say that it is conformable to the principles of monarchy or of democracy. But that means nothing. If there are persons in whose minds these words are associated with an idea of approbation, there are others who attach contrary ideas to them. Let these two parties begin to quarrel, the dispute will never come to an end, except through the weariness of the combatants. For, before beginning a true examination, we must renounce these impassioned terms, and calculate the effects of the proposed law in good and evil.

Blackstone admires in the British constitution the combination of the three forms of government; and he hence concludes that it must possess the collected good qualities of monarchy, aristocracy, and democracy. How happened it that he did not perceive, that without changing his premises, a conclusion might be drawn from them, diametrically opposite, yet equally just; to wit, that the British constitution must unite all the particular *faults* of democracy, aristocracy, and monarchy?

To the word *independence*, there are attached certain accessory ideas of dignity and virtue; to the word *dependence*, accessory ideas of inferiority and corruption. Hence it is that the panegyrists of the British constitution admire the *independence* of the three powers of which the legislature is composed. This, in their eyes, is the masterpiece of politics; the happiest trait in that whole scheme of government. On the other side, those who would detract from the merits of that constitution, are always insisting upon the actual *dependence* of one or the other of its branches. Neither the praise nor the censure contain any reasons.

As to the fact, the pretended independence does not exist. The king and the greater part of the lords have a direct influence upon the election of the House of Commons. The king has the power of dissolving that House at any moment; a power of no little efficacy. The king exercises a direct influence by honourable and lucrative employments, which he gives or takes away at pleasure. On the other side, the king is dependent upon the two Houses, and particularly upon the Commons, since he cannot maintain himself without money and troops,—two principal and essential matters which are wholly under the control of the representatives of the people. What pretence has the House of Lords to be called independent, while the king can augment its number at pleasure, and change the vote in his favour by the creation of new lords; exercising too, as he does, an additional influence on the temporal peers, by the prospect of advancement in the ranks of the peerage; and on the bishops, by the bait of ecclesiastical promotion?

Instead of reasoning upon a deceptive word, let us consider effects. It is the reciprocal dependence of these three powers which produces their agreement; which subjects them to fixed rules, which gives them a steady and systematic operation. Hence the necessity of mutual respect, attention, concession, and moderation. If they were absolutely independent, there would be continual shocks between them. It would often be necessary to appeal to force; and the result would be a state of anarchy.

I cannot refrain from giving two other examples of this error of reasoning, founded upon the misuse of terms.

If we attempt a theory upon the subject of *national representation*, in following out all that appears to be a natural consequence of that abstract idea, we come at last to the conclusion that *universal suffrage* ought to be established; and to the additional conclusion that the representatives ought to be re-chosen as frequently as possible, in order that the national representation may deserve to be esteemed such.

In deciding these same questions according to the principle of utility, it will not do to reason upon words; we must look only at effects. In the election of a legislative assembly, the right of suffrage should not be allowed except to those who are esteemed by the nation fit to exercise it; for a choice made by men who do not possess the national confidence will weaken the confidence of the nation in the assembly so chosen.

Men who would not be thought fit to be electors, are those who cannot be presumed to possess political integrity, and a sufficient degree of knowledge. Now we cannot presume upon the political integrity of those whom want exposes to the temptation of selling themselves; nor of those who have no fixed abode; nor of those who have been found guilty in the courts of justice of certain offences forbidden by the law. We cannot presume a sufficient degree of knowledge in women, whom their domestic condition withdraws from the conduct of public affairs; in children and adults beneath a certain age; in those who are deprived by their poverty of the first elements of education, &c. &c.

It is according to these principles, and others like them, that we ought to fix the conditions necessary for becoming an elector; and it is in like manner, upon the advantages and disadvantages of frequent elections, without paying any attention to arguments drawn from abstract terms, that we ought to reason in establishing the duration of a legislative assembly.

The last example I shall give will be taken from *contracts;* I mean those political fictions to which this name has been applied by their authors.

When Locke and Rousseau reason upon this pretended contract;

when they affirm that the social or political contract includes such and such a clause, can they prove it otherwise than by the general utility which is supposed to result from it? Grant that this contract which has never been reduced to writing is, however, in full existence. On what depends all its force? Is it not upon its utility? Why ought we to fulfil our engagements? Because the faith of promises is the basis of society. It is for the advantage of all that the promises of every individual should be faithfully observed. There would no longer be any security among men, no commerce, no confidence;—it would be necessary to go back to the woods, if engagements did not possess an obligatory force. It is the same with these political contracts. It is their utility which makes them binding. When they become injurious, they lose their force. If a king had taken an oath to render his subjects unhappy, would such an engage-be valid? If the people were sworn to obey him at all events, would they be bound to suffer themselves to be exterminated by a Nero or a Caligula, rather than violate their promise? If there resulted from the contract effects universally injurious, could there be any sufficient reason for maintaining it? It cannot be denied, then, that the validity of a contract is at bottom only a question of utility—a little wrapped up, a little disguised, and, in consequence, more susceptible of false interpretations.

10. *An imaginary Law is not a Reason.*

Natural law, *natural rights*, are two kinds of fictions or metaphors, which play so great a part in books of legislation that they deserve to be examined by themselves.

The primitive sense of the word *law*, and the ordinary meaning of the word, is—the will or command of a legislator. The *law of nature* is a figurative expression, in which nature is represented as a being; and such and such a disposition is attributed to her, which is figuratively called a law. In this sense, all the general inclinations of men, all those which appear to exist independently of human societies, and from which must proceed the establishment of political and civil law, are called *laws of nature.* This is the true sense of the phrase.

But this is not the way in which it is understood. Authors have taken it in a direct sense; as if there had been a real code of natural laws. They appeal to these laws; they cite them, and they oppose them, clause by clause, to the enactments of legislators. They do not see that these natural laws are laws of their own invention; that they are all at odds among themselves as to the contents of this pretended code; that they affirm without proof; that systems are as numerous as authors; and that, in reasoning in this manner, it is necessary to be always beginning anew, because every one can advance what he pleases touching laws which are only imaginary, and so keep on disputing for ever.

What is natural to man is sentiments of pleasure or pain, what are called inclinations. But to call these sentiments and these inclinations *laws*, is to introduce a false and dangerous idea. It is to set language in opposition to itself; for it is necessary to make *laws* precisely for the purpose of restraining these inclinations. Instead of regarding them as laws, they must be submitted to laws. It is against the strongest natural inclinations that it is necessary to have laws the most repressive. If there were a law of nature which directed all men towards their common good, laws would be useless; it would be employing a creeper to uphold an oak; it would be kindling a torch to add light to the sun.

Blackstone, in speaking of the obligation of parents to provide for the support of their children, says, "that it is a principle of natural law, a duty imposed by nature itself, and by the proper act of the parents in bringing the children into the world. Montesquieu," he adds, "observes with reason, that the natural obligation of the father to support his children, is what has caused the establishment of marriage, which points out the person who ought to fulfil this obligation." (Book i. ch. 16.)

Parents *are inclined* to support their children; parents *ought* to support their children; these are two distinct propositions.

The first does not suppose the second; the second does not suppose the first. There are, without doubt, the strongest reasons for imposing upon parents the obligation to bring up their children. Why have not Blackstone and Montesquieu mentioned those reasons? Why do they refer us to what they call the law of nature? What is this law of nature, which needs to be propped up by a secondary law from another legislator? If this natural obligation exists, as Montesquieu says it does, far from serving as the foundation of marriage, it proves its inutility,—at least for the end which he assigns. One of the objects of marriage is, precisely to supply the insufficiency of natural affection. It is designed to convert into obligation that inclination of parents, which would not always be sufficiently strong to surmount the pains and embarrassments of education.

Men are very well disposed to provide for their own support. It has not been necessary to make laws to oblige them to that. If the disposition of parents to provide for the support of their children had been constantly and universally as strong, legislators never would have thought of turning it into an obligation.

The exposure of infants, so common in ancient Greece, is still practised in China, and to a greater extent. To abolish this practice, would it not be necessary to allege other reasons besides this pretended law of nature, which here is evidently at fault?

The word *rights*, the same as the word *law*, has two senses; the one a proper sense, the other a metaphorical sense. *Rights*, properly so called, are the creatures of *law* properly so called; real laws give birth to real rights. *Natural rights* are the creatures of natural law; they are a metaphor which derives its origin from another metaphor.

What there is natural in man is means,—faculties. But to call these means, these faculties, *natural rights*, is again to put language in opposition to itself. For *rights* are established to insure the exercise of means and faculties. The right is the *guarantee;* the faculty is the thing guaranteed. How can we understand each other with a language which confounds under the same term things so different? Where would be the nomenclature of the arts, if we gave to the *mechanic* who makes an article the same name as to the article itself?

Real rights are always spoken of in a legal sense; natural rights are often spoken of in a sense that may be called anti-legal. When it is said, for example, that *law cannot avail against natural rights,* the word rights is employed in a sense above the law; for, in this use of it, we acknowledge rights which attack the law; which overturn it, which annul it. In this anti-legal sense, the word *right* is the greatest enemy of reason, and the most terrible destroyer of governments.

There is no reasoning with fanatics, armed with *natural rights;* which each one understands as he pleases, and applies as he sees fit; of which nothing can be yielded, nor retrenched; which are inflexible, at the same time that they are unintelligible; which are consecrated as dogmas, from which it is a crime to vary. Instead of examining laws by their effects, instead of judging them as good or as bad, they consider them in relation to these pretended natural rights; that is to say, they substitute for the reasoning of experience the chimeras of their own imaginations.

This is not a harmless error; it passes from speculation into practice. "Those laws must be obeyed, which are accordant with nature; the others are null in fact; and instead of obeying them, they ought to be resisted. The moment natural rights are attacked, every good citizen ought to rouse up in their defence. These rights, evident in themselves, do not need to be proved; it is sufficient to declare them. How prove what is evident already? To doubt implies a want of sense, or a fault of intellect," &c.

But not to be accused of gratuitously ascribing such seditious maxims to these inspired politicians of nature, I shall cite a passage from Blackstone, directly to the point; and I choose Blackstone, because he is, of all writers, the one who has shown the most profound respect for the authority of governments. In speaking of these pretended laws of nature, and of the laws of revelation, he says: "Human laws must not be permitted to contradict these; if a human law commands a thing forbidden by the natural or divine law, we are bound to transgress that human law," &c. (1 Comm. p. 43.)

Is not this arming every fanatic against all governments? In the immense variety of ideas respecting natural and Divine law, cannot some reason be found for resisting all human laws? Is there a single state which can maintain itself a day, if each individual holds himself bound in conscience to resist the laws, whenever they are not conformed to his particular ideas of natural or Divine law? What a cut-throat scene of it we should have between all the interpreters of the code of nature, and all the interpreters of the law of God!

"The pursuit of happiness is a natural right." The pursuit of happiness is certainly a natural inclination; but can it be declared to be a right? That depends on the way in which it is pursued. The assassin pursues his happiness, or what he esteems such, by committing an assassination. Has he a right to do so? If not, why declare that he has? What tendency is there in such a declaration to render men more happy or more wise?

Turgot was a great man; but he had adopted the general opinion without examining it. Inalienable and natural rights were the despotism or the dogmatism which he wished to exercise, without himself perceiving it. If he saw no reason to doubt a proposition; if he judged it evidently true; he referred it, without going further, to natural right, to eternal justice. Henceforward he made use of it as an article of faith, which he was no longer permitted to examine.

Utility having been often badly applied, understood in a narrow sense, and having lent its name to crimes, has appeared contrary to eternal justice. It thus became degraded, and acquired a mercenary reputation. It needs courage to restore it to honour, and to re-establish reasoning upon its true basis.

I propose a treaty of conciliation with the partisans of natural rights. If *nature* has made such or such a law, those who cite it with so much confidence, those who have modestly taken upon themselves to be its interpreters, must suppose that nature had some reasons for her law. Would it not be surer, shorter and more persuasive, to give us those reasons directly, instead of urging upon us the will of this unknown legislator, as itself an authority?

Here would be the place to remark the false methods of argument, which especially prevail in deliberative assemblies—personalities, imputations of bad motives, declamations, delays. But what has been said above is enough to show what is reasoning, according to the principle of utility, and what is not.

All these false methods of reasoning can always be reduced to one or the other of the two false principles. This fundamental distinction is very useful in getting rid of words, and rendering ideas more clear. To refer such or such an argument to one or another of the false principles, is like tying weeds into bundles, to be thrown into the fire.

I conclude with a general observation. The language of error is always obscure and indefinite. An abundance of words serves to cover a paucity and a falsity of ideas. The oftener terms are changed, the easier it is to delude the reader. The language of truth is uniform and simple. The same ideas are always expressed by the same terms. Everything is referred to pleasures or to pains. Every expression is avoided which tends to disguise or intercept the familiar idea, that *from such and such actions result such and such pleasures and pains*. Trust not to me, but to experience, and especially your own. *Of two opposite methods of action, do you desire to know which should have the preference? Calculate their effects in good and evil, and prefer that which promises the greater sum of good.*

PRINCIPLES OF THE CIVIL CODE.

INTRODUCTION.

BY DUMONT.

Of all the branches of legislation, civil law is that which has the least attraction for those who do not study jurisprudence as a profession. But this is not saying enough. In fact, it inspires a kind of terror. Curiosity has for a long time been ardently exercised upon political economy, upon penal law, and upon the principles of government. Celebrated works have given credit to those studies; and under the penalty of confessing an humbling inferiority, it is necessary to have some information, and to express some opinions about them. But civil law has not yet come out of the narrow enclosure of the bar. Its commentators sleep in the dust of libraries, by the side of its controversialists. The public knows not even the names of its sects; and regards with a mute and ignorant respect those numerous folios, those enormous compilations, ornamented with the pompous titles of *Bodies of Law*, and *Collections of Universal Jurisprudence.*

The general repugnance against this study results from the manner in which it has been treated. The works above alluded to bear the same relation to the science of law which was borne to the natural sciences by the works of the scholastic writers, before the introduction of experimental philosophy. They who attribute the dryness and obscurity of those works to the nature of the subject, are altogether too indulgent.

What is it of which this part of the law treats? It treats of everything that is most interesting to men: of their security; of their property; of their mutual and daily transactions; of their domestic condition, in the relations of father, of children, of husband, and of wife. Here it is that *rights* and *obligations* spring up; for all the objects of law may be reduced, without mystery, to these two terms.

The civil law is, in fact, only another aspect of the penal law; one cannot be understood without the other. To establish *rights*, is to grant permissions; it is to make prohibitions; it is, in one word, to create offences. To commit a private offence is to violate an obligation which we owe to an individual,—a right which he has in regard to us. To commit a public offence is to violate an obligation which we owe to the public,—a right which the public has in regard to us. Civil law, then, is only penal law viewed under another aspect. If I consider a law at the moment when it confers a right, or imposes an obligation, this is the civil point of view. If I consider a law in its sanction, in its effects as regards the violation of that right, the breaking through that obligation, that is the penal point of view.

What is to be understood by *principles of civil law?* They are the *motives* of laws; the knowledge of the true *reasons* which ought to guide the legislator in the distribution of the rights which he confers, and the obligations which he imposes.

We might search in vain through the libraries of law books, for a volume in which it has been attempted to found laws upon reasons. The *theory of civil laws* by Linguet, promises much in its title, which it is very far from performing. It is the production of a disordered imagination, in the service of a bad heart. The author wishes to reduce all governments to the model of oriental despotism, and to strike out of them all notions of liberty and humanity,—in his view mournful spectres, the sight of which appears to torment him.

The disputes of jurisprudence have produced, among the

lawyers, a kind of unbelievers, who have doubted whether law has any principles. According to them, everything is arbitrary. The law is good because it is the law; because a decision, of whatever kind, produces the great advantage of peace. There is a little truth in this opinion, and a great deal of error. It will be seen in the following chapters that the principle of utility extends to this part of the law, as to all others. But its application is difficult; it demands an intimate knowledge of human nature.

The first ray of light which struck the mind of Bentham, in the study of law, was the perception that *natural rights*, the *original pact*, the *moral sense*, the *notion of just and unjust*, which are used to explain everything, were at bottom nothing but those *innate ideas* of which Locke has so clearly shown the falsity. He saw that authors were going round in a vicious circle. Familiar with the method of Bacon and of Newton, he resolved to transfer it to the subject of legislation; he resolved to make jurisprudence an experimental science. He avoided all dogmatic words; he rejected everything which did not express a sensation of pain or pleasure; he refused to admit, for example, that property was an inherent right, or a natural right, because these terms explained nothing and proved nothing. The words *justice* and *injustice* had, in his estimation, a similar inconvenience,—that of prejudging questions, instead of throwing light upon them. When he proposes a law, he does not pretend to find a corresponding law in the code of nature, and by a common piece of legerdemain to present, as a thing made already, the very thing he wishes to make. When he explains *obligations*, he does not wrap himself up in mysterious reasons; he admits no supposition; he shows plainly that every obligation ought to be founded either upon a precedent service received by the person obligated; upon a superior need on the part of him in whose favour the obligation is imposed; or upon a mutual agreement which derives all its force from its utility. Thus, always guided by experience and observation, he considers in laws nothing but the effects they produce upon the faculties of man as a sensitive being; and he always gives *pains to be avoided* as the only arguments of real value.

The lawyers are always reasoning upon fictions, and giving to those fictions the same effect as to realities. They admit, for example, *contracts* which never have existed; and *quasi contracts* which have not even an appearance of existence. In certain cases they admit a *civil death*, in others they deny the *natural death*: such a dead man is not dead; such a living man is not living. A person who is absent is taken to be present; a person who is present is regarded as absent. A province is not where it is; a country does not belong to those who own it. Men are sometimes *things*, and as such are not susceptible of rights. *Things* are sometimes beings who have rights, and who are submitted to obligations. They acknowledge imprescriptible rights, against which prescription has always prevailed; inalienable rights which have always been alienated; and that *which is not*, in their eyes, is always of more avail than that *which is*. Take away these fictions, or rather these falsehoods, and they would not know where they were. Accustomed to these false supports, they cannot sustain themselves in any other way. Bentham has rejected all these puerile arguments; he makes no gratuitous suppositions, he uses no arbitrary definitions; no reason which is not the expression of a fact; no fact which is not a statement of good or bad effects.

It is by this logical method of reasoning that he has made a new science of civil law; new and even paradoxical for those who have been bred in the opinions of the old schools; but simple, natural, and even familiar, to those who have not been bewildered by false systems. A translation of this book will have, in all languages, the same sense and the same force, because it appeals to the universal experience of men; while technical reasons—reasons founded upon abstract terms, upon arbitrary definitions having only a local value, and consisting only in words—vanish when one attempts to find synonyms by which to translate them. So the African tribes, who use shells for money, become conscious of their poverty the moment they go beyond their own boundaries, and offer their conventional riches to strangers.

I ought to add that Bentham made frequent digressions upon

the laws of England, which I have suppressed, for they have only a local interest. There are cases, however, where his observations would have lacked a foundation if I had omitted to mention the particular laws which were their object. In seeking to be more clear, to develop that which in the original was often only an allusion, I may have made some mistakes, which it would be unjust to impute to the author. These laws are so difficult to understand, that it is dangerous for an Englishman who is not a lawyer to run the risk of speaking about them—a risk which, for obvious reasons, must be still greater in the case of a foreigner.

PART FIRST.

OBJECTS OF THE CIVIL LAW.

CHAPTER I.

Rights and Obligations.

All the objects which the legislator is called upon to distribute among the members of the community may be reduced to two classes:—

1st. *Rights.*

2nd. *Obligations.*

Rights are in themselves advantages, benefits, for him who enjoys them. Obligations, on the contrary, are duties, charges, onerous to him who ought to fulfil them.

Rights and obligations, though distinct and opposite in their nature, are simultaneous in their origin, and inseparable in their existence. In the nature of things, the law cannot grant a benefit to one without imposing, at the same time, some burden upon another; or, in other words, it is not possible to create a right in favour of one, except by creating a corresponding obligation mposed upon another. How confer upon me the right of property in a piece of land? By imposing upon all others an obligation not to touch its produce. How confer upon me a right of command? By imposing upon a district, or a number of persons, the obligation to obey me.

The legislator ought to confer rights with pleasure, since they are in themselves a good; he ought to impose obligations with reluctance, since they are in themselves an evil. According to the principle of utility, he ought never to impose a burden except for the purpose of conferring a benefit of a clearly greater value.

By creating obligations, the law to the same extent trenches upon liberty. It converts into offences acts which would otherwise be permitted and unpunishable. The law creates an offence either by a positive command or by a prohibition.

These retrenchments of liberty are inevitable. It is impossible to create rights, to impose obligations, to protect the person, life, reputation, property, subsistence, liberty itself, except at the expense of liberty.

But every restriction imposed upon liberty is subject to be followed by a natural sentiment of pain, greater or less; and that independently of an infinite variety of inconveniences and sufferings, which may result from the particular manner of this restriction. It follows, then, that no restriction ought to be imposed, no power conferred, no coercive law sanctioned, without a sufficient and specific reason. There is always a reason against every coercive law—a reason which, in default of any opposing reason, will always be sufficient in itself; and that reason is, that such a law is an attack upon liberty. He who proposes a coercive law ought to be ready to prove, not only that there is a specific reason in favour of it, but that this reason is of more weight than the general reason against every such law.

The proposition that every law is contrary to liberty,* though as clear as evidence can make it, is not generally acknowledged. On the contrary, those among the friends of liberty who are more ardent than enlightened, make it a duty of conscience to combat this truth. And how? They pervert language; they refuse to employ the word *liberty* in its common acceptation; they speak a tongue peculiar to themselves. This is the definition they give of liberty: *Liberty consists in the right of doing everything which is not injurious to another*. But is this the ordinary sense of the word? Is not the liberty to do evil liberty? If not, what is it? What word can we use in speaking of it? Do we not say that it

* Those laws must be excepted by which restrictive laws are revoked, laws which *permit* what other laws had forbidden.

is necessary to take away liberty from idiots and bad men, because they abuse it?

According to this definition, I can never know whether I have the liberty to do an action until I have examined all its consequences. If it seems to me injurious to a single individual, even though the law permit it, or perhaps command it, I should not be at liberty to do it. An officer of justice would not be at liberty to punish a robber, unless, indeed, he were sure that this punishment could not hurt the robber! Such are the absurdities which this definition implies.

What does simple reason tell us? Let us attempt to establish a series of true propositions on this subject.

The only object of government ought to be the greatest possible happiness of the community.

The happiness of an individual is increased in proportion as his sufferings are lighter and fewer, and his enjoyments greater and more numerous.

The care of his enjoyments ought to be left almost entirely to the individual. The principal function of government is to guard against pains.

It fulfils this object by creating rights, which it confers upon individuals: rights of personal security, rights of protection for honour, rights of property, rights of receiving aid in case of need. To these rights correspond offences of different kinds. The law cannot create rights except by creating corresponding obligations. It cannot create rights and obligations without creating offences. It cannot command nor forbid without restraining the liberty of individuals.

It appears, then, that the citizen cannot acquire rights except by sacrificing a part of his liberty. But even under a bad government there is no proportion between the acquisition and the sacrifice. Government approaches to perfection in proportion as the sacrifice is less and the acquisition more.

CHAPTER II.

Ends of Civil Law.

In the distribution of rights and obligations, the legislator, as we have said, should have for his end the happiness of society. Investigating more distinctly in what that happiness consists, we shall find four subordinate ends :—

Subsistence.
Abundance.
Equality.
Security.

The more perfect enjoyment is in all these respects, the greater is the sum of social happiness: and especially of that happiness which depends upon the laws.

We may hence conclude that all the functions of law may be referred to these four heads:—To provide subsistence; to produce abundance; to favour equality; to maintain security.

This division has not all the exactness which might be desired. The limits which separate these objects are not always easy to be determined. They approach each other at different points, and mingle together. But it is enough to justify this division, that it is the most complete we can make; and that, in fact, we are generally called to consider each of the objects which it contains, separately and distinct from all the others.

Subsistence, for example, is included in abundance; still it is very necessary to consider it separately; because the laws ought to do many things for subsistence which they ought not to attempt for the sake of abundance.

Security admits as many distinctions as there are kinds of actions which may be hostile to it. It relates to the person, the honour, to property, to condition. Acts injurious to security, branded by prohibition of law, receive the quality of offences.

Of these objects of the law, security is the only one which necessarily embraces the future. Subsistence, abundance, equality, may be considered in relation to a single moment of present time; but security implies a given extension of future time in respect to all that good which it embraces. Security, then, is the pre-eminent object.

I have mentioned equality as one of the objects of law. In an arrangement designed to give to all men the greatest possible sum of good, there is no reason why the law should seek to give more to one individual than to another. There are abundance of reasons why it should not; for the advantages acquired on one side, never can be an equivalent for the disadvantages felt upon the other. The pleasure is exclusively for the party favoured; the pain for all who do not share the favour.

Equality may be promoted either by protecting it where it exists, or by seeking to produce it. In this latter case, the greatest caution is necessary; for a single error may overturn social order.*

Some persons may be astonished to find that *Liberty* is not ranked among the principal objects of law. But a clear idea of liberty will lead us to regard it as a branch of security. Personal liberty is security against a certain kind of injuries which affect the person. As to what is called *political liberty*, it is another branch of security,—security against injustice from the ministers of government. What concerns this object belongs not to civil, but to constitutional law.

CHAPTER III.

Relations between these Ends.

THESE four objects of law are very distinct in idea, but they are much less so in practice. The same law may advance several of them; because they are often united. That law, for example,

* Equality may be considered in relation to all the advantages which depend upon laws. Political equality is an equality of political rights; civil equality is an equality of civil rights. When used by itself, the word is commonly understood to refer to the distribution of property. It is so used in this treatise.

which favours security, favours, at the same time, subsistence and abundance.

But there are circumstances in which it is impossible to unite these objects. It will sometimes happen that a measure suggested by one of these principles will be condemned by another. Equality, for example, might require a distribution of property which would be incompatible with security.

When this contradiction exists between two of these ends, it is necessary to find some means of deciding the pre-eminence; otherwise these principles, instead of guiding us in our researches, will only serve to augment the confusion.

At the first glance we see subsistence and security arising together to the same level; abundance and equality are manifestly of inferior importance. In fact, without security, equality could not last a day; without subsistence, abundance could not exist at all. The two first objects are life itself; the two latter, the ornaments of life.

In legislation, the most important object is security. Though no laws were made directly for subsistence, it might easily be imagined that no one would neglect it. But unless laws are made directly for security, it would be quite useless to make them for subsistence. You may order production; you may command cultivation; and you will have done nothing. But assure to the cultivator the fruits of his industry, and perhaps in that alone you will have done enough.

Security, as we have said, has many branches; and some branches of it must yield to others. For example, liberty, which is a branch of security, ought to yield to a consideration of the general security, since laws cannot be made except at the expense of liberty.

We cannot arrive at the greatest good, except by the sacrifice of some subordinate good. All the difficulty consists in distinguishing that object which, according to the occasion, merits pre-eminence. For each, in its turn, demands it; and a very complicated calculation is sometimes necessary to avoid being deceived as to the preference due to one or the other.

Equality ought not to be favoured except in the cases in which it does not interfere with security; in which it does not thwart the expectations which the law itself has produced, in which it does not derange the order already established.

If all property were equally divided, at fixed periods, the sure and certain consequence would be, that presently there would be no property to divide. All would shortly be destroyed. Those whom it was intended to favour, would not suffer less from the division than those at whose expense it was made. If the lot of the industrious was not better than the lot of the idle, there would be no longer any motives for industry.

To lay down as a principle that all men ought to enjoy a perfect *equality of rights*, would be, by a necessary connection of consequences, to render all legislation impossible. The laws are constantly establishing inequalities, since they cannot give rights to one without imposing obligations upon another. To say that all men—that is, all human beings—have equal rights, is to say that there is no such thing as subordination. The son then has the same rights with his father; he has the same right to govern and punish his father that his father has to govern and punish him. He has as many rights in the house of his father as the father himself. The maniac has the same right to shut up others that others have to shut up him. The idiot has the same right to govern his family that his family have to govern him. All this is fully implied in the absolute equality of rights. It means this, or else it means nothing. I know very well that those who maintain this doctrine of the equality of rights, not being themselves either fools or idiots, have no intention of establishing this absolute equality. They have, in their own minds, restrictions, modifications, explanations. But if they themselves cannot speak in an intelligible manner, will the ignorant and excited multitude understand them better than they understand themselves?

CHAPTER IV.

Laws relatively to Subsistence.

What can the law do for subsistence? Nothing directly. All it can do is to create *motives*, that is, punishments or rewards, by the force of which men may be led to provide subsistence for themselves. But nature herself has created these motives, and has given them a sufficient energy. Before the idea of laws existed, *needs* and *enjoyments* had done in that respect all that the best concerted laws could do. Need, armed with pains of all kinds, even death itself, commanded labour, excited courage, inspired foresight, developed all the faculties of man. Enjoyment, the inseparable companion of every need satisfied, formed an inexhaustible fund of rewards for those who surmounted obstacles and fulfilled the end of nature. The force of the physical sanction being sufficient, the employment of the political sanction would be superfluous.

Besides, the motives which depend on laws are more or less precarious in their operation. It is a consequence of the imperfection of the laws themselves; or of the difficulty of proving the facts in order to apply punishment or reward. The hope of impunity conceals itself at the bottom of the heart during all the intermediate steps which it is necessary to take before arriving at the enforcement of the law. But the natural effects, which may be regarded as nature's punishments and rewards, scarcely admit of any uncertainty. There is no evasion, no delay, no favour. Experience announces the event, and experience confirms it. Each day strengthens the lesson of the day before; and the uniformity of this process leaves no room for doubt. What could be added by direct laws to the constant and irresistible power of these natural motives?

But the laws provide for subsistence indirectly, by protecting men while they labour, and by making them sure of the fruits of their labour. *Security* for the labourer, *security* for the fruits of labour; such is the benefit of laws; and it is an inestimable benefit.

CHAPTER V.

Laws relatively to Abundance.

SHALL laws be made directing individuals not to confine themselves to mere subsistence, but to seek abundance? No! That would be a very superfluous employment of artificial means, where natural means suffice. The attraction of pleasure; the succession of wants; the active desire of increasing happiness, will procure unceasingly, under the reign of security, new efforts towards new acquisitions. Wants, enjoyments, those universal agents of society, having begun with gathering the first sheaf of corn, proceed little by little, to build magazines of abundance, always increasing but never filled. Desires extend with means. The horizon elevates itself as we advance; and each new want, attended on the one hand by pain, on the other by pleasure, becomes a new principle of action. Opulence, which is only a comparative term, does not arrest this movement once begun. On the contrary, the greater our means, the greater the scale on which we labour; the greater is the recompense, and, consequently, the greater also the force of motive which animates to labour. Now what is the wealth of society, if not the sum of all individual wealth? And what more is necessary than the force of these natural motives, to carry wealth, by successive movements, to the highest possible point?

It appears that abundance is formed little by little, by the continued operation of the same causes which produce subsistence. Those who blame abundance under the name of luxury, have never looked at it from this point of view.

Bad seasons, wars, accidents of all kinds, attack so often the fund of subsistence, that a society which had nothing superfluous, and even if it had a good deal that was superfluous, would often be exposed to want what is necessary. We see this among savage tribes; it was often seen among all nations, during the times of ancient poverty. It is what happens even now, in countries little favoured by nature, such as Sweden; and in those where government restrains the operations of commerce, instead of confining itself to protection. But countries in which luxury abounds, and where governments are enlightened, are above the risk of famine. Such is the happy situation of England. With a free commerce, toys useless in themselves have their utility, as the means of obtaining bread. Manufactures of luxury furnish an assurance against famine. A brewery or a starch-factory might be changed into a means of subsistence.

How often have we heard declamations against dogs and horses, as devouring the food of men! Such declaimers rise but one degree above those apostles of disinterestedness, who set fire to the magazines in order to cause an abundance of corn.

CHAPTER VI.

Pathological Propositions upon which the good of Equality is founded.

Pathology is a term used in medicine. It has not been introduced into morals, where it is equally needed, though in a somewhat different sense. By *pathology*, I mean the study and the knowledge of the sensations, affections, passions, and of their effects upon happiness. Legislation, which hitherto has been founded in a great measure only upon the quicksands of prejudice and instinct, ought at last to be built upon the immoveable basis of sensations and experience. It is necessary to have a moral thermometer to make perceptible all the degrees of happiness and misery. This is a term of perfection which it is not possible to reach; but it is well to have it before our eyes. I know that a scrupulous examination of more or less, in the matter of pain or pleasure, will at first appear a minute undertaking. It will be said that in human affairs it is necessary to act in gross; to be contented with a vague approximation. This is the language of indifference or of incapacity. The sensations of men are sufficiently regular to become the objects of a science and an art. Yet hitherto we have seen but essays, blind attempts, and irregular efforts not well followed up. Medicine has for its foundation the axioms of physical pathology. Morality is the medicine of the soul; and legislation, which is the practical part of it, ought to have for its foundation the axioms of mental pathology.

To judge of the effect of a portion of wealth upon happiness, it is necessary to consider it in three different states:—

1st. When it has always been in the hands of the holder.

2nd. When it is leaving his hands.

3rd. When it is coming into them.

It is to be observed in general, that in speaking of the effect of a portion of wealth upon happiness, abstraction is always to be made of the particular sensibility of individuals, and of the exterior circumstances in which they may be placed. Differences of character are inscrutable; and such is the diversity of circumstances, that they are never the same for two individuals. Unless we begin by dropping these two considerations, it will be impossible to announce any general proposition. But though each of these propositions may prove false or inexact in a given individual case, that will furnish no argument against their speculative truth and practical utility. It is enough for the justification of these propositions—1st, If they approach nearer the truth than any others which can be substituted for them; 2nd, If with less inconvenience than any others they can be made the basis of legislation.

I. Let us pass to the first case. The object being to examine the effect of a portion of wealth, when it has always been in the hands of the holder, we may lay down the following propositions:—

1st. *Each portion of wealth has a corresponding portion of happiness.*

2nd. *Of two individuals with unequal fortunes, he who has the most wealth has the most happiness.*

3rd. *The excess in happiness of the richer will not be so great as the excess of his wealth.*

4th. For the same reasons, *the greater the disproportion is between the two masses of wealth, the less is it probable that there exists a disproportion equally great between the corresponding masses of happiness.*

5th. *The nearer the actual proportion approaches to equality, the greater will be the total mass of happiness.*

It is not necessary to limit what is here said of wealth to the condition of those who are called wealthy. This word has a more extensive signification. It embraces everything which serves either for subsistence or abundance. It is for the sake of brevity that the phrase *portion of wealth* is used instead of *portion of the matter of wealth.*

I have said that for *each portion of wealth there is a corresponding portion of happiness.* To speak more exactly, it ought rather to be said, *a certain chance of happiness.* For the efficacy of a cause of happiness is always precarious; or, in other words, a cause of happiness has not its ordinary effect, nor the same effect, upon all persons. Here is the place for making an application of what has been said concerning the sensibility and the character of individuals, and the variety of circumstances in which they are found.

The second proposition is a direct consequence of the first. *Of two individuals, he who is the richer is the happier or has the greater chance of being so.* This is a fact proved by the experience of all the world. The first who doubts it shall be the very witness I will call to prove it. Let him give all his superfluous wealth to the first comer who asks him for it; for this superfluity, according to his system, is but dust in his hands; it is a burden and nothing more. The manna of the desert putrefied, if any one collected a greater quantity than he could eat. If wealth resembled that manna, and after passing a certain point was no longer productive in happiness, no one would wish for it; and the desire of accumulation would be a thing unknown.

The third proposition is less likely to be disputed. Put on one side a thousand farmers, having enough to live upon, and a little more. Put on the other side a king, or, not to be encumbered with the cares of government, a prince, well portioned, himself as rich as all the farmers taken together. It is probable, I say, that his happiness is greater than the average happiness of the thousand farmers; but it is by no means probable that it is equal to the sum total of their happiness, or, what amounts to the same thing, a thousand times greater than the average happiness of one of them. It would be remarkable if his happiness were ten times, or even five times greater. The man who is born in the bosom of opulence, is not so sensible of its pleasures as he who is the artisan of his own fortune. It is the pleasure of acquisition, not the satisfaction of possessing, which gives the greatest delights. The one is a lively sentiment, pricked on by the desires, and by anterior privations, which rushes toward an unknown good; the other is a feeble sentiment, weakened by use, which is not animated by contrasts, and which borrows nothing from the imagination.

II. Passing to the second case, let us examine the effect of a portion of wealth, when it enters for the first time into the hands of a new possessor. It is to be observed that we must lay expectation out of view. It is necessary to suppose that this augmentation of fortune comes unexpectedly, as a gift of chance.

1st. *A portion of wealth may be so far divided as to produce no happiness at all for any of the participants.* This is what would happen, rigorously speaking, if the portion of each was less in value than the smallest known coin. But it is not necessary to carry the thing to that extreme, in order to make the proposition true.

2nd. *Among participants of equal fortunes, the more perfectly equality is preserved in the distribution of a new portion of wealth, the greater will be the total mass of happiness.*

3rd. *Among participants of unequal fortunes, the more the distribution of new wealth tends to do away that inequality, the greater will be the total mass of happiness.*

III. The third case requires us to examine the effect produced by a portion of wealth which is leaving the hands of its former possessor. Here, too, we must lay expectation out of view, and suppose the loss to be unforeseen;—and a loss almost always is so, because every man naturally expects to keep what he has.

This expectation is founded upon the ordinary course of things. For in a general view of human affairs, wealth already acquired is not only preserved, but increased. This is proved by the extreme difference between the primitive poverty of every community and its actual wealth.

1st. *The loss of a portion of wealth will produce, in the total happiness of the loser, a defalcation greater or less, according to the proportion of the part lost to the part which remains.*

Take away from a man the fourth part of his fortune, and you take away the fourth part of his happiness, and so on.*

But there are cases in which the proportion would not be the same. If, in taking away from me three-fourths of my fortune, you take away what is necessary for my physical support, and if, in taking away half of it, you would have left that necessary portion untouched, the defalcation of happiness, instead of being twice as great in the first case as in the second, will be four times, ten times, indefinitely greater.

2nd. *This granted, fortunes being equal, the greater the number of persons among whom a loss is shared, the less considerable will be the defalcation from the sum total of happiness.*

3rd. *After passing a certain point, division renders the several quotas impalpable, and the defalcation in the sum total of happiness amounts to nothing.*

4th. *Fortunes being unequal, the loss of happiness produced by a given loss of wealth will become less in proportion as the distribution of the loss shall tend towards the production of an exact equality.* But in this case we must lay out of view the inconveniences attendant on the violation of security.

Governments, profiting by the progress of knowledge, have

* It is to this head that the evils of deep play ought to be referred. Though the chances, so far as relates to money, are equal, in regard to pleasure, they are always unfavourable. I have a thousand pounds. The stake is five hundred. If I lose, my fortune is diminished one-half; if I gain, it is increased only by a third. Suppose the stake to be a thousand pounds. If I gain, my happiness is not doubled with my fortune; if I lose, my happiness is destroyed, I am reduced to indigence.

favoured, in many respects, the principle of equality in the distribution of losses. It is thus that they have taken under the protection of the laws *policies of insurance*, those useful contracts by which individuals assess themselves beforehand to provide against possible losses. The principle of insurance, founded upon a calculation of probabilities, is but the art of distributing losses among so great a number of associates as to make them very light, and almost nothing.

The same spirit has influenced sovereigns when they have indemnified, at the expense of the state, those of their subjects who have suffered either by public calamities or by the devastations of war. We have seen nothing of this kind wiser or better managed than the administration of the great Frederic. It is one of the finest points of view under which the social art can be considered.

Some attempts have been made to indemnify individuals for losses caused by the offences of malefactors. But examples of this kind are yet very rare. It is an object which merits the attention of legislators; for it is the means of reducing almost to nothing the evil of offences which attack property. To prevent it from becoming injurious, such a system must be arranged with care. It will not do to encourage indolence and imprudence in the neglect of precautions against offences, by making them sure of an indemnification; and it is necessary to guard even more cautiously against fraud and secret connivances which might counterfeit offences, and even produce them, for the sake of the indemnity. The utility of this remedial process would depend entirely on the way in which it was administered; yet the rejection of a means so salutary can only originate in a culpable indifference, anxious to save itself the trouble of discovering expedients.

The principles we have laid down may equally serve to regulate the distribution of a loss among many persons charged with a common responsibility. If their respective contributions correspond to the respective quantity of their fortunes, their relative state will be the same as before; but if it is desired to improve this occasion for the purposes of an approach towards equality, it is necessary to adopt a different proportion. To levy an equal impost, without regard to differences of fortune, would be a third plan, which would be agreeable neither to equality nor security.

To place this subject in a clearer light, I shall present a mixed case, in which it is necessary to decide between two individuals, of whom one demands a profit at the expense of the other. The question is to determine the effect of a portion of wealth which, passing into the hands of one individual under the form of gain, must come out of the hands of another in the form of loss.

1st. *Among competitors of equal fortunes, when that which is gained by one must be lost by another, the arrangement productive of the greatest sum of good will be that which favours the old possessor to the exclusion of the new demandant.*

For, in the first place, the sum to be lost, bearing a greater proportion to the reduced fortune than the same sum to the augmented fortune, the diminution of happiness for the one will be greater than the augmentation of happiness for the other; in one word, equality will be violated by the contrary arrangement.*

In the second place, the loser will experience a pain of disappointment; the other merely does not gain. Now the negative evil of not acquiring is not equal to the positive evil of losing. If it were, as every man would experience this evil for all that he does not acquire, the causes of suffering would be infinite, and men would be infinitely miserable.

In the third place, men in general appear to be more sensitive to pain than to pleasure, even when the cause is equal. To such a degree, indeed, does this extend, that a loss which diminishes a man's fortune by one-fourth, will take away more happiness than he could gain by doubling his property.

2nd. *Fortunes being unequal, if the loser is the poorer, the evil of the loss will be aggravated by that inequality.*

3rd. *If the loser is the richer, the evil done by an attack upon security will be compensated in part by a good which will be great in proportion to the progress towards equality.*

* See the note upon gaming. This case is exactly the same.

By the aid of these maxims, which, to a certain point, have the character and the certainty of mathematical propositions, there might be at last produced a regular and constant art of indemnities and satisfactions. Legislators have frequently shown a disposition to promote equality under the name of *equity*, a word to which a greater latitude has been given than to *justice*. But this idea of equity, vague and half developed, has rather appeared an affair of instinct than of calculation. It was only by much patience and method that it was found possible to reduce to rigorous propositions an incoherent multitude of confused sentiments.

CHAPTER VII.

Of Security.

We come now to the principal object of law,—the care of security. That inestimable good, the distinctive index of civilization, is entirely the work of law. Without law there is no security; and, consequently, no abundance, and not even a certainty of subsistence; and the only equality which can exist in such a state of things is an equality of misery.

To form a just idea of the benefits of law, it is only necessary to consider the condition of savages. They strive incessantly against famine; which sometimes cuts off entire tribes. Rivalry for subsistence produces among them the most cruel wars; and, like beasts of prey, men pursue men, as a means of sustenance. The fear of this terrible calamity silences the softer sentiments of nature; pity unites with insensibility in putting to death the old men who can hunt no longer.

Let us now examine what passes at those terrible epochs when civilized society returns almost to the savage state; that is, during war, when the laws on which security depends are in part suspended. Every instant of its duration is fertile in calamities; at every step which it prints upon the earth, at every movement which it makes, the existing mass of riches, the fund of abundance and of subsistence, decreases and disappears. The cottage is ravaged as well as the palace; and how often the rage, the caprice even of a moment, delivers up to destruction the slow produce of the labours of an age!

Law alone has done that which all the natural sentiments united have not the power to do. Law alone is able to create a fixed and durable possession which merits the name of property. Law alone can accustom men to bow their heads under the yoke of foresight, hard at first to bear, but afterwards light and agreeable. Nothing but law can encourage men to labours superfluous for the present, and which can be enjoyed only in the future. Economy has as many enemies as there are dissipators—men who wish to enjoy without giving themselves the trouble of producing. Labour is too painful for idleness; it is too slow for impatience. Fraud and injustice secretly conspire to appropriate its fruits. Insolence and audacity think to ravish them by open force. Thus security is assailed on every side—ever threatened, never tranquil, it exists in the midst of alarms. The legislator needs a vigilance always sustained, a power always in action, to defend it against this crowd of indefatigable enemies.

Law does not say to man, *Labour, and I will reward you;* but it says: *Labour, and I will assure to you the enjoyment of the fruits of your labour—that natural and sufficient recompense which without me you cannot preserve; I will insure it by arresting the hand which may seek to ravish it from you.* If industry creates, it is law which preserves; if at the first moment we owe all to labour, at the second moment, and at every other, we are indebted for everything to law.

To form a precise idea of the extent which ought to be given to the principle of security, we must consider that man is not like the animals, limited to the present, whether as respects suffering or enjoyment; but that he is susceptible of pains and pleasures by anticipation; and that it is not enough to secure him from actual loss, but it is necessary also to guarantee him, as far as possible, against future loss. It is necessary to prolong the idea of his security through all the perspective which his imagination is capable of measuring.

This presentiment, which has so marked an influence upon the fate of man, is called *expectation.* It is hence that we have the power of forming a general plan of conduct; it is hence that the successive instants which compose the duration of life are not like isolated and independent points, but become continuous parts of a whole. *Expectation* is a chain which unites our present existence to our future existence, and which passes beyond us to the generation which is to follow. The sensibility of man extends through all the links of this chain.

The principle of security extends to the maintenance of all these expectations; it requires that events, so far as they depend upon laws, should conform to the expectations which law itself has created.

Every attack upon this sentiment produces a distinct and special evil, which may be called a *pain of disappointment.*

It is a proof of great confusion in the ideas of lawyers, that they have never given any particular attention to a sentiment which exercises so powerful an influence upon human life. The word *expectation* is scarcely found in their vocabulary. Scarce a single argument founded upon that principle appears in their writings. They have followed it, without doubt, in many respects; but they have followed it by instinct rather than by reason. If they had known its extreme importance they would not have failed to *name* it and to mark it, instead of leaving it unnoticed in the crowd.

CHAPTER VIII.

Of Property.

The better to understand the advantages of law, let us endeavour to form a clear idea of *property.* We shall see that there is no such thing as natural property, and that it is entirely the work of law.

Property is nothing but a basis of expectation; the expectation of deriving certain advantages from a thing which we are said to possess, in consequence of the relation in which we stand towards it.

There is no image, no painting, no visible trait, which can express the relation that constitutes property. It is not material, it is metaphysical; it is a mere conception of the mind.

To have a thing in our hands, to keep it, to make it, to sell it, to work it up into something else; to use it—none of these physical circumstances, nor all united, convey the idea of property. A piece of stuff which is actually in the Indies may belong to me, while the dress I wear may not. The aliment which is incorporated into my very body may belong to another, to whom I am bound to account for it.

The idea of property consists in an established expectation; in the persuasion of being able to draw such or such an advantage from the thing possessed, according to the nature of the case. Now this expectation, this persuasion, can only be the work of law. I cannot count upon the enjoyment of that which I regard as mine, except through the promise of the law which guarantees it to me. It is law alone which permits me to forget my natural weakness. It is only through the protection of law that I am able to inclose a field, and to give myself up to its cultivation with the sure though distant hope of harvest.

But it may be asked, What is it that serves as a basis to law, upon which to begin operations, when it adopts objects which, under the name of property, it promises to protect? Have not men, in the primitive state, a *natural* expectation of enjoying certain things,—an expectation drawn from sources anterior to law?

Yes. There have been from the beginning, and there always will be, circumstances in which a man may secure himself, by his own means, in the enjoyment of certain things. But the catalogue of these cases is very limited. The savage who has killed a deer may hope to keep it for himself, so long as his cave is undiscovered; so long as he watches to defend it, and is stronger than his rivals; but that is all. How miserable and precarious is such a possession! If we suppose the least agreement among savages to respect the acquisitions of each other, we see the introduction of a principle to which no name can be given but that of law. A feeble and momentary expectation may result from time to time from circumstances purely physical; but a strong and permanent expectation can result only from law. That which, in the natural state, was an almost invisible thread, in the social state becomes a cable.

Property and law are born together, and die together. Before laws were made there was no property; take away laws, and property ceases.

As regards property, security consists in receiving no check, no shock, no derangement to the expectation founded on the laws, of enjoying such and such a portion of good. The legislator owes the greatest respect to this expectation which he has himself produced. When he does not contradict it, he does what is essential to the happiness of society; when he disturbs it, he always produces a proportionate sum of evil.

CHAPTER IX.

Answer to an Objection.

But perhaps the laws of property are good for those who have property, and oppressive to those who have none. The poor man, perhaps, is more miserable than he would be without laws.

The laws, in creating property, have created riches only in relation to poverty. Poverty is not the work of the laws; it is the primitive condition of the human race. The man who subsists only from day to day is precisely the man of nature—the savage. The poor man, in civilized society, obtains nothing, I admit, except by painful labour; but, in the natural state, can he obtain anything except by the sweat of his brow? Has not the chase its fatigues, fishing its dangers, and war its uncertainties? And if man seems to love this adventurous life; if he has an instinct warm for this kind of perils; if the savage enjoys with delight an idleness so dearly bought;—must we thence conclude that he is happier than our cultivators? No. Their labour is more uniform, but their reward is more sure; the woman's lot is far more agreeable; childhood and old age have more resources; the species multiplies in a proportion a thousand times greater,—and that alone suffices to show on which side is the superiority of happiness. Thus the laws, in creating riches, are the benefactors of those who remain in the poverty of nature. All participate more or less in the pleasures, the advantages, and the resources of civilized society. The industry and the labour of the poor place them among the candidates of fortune. And have they not the pleasures of acquisition? Does not hope mix with their labours? Is the security which the law gives of no importance to them? Those who look down from above upon the inferior ranks see all objects smaller; but towards the base of the pyramid it is the summit which in turn is lost. Comparisons are never dreamed of; the wish of what seems impossible does not torment. So that, in fact, all things considered, the protection of the laws may contribute as much to the happiness of the cottage as to the security of the palace.

It is astonishing that a writer so judicious as Beccaria has interposed, in a work dictated by the soundest philosophy, a doubt subversive of social order. *The right of property,* he says, *is a terrible right, which perhaps is not necessary.* Tyrannical and sanguinary laws have been founded upon that right; it has been frightfully abused; but the right itself presents only ideas of pleasure, abundance, and security. It is that right which has vanquished the natural aversion to labour; which has given to man the empire of the earth; which has brought to an end the migratory life of nations; which has produced the love of country and a regard for posterity. Men universally desire to enjoy speedily—to enjoy without labour. It is that desire which is terrible; since it arms all who have not against all who have. The law which restrains that desire is the noblest triumph of humanity over itself.

CHAPTER X.

Analysis of the Evils which result from Attacks upon Property.

We have already seen that subsistence depends upon the laws which assure to the labourer the produce of his labour. But it is desirable more exactly to analyze the evils which result from violations of property. They may be reduced to four heads.

1st. *Evil of Non-Possession.*—If the acquisition of a portion of wealth is a good, it follows that the non-possession of it is an evil, though only a negative evil. Thus, although men in the condition of primitive poverty may not have specially felt the want of a good which they knew not, yet it is clear that they have lost all the happiness which might have resulted from its possession, and of which we have the enjoyment. The loss of a portion of good, though we knew nothing of it, is still a loss. Are you doing me no harm when, by false representations, you deter my friend from conferring upon me a favour which I did not expect? In what consists the harm? In the negative evil which results from not possessing that which, but for your falsehoods, I should have had.

2nd. *Pain of Losing.*—Everything which I possess, or to which I have a title, I consider in my own mind as destined always to belong to me. I make it the basis of my expectations, and of the hopes of those dependent upon me; and I form my plan of life accordingly. Every part of my property may have, in my estimation, besides its intrinsic value, a value of affection—as an inheritance from my ancestors, as the reward of my own labour, or as the future dependence of my children. Everything about it represents to my eye that part of myself which I have put into it—those cares, that industry, that economy which denied itself present pleasures to make provision for the future. Thus our property becomes a part of our being, and cannot be torn from us without rending us to the quick.

3rd. *Fear of Losing.*—To regret for what we have lost is joined inquietude as to what we possess, and even as to what we may acquire. For the greater part of the objects which compose subsistence and abundance being perishable matters, future acquisitions are a necessary supplement to present possessions. When insecurity reaches a certain point, the fear of losing prevents us from enjoying what we possess already. The care of preserving condemns us to a thousand sad and painful precautions, which yet are always liable to fail of their end. Treasures are hidden or conveyed away. Enjoyment becomes sombre, furtive, and solitary. It fears to show itself, lest cupidity should be informed of a chance to plunder.

4th. *Deadening of Industry.*—When I despair of making myself sure of the produce of my labour, I only seek to exist from day to day. I am unwilling to give myself cares which will only be profitable to my enemies. Besides, the will to labour is not enough; means are wanting. While waiting to reap, in the meantime I must live. A single loss may deprive me of the capacity of action, without having quenched the spirit of industry, or without having paralyzed my will. Thus the three first evils affect the passive faculties of the individual, while the fourth extends to his active faculties, and more or less benumbs them.

It appears from this analysis that the two first evils do not go beyond the individual injured; while the two latter spread through society, and occupy an indefinite space. An attack upon the property of an individual excites alarm among other proprietors. This sentiment spreads from neighbour to neighbour, till at last the contagion possesses the entire body of the state.

Power and *will* must unite for the development of industry. Will depends upon encouragement; *power* upon means. These means are what is called, in the language of political economy, *productive capital.* When the question relates only to an individual, his productive capital may be annihilated by a single loss, while his spirit of industry is not extinguished, nor even weakened. When the question is of a nation, the annihilation of its productive capital is impossible; but a long time before that fatal term is approached, the evil may infect the will; and the spirit of industry may fall into a fatal lethargy, in the midst of natural resources offered by a rich and fertile soil. The will, however, is excited by so many stimulants, that it resists an abundance of discouragements and losses. A transitory calamity, though great, never destroys the spirit of industry. It is seen to spring up, after devouring wars which have impoverished nations, as a robust oak, mutilated by tempests, repairs its losses in a few years and covers itself with new branches. Nothing is sufficient to deaden industry, except the operation of a domestic and permanent cause, such as a tyrannical government, bad legislation, an intolerant religion which drives men from the country, or a minute superstition which stupifies them.

A first act of violence produces immediately a certain degree of apprehension; some timid spirits are already discouraged. A second violence, which soon succeeds, spreads a more considerable alarm. The more prudent begin to retrench their enterprises, and little by little to abandon an uncertain career. In proportion as these attacks are repeated, and the system of oppression takes a more habitual character, the dispersion increases. Those who fly are not replaced; those who remain fall into a state of languor. Thus the field of industry, beaten by perpetual storms, at last becomes a desert.

Asia Minor, Greece, Egypt, the coasts of Africa, so rich in agriculture, in commerce, and in population, at the flourishing epoch of the Roman empire, what have they become under the absurd despotism of the Turkish government? Palaces have been changed into cabins, and cities into hamlets. That government, odious to every thinking man, has never known that a state cannot grow rich except by an inviolable respect for property. It has never had but two secrets of statesmanship,—to sponge the people, and to stupify them. Thus the finest countries of the earth, wasted, barren, and almost abandoned, can hardly be recognised under the hands of barbarous conquerors.

These evils ought not to be attributed to foreign causes. Civil wars, invasions, natural scourges, may dissipate wealth, put the arts to flight, and swallow up cities. But choked harbours are opened again; communications are re-established; manufactures revive; cities rise from their ruins. All ravages are repaired by time, while men continue to be men; but there are no men to be found in those unhappy countries, where the slow but fatal despair of long insecurity has destroyed all the active faculties of the soul.

If we trace the history of this contagion, we shall see its first attacks directed against that part of society which is easy and well off. Opulence is the object of the first depredations. Apparent superfluity vanishes little by little. Absolute need makes itself be obeyed in spite of obstacles. We must live; but when man limits himself to living, the state languishes, and the lamp of industry throws out only a dying flame. Besides, abundance is never so distinct from subsistence, that one can be destroyed without a dangerous blow at the other. While some lose only what is superfluous, others lose a part of what is necessary; for by the infinitely complicated system of economical connections, the opulence of a part of the citizens is the only fund upon which a part more numerous depends for subsistence.

But another picture may be traced, more smiling and not less instructive. It is the picture of the progress of *security*, and of prosperity, its inseparable companion. North America presents to us a most striking contrast. Savage nature may be seen there, side by side with civilized nature. The interior of that immense region offers only a frightful solitude, impenetrable forests or sterile plains, stagnant waters and impure vapours; such is the earth when left to itself. The fierce tribes which rove through those deserts without fixed habitations, always occupied with the pursuit of game, and animated against each other by implacable rivalries, meet only for combat, and often succeed in destroying each other. The beasts of the forest are not so dangerous to man as he is to himself. But on the borders of these frightful solitudes, what different sights are seen! We appear to comprehend in the same view the two empires of good and evil. Forests give place to cultivated fields; morasses are dried up, and the surface, grown firm, is covered with meadows, pastures, domestic animals, habitations healthy and smiling. Rising cities are built upon regular plans; roads are constructed to communicate between them; everything announces that men, seeking the means of intercourse, have ceased to fear and to murder each other. Harbours filled with vessels receive all the productions of the earth, and assist in the exchange of all kinds of riches. A numerous people, living upon their labour in peace and abundance, has succeeded to a few tribes of hunters, always placed between war and famine. What has wrought these prodigies? Who has renewed the surface of the earth? Who has given to man this domain over nature—over nature embellished, fertilized, and perfected? That beneficent genius is *Security*. It is security which has wrought this great metamorphosis. And how rapid are its operations? It is not yet two centuries since William Penn landed upon those savage coasts, with a colony of true conquerors, men of peace, who did not soil their establishments with blood, and who made themselves respected by acts of beneficence and justice.

CHAPTER XI.

Opposition between Security and Equality.

In consulting the grand principle of security, what ought the legislator to decree respecting the mass of property already existing?

He ought to maintain the distribution as it is actually established. It is this which, under the name of *justice*, is regarded as his first duty. This is a general and simple rule, which applies itself to all states; and which adapts itself to all places, even those of the most opposite character. There is nothing more different than the state of property in America, in England, in Hungary, and in Russia. Generally, in the first of these countries, the cultivator is a proprietor; in the second, a tenant; in the third, attached to the glebe; in the fourth, a slave. However, the supreme principle of security commands the preservation of all these distributions, though their nature is so different, and though they do not produce the same sum of happiness. How make another distribution without taking away from each that which he has? And how despoil any without attacking the security of all? When your new repartition is disarranged—that is to say, the day after its establishment—how avoid making a second? Why not correct it in the same way? And in the meantime, what becomes of security? Where is happiness? Where is industry?

When security and equality are in conflict, it will not do to hesitate a moment. Equality must yield. The first is the foundation of life; subsistence, abundance, happiness, everything depends upon it. Equality produces only a certain portion of good. Besides, whatever we may do, it will never be perfect; it may exist a day; but the revolutions of the morrow will overturn it. The establishment of perfect equality is a chimera; all we can do is to diminish inequality.

If violent causes, such as a revolution of government, a division, or a conquest, should bring about an overturn of property, it would be a great calamity; but it would be transitory; it would diminish; it would repair itself in time. Industry is a vigorous plant which resists many amputations, and through which a nutritious sap begins to circulate with the first rays of returning summer. But if property should be overturned with the direct intention of establishing an equality of possessions, the evil would be irreparable. No more security, no more industry, no more abundance! Society would return to the savage state whence it emerged.

If equality ought to prevail to-day it ought to prevail always. Yet it cannot be preserved except by renewing the violence by which it was established. It will need an army of inquisitors and executioners as deaf to favour as to pity; insensible to the seductions of pleasure; inaccessible to personal interest; endowed with all the virtues, though in a service which destroys them all. The levelling apparatus ought to go incessantly backward and forward, cutting off all that rises above the line prescribed. A ceaseless vigilance would be necessary to give to those who had dissipated their portion, and to take from those who by labour had augmented theirs. In such an order of things there would be only one wise course for the governed,—that of prodigality; there would be but one foolish course,—that of industry. This pretended remedy, seemingly so pleasant, would be a mortal poison, a burning cautery, which would consume till it destroyed the last fibre of life. The hostile sword in its greatest furies is a thousand times less dreadful. It inflicts but partial evils, which time effaces and industry repairs.

Some small societies, in the first effervescence of religious enthusiasm, have established the community of goods as a fundamental principle. Does any one imagine that happiness was gained by that arrangement? For the sweet power of reward is substituted the sad impulses of pain. Labour, so easy and so light, when animated by hope, it is necessary under these systems to represent as a penitential means of escaping eternal punishment. So long as the religious impulse preserves its power, all labour, but all groan. So soon as it begins to grow weak, the society divides into two classes: one composed of degraded fanatics, contracting all the vices of an unhappy superstition; the others, lazy rogues, who are supported in a holy indolence by the dupes who surround them. The word equality becomes a mere pretext—a cover to the robbery which idleness perpetrates upon industry.

Those ideas of benevolence and of concord which have seduced some ardent souls into an admiration of this system are only chimeras of the imagination. In the distribution of labours, what motive could determine any to embrace the more painful? Who would undertake gross and disagreeable functions? Who would be content with his lot? Who would not find the burden of his neighbour lighter than his own? How many frauds would be contrived in order to lay upon others the labour from which all would endeavour to exempt themselves? And, in the division, how impossible to satisfy all; to preserve the appearances of equality; to prevent jealousies, quarrels, rivalries, preferences. Who would settle the numberless disputes for ever breaking out? What an apparatus of penal laws would be necessary as a substitute for the sweet liberty of choice, and the natural recompense of labour! One half the society would not suffice to regulate the other half. Thus this absurd and unjust system would only be able to maintain itself by means of a political and religious slavery, such as that of the Helots at Lacedæmon and the Indians of Paraguay, in the establishments of the Jesuits. Sublime invention of legislators, which, to accomplish a plan of equality, makes two corresponding lots of good and of evil, and puts all the pain on one side and all the enjoyment on the other!

CHAPTER XII.

Means of uniting Security and Equality.

Is it necessary that between these two rivals, *Security* and *Equality*, there should be an opposition, an eternal war? To a certain point they are incompatible; but with a little patience and address they may, in a great measure, be reconciled.

The only mediator between these contrary interests is time. Do you wish to follow the counsels of equality without contravening those of security?—await the natural epoch which puts an end to hopes and fears, the epoch of death.

When property by the death of the proprietor ceases to have an owner, the law can interfere in its distribution, either by limiting in certain respects the testamentary power, in order to prevent too great an accumulation of wealth in the hands of an individual; or by regulating the succession in favour of equality in cases where the deceased has left no consort, nor relation in the direct line, and has made no will. The question then relates to new acquirers who have formed no expectations; and equality may do what is best for all without disappointing any. At present I only indicate the principle: the development of it may be seen in the second book.

When the question is to correct a kind of civil inequality, such as slavery, it is necessary to pay the same attention to the right of property; to submit it to a slow operation, and to advance towards the subordinate object without sacrificing the principal object. Men who are rendered free by these gradations, will be much more capable of being so than if you had taught them to tread justice under foot, for the sake of introducing a new social order.

It is worthy of remark that, in a nation prosperous in its agriculture, its manufactures, and its commerce, there is a continual progress towards equality. If the laws do nothing to combat it, if they do not maintain certain monopolies, if they put no shackles upon industry and trade, if they do not permit entails, we see great properties divided little by little, without effort, without revolution, without shock, and a much greater number of men coming to participate in the moderate favours of fortune. This is the natural result of the opposite habits which are formed in opulence and in poverty. The first, prodigal and vain, wishes only to enjoy without labour; the second, accustomed to obscurity and privations, finds pleasures even in labour and economy. Thence the change which has been made in Europe by the progress of arts and commerce, in spite of legal obstacles. We are at no great distance from those ages of feudality, when the world was divided into two classes: a few great proprietors, who were everything, and a multitude of serfs, who were nothing. These pyramidal heights have disappeared or have fallen; and from their ruins industrious men have formed those new establishments, the great number of which attests the comparative happiness of modern civilization. Thus we may conclude that *Security*, while preserving its place as the supreme principle, leads indirectly to *Equality;* while equality, if taken as the basis of the social arrangement, will destroy both itself and security at the same time.

CHAPTER XIII.

Sacrifice of Security to Security.

This title appears at first enigmatical, but the sense of the enigma may easily be found.

There is an important distinction between the ideal perfection of security, and its practicable perfection. The first would demand that nothing should ever be taken from anybody. The second is satisfied, if nothing is taken beyond what is necessary for the preservation of the rest.

This sacrifice is not an attack upon security; it is simply a defalcation. An attack is an unexpected shock, an evil which cannot be calculated, an irregularity which has no fixed principle. It seems to put all the rest in peril; it produces a general alarm. But a defalcation is a fixed, regular, and necessary deduction, which is expected; which produces only an evil of the first order; but no danger, no alarm, no discouragement to industry. The same sum of money, according to the way in which it is levied, will have one or the other of these characters; and will consequently produce either the deadening effects of insecurity, or the vivifying results of confidence.

The necessity of these defalcations is evident. To labour, and to guard the labourers, are two different operations, which cannot be performed at the same time, by the same persons. It is necessary that those who produce wealth by labour should lay aside some portion of it, to support the guardians of the state. Wealth can only be defended at its own expense.

Society, attacked by enemies, whether foreign or domestic, can only maintain itself at the expense of security,—not the security of those enemies alone, but the security even of the very persons to whom protection is extended.

If there are men who do not perceive this necessary connection, it is because in this matter, as in many others, the want of to-day eclipses that of yesterday. The whole of government is but a tissue of sacrifices. The best is that in which these sacrifices are reduced to their lowest term. The practical perfection of security is a quantity which tends without ceasing to approach an ideal perfection.

"It is not necessary to increase the real wants of the people, to satisfy imaginary wants of state."

"Imaginary wants are those created by the passions and the weaknesses of men who govern, by the charm of an extraordinary project, the disordered love of empty glory, and a certain powerlessness of mind to resist the suggestions of fancy. It has often happened that unquiet spirits, placed by the prince at the head of affairs, have imagined that the wants of their own little souls were wants of the state."*

The author of the *Persian Letters* has written too many chapters in the *Spirit of Laws*. What do we learn from this satirical description? If Montesquieu had condescended to give us a simple enumeration of the true wants of the state, we should have known much better what he meant by imaginary wants.

I proceed to give a catalogue of the cases in which the sacrifice of some portion of security, so far as property is concerned, is necessary, to preserve the greater mass of it.

1st. General wants of the state for its defence against exterior enemies.

2nd. General wants of the state for its defence against violators of the laws, or internal enemies.

3rd. General wants of the state to furnish means of affording aid in cases of physical calamity.

4th. Amends levied upon delinquents, either as punishment, or as an indemnity in favour of the parties injured.

5th. A tax upon the property of individuals to furnish the ability of applying remedies to the evils above mentioned, by means of courts of justice, institutions of police, and an armed force.

6th. Limitation of the rights of property, or of the use which each proprietor may make of his own goods, so as to prevent

* *Spirit of Laws*, book xiii. c. i.

him from employing them to his own injury or to that of others.*

In all these cases the necessity is too palpable to need any proofs. But it must be noticed that the same reserves will equally apply to the other branches of security. It is not possible, for example, to maintain the rights of person and of honour, except by penal laws; and penal laws can hardly be executed, except at the expense of person or of honour.

CHAPTER XIV.

Of some Cases liable to be contested.

OUGHT we to reckon among those wants of the state which ought to be provided for by forced contributions, the care of the indigent, public worship, and the cultivation of the arts and sciences?

* We possess a general right of property over a thing when we can apply it to every use, except certain uses which are forbidden for special reasons. These reasons may be referred to three heads :—

1st. Private detriment, when a given use of a thing would injure some other individual, either in his fortune or otherwise.

2nd. Public detriment, that which may result to the community in general.

3rd. Detriment to the individual himself.

This sword is mine in full property; but however complete that right of property may be, as respects a thousand uses, I ought not to employ it to wound my neighbour, nor to cut his dress, nor to hold it up as a signal of insurrection. If I am a minor or a maniac, it may be taken from me, lest I should injure myself.

An absolute and unlimited right of property over any object, would be the right to commit almost every crime. If I had such a right over a stick which I had cut, I might employ it as a club to beat the passers-by, or convert it into a sceptre as a sign of royalty, or into an idol offensive to the national religion.

Section I.

Indigence.

In the highest state of social prosperity, the great mass of citizens will have no resource except their daily industry; and consequently will be always near indigence, always ready to be thrown into a state of destitution, by accidents, such as revolutions of commerce, natural calamities, and especially sickness. Infancy has no means of subsisting by its own strength; the feebleness of old age is equally destitute. These two extremes of life are alike in weakness. If natural instinct, humanity, shame, and the aid of the law, assure to children and old men the care and protection of their relatives, still these resources are precarious, and those who give may soon themselves be reduced to want. A numerous family, supported in abundance by the labour of the father and mother, may lose at any instant half its resources by the death of one parent, and the whole by the death of the other.

Old age is yet worse provided for. Love which descends has more force than love which ascends. Gratitude is less powerful than instinct. Hope attaches to feeble beings who are beginning life; it promises nothing for those who are ending it. But suppose—what is not uncommon—suppose all possible care for the old; the idea of changing the part of a giver for that of a receiver will always shed more or less of bitterness into the benefits received, especially at that epoch of decline when the morbid sensibility of the soul renders painful changes indifferent in themselves.

This aspect of society is the saddest of all. It presents that long catalogue of evils which end in indigence, and consequently in death, under its most terrible forms. This is the centre towards which inertia alone, that force which acts without relaxation, makes the lot of every mortal gravitate. Not to be drawn into the abyss, it is necessary to mount up by a continual effort; and we see by our side the most diligent and the most virtuous sometimes slipping by one false step, and sometimes thrown headlong by inevitable reverses.

There are only two means, independently of the laws, of making head against these evils, viz., *savings* and *voluntary contributions*.

If these two resources would always suffice, we ought, by all means, to avoid any legal interference for the succour of the poor. A law which offers to indigence an aid independent of industry is, to a certain extent, a law against industry—or at least against frugality. The motives to labour and economy are—present need and the fear of future need. The law which takes away that need and that fear is an encouragement to idleness and dissipation. Such is the reproach which is cast, and not without reason, upon most of the establishments created in favour of the poor.

But a slight examination will be enough to convince us that the two means of succour, independent of the laws, are not sufficient.

With respect to *savings*—if the greatest efforts of industry will not suffice for the daily support of a numerous class, how can that class lay by for the future? A second class may pay their daily expenses by their daily labour; but they will have nothing superfluous to lay aside against the necessities of a distant day. There will remain then only a third class, which, by economizing during the age of labour, may, perhaps, be able to provide for the time when they can labour no longer. It is only these last to whom poverty can be ascribed as a sort of crime. "Economy," it will be said, "is a duty. If they have neglected it, so much the worse for them. If misery and death await them, they have nobody to accuse but themselves. Their catastrophe, however, will not be an unmixed evil. It will serve as a lesson to prodigals. It is the execution of a law established by nature—a law which is not, like that of men, subject to uncertainty or injustice. Punishment does not fall save on the guilty, and it is exactly proportioned to the fault."

This severe language might be justifiable if the object of the law were vengeance. But vengeance is condemned by the principle of utility, as an impure motive founded upon antipathy. What will be the fruit of these evils, this abandonment and this indigence, which you regard in your anger as a just punishment of prodigality? Are you sure that these sacrificed victims will prevent, by their example, the faults which have led them into misfortune? To think so would manifest a great ignorance of the human heart. The distress, the death of some prodigals, if we ought so to call those unfortunates who have not known how to deny themselves some of the little pleasures of their condition, who have not known the painful art of striving by reflection against the temptations of every moment—their distress, I say, even their death, will have but little influence, in the way of instruction, upon the laborious classes of society. That sad spectacle, the details of which for the most part would be concealed by shame, would not, like the punishment of malefactors, have a publicity which would attract a general attention, and not suffer its cause to be unknown. Would those to whom the lesson was most necessary know how to give a fit interpretation to the event? Would they always seize upon the supposed connection between imprudence as the cause, and misfortune as the effect? Might they not attribute the catastrophe to accidents unforeseen, and impossible to be foreseen? In place of saying, "Here is a man who has been the author of his own destruction; his indigence ought to impel me to labour and frugality,"—would they not often say, and with apparent reason, "Here is an unfortunate man, who has given himself a deal of trouble to no purpose, and whose case is a striking proof of the vanity of human prudence!" This would be bad reasoning, no doubt; but must an error of logic be punished so rigorously—a mere want of reflection, and that too in a class of men more often called upon to exercise their muscles than their minds?

Besides, what shall we think of a punishment delayed in its execution till the very end of life, and which must begin to vanquish, at the other extremity of it—that is, in youth—the influence of the most imperious motives? How feeble grows this pretended lesson in the distance! How little resemblance there is between the old man and the young man! What is the example of the one to the other? In youth the idea of immediate good or evil, occupying all the sphere of reflection, excludes the idea of distant good and evil. If you wish to act upon the young, place the motive near. Show them, for example, a marriage, or some other pleasure, in perspective. But a pain placed at a distance, beyond their intellectual horizon, is quite thrown away. You want to determine men who think very little; and to draw instruction from the misfortunes of others, it is necessary to think much. To what purpose employ a political means, designed to operate upon a class having the least foresight, and yet of a nature to be efficacious only with philosophers?

To recapitulate. The resource of savings is insufficient. 1st, It evidently is so for those who do not gain enough to subsist upon; 2nd, It is equally so for those who gain a mere subsistence. As to the third class, which embraces all not included in the first two, savings are not naturally insufficient, but they become so through the deficiency of human prudence.

Let us now pass to the other resource—*voluntary contributions.* That, too, has many imperfections.

1st. Its uncertainty. It will experience daily vicissitudes, like the fortune and the liberality of the individuals on whom it depends. Is it insufficient? Such junctures are marked by misery and death. Is it superabundant? It will offer a reward to idleness and profusion.

2nd. The inequality of the burden. This supply for the wants of the poor is levied entirely at the expense of the more humane and the more virtuous, often without any proportion to their means; while the avaricious calumniate the poor, to cover their refusal with a varnish of system and of reason. Such an arrangement is a favour granted to selfishness, and a punishment to humanity, that first of virtues.

I say a punishment; for though these contributions are called voluntary, what is the motive whence they emanate? If it is not a religious or a political fear, it is sympathy, tender but sad, which presides over these generous actions. It is not the hope of a pleasure which is bought at this price; it is the torment of pity, which is sought to be avoided. Thus it has been noticed in

Scotland, a country where indigence is limited to this sad resource, that paupers derive their principal support from the class nearest to pauperism.

3rd. The inconveniences of the distribution. If these contributions are abandoned to chance, as in the case of alms asked on the highway; if they are left to be paid, as occasion occurs, without any person intermediate between him who gives and him who asks, the uncertainty as to the sufficiency of these gifts is aggravated by another uncertainty. How appreciate in a multitude of cases the degree of want and of need? May not the poor widow's farthing go to increase the ephemeral treasure of the impure woman? How many generous souls like Sidney will be found, who will repel the vivifying draught from their parched lips, to say, *I can yet wait; first minister to that unfortunate, for his distress is greater than mine.* Every one knows that in the distribution of these gratuitous gifts, it is not modest virtue, it is not true poverty, often mute and bashful, which obtains the larger part. There needs as much of management and intrigue to succeed upon this obscure theatre, as upon the brilliant scene of the world. He who knows how to importune, to flatter, to lie, to mix boldness with baseness, and to vary his impostures according to the occasion, will have success such as the virtuous poor, devoid of artifice, and preserving their honour in their poverty, will not attain.

Les vrais talents se taisent et s'enfuient,
Découragés des affronts qu'ils essuient.
Les faux talents sont hardis, effrontés,
Souples, adroits, et jamais rebutes.

Discouraged by affronts, true talents fly,
And hide themselves in silence. Hardy and bold,
Adroit and supple too, false talents brave
Repulses.

What Voltaire says of talents may be applied to mendicity. In the division of voluntary contributions, the lot of the honest and virtuous poor is seldom equal to that of the impudent and obstreperous beggar.

Suppose that these contributions are put into a common fund to be distributed by persons appointed for that purpose. This method is far preferable, since it admits a regular examination of wants and claims, and tends to proportion the aid accordingly; but it has also a tendency to diminish liberalities. That gift which is going to pass through the hands of a stranger, of which I shall not follow the application, of which I shall not have the pleasure nor the immediate merit, has something abstract about it which chills sentiment. That which I give myself, I give at the moment when I am moved, when the cry of the poor is re-echoed in my heart, when there is only I to succour him. What I put into a general contribution may not have a destination agreeable to my desires; that poor coin which is much for me and my family will be but a drop to that mass of contributions on the one hand, and that multitude of wants on the other; let the rich sustain the poor! This is the way that many people reason, and it is on this account that contributions succeed better when taken for a particular class of individuals, than for an indefinite multitude like the entire mass of the poor; yet it is for that mass that a permanent aid must be provided.

It seems to me, after these observations, that we may lay it down as a general principle that the legislator ought to establish a regular contribution for the wants of indigence, it being understood that those only are to be regarded as indigent who are in want of what is absolutely necessary. From this definition of the indigent, it follows that their title as indigent is stronger than the title of the proprietor of superfluities as proprietor. For the pain of death, which would presently fall upon the starving poor, would be always a more serious evil than the pain of disappointment which falls upon the rich when a portion of his superfluity is taken from him.*

In the amount of the legal contribution we ought not to go

* When this tax is put upon a regular footing, and each proprietor knows beforehand what he must contribute, the pain of disappointment vanishes, and gives place to another, different in its nature, and less in degree.

beyond what is simply necessary. To go beyond that would be taxing industry for the support of idleness. Those establishments which furnish more than is absolutely necessary are not good, except so far as they are supported at the expense of individuals, for individuals can make a discrimination in the distribution of these aids, and apply them to specific classes.

The details of the manner of assessing this contribution, and distributing its produce, belong to political economy, as also the inquiry into the means of encouraging a spirit of economy and foresight in the lower classes of society. We have some instructive memoirs upon this interesting subject, but no treatise which embraces the whole question. Such a work should begin with the theory of poverty—that is, by a classification of the indigent and of the causes which bring on indigence, and thence proceed to suggest precautions and remedies.

Section II.

The Expenses of Public Worship.

If the ministers of religion are considered as charged with maintaining one of the sanctions of morality (the religious sanction), the expense of their support ought to be referred to the same branch of administration with justice and the police, viz., the support of internal security. The clergy are a body of inspectors and moral instructors, who form, so to speak, the advanced guard of the law. They have no power against offences, but they combat the vices from which offences originate, and thus render the exercise of authority more rare by maintaining morals and subordination. If they were charged with all the functions which might properly be assigned to them in the education of the inferior classes, in the promulgation of the laws, in the performance of divers public acts, the utility of their ministry would be more manifest. The more real services they rendered to the state the less would they be subject to those maladies of dogmatism and of controversy which spring from the desire of making themselves distinguished and from the want of power to be useful. It is necessary to direct their activity and their ambition towards salutary objects to prevent them from becoming mischievous.

In this point of view, even those who do not acknowledge the truth of religion cannot complain at being called upon to contribute towards its support, since they participate in its advantages.

But if there exists a great diversity of worship and religion, and the legislator is not fettered by an anterior establishment or particular considerations, it will be more conformable to liberty and equality to apply the contributions of each religious community to the support of their own church. It is true that in this arrangement we have cause to fear a spirit of proselytism on the part of the clergy; but it is equally probable that a useful emulation will result from their reciprocal efforts, and that the balance of their influence will establish a kind of equilibrium in that fluid of opinions subject to such dangerous tempests.

We can imagine a very unfortunate case, that of a people to whom the legislator forbids the public exercise of their religion, and at the same time imposes upon them the obligation of supporting a religion which they regard as hostile to their own. This would be a double violation of security. There would gradually be formed among this people an habitual sentiment of hatred against the government, a desire of change, a ferocious courage, a profound secrecy. The people, deprived of all the advantages of a public religion, of known guides and of avowed priests, would be delivered up to ignorant and fanatical leaders, and as the maintenance of their worship would be a school of conspiracy, the faith of oaths, instead of being the safeguard of the state, would become its terror; instead of binding the citizens to the government, it would unite them against it, so much so that such a people would become as formidable through their virtues as their vices. This is not an imaginary case, as the history of Ireland will show.

SECTION III.

The Cultivation of the Arts and Sciences.

I shall not speak here of what ought to be done for what are called the *useful arts and sciences;* nobody doubts that objects of public utility ought to be sustained and encouraged by public contributions.

But when the question relates to the cultivation of the fine arts, the embellishment of a country, edifices of luxury, objects of ornament and pleasure—in one word, to works of superfluity—ought we to raise forced contributions for their support? Can taxes be justified for this brilliant, but superfluous end?

I do not desire to undertake here the support of the agreeable against the useful;* nor to argue that the people should be distressed in order to give *fêtes* to a court, or pensions to buffoons. But one or two reflections may be offered by way of apology.

1st. The expense which is, or can be, incurred for these objects is commonly a trifling affair compared to the mass of necessary contributions. Let any one undertake to restore to each his quota of this superfluous expense, and would it not be almost impalpable?

2nd. This superfluous part of the contributions being confounded with the mass of those which are necessary, the levy is imperceptible; it excites no separate sensation which can give room to a distinct complaint; and the evil of the first order, limited to a sum so moderate, is not sufficient to produce an evil of the second order.

3rd. This luxury of taste may have a palpable utility by bringing together a concourse of strangers who spend their

* Not that there is any real opposition between them; everything that gives pleasure is useful; but in common language, that is exclusively called useful which produces a permanent utility; while the word *agreeable* is limited to an immediate utility, or a present pleasure. Many things, in fact, which we refuse to call *useful*, have a much more certain utility than some others, to which that epithet is usually applied.

money in the country. Little by little all nations become tributary to her who holds the sceptre of the fashions. A country fertile in amusements may be looked upon as a great theatre, which is in part supported at the expense of a crowd of curious spectators drawn to it from all parts.

It may happen, too, that this pre-eminence in objects of amusement, literature, and taste, tends to gain for a people the good will of other nations. Athens, which was called the eye of Greece, was saved more than once by the sentiment of respect which superiority of civilization inspired. The halo of glory which encircled that home of the arts served a long time to hide its weakness; and everything which was not barbarian was interested in the preservation of a city, the centre of politeness and of intellectual pleasures.

But, after all, it must be admitted that this seducing object may be abandoned without risk to the sole resource of voluntary contributions. At least, everything essential ought to be provided for before giving one's self up to expenses of pure ornament. It will be time to provide for actors, painters, and architects after the public faith is satisfied; when individuals have been indemnified for the losses occasioned by war, crimes, and physical calamities; when the support of the indigent is provided for; till then, all such expense would be an unjust preference granted to brilliant accessaries over objects of necessity.

Such expenses, under such circumstances, are very contrary to the interest of a sovereign, because the reproaches they occasion will always be much exaggerated; for it needs no sagacity to invent them, but only passion and humour to set them distinctly forth. It is well known what efficacy they have had when wrought into pieces of popular eloquence, and employed to stir up the people against regal government. Though it be true that everything conspires to throw kings into this illusion,—so far as regards the luxury of amusements, have they ever fallen into excesses so great as those of many republics? Athens, at an epoch of most pressing dangers, despised alike the eloquence of Demosthenes and the threats of Philip, engrossed with a need more urgent than defence, an object more essential than the maintenance of liberty. The gravest of crimes was the diversion, even for wants of the state, of the funds destined to the support of the theatres. And at Rome, was not the passion for spectacles carried to an equal extreme? It was necessary to lavish the treasures of the world, and the spoils of nations, to captivate the suffrages of the sovereign people. Terror spread through a whole country, whenever a pro-consul was about to give a spectacle at Rome; an hour of the magnificences of the circus cast into despair a hundred thousand inhabitants of the provinces.

CHAPTER XV.

Examples of Attacks upon Security.

It will be useful to give some examples of what I mean by *attacks upon security*. It will be a means of putting principles in a clearer light, and of showing that what is unjust in morals cannot be innocent in politics. Nothing is more common than to authorize under one name what would be odious under another.

And here I cannot help observing the bad effects of one branch of classical education. We are accustomed from our earliest youth to see in the history of the Roman people public acts of injustice, atrocious in themselves, always coloured with specious names, always accompanied by a proud eulogy on Roman virtues. The abolition of debts plays a great part from the earliest times of the republic. A withdrawal of the people to Mount Aventine, when the enemy was at the gates of Rome, forced the Senate to pass a sponge over the rights of creditors. The historian excites all our interest in favour of the fraudulent debtors who paid their debts by a bankruptcy, and does not fail to render odious those who were despoiled by an act of violence. And what was gained by that injustice? Usury, which had served as a pretext for the robbery, could not but be augmented the very next day after the catastrophe; for the exorbitant rate of interest was only the price of the risk caused by the uncertainty of engagements. The foundation of the Roman colonies has been celebrated as a work of profound policy. It always consisted in despoiling a part of the lawful proprietors of a conquered country to create establishments in the way of favour or reward.

This proceeding, so cruel in its immediate effects, was yet more fatal in its consequences. The Romans, accustomed to violate all the rights of property, knew not where to check themselves in this career. Thence the perpetual demand for a new division of lands, which was ever the fire-brand of the seditious, and which contributed under the triumvirate to a frightful system of general confiscations.

The history of the republics of Greece is full of facts of the same kind, always presented in a manner plausible enough to lead astray superficial inquirers. What abuse of reasoning has there been upon that division of lands brought about by Lycurgus, to serve as a basis for his community of warriors; in which, by an inequality the most shocking, all the rights are on one side, and all the servitude on the other!

These *attacks upon security*, which have found so many officious defenders when the question has been of the Greeks and the Romans, have not experienced the same indulgence when the monarchs of the East have been the actors. The despotism of an individual has nothing seducing in it; because it confines itself too evidently to his person alone; there are a million chances of suffering from it, to one of enjoying. But the despotism exercised by a multitude deceives weak minds by a false image of the public good. We place ourselves in imagination among the great number that commands, instead of supposing ourselves among the small number that yields and suffers. Let us, then, leave in peace the sultans and the viziers. We may be sure their injustice will not be glossed over by the flatteries of historians. Their reputation serves as an antidote to their example.

We may dispense, for the same reason, with insisting upon such attacks upon security as national bankruptcies; but we may remark, in passing, a curious effect of fidelity to engagements upon the authority of the government itself. In England, since the Revolution, the engagements of the state have always been sacred; so that individuals who lend to the government never demand any other pledge than the national credit; and the collection of the imposts assigned to pay the interest of the debt has always remained in the hands of the king. In France, under the monarchy, violations of the public faith were so frequent, that those who made advances to the government were in the habit, from an early period, of requiring the collection of the imposts to be intrusted to them, and of paying themselves with their own hands. But this arrangement cost the people dear; for the public creditor had no interest to consult their convenience; and it cost the prince yet dearer, since it deprived him of the affections of the people. When, in 1787, the announcement of a deficient revenue alarmed all the creditors of the state, that class so interested in England, in the maintenance of government, showed itself in France, ardent for a revolution. All thought they saw their own security in taking away from the sovereign the administration of the finances, and placing them in the hands of a national council. It is well known how far the event answered to their hopes. But it is not the less interesting to observe that the fall of that monarchy, which appeared so immoveable, was owing, in no small measure, to the distrust which so many violations of the public faith had caused.

But among the many *attacks upon security* committed through ignorance, inadvertence, or false reasons, it will suffice to note some individual cases.

1st. We may regard as such, *taxes unequally levied*,—those disproportioned imposts which spare the rich at the expense of the poor. The weight of this evil is aggravated by the sentiment of injustice at the idea of paying more than one's fair proportion.

Corvées are the height of inequality; since they fall entirely upon those who have only their hands for their patrimony.

So are imposts levied upon an uncertain fund; upon persons who may have nothing to pay with. In that case, the evil takes another turn. Indigence may protect us from paying the tax, but it subjects us at the same time to the gravest evils. The sufferings of want take the place of the inconveniences of the impost. This is the reason why a poll-tax is so unjust. It is possible to have a head, and to have nothing else.

Imposts which fetter industry, such as monopolies, and exclusive companies. The true method of estimating these imposts is, not to consider what income they pay, but what they prevent from being paid.

Imposts upon necessaries. What physical privations, what maladies, what deaths they produce, no man can tell! These sufferings, caused by the fault of the government, are confounded with natural evils which it cannot prevent.

Imposts upon private sales. Generally speaking, it is necessity which causes these sales; and the tax-gatherer, coming in at an epoch of distress, levies an extraordinary tribute upon an unfortunate individual.

Imposts upon public sales, or sales at auction. Here the distress is fully proved; often it is extreme, and the fiscal injustice is most manifest.

Taxes upon law proceedings. They include all kinds of attacks upon security, since they are equivalent to refusing the protection of the law to all those who cannot pay for it. They consequently offer a hope of impunity to crime. It is only necessary to choose as objects of injustice individuals who cannot afford the advances necessary to a judicial prosecution, or who are not rich enough to run the risk.

2nd. *A forced Elevation of the Value of Money.*—This is a bankruptcy, since the government does not pay all that it owes; a fraudulent bankruptcy, since there is a semblance of paying; and a foolish fraud, which deceives nobody. As far as it goes, it is equivalent to an abolition of debts. The theft which the government commits upon its own creditors, it authorizes every debtor to commit upon his, though without any profit from it to the public treasury. And when this course of injustice is completed; after this operation has enfeebled confidence, ruined honest men, enriched rogues, deranged commerce, disordered taxation, and caused a thousand individual evils, it does not leave the least advantage to the government which it has dishonoured. Expense and income presently return to the same proportions as before.

3rd. *Forced Reduction of the Rate of Interest.*—Regarded as a question of political economy, reducing the rate of interest by law is injurious to wealth, because it is prohibiting the payment of any premium for the introduction of foreign capital; it is prohibiting, in many cases, new branches of commerce, and even old ones, if the legal interest is not sufficient to balance the risks of the capital employed. But with a more immediate view to security, it is taking away from lenders to give to borrowers. Let the rate of interest be reduced by law a fifth part below its natural level, and the event is the same to the lenders as if they were plundered every year by robbers of the fifth part of their fortunes.

If the legislator finds it good to take away from a particular class of citizens a fifth part of their revenue, why stop there? Why not take away another fifth part, and still another? If the first reduction answered its end, a further reduction will answer it in the same proportion; and if the measure is good in one case, why should it be bad in the other? Wherever we stop, it is necessary to have a reason for stopping; but whatever reason prevents the second step will be just as good to prevent the first. This operation is exactly the same as diminishing rents under the pretext that the proprietors are useless consumers, and the farmers productive labourers. If you shake the principle of security as respects one class of citizens, you shake it for all. The bundle of rods is its emblem.

4th. *General Confiscations.*—I refer to this head vexations exercised upon a sect, upon a party, upon a class of men, under the vague pretext of some political crime—a pretext so vague that, while it is pretended that the confiscation is a punishment, there is often room to believe that the crime has been created for the sake of the confiscation. History presents many examples of such robbery. The Jews have often been its object; they were too rich not to be always guilty. Financiers and farmers of the public revenue, for the same reason, have been often subjected to what were called *chambers of fire* (*chambres ardentes*). While the order of succession remained unfixed, everybody at the sovereign's death might become guilty; and the spoils of the vanquished formed, in the hands of the successor, a treasure of rewards. In a republic torn by factions, each half of the nation denounces the other as traitors; and let the system of confiscations be once introduced, and parties, as at Rome, become in turn the devourers of each other.

The crimes of the powerful, and especially the crimes of the popular party in democracies, have always found apologists. "The greater part of these great fortunes," it is said, "have been founded upon injustice; and what has been plundered from the public may as well be restored to the public." To reason in this way is to open an unlimited career to tyranny. It is a permission to presume crime instead of proving it. According to this logic, it is impossible for a rich man to be innocent. Ought a punishment so severe as confiscation to be inflicted in gross, without examination, without detail, without proof? Does a procedure which would be declared atrocious if employed against an individual, become lawful when directed against a whole class of citizens? Can we make ourselves deaf to the evil we are doing because of the number of the sufferers whose cries are mingled together in this common shipwreck? To plunder great proprietors, under the pretext that some of their ancestors have acquired their opulence by unjust means, is like bombarding a city because some robbers are thought to be concealed in it.

5th. *Dissolution of Convents and of Monastic Orders.*—The decree for their abolition was signed by reason itself; but its execution should not have been abandoned to prejudice and to avarice. It would have been enough to have forbidden these societies to admit new members. In that case they would have died away gradually. Individuals would have suffered no privation. The revenues as they fell in might have been appropriated to some useful object; and philosophy would have applauded an operation excellent in principle and mild in its execution. But this slow process is not that which cupidity loves. It would seem as if sovereigns, in dissolving these societies, had wished to punish the members for some wrong they had done. In place of regarding them as orphans and invalids, deserving all the compassion of the legislator, they were looked upon as enemies, who were treated with clemency even when they were stripped of all their wealth and reduced to absolute want.

6th. *Suppression of Pensions and Places without Indemnity to the Possessors.*—This attack upon security merits the rather a particular mention, because, instead of being blamed as an injustice, it is often approved as an act of economy and reform. Envy is never so much at its ease as when it can conceal itself under the mask of patriotism and the public good. But the public good requires only the abolition of sinecures; it does not demand the ruin of the persons who hold them.

The principle of security requires that reform should be attended with complete indemnity. The only benefit that can be lawfully drawn from it is the conversion of a perpetual into a life annuity.

Is it said that the immediate suppression of these places will be a gain to the public? This argument is sophistical. The sum in question would doubtless be a gain, considered in itself, if it came from abroad, or if it were acquired by commerce; but it is not a gain when taken from the hands of certain individuals, who are themselves a part of the public. Would a family be the richer because the father had taken everything from one of his children, the better to endow the others? Even in such a case, the spoils of one child would increase the inheritance of his brothers, and the evil would not be a total loss; it would produce a portion of good. But when the question is of the public, the profit of a place suppressed is divided among the whole community, while the loss falls entirely upon one. The gain, spread among the multitude, is divided into impalpable parts; the loss is wholly felt by him who alone supports it. The result of the operation is this—it does not enrich the party that gains, and it reduces him who loses to poverty. Instead of one place suppressed, suppose a thousand, ten thousand, a hundred thousand. The total disadvantage will remain the same. The plunder taken from thousands of individuals must be divided among millions. Your streets will everywhere present unfortunate citizens whom you will have plunged into indigence; and you will hardly see an individual who will be sensibly the richer by virtue of these cruel operations. Groans of pain and cries of despair will resound on every side. The cries of joy, if there are any, will not be expressions of happiness, but of that antipathy which rejoices in the misery of its victims. Ministers of kings and of the people, it is not by the wretchedness of individuals that you will produce the happiness of nations! The altar of the public good demands barbarous sacrifices as little as the altar of the Divinity.

I cannot yet quit the subject; for the establishment of the principle of security demands that error should be pursued into all its retreats.

What means do men take to deceive themselves or to deceive the people on the subject of such great injustice? They have recourse to certain pompous maxims which are a mixture of truth and falsehood, and which give to a question, simple in itself, an air of depth and political mystery. The interest of individuals, it is said, ought to yield to the public interest. But what does that mean? Is not one individual as much a part of the public as another? This public interest, which you introduce as a person, is only an abstract term; it represents nothing but the mass of individual interests. It is necessary to take them all into account, instead of considering some as all, and the others as nothing. If it is a good thing to sacrifice the fortune of one individual to augment that of others, it will be yet better to sacrifice a second, a third, a hundred, a thousand, an unlimited number; for whatever may be the number of those you have sacrificed, you will always have the same reason to add one more. In one word, the interest of everybody is sacred, or the interest of nobody.

Individual interests are the only real interests. Take care of the individuals; never molest them, never suffer any one to molest them, and you will have done enough for the public. Would it be believed that there are men so absurd as to love posterity better than the present generation; to prefer the man who is not to the man who is; to torment the living under pretext of doing good to those who are not born, and who perhaps never will be?

Upon a multitude of occasions, men who have suffered by the operation of a law have not dared to complain, or have not been listened to, by reason of this false and obscure notion, that private interest ought to yield to public interest. But if it comes to a question of generosity, who is loudest called upon to exercise it,—the whole towards one, or one towards the whole? An evil felt, and a benefit not felt; such is the result of these admirable operations by which individuals are sacrificed to the public!

I shall conclude by a general observation of great importance The more the principle of property is respected the stronger hold it takes on the popular mind. Slight attacks upon this principle prepare the way for heavier ones. A long time has been necessary to carry property to the point where we now see it in civilized societies; but a fatal experience has shown with what facility it can be shaken, and how easily the savage instinct of plunder gets the better of the laws. Governments and the people are, in this respect, like tamed lions; let them but taste a drop of blood, and their native ferocity revives.

Si torrida parvus
Venit in ora cruor, rediunt rabiesque furorque;
Admonitæque tument gustato sanguine fauces,
Fervet, et a trepido vix abstinet ora magistro.

LUCAN, iv.

If but a little blood
Touch his hot mouth, fury and rage return;
His counselled jaws swell with the tasted gore;
He raves; and from his trembling keeper scarce
Restrains his teeth.

CHAPTER XVI.

Forced Exchanges.

"Astyages, in Xenophon's *Cyropædia*, asks Cyrus to give an account of his last lesson. Cyrus answers thus: 'One of the boys in our school who had a coat too small for him gave it to one of his companions a little smaller than himself, and took away his coat, which was too large. The preceptor made me the judge of this dispute, and I decided that the matter should be left as it was, since both parties seemed to be better accommodated than before. Upon which the preceptor pointed out to me that I had done wrong, for I had been satisfied with considering the convenience of the thing, whereas I ought first to have looked at the justice of it; and justice never would allow violence to be done to any one's property.'"—*Montaigne's Essays*, book i. ch. xxiv.

What ought we to think of this decision? At the first view it would appear that a forced exchange is not contrary to security, provided an equal value is given. How can I be said to lose in consequence of a law, if, after it has had its full effect, the amount of my property remains the same as before? If one has gained, and the other has not lost, the operation seems to be a good one.

No; it is not. He whom you suppose to have lost nothing by a forced exchange, in reality has lost; since everything moveable or immoveable has different values for different persons, according to circumstances, and every one expects to enjoy the favourable circumstances which may augment the value of such or such a part of his property. If the house that Peter occupies would be more valuable to Paul, that is no reason why Paul should be gratified by forcing Peter to yield the house to him for the sum which it is worth to himself. That would be to deprive Peter of the benefit which he has a right to derive from the very circumstance that the house is worth more to Paul.

And suppose Paul should say that for the sake of peace he

had offered a price above the ordinary value, and that Peter refuses it out of pure obstinacy, still it might be replied to him, "This surplus of price which you pretend to have offered is only a supposition of yours." The opposite supposition is just as probable. For if you had really offered more than the house is worth, he would have hastened to seize so favourable a circumstance, which might not occur again, and the bargain would have been soon concluded. If he did not accept your offer it is a proof that you were deceived in your estimate, and that if the house were taken from him on the conditions you propose, it would be an injury to his fortune, if not to what he possesses, at least to what he has a right to acquire.

No, Paul will reply; he knows that my estimate is higher than anything he can expect in the ordinary course of things; but he also knows my necessity, and he refuses a reasonable offer in hopes to derive an unfair advantage from my situation.

I perceive a principle which may serve to settle this difference between Paul and Peter. Things must be distinguished into two classes, those which ordinarily have only their intrinsic value, and those which are susceptible of a value of affection. Houses of the common sort, fields cultivated in the usual way, a crop of hay or corn, and ordinary kinds of manufactures, seem to belong to the first class. To the second may be referred pleasure-grounds and gardens, libraries, pictures, statues, collections of natural history. A forced exchange of such objects should never be permitted. The value they derive from a sentiment of affection cannot be appreciated. But objects of the first class may be submitted to forced exchanges whenever it is the only means to prevent great losses. I possess a piece of land from which I derive a considerable revenue, but which I can approach only by a road running along the edge of a river. The river overflows and washes away the road. My neighbour obstinately refuses me a passage along a strip of land which is not worth the hundredth part of my field. Ought I to lose my all through the caprice or hostility of an unreasonable neighbour?

But to prevent the abuse of a principle so delicate, rigorous rules ought to be laid down. I say, then, that forced exchanges ought to be permitted to prevent a great loss, as in the case of a field rendered inaccessible except by a passage through another.

By observing all the scruples of the English legislators in this behalf, we may perceive the respect which is paid in that country to the rights of property. If a new road is to be opened, an Act of Parliament must be first obtained. All interested are heard, and the legislature, not content with assigning an equitable satisfaction to the proprietors, protects houses, gardens, and such other objects as may have a value of affection, by special exceptions in the Act.

Forced exchanges may also be justified whenever the obstinacy of an individual or of a small number are clearly hostile to the advantage of a great number. So in the matter of the English Inclosure Acts, the opposition of a few has not been suffered to prevail, and the sale of houses is often compelled by the law where the convenience or the health of cities requires it.

The question is of forced *exchanges*, not of forced transfers, for a transfer is not an exchange; and a forced transfer without equivalent, even for the benefit of the state, would be a mere injustice, an act of power devoid of that tenderness which the principle of utility ever demands.

CHAPTER XVII.

Power of the Laws over Expectation.

The legislator is not master of the dispositions of the human heart, he is only their interpreter and their minister. The goodness of the laws depends upon their conformity to general *expectation*. The legislator ought to be well acquainted with the progress of this expectation, in order to act in concert with it. This should be the end; let us inquire into the conditions necessary to attain it.

1st. The first of these conditions, but at the same time the most difficult to fulfil, is this, *that the laws should be anterior to expecta-*

tion. If we could suppose a new people, a generation of children, the legislator finding no expectations already formed in contradiction to his views, might fashion them at his pleasure, as the statuary does a block of marble. But as there exists already among all people a multitude of expectations founded upon ancient laws or ancient usages, the legislator is forced to follow a system of conciliation and of humouring which constantly fetters him.

The very first laws found some expectations already formed. For we have seen that prior to laws there existed a feeble kind of property—that is, a sort of expectation of preserving what had been acquired. The laws received their first determination from these anterior expectations, they have produced new ones, and have gradually formed the channel of our desires and hopes. No changes can be made in the laws of property without deranging, more or less, this established current, and without opposing more or less resistance to it.

Do you find it necessary to establish a law contrary to the actual expectations of men? If it is possible, you should so arrange matters that this law will not begin to take effect except at a remote period. The present generation will not feel the change, and the rising generation will be prepared for it. You will find among the young auxiliaries against old opinions, you will not wound actual interests, because time will be allowed to prepare for a new order of things. Everything will become easy to you, because you will have prevented the birth of those expectations which otherwise you would have been compelled to contradict.

2nd. The second condition is, *that the laws should be known.* A law which is unknown can have no effect upon expectation, it will not even serve to prevent a contrary expectation.

This condition, it will be said, does not depend upon the nature of the law, but on the measures which are taken to make it public. These measures may be sufficient for their object, whether the law be so or not.

This reasoning is more specious than true. There are some

laws so made as to be more easily known than others. These are laws conformable to expectations already formed, laws which rest upon *natural expectations.* This natural expectation, that is, this expectation produced by previous habits, may be founded upon a superstition, upon a hurtful prejudice, or upon a perception of utility, it makes no difference which, the law which is conformed to it is easily borne in mind; in fact, it was in the mind before it received the sanction of the legislator. But a law contrary to this natural expectation is difficult to be understood, and still more difficult to be remembered. Another arrangement always suggests itself, while the law, strange to all, and without any root in the mind, tends constantly to slip from a place to which it has only an artificial adhesion.

Codes of ritual law have this inconvenience among others, that the fantastic and arbitrary rules of which they are composed, never well known, fatigue the understanding and the memory; so that man, always fearful, always in fault, always defiled by some imaginary sin, can never count upon innocence, and lives in perpetual need of absolution.

Expectation naturally directs itself towards the laws which are most important to society. The stranger who commits a theft, a forgery, an assassination, should not be suffered to plead ignorance of the laws of the country, since he could not be ignorant that acts so manifestly hurtful were crimes everywhere.

3rd. The third condition is, *that the laws should be consistent.* This principle is closely connected with the preceding, but it serves to place a great truth in a new light. When the laws have established a certain arrangement upon a principle generally admitted, every additional arrangement which is consistent with that principle will prove to be conformable to the general expectation. Every analogous law is presumed, as it were, beforehand. Each new application of the principle contributes to strengthen it. But a law which has not this character remains isolated in the mind; and the influence of the principle to which it is opposed is a force which tends, without ceasing, to drive it from the memory.

That upon a man's death his property should go to the next of kin, is a rule generally admitted, and according to which expectations are naturally formed. A law directing the order of succession, which should conform to this principle, would obtain a general approbation, and would be universally understood. But the more this principle is obscured, by admitting exceptions, the more difficult it is to understand the law and to remember it. The English *Common Law* affords us a striking example. It is so complicated in its provisions regulating the descent of property, it admits distinctions so singular, the decisions which serve to regulate it are so subtle, that not only is it impossible for simple good sense to presume its regulations beforehand, but it is very difficult to discover them at all. It is a profound study, like that of the most abstract sciences, confined to a small number of privileged men. It has been even necessary to sub-divide it, for no lawyer pretends to understand the whole of it. Such has been the fruit of too superstitious a respect for antiquity!

When new laws are made in opposition to a principle established by the old ones, the stronger that principle is, the more odious will the inconsistency appear. A contradiction of sentiment results from it, and disappointed expectations accuse the legislator of tyranny.

In Turkey, when an officer of the government dies, the Sultan takes possession of his entire fortune, and his children fall at once from the height of opulence to the depths of poverty. This law, which overturns all natural expectations, was perhaps borrowed from some other oriental government, in which it was less inconsistent and less odious, because the sovereign entrusted employments only to eunuchs.

4th. The fourth condition is, that *the laws should be consistent with the principle of utility;* for utility is a point towards which all expectations have a natural tendency.

It is true that a law conformable to utility may happen to be contrary to public opinion; but this is only an accidental and transitory circumstance. All minds will be reconciled to the law so soon as its utility is made obvious. As soon as the veil which conceals it is raised, expectation will be satisfied, and the public opinion be gained over. Now, it is plain that the more the laws are conformed to utility, the more manifest it is possible for their utility to become. If we ascribe to a thing a quality which it does not possess, the triumph of error can exist but for a time—a single ray of light will suffice to dissipate it. But a quality which actually exists, although not known, may chance to be discovered at any instant. At the first moment, an innovation is surrounded by an impure atmosphere; a mass of clouds formed by caprices and prejudices float about it; and the appearance of things is changed by the refractions it undergoes in the passage through so deceitful a medium. It needs time for the sight to grow strong, and to acquire the power of separating from the object all that is foreign to it. But, little by little, truth gains the ascendant. If the first attempt does not succeed, the second will be more fortunate, because it will be better known where lies the difficulty which it is necessary to conquer. The plan which favours the most interests cannot fail in the end to gain the most suffrages; and the useful novelty, which at first was repulsed with affright, becomes presently so familiar that no one recollects its commencement.

5th. The fifth condition is *method in the laws*. The bad arrangement of a code of laws may produce, by its effect upon expectation, the same inconveniences with incoherence and inconsistency. There may result from it the same difficulty of understanding the law, and of remembering it. Every man has his limited measure of understanding. The more complex the law is, the more it is above the faculties of a great number. In the same proportion it is less known; it has less hold upon men; it does not present itself to their minds upon the necessary occasions; or, what is yet worse, it deceives them, and produces false expectations. Both the style and the method should be simple; the law ought to be a manual of instruction for each individual; and every one should be enabled to consult it in doubtful cases, without the aid of an interpreter.

The more the laws conform to the principle of utility the

simpler they will become; for a system founded upon a single principle may be as simple in form as in substance. It is only such a system which is susceptible of a natural method, and a familiar nomenclature.

6th. To become the controller of expectation, the law ought to present itself to the mind as *certain to be executed;* at least, no reason for presuming the contrary ought to appear.

Is there ground for supposing that the law will not be executed? An expectation is formed contrary to the law itself. The law, then, is useless. It never exercises its power except to punish; and these inefficacious punishments are an additional reproach to the law. Contemptible in its weakness, odious in its force, it is always bad, whether it reaches the guilty or suffers him to escape.

This principle has often been absurdly disregarded. For example, during Law's paper-money system, when the citizens of France were forbidden to keep in their houses more than a certain sum in coin,—could not everybody presume on the success of disobedience?

How many mercantile prohibitions are vicious in this particular! A multitude of rules easily eluded, form, so to speak, a lottery of immorality, in which individuals stake their money against the legislator and the custom-house.

It is in accordance with this principle that the domestic authority has been established in the hands of the husband. If it had been given to the woman, the physical power being on one side, and the legal power on the other, the discord would have been eternal. If an equality had been established between them, this nominal equality could never have been maintained, because of two opposite wills one or the other must have the sway. The existing arrangement is most favourable to the peace of families, because, in making the physical and legal power operate in concert, everything is combined which is necessary for effectual action.

This principle affords a great assistance towards the resolution of certain problems which have very much embarrassed the lawyers; such, for instance, as this—in what cases ought a *thing found* to belong to the finder? The easier it would be to appropriate the thing in spite of the law, the more expedient is it not to make a law which will disappoint expectation; or in other terms, the easier it is to elude the law, the more cruel it would be to make a law which, presenting itself to the mind as almost impossible to be executed, would do nothing but evil, when by chance it should happen to be executed. This may be made clearer by an example:—Should I find a diamond in the ground, my first idea would be to regard it as my own; and an expectation of keeping it would be formed at the same instant, not only through the bent of desire, but also by analogy with habitual ideas of property. 1st. I have the physical possession of it, and this possession alone is a title where there is no opposing title. 2nd. There is something of mine in the discovery; it is I who have drawn this diamond from the dirt, where, unknown to all the world, it had no value. 3rd. I may flatter myself with the idea of keeping it, without the aid of the law, and even in spite of the law; since it will be enough to conceal it till I have a pretext for producing it under some other title. Now, should the law undertake to bestow the diamond upon some other person than me, it could not prevent this first movement of expectation, this hope of keeping it; and in taking it away from me, it would make me experience that pain of disappointment commonly called *injustice* or *tyranny*. This reason would be sufficient for causing the thing to be given to the finder, unless some stronger reason can be offered to the contrary.

This rule may vary according to the natural chance of keeping the thing found without the aid of the law. A shipwrecked vessel which I may have been the first to see upon the coast; a mine; an island which I may have discovered; are objects as to which an anterior law may prevent any idea of property, because it is impossible for me secretly to appropriate them to my own use. The law which refused them to me, being easily executed, would have its full and entire effect upon my mind; to such a degree, that if the question turned on this principle alone, the legislator would be at liberty to give or refuse the thing to the discoverer, as he saw fit. But there is a particular reason for showing some favour to the discoverer, which is, that a reward given to industry tends to augment the general wealth. When all the profit of discovery passes to the public treasury, that all is generally very little.

7th. The seventh and last condition necessary to produce a conformity between expectation and the laws, requires that the *laws should be literally followed.* This condition depends partly on the laws, and partly on the judges. If the laws do not harmonize with the ideas of the people, if the code of a barbarous age still prevails in an era of civilization; the tribunals, little by little, will drop old principles, and insensibly substitute new maxims. Thence will result a kind of contest between laws that are growing obsolete, and usage that is taking their place; and a feebleness in the effect of the laws upon expectation, will be a consequence of this uncertainty.

The word *interpretation* has a very different meaning in the mouth of a lawyer, from what it has when employed by other people. To interpret a passage in an author, is to bring out of it the sense which the writer had in his mind; to interpret a law, in the sense at least of the Roman lawyers, is often to get rid of the intention clearly and plainly expressed, and to substitute some other for it, in the presumption that this new sense was the actual intention of the legislator!

With such a method of proceeding, there is no security. Where the law is fixed, though it be difficult, obscure, incoherent,—the citizen always has a chance to know it. It gives a confused intimation, less efficacious than it might be, yet always useful; we see at least the limits of the evil it can do. But let a judge dare to arrogate to himself the power of interpreting the laws, that is to say, of substituting his will for that of the legislator, and everything becomes arbitrary; no one can foresee the course which caprice will take. The question is no longer of the actual evil; however great that may be, it is small in comparison with the magnitude of possible consequences. The serpent, it is said, can pass his whole body wherever he can introduce his head. As respects legal tyranny, it is this subtle head of which we must take care, lest presently we see it followed by all the tortuous folds of abuse. It is not the evil only which we ought to distrust,—it is the good even which springs from such means. Every usurpation of a power above the law, though useful in its immediate effects, as regards the future ought to be an object of terror. There are bounds, and even narrow bounds, to the good which can result from such arbitrary proceedings; there are no bounds to the possible evil; there are no bounds to the alarm. An indistinct danger hovers over every head.

Without speaking of ignorance and caprice, how many facilities does this arbitrary system afford to partiality! The judge, now conforming to the law, and now explaining it away, can always decide a case to suit his own designs. He is always sure of saving himself, either by the literal sense or the interpretation, He is a charlatan who astonishes the spectators by making sweet and bitter run from the same cup.

One of the most eminent characteristics of the English tribunal is their scrupulous fidelity in following the declared will of the legislator; and in directing themselves as much as possible, by former judgments, in that imperfect part of English legislation which depends upon custom. This rigid observation of the laws may have considerable inconveniences in an incomplete system, but it is the true spirit of liberty which inspires the English with so much horror for what they call *ex post facto laws.*

All the conditions which constitute the goodness of the laws have so intimate a connection that the fulfilment of one supposes the fulfilment of the others. Intrinsic utility; apparent utility; consistency; simplicity; facility of being known; probability of execution; all these qualities may be reciprocally considered as the cause or the effect of each other.

If that obscure system called *custom* were no longer permitted, and everything were reduced to written law; if the laws which concern every member of the community were arranged in one volume, and those which concern particular classes in little separate collections; if the general code were universally disseminated; had it become, as among the Hebrews, a part of worship and a manual of education; if a knowledge of it were required as preliminary to the enjoyment of political rights;—the law would then be truly known; every deviation from it would be manifest; every citizen would become its guardian; its violation would not be a mystery, its explanation would not be a monopoly; and fraud and chicane would no longer be able to elude it.

It is further necessary that the style of the laws should be as simple as their provisions; that it should make use of common language; that its forms should have no artificial complexity. If the style of the code differed from that of other books, it should be by a greater clearness, by a greater precision, by a greater familiarity; because it is designed for all understandings, and particularly for the least enlightened class.

After having imagined such a system of laws, if we proceed to compare it with what actually exists, the sentiment that results is far from favourable to our institutions. But however bad existing laws may be, let us distrust the declamations of chagrin and the exaggerations of complaint. He who is so limited in his views, or so passionate in his ideas of reform as to desire a revolt, or to bring the established system into general contempt, is unworthy to be heard at the tribunal of an enlightened public. Who can enumerate the benefits of law, I do not say under the best government, but under the worst? Are we not indebted to it for all we have of security, property, industry, and abundance? Are we not indebted to it for peace between citizens, for the sanctity of marriage, and the sweet perpetuity of families? The good which the law produces is universal; it is enjoyed every day and every moment. Its evils are transient accidents. But the good is not perceived; we enjoy it without referring it to its true cause, as if it appertained to the ordinary course of nature; while evils are vividly felt, and, in the description of them, the suffering which is spread over a great space and a long series of years, is accumulated by the imagination upon a single moment. How many reasons we have to love the laws in spite of their imperfections!

PART SECOND.

DISTRIBUTION OF PROPERTY.

CHAPTER I.

Titles which constitute Property.

We have already shown the reasons which induce the legislator to sanction property. But hitherto we have viewed wealth only in the mass; it is now necessary to descend to details, to take the individual objects which compose it, and to seek the principles which ought to govern the distribution of property, at the time when it presents itself to the law, to be appropriated to such or such individuals. These principles are the same which we have already laid down, viz., *Subsistence*, *Abundance*, *Equality*, *Security*. Where they agree, the decision is easy; when they differ, we must learn to distinguish where the preference should be given.

I. Actual Possession.—Actual possession is a title to property which precedes all others, and may hold the place of them. It will always be good against every man who has no other to oppose to it. Arbitrarily to take away from him who has, for the sake of giving to him who has not, is to create a loss on one side and a gain on the other. But, first, the value of the resulting pleasure will not be equal to the amount of the resulting pain; second, such an act of violence, by its attack upon security, will spread alarm among all proprietors. It appears, then, that actual possession is a title founded upon good of the first order, and good of the second order.

What is called the right of the *first occupant*, or of original discovery, amounts to the same thing. When the right of property is awarded to the first occupant,—1st. He is spared the pain of disappointment, the pain he would have felt at seeing himself deprived of a thing of which he had been the first to take possession. 2nd. The contests are prevented which might take place between the first occupant and a succession of competitors for the possession. 3rd. Certain enjoyments are produced, which otherwise would have had no existence; for the first occupant, if he had no right of possession, dreading to lose what he had found, would not dare to enjoy it openly, for fear of betraying himself; and whatever he could not instantly consume would be valueless to him. 4th. The enjoyment thus bestowed upon a discoverer is a spur to the industry of others, who will be encouraged to seek like enjoyments for themselves; and these individual acquisitions will result in general wealth. 5th. If unappropriated things did not belong to the first occupant, they would always be the prey of the strongest, and the weak would be for ever oppressed.

All these reasons do not present themselves distinctly to men's minds; but they are perceived in a confused manner, as it were instinctively. Such, they say, is the decree of reason, equity, and justice. These words, which everybody repeats and nobody explains, express nothing but a sentiment of approbation; but this approbation, founded upon solid reasons, acquires a new force when distinctly supported upon the principle of utility.

The title of original occupation formed the primitive foundation of property. It will still serve as regards islands newly risen from the waters, or lands newly discovered, saving the right of government, which is a peculiar incident of sovereignty.

II. Ancient Possession in Good Faith.—Possession, after a certain period fixed by the law, ought to prevail over all other titles. If you have suffered that period to elapse without putting in a claim, it is a proof, either that you were ignorant of the existence of your right, or that you had no intention to avail yourself of it. In these two cases there is no expectation on your part, no desire to gain possession; and on my part there is an expectation and a desire to preserve it. To leave the possession with me will not be contrary to security; but it will be an attack upon security to transfer the possession to you, for it will give inquietude to all possessors who are obliged to rely for their title upon ancient possession in good faith.

But what length of time is necessary to produce this displacement of expectation? or, in other words, what period is necessary to legitimate property in the hands of a possessor, and to extinguish every opposite title? To this inquiry, no exact answer can be given. It is necessary to draw at hazard the line of demarcation, according to the kind and value of the property in question. If this line does not always prevent the pain of disappointment among those actually interested, it will at least prevent all evil of the second order. The law informs me that if during one year, ten years, or twenty years, I neglect to claim my right, the loss of that right will be the result of my negligence. This threat, the effects of which I can prevent, is not calculated to disturb my security.

I suppose that the possession is in good faith, that is, that the possessor believes himself to have a title. If not so, to confirm it would not be to favour security, but to reward crime. The age of Nestor ought not to be sufficient to insure to the fraudulent usurper the wages and the pay of his iniquity. Why should there be a time when the malefactor can become tranquil? Why should he enjoy the fruits of his offence under the protection of the laws he has violated?

With respect to heirs, a distinction must be taken. Are they possessors in good faith, believing themselves to have a title? The same reasons can then be alleged in their behalf as in behalf of the former proprietoı, and they have the possession beside, which inclines the balance in their favour. Are they possessors in bad faith, as their ancestor was? Then they are his accomplices, and impunity ought never to become the privilege of fraud.

This second title is what is commonly called *Prescription.*

The *reasons* on which it is founded are the prevention of disappointment and the general security of proprietors.

III. Possession of the Contents and Produce of Land.—The property of a field includes everything which the field contains, and everything which it produces. We understand by *contents* everything beneath the surface, such as mines and quarries; by produce, everything that belongs to the vegetable kingdom. All possible reasons,—security, subsistence, the augmentation of general wealth, the good of peace,—combine to give this extent to the right of property in land.

IV. Possession of what Land supports, and of what it receives.—If my land has supported animals, it is to me that they owe their sustenance. Their existence would be a loss to me if the possession of the animals themselves did not secure me an indemnity. If the law gave them to another it would be a pure loss on my part and a pure gain on his—an arrangement as contrary to equality as to security. It would then become my interest to diminish their number and to prevent their multiplication, which would be manifestly to the detriment of the general wealth.

If chance has thrown upon land things which have not yet received the stamp of property, or which have lost the impress of it, as a whale driven on shore by a storm, the scattered fragments of a wreck, or trees torn up by the roots, such things ought to belong to the owner of the land. The reason of this preference is, that he is so situated as to derive a profit from them without any individual being subjected to a loss; they cannot be taken from him without occasioning a pain of disappointment, and finally, no other person can take them without occupying his land and trespassing upon his rights. He has all the reasons of a first occupant in his favour.

V. Possession of adjacent Lands.—If water which has covered unappropriated land leaves it, to whom shall the new land belong? There are many reasons for giving it to the proprietors of the adjacent lands. 1st. They only can occupy it without trespassing upon the property of others. 2nd. They only have formed some expectation of possessing it, or can look upon themselves as having a claim to it. 3rd. The chance of gaining by the retreat of the waters is no more than an indemnity for the chance of losing by their invasion. 4th. The property in land gained from the water will operate as a reward calculated to stimulate the labour necessary to this kind of conquest.*

VI. Ameliorations of one's own Property.—If I have applied my labour to one of those things which already belong to me, my title acquires a new force. I have sowed and gathered these vegetables, the produce of my land; I have taken care of these animals, I have dug these roots, I have cut these trees and shaped them. If I should have suffered at seeing these things taken from me before I had bestowed any pains upon them, how much more shall I suffer after the efforts of my industry have given them a new value, and have fortified my attachment to them and my expectation of keeping them? This fund for future enjoyment, which labour constantly increases, could not exist without security.

VII. Possession in good Faith with Amelioration of another's Property.—But, if I have applied my labour to a thing belonging to another, treating it as if it belonged to me, for example, if I have made cloth of your wool, to which of us shall the manufacture belong? Before answering, it is necessary to ascertain the state of the facts. Is it in good faith or bad faith that I have treated the thing as my property? If I have

* Such is the theory. In practice, many details will be required, otherwise this concession will resemble that famous partition of the new world, which a pope made between the Spanish and Portuguese. Suppose the water quits a bay, which has many proprietors on its shores; shall the distribution be regulated according to the quantity of land which each possesses, or to the extent of his shore? Lines of demarcation will be necessary; but it will not answer to wait till the event has arrived, and the value of the land is known, for then all will entertain hopes, which some only can realize. The event must be anticipated, and expectation not yet formed will then be docile in the hands of the legislator.

acted in bad faith, to give me the production would be to reward crime; if I have acted in good faith, it remains to inquire which of the two values is the greater, the original value of the thing worked upon or the additional value of the labour bestowed upon it? How long since the first owner lost it? How long have I possessed it? To whom belongs the place in which it is at the moment when it is reclaimed,—to me, to the former possessor, or to a stranger?

The principle of caprice, without regard to the comparative amount of pains and pleasures, gives everything to one of the parties without paying any attention to the other. The principle of utility anxious to reduce to the least term an inevitable inconvenience, weighs the two interests, seeks the means of reconciling them, and directs indemnities. It grants the thing itself to that claimant who would suffer the greater loss if his demand were refused, upon the condition, however, of giving to the other a sufficient indemnification.

It is according to these same principles that we must answer the same question in relation to things which become mixed and confounded, as metal of yours and mine which has run together in the melting-pot, or liquors of mine which have been poured into the same recipient with yours. There are great debates among the Roman jurists who shall have the whole; the *Sabinians* wish to give the whole to me, the *Proculeians* wish to give the whole to you. Which is right? Neither. Either decision would still leave one of the parties a sufferer. A single question might cut short all these debates—Which of the two, in losing what belonged to him, would lose the most? Let him have the possession, and let the other have an indemnity.

The English lawyers have cut this Gordian knot. They have not troubled themselves to examine on which side would be the greater injury, they make no account of good faith or of bad faith, they make no inquiry as to the greater value or the stronger expectation. They decide that the property of movable effects shall always be given to the actual possessor, on condition, however, of indemnifying the other claimant.

VIII. Exploration of Mines in the Land of Another.—Your land has hidden treasures in its bosom; but, because you lack the knowledge or the means, or have little confidence of success, you do not dare to undertake the enterprise of mining, and the treasures remain buried. If I, a stranger to your land, have all the means of exploration which you want, and I wish to undertake it, ought the right to be granted to me without your consent? Why not? Under your hands these buried riches are of no use to anybody; in mine they will acquire a great value—thrown into circulation they will animate industry. What wrong is done to you? You lose nothing. The surface, the only thing which you put to any use, may still remain in the same condition. But the law, attentive to the interests of all, ought to secure you a share, greater or less, of the produce; for, though this treasure might be of no actual value in your hands, still you would have an expectation of sometime profiting by it, and you ought not to be deprived of that chance without indemnity.

Such is the English law. Under certain conditions, it allows a vein, discovered in one field, to be followed into another by any one who is willing to undertake the enterprise.

IX. Liberty of Fishing in Great Waters.—Great lakes, great rivers, great bays, and especially the ocean, are not occupied by exclusive proprietors. They are considered as belonging to nobody, or rather as belonging to all.

There are no reasons for limiting the ocean fisheries. The multiplication of most kinds of fish appears to be inexhaustible. In this matter the prodigality, the magnificence of nature almost surpasses conception. The indefatigable Leuwenhoek has estimated that the spawn of a single cod is capable of producing six millions of codlings. What we can take or consume out of this immense magazine of food is absolutely nothing when compared with the destruction produced by physical causes, which we can neither lessen nor prevent. Man on the ocean, with his wherry and his nets, is but a feeble rival of the great rulers of the sea. Sharks cause more ravages among the small fish than he does.

As to the fish of rivers, lakes, and small bays, the laws take precautions for their preservation, at once necessary and efficacious.

Where there is no occasion for jealousy, and no fear that the number of competitors will diminish the fund of wealth, it is better to leave to every one the right of first occupancy, and to encourage every kind of labour that tends to augment the general abundance.

X. Liberty of Hunting upon Unappropriated Grounds.—It is the same with unappropriated lands, uncultivated wastes and savage forests. In those vast countries which are not peopled in proportion to their extent, these unappropriated tracts are often of great size, and the right of hunting may be exercised without limit. Man there is only a rival of the beasts of prey, and the chase enlarges the fund of subsistence without injuring anybody.

But in civilized societies, where agriculture has made great progress, and where unappropriated lands bear only a small proportion to those which have received the impress of possession, there are many reasons against allowing this right of chase.

First inconvenience.—In those countries where the population is numerous, the destruction of wild animals may go on faster than their reproduction. Render the chase free, and the animals which are the object of it would sensibly diminish, and even be annihilated. The sportsman would presently have as much trouble to obtain a single partridge as he now has to get a hundred, and the price would be enhanced a hundred-fold. He would suffer no loss himself, but he would furnish to society only a hundredth part the value which he now furnishes. In simpler terms, the pleasure of eating partridges would be reduced a hundred-fold.

Second inconvenience.—The chase, without being more productive than other labours, has unhappily more attractions. Sport is combined with labour, idleness with exercise, and glory with danger. The charm of a profession so well adapted to all the natural tastes of man will draw into this pursuit a great number of competitors; by their competition they will reduce the profits of this employment to a mere subsistence; and in general this class of adventurers will be poor.

Third inconvenience.—The chase having particular seasons, there will be intervals during which the huntsman will be unemployed. He will not easily return from a wandering to a sedentary life, from independence to subjection, and from a habit of idleness to a habit of labour. Accustomed, like the gambler, to live upon chances and hope, a small fixed income has few attractions for him. The want and idleness of such a condition naturally lead to crime.

Fourth inconvenience.—The very exercise of this profession is naturally fertile in offences. The quarrels, the lawsuits, the prosecutions, the convictions, the imprisonments and other punishments which it causes, are more than sufficient to counterbalance its pleasures. The hunter, tired with vainly waiting for his prey on the highways, secretly spies out the game in the neighbouring enclosures. Does he think himself observed? He turns aside and waits, for he is an adept in patience and stratagem. Does he see no witnesses? He respects boundaries no longer; he jumps the ditches, he leaps the hedges, he devastates enclosures; and his cupidity betraying him into imprudences, he gets himself into perilous positions, whence he cannot escape without disaster or crime. If hunting were permitted on the high roads, there would be needed an army of guards to restrain the wanderings of the hunters.

Fifth inconvenience.—If this right of chase, so little advantageous when confined within such narrow limits, is still suffered to exist, the civil and penal code will need an assortment of laws to limit its exercise and to punish its excesses. This multiplication of laws is always an evil, because laws cannot be multiplied without being weakened. Besides, the severity necessary to prevent offences so easy and so attractive gives an odious character to property, and places the opulent in a state of war with their poor neighbours. The way to cut this matter short is not to regulate the right, but to suppress it.

The prohibitive law being once known, no expectations will be formed of enjoying this privilege. Partridges will no more be coveted than pullets, and even in the minds of the multitude poaching will not be distinguished from theft.

It is true that at the present day popular ideas are in favour of this right of hunting; but if a condescension is due to popular ideas, it is only upon occasions when they have a great power, and when there is little hope of changing them. Let pains be taken to enlighten the people, to make the motives of the law evident, to exhibit it as a means of peace and security, to show that the exercise of this right reduces itself almost to nothing, that the life of a hunter is miserable, that this ungrateful profession constantly exposes him who follows it to the commission of offences and his family to poverty and shame; and I dare to affirm that popular ideas, pressed by the continuous and mild force of reason, would presently assume a new direction.*

There are animals whose value does not compensate the damage they do; such as foxes, wolves, bears, and all beasts of prey, the enemies of the animals subject to man. So far from preserving, it is an object to destroy them. One means for this end is, to give all a right to destroy them, and a property in the beast when slain, without regard to the ownership of the land. Every hunter who attacks these hurtful animals ought to be considered as employed by the police. But this exception ought to be admitted only in case of animals capable of much mischief.

* We may observe, that of the five inconveniences above enumerated with which the right of free hunting is said to be attended, the *second*, *third*, and *fourth* resolve themselves into this, viz., that in a civilized community, the business of hunting is a private loss and a public inconvenience. This being granted—and the fact is doubtless so—if by permitting free hunting, that annihilation of wild game, which is described as the *first* inconvenience, can be brought about, it will be a decided benefit; and when hunting ceases for want of game, of course all the evils which go to make up the inconveniences of its existence will disappear with it. This is a view of the case which the author seems not to have taken. That a right of free hunting would operate in this way, the example of *Massachusetts* clearly proves, a state in which game and sportsmen are equally rare, and game laws are unknown.—*Translator.*

CHAPTER II.

Title by Consent.

It may happen that possessing a thing by a lawful title, we wish to dispossess ourselves of it, and to abandon its enjoyment to another. Shall such an arrangement be confirmed by the law? Doubtless it shall be. All the reasons which plead in favour of the old proprietor change sides with the transfer, and then plead in favour of the new one. Besides, the former proprietor must have had some motive for abandoning his property. *Motive* is *pleasure*, or equivalent; *pleasure of friendship* or of benevolence, if the thing was given for nothing; *pleasure of acquisition*, if it was a means of exchange; *pleasure of security*, if it was given to ward off some evil; *pleasure of reputation*, if the object was to acquire the esteem of others. It seems, then, that the transfer must increase the enjoyment of the parties interested in it. The acquirer stands in the place of the conferrer as to the old advantages, and the conferrer acquires a new advantage. We may then lay it down as a general maxim, that *every alienation imports advantage*. A good of some sort is always the result of it.

When the question is of an exchange, there are then two alienations, of which each has its separate advantages. The advantage for each of the contracting parties is, the difference to him between the value of the thing he gives, and that of the thing he acquires. In every transaction of this sort there are two new masses of enjoyment. In this the good of commerce consists.

In all the arts, there are many things which cannot be produced except by the concourse of a great number of workmen. In all these cases the labour of an individual would have no value, either for himself or for others, if it could not be exchanged.

II. Cases in which Exchanges should be Invalid.—But there are cases in which the law ought not to sanction exchanges, and in which the interests of the parties ought to be regulated, as if the bargain had not taken place; because, instead of being advantageous, the exchange would be injurious to one of the parties, or to the public. We may arrange all the causes which invalidate exchanges under the nine following heads:—

1st. Concealment.
2nd. Fraud.
3rd. Coercion.
4th. Subornation.
5th. Erroneous idea of legal obligation.
6th. Erroneous idea of value.
7th. Incapacity.
8th. Probable inconvenience to the public.
9th. Want of right on the part of the conferrer.

1st. *Concealment.*—If the thing acquired proves of less value than the acquirer had expected, he experiences regret, and feels a pain of disappointment. If the value is not equal to what he gave in exchange, instead of gaining, he has lost. It is true that the other party has gained; but the *good of gain* is not equivalent to the *evil of loss.* I have paid ten guineas for a horse, which would be worth that sum if he were sound; but, as his wind is broken, he is worth but two guineas. The seller has gained eight guineas, which I have lost; but, if the interests of the two parties be weighed together, the trade, on the whole, is not productive of pleasure, but the contrary.

But if at the time of the sale this inferiority of value was unknown to the former proprietor, why should the exchange be void? Why oblige him to make a disadvantageous re-exchange? The loss must fall on somebody, and why on him more than another? And even suppose that he knew the circumstance which lessened the value of the thing, was he obliged to communicate it without being asked?

The two following questions arise in every case of invalidity resulting from concealment:—Did the seller know of the existence of the fault? Was it a case in which he ought to have told of it? The solution of these questions demands too many details and researches to find a place here, especially as an answer cannot be given which embraces every case, but divers modifications are necessary, according to the different kinds of things.

2nd. *Fraud.*—This case is simpler than the preceding. A fraudulent acquisition ought never to be permitted when it can be hindered. Fraud is an offence which borders upon theft. You asked the seller if the horse was broken-winded; he replied in the negative, knowing the contrary. To sanction such a trade would be to reward crime. Add the reason in the preceding case, namely, an evil to the purchaser greater than the good to the seller, and it will then appear that this cause of invalidity is well founded.

3rd. It is the same with *coercion.* A seller whose horse is worth but two guineas has constrained you, by violence and threats, to give ten guineas. Suppose you would have been willing to pay two guineas, the surplus is so much gained by an offence. It is true that this loss was an advantage to you in comparison with the evil you were threatened with in case of refusal; but neither this comparative advantage, nor the gain of the delinquent, can counterbalance the evil of the offence.

4th. It is the same with *subornation;* by which I understand the price of a service, which consists in committing an offence, as money promised to a man to engage him to give a false deposition. There are two advantages in such a bargain, that of the suborned and that of the suborner; but these two advantages are not at all equal to the evil of the offence.

It may be observed in passing, that in the case of fraud, of undue coercion, and of subornation, the law, not content with annulling the act, opposes to it a stronger counter-weight of punishment.

5th. *Erroneous Idea of Legal Obligation.*—You have delivered your horse to a man, under an erroneous idea that your manager had sold him. Or you have delivered your horse to a man under the impression that he was authorized by the government to take him for the use of the state; in one word, you imagine yourself obliged to sell, when no such obligation exists. If after the discovery of the mistake the alienation should be confirmed, the buyer would make an unexpected gain, while the seller would experience an unexpected loss. But we have seen that the *good of gain* is not equivalent to the *evil of loss*. Besides, this case may be classed with that of coercion.

6th. *Erroneous Idea of Value.*—If, in alienating a thing, I was ignorant of a circumstance which tended to augment its value, upon discovering my error, I shall experience the regret of loss. But is that a reason for invalidating the contract? On the one side, if such causes of nullity are admitted without restriction, there is the risk of a great discouragement to exchanges; for what security of acquisition do I have, if the seller can break the trade, under the pretence of not knowing what he was about? On the other side, there would be the pain of a very lively regret, if after having sold a diamond as a morsel of crystal, there were no means of recovering it. To hold an equal balance between the parties, we must conform to the diversity of circumstances and of things. We must always examine if the ignorance of the seller were not the result of negligence; and even should the case require the avoidance of the sale, it will always be necessary to provide for the security of the person whose interest it would be to have the bargain confirmed.

But it may be that a trade exempt from all these faults turns out to be disadvantageous. You bought a horse for the sake of a journey which you do not make. When you are ready to set out, the horse falls sick and dies. You set out, and the horse throws you and breaks your leg. You mount the horse, but only to go on the highway to rob. The fancy which made you buy him was transitory, and, being past, leaves you a loser. These eventual cases may be multiplied indefinitely,—cases in which a thing acquired on account of its value becomes useless, or onerous, or fatal to the acquirer, or to another. Are not these exceptions to the axiom that every exchange imports an advantage? Are not these reasonable grounds for invalidating the contract?

No. All these unfavourable events are only matters of accident, posterior to the sale. The common case is, that the thing is worth what it costs. The total advantage of useful exchanges is far more than equivalent to the total disadvantage of such as are unfavourable. The gains of commere are greater than the losses, since the world is now richer than in the savage state. Alienations in general ought, then, to be maintained. But to annul alienations, on account of accidental losses, would be to interdict alienations in general; for nobody would wish to sell, nobody would wish to buy, if the transaction could be annulled at any moment, on account of some subsequent event impossible to be foreseen or prevented.

7th. There are cases in which the legislator foresees the evil of conventions, and prohibits them beforehand. It is thus that in many countries prodigals are *incapacitated* to contract, that is, all contracts with them are declared void. But the danger of such contracts, that is, the disposition which renders the prodigal unfit to manage his own affairs, is always previously made known. Every one has notice, or at least might have, of the incapacity which the guardian hand of justice has imposed.

In all countries there has been established an incapacity to contract in the two analogous cases of infancy and madness; I say analogous, for what a child is, for a period which may be sufficiently well determined, though always by a demarcation more or less arbitrary, the madman is, for a time indeterminate, or perpetual. The reasons are the same as in the preceding case. Minors and persons of unsound understanding are, by their condition, either ignorant, rash, or prodigal. This is presumed by a general induction, which does not need to be sustained by particular proofs.

It is plain that in these three cases the incapacity ought to extend only to things of a certain importance. To apply them to little objects of daily consumption would be condemning these three classes to die of famine.

8th. The law sometimes invalidates contracts in consideration of some *public inconvenience* likely to result from them.

I have a landed property situated on the boundary of the state. If acquired by the neighbouring power it might become the seat of hostile intrigues, or might favour preparations dangerous to my country. Whether I have or have not such an intent, the law ought to provide for the public interest. It ought to prevent the evil by refusing beforehand to give a sanction to such sales.*

The restraints which it has been thought fit to put upon the sale of drugs which operate as poisons may be referred to this head. It would be the same of a prohibition to sell murderous arms, such as stilettoes, so frequently used in Italy in the most common quarrels.

It is to this same motive, well or ill founded, that we ought to refer all prohibitions relative to the introduction or sale of certain species of merchandise.†

In most of these cases the custom is to say, that the *contract is void in itself.* We need but open the law books to see what nonsense has been gravely uttered upon this subject, and to discover into what absurdities the lawyers have fallen, from not having seized upon the sole cause of the invalidity of contracts made under these circumstances, to wit, that they are attended by more evil than good.

Having said that these contracts are *void in themselves* to be consistent, it seems to follow that they ought not to have any effect; that they ought to be annihilated; and that no trace of them should be left. However, there are abundance of cases in which it will be sufficient to modify them, and to correct their inequality by compensations without altering the substance of the original contract.

No contract is void in itself; none is valid in itself. It is the law which, in either case, grants or refuses validity. But for

* Most nations, perhaps without thinking of it, have obviated this danger by a general law, which forbids strangers to acquire lands. But that is going too far. The reason of the prohibition does not extend beyond the particular case above mentioned. The stranger who wishes to buy immoveable property, gives the country of his choice the most unequivocal proof of his affection, and the surest pledge of good conduct. Even if we look no further than to finance, the state cannot but gain by such purchases.

† Under this head fall the laws prohibiting the traffic in ardent spirits. —*Translator.*

granting or refusing it, reasons are necessary. Equivocal generation is banished from sound physiology; perhaps some day it will be banished from jurisprudence. This *void in itself* is precisely an equivocal generation.

III. Obstacles to the Alienation of Land.—To say that the power of alienation is useful, is also to say that all arrangements which tend to prevent it are generally pernicious.

It is with respect to immoveables that this inconsistency has chiefly been displayed, whether by entails or by inalienable foundations, described by English lawyers as grants in mortmain; yet, besides the general reasons already given, there are some particular ones in favour of the free alienation of land.

1st. He who seeks to get rid of a landed estate shows sufficiently that it is not for his advantage to keep it. He either cannot or will not spend anything for its improvement; indeed, it often happens that he cannot help sacrificing its future value to satisfy a present want. On the contrary, he who seeks to acquire an estate certainly has no intention of diminishing its value, and he probably means to increase it.

It is true that the same capital which would be employed in the improvement of a landed estate might otherwise be employed in commerce; but, although the advantage of these two employments might be the same to an individual, they would not be the same to the state. That portion of wealth which is applied to agriculture is more fixed; that which is applied to commerce is more fugitive. The first is immoveable; the second can be transported at the pleasure of the proprietor.

2nd. By mortgaging an immoveable estate a productive capital may be raised. Thus one portion of the value of a landed estate may be employed in the improvement of the other portion of it; an enterprise which, perhaps, without that resource, could not be undertaken. To prevent the free alienation of lands is to diminish the productive capital which might be employed in their improvement nearly to the amount of their saleable value; for a thing cannot be mortgaged unless it can be alienated.

It is true that we speak here only of loans; and there is no new capital created by a loan. This same capital, in other hands, might receive a destination not less useful; but it is to be observed that the more means there are for employing capital the greater amount of it will come into a country. That which comes from abroad forms a net addition to the domestic supply.

These restrainsts upon alienation, though condemned by the soundest notions of political economy, are to be found almost everywhere. It is true that they have gradually diminished in proportion as governments have better understood the interests of agriculture and commerce; but there are still three causes which operate to maintain them.

The first is, the desire of preventing prodigality. But to obviate this evil, it is not necessary to prevent the sale of lands; it will be sufficient to protect their value by not leaving it at the disposal of the prodigal.

The second is, family pride, joined to that agreeable illusion, which paints the successive existence of our descendants as the prolongation of our own. The imagination is not satisfied with the idea of leaving our children the same value; they must possess the same lands, the same houses, the same natural objects. This continuity of possession appears a continuity of enjoyment, and gives support to a feeling chimerical and absurd.

The third cause is, the love of power, the desire of ruling after death. The preceding motive supposes a posterity, this does not. It is to this cause that we must refer all foundations, both those which have an object of utility, well or ill understood, and those of pure fancy.

If a foundation consists merely in the distribution of benefits without imposing any conditions, and without exacting any service, it appears sufficiently innocent, and its continuation is not an evil. We must except foundations for distributing alms without distinction and discernment, which serve merely to promote mendicity and idleness. The best of these establishments are those in favour of such poor as were once of a better condition. They are a means of providing for such unfortunates a more liberal support than public charity would allow.

As to foundations, the benefits of which are not granted except on the fulfilment of certain duties, such as convents, colleges, and churches, their tendency is useful, indifferent, or injurious, according to the nature of the services exacted.

It is a singularity which merits observation, that in general, these foundations, these particular laws, which the individual establishes by the indulgence of the sovereign, have been treated with more respect than the public laws, which are immediately derived from the sovereign himself. When a legislator has wished to tie up the hands of posterity, such a proceeding has appeared absurd or futile. The obscurest individuals have arrogated that privilege, and no one has dared to attack it!

It would seem that lands left to corporations, convents, and churches, must necessarily decline in value. Indifferent towards successors, who are not allied to him by blood, each transient proprietor will be apt to exhaust as much as he can a possession which he enjoys only for life; and, in old age especially, to neglect the necessary repairs. This sometimes happens. We must be just, however, to religious communities. They are oftener distinguished for good than for bad economy. If their situation inflames cupidity and avarice, it represses pride and prodigality. If there are causes which nourish among them a spirit of selfishness, there are others which combat that sentiment by creating an *esprit de corps*, a warm attachment to the profession to which they belong.

It is scarcely necessary to mention public property,—that is, those things the use of which is public, such as roads, churches, markets. To fulfil their end, it is necessary that their duration should be indefinite, with provision, however, for permitting those successive changes which circumstances may require.

CHAPTER III.

Title by Succession.

After the decease of an individual, how ought his goods to be disposed of?

In framing a law of succession, the legislator ought to have three objects in view:—1st, Provision for the subsistence of the rising generation; 2nd, Prevention of disappointment; 3rd, The equalization of fortunes.

Man is not a solitary being. With a very small number of exceptions, every man has about him a circle of companions, more or less extensive, who are united to him by the ties of kindred or of marriage, by friendship or by services, and who share with him, *in fact*, the enjoyment of those goods which *in law* belong to him exclusively. His fortune is commonly the sole fund of subsistence on which many others depend. To prevent the calamities of which they would be the victims, if death in taking away their friend took from them at the same time the supplies which they draw from his fortune, it is necessary to know who habitually enjoy these supplies, and in what proportions. Now, since these are facts which it would be impossible to establish by direct proofs, without becoming involved in embarrassing procedures and infinite contests, it is necessary to resort to general presumptions, as the only basis upon which a decision can be established. The share which each survivor was accustomed to enjoy in the property of the deceased may be presumed from the degree of affection which ought to have subsisted between them; and this degree of affection may be presumed from nearness of relationship.

If relationship were the only consideration, the law of succession would be very simple. In the *first* degree of relationship are all those who are connected with you without any other person intervening: your wife, or husband, your father, your mother, and your children. In the *second* degree are those whose connection with you demands the intervention of a single person, or the joint intervention of two persons: your grandfathers, your grandmothers, your brothers, your sisters, and your grandchildren. In the *third* degree are those whose relationship supposes two intermediate generations: your great-grandfathers, your great-grandmothers, your great-grandchildren, your uncles and aunts, nephews and nieces.

But this arrangement, though quite perfect as respects simplicity and regularity, will not answer the political and moral ends to be aimed at by the legislator. It does not correspond to the degree of affection of which, if employed, it must be taken as a presumptive proof; and it will not accomplish the principal object, which is to provide for the wants of the rising generation. Let us leave, then, this genealogical arrangement, and adopt one founded upon utility. It consists in *always giving to the descending line, however long, a preference over the ascending and composite lines.*

Still, it must happen that the presumptions of affection or of want, which serve as a foundation to these rules, will often fail in practice; and that, in consequence, the rules themselves will not accomplish their end. But the power of making a will offers, as we shall see, an efficacious remedy for the imperfections of the general law; and that is the principal reason for sanctioning such a power.

These are the general principles; but how ought they to be applied in detail, when it is necessary to decide between several claimants?

The model of a law will serve instead of a great number of discussions.

ARTICLE I. *No distinction between the sexes; what is said of one extends to the other. The portion of the one shall be always equal to that of the other.*

Reason.—Good of equality. If there were any difference, it ought to be in favour of the feebler—in favour of women—who have more wants and fewer means of acquisition, or of employing profitably what they possess. But the stronger have had all the preferences. Why? Because the stronger have made the laws.

ARTICLE II. *After the husband's death, the widow shall retain half the common property; unless some different arrangement was made by the marriage contract.*

ARTICLE III. *The other half shall be distributed among the children in equal proportions.*

Reasons.—1st. Equality of affection on the part of the father. 2nd. Equality of co-occupation on the part of the children. 3rd. Equality of wants. 4th. Equality of all imaginable reasons on one side and the other. Differences of age, of temperament, of talent, and of strength, may produce some differences in point of wants; but it is not possible for the law to appreciate them. The father must provide for them by the exercise of his right to make a will.

ARTICLE IV. *If a child dies before his father, leaving children, his share shall be divided among his children in equal proportions; and so of all descendants.*

This distribution by stocks is preferred to that by heads, for two reasons. 1st. To prevent disappointment. That the part of the eldest should be diminished by the birth of each younger child is a natural event, to which his expectation will conform itself. But in general, when one of the children begins to exercise his reproductive faculty, that of the father is almost at its end. At that time the children suppose themselves arrived at the point where the diminution of their respective portions ceases. But if each grandson and granddaughter were to produce the same diminution which each son and daughter had produced, the diminution would have no bounds. There would no longer be any certainty according to which they could arrange their plan of life. 2nd. The grandchildren have, as an immediate resource, the property of their deceased father. Their habit of co-occupation, detached from their grandfather, must have been exercised in preference, if not exclusively, upon the fund of their father's industry. Add to this, that they have in the property of their mother and her relations a resource, in which the other descendants of their grandfather have no share.

ARTICLE V. *If there are no descendants, the property shall go in common to the father and mother.*

Why to descendants before all others? 1st. *Superiority of affection.* Every other arrangement would be contrary to the inclination of the father. We love those better who depend upon us than those upon whom we depend. It is sweeter to govern than to obey. 2nd. *Superiority of need.* It is certain that our children cannot exist without us, or some one who fills our place. It is probable that our parents may exist without us, as they did exist before us.

Why should the succession pass to the father and mother, rather than to the brothers and sisters? 1st. The relationship being more immediate, is a presumption of superior affection. 2nd. It is a recompense for services rendered, or rather an indemnity for the pains and expense of educating the child. The relationship between me and my brother consists in our common relationship to the same father and mother; and the reason why he is more dear to me than another companion with whom I have passed an equal portion of my life is, his being dearer to those who have my first affections. It is not certain that I am indebted to him for anything, but it is certain that I am indebted to them for everything. Thus, whenever the stronger title of my own children does not intervene, I owe compensations to my parents, to which a brother can have no claim.

ARTICLE VI. *If one of the parents is dead, the share of the deceased shall go to his or her descendants, in the same way as it would have gone, had there been any, to the descendants of the deceased child.*

In poor families, whose only property is household furniture, it will be better that the whole should go to the individual survivor, whether father or mother, with the condition of providing for the support of the children. The expense of the sale and the dispersion of the property would ruin the survivor, while the parts, too small to serve as capital, would soon be dissipated.

ARTICLE VII. *Failing such descendants, the whole property shall go to the surviving parent.*

ARTICLE VIII. *If both father and mother are dead, the property, shall be divided as above among their descendants.*

ARTICLE IX. *But the part of the half-blood shall be only half as great as the part of the whole-blood.*

Reason.—Superiority of affection. Two ties attach me to my brother, but only one to my half-brother.

ARTICLE X. *In defect of relations in these degrees, the property shall go into the public treasury.*

ARTICLE XI. *Under condition, however, of distributing the interest in the form of life annuities among all the relations in the ascending line in equal shares.*

The tenth and eleventh articles may be adopted or not, according to the condition of the public revenue; but I cannot discover any solid objection against this fiscal resource. It may be said that the collateral relations who will be excluded by this arrangement may be in want. But this is too casual an accident to found a general rule upon. They have, as a natural resource, the property of their respective parents, and they do not form their expectations or fix their plan of life upon this basis. On the part even of an uncle, the expectation of inheriting from a nephew can be but feeble; and a positive law will be enough to extinguish it without violence, or to prevent it being formed. The uncle has not the titles of the father and grandfather. It is true that, in case of their death, the uncle may have taken their place, and acted as a father to his nephew. This is a circumstance which merits the attention of the legislator. The power of making a will would be a remedy for cases of this sort; but that means of obviating the inconveniences of the general law would be unavailing when the nephew died at an age too tender to allow the exercise of that power. If, then, it were determined to soften this fiscal regulation, the first exception should be in favour of the uncle, whether as regards the principal, or only the interest of the property.

ARTICLE XII. *To effect a division among the heirs, the property shall be sold at auction; reserving to them the right of making such other arrangement as they may think proper.*

This is the only means of preventing a community of goods, an arrangement the pernicious consequences of which will presently be pointed out. Such of the property as may have a value of affection, will find its true price from the competition of the heirs, and will turn to the common advantage, without producing those disputes which occasion durable animosities in families.

Article XIII. *Until sale and division be made, the whole property shall be intrusted to the keeping of the oldest male heir of full age; reserving to the court to make other arrangements, through apprehension of bad management, specified on the hearing of the case.*

Women in general are less fit for affairs of money and business than men. But an individual woman may have a superior aptitude; if pointed out by the general wish of the relations, she ought to have the preference.

Article XIV. *In defect of a male heir of full age, the property shall be intrusted to the guardian of the oldest male heir, reserving a discretionary power as in the preceding article.*

Article XV. *The succession which falls to the treasury, for want of natural heirs, shall also be sold at auction.*

The government is incapable of managing specific property to advantage. The administration of such property belonging to a government costs much, brings in little, and is certain to undergo a rapid deterioration. This is a truth which Adam Smith has demonstrated.

This project of a law appears to be simple, precise, and easy to be comprehended; it gives little room for fraud, chicanery, or diversity of interpretation; and finally, it is analogous to the affections of the human heart, to those habitual inclinations which spring from the social relations; and therefore it is likely to conciliate both the affections of those who judge by sentiment and the esteem of those who appreciate reasons.

Those who accuse this plan of being too simple, and who declare that at this rate the law would no longer be a science, may find wherewith to be satisfied, astonished, and delighted, in the labyrinth of the English common law of successions.

To give the reader an idea of the English common law on this subject, it would be necessary to begin with a dictionary of new words; and presently, when they should discover the absurdities, the subtilties, the cruelties, the frauds, with which that system abounds, they would imagine that I had written a satire, and that I wished to insult a nation otherwise so justly renowned for its wisdom.

It is to be observed, however, that the right of making a will reduces this evil within tolerably narrow limits. It is only the succession to the property of intestates which is obliged to pass through the crooked roads of the common law. Wills in that country may be compared to arbitrary pardons, which correct the severity of penal laws.

CHAPTER IV.

Testaments.

1st. The law, not knowing individuals, cannot accommodate itself to the diversity of their wants. All that can be exacted from it is to offer the best possible chance of satisfying those wants. It is for each proprietor, who can and who ought to know the particular circumstances in which those who depend upon him will be placed at his death, to correct the imperfections of the law in all those cases which it cannot foresee. The power of making a will is an instrument intrusted to the hands of individuals, to prevent private calamities.

2nd. The same power may be considered as an instrument of authority, intrusted to individuals for the encouragement of virtue in their families and the repression of vice. It is true that this means may be employed for the contrary purpose; but, fortunately, such cases are an exception. The interest of each member of a family is, that the conduct of every other member should be conformable to virtue, that is, to general utility. The passions may occasion accidental deviations; but the law must be arranged in conformity to the ordinary course of things. Virtue is the dominant regulator of society; even vicious parents are as jealous as others of the honour and the reputation of their children. A man little scrupulous in his own conduct would be shocked to have his secret practices disclosed to his family; at home he is still the apostle of probity; he disregards it in his own behaviour, but he wishes it in those about him. In this point of view, every proprietor is entitled to the confidence of the law. Clothed with the power of making a will, which is a branch of penal and remunerative legislation, he may be considered as a magistrate appointed to preserve good order in that little state called a family. This magistrate may be guilty of partiality and injustice; and as he is restrained in the exercise of his power neither by publicity nor by responsibility, he would seem to be very likely to abuse it. But that danger is more than counterbalanced by the ties of interest and affection, which put his inclination in accord with his duty. His natural attachment to his children and his relatives is as secure a pledge for his good conduct as any that can be obtained for that of the political magistrate; to such a degree that, all things considered, the authority of this non-commissioned magistrate, besides being absolutely necessary to children of tender age, will oftener be found salutary than hurtful, even to adults.

3rd. The power of making a will is advantageous under another aspect, as a means of governing—not for the good of those who obey, as in the preceding article, but for the good of him who commands. In this way the power of the present generation is extended over a portion of the future, and to a certain extent the wealth of each proprietor is doubled. By means of an order not payable till after his death, he procures for himself an infinity of advantages beyond what his actual means would furnish. By continuing the submission of children beyond the term of minority, the indemnity for paternal cares is increased, and an additional assurance against ingratitude is secured to the father; and though it would be agreeable to think that such precautions are superfluous, yet when we recollect the infirmities of old age, we must be satisfied that it is necessary not to deprive it of this counterpoise of factitious attractions. In the rapid descent of life, every support on which man can lean should be left untouched, and it is well that interest serve as a monitor to duty.

Ingratitude on the part of children and contempt for old age are not common vices in civilized society; but we must recollect that everywhere, more or less, the power of making a will exists. Are these vices most frequent where this power is most limited? We might decide the question by observing what passes in poor families, where there is but little to give in legacies; but even that method of judging would be deceptive, for the influence of this power, established in society by the laws, tends to form general manners, and general manners thus formed determine the sentiments of individuals. This power given to fathers renders the paternal authority more respectable, and those fathers whose indigence does not permit them to exercise it, unconsciously profit by the general habit of submission to which it has given rise.

But in making the father a magistrate we must take care not to make him a tyrant. If children have their faults he may have his, and though we give him the power of correction, it does not follow that he should have the right to punish by starvation. The institution called in France a *légitime*, by which each child is protected against a total disinheritance, is a convenient medium between domestic anarchy and paternal tyranny. Even this provision the father should have the power of taking away, for causes specified in the law and judicially proved.

There is still another question. In default of natural heirs, shall the proprietor have the right of leaving his property to whomsoever he chooses, either to distant relations or to strangers? In that case the fiscal resource spoken of in the preceding chapter will be greatly diminished, it will apply only to the case of intestates. Here the reasons of utility divide. We must endeavour to find some middle course.

It may be said that, in default of kin, the services of strangers are necessary to a man, and his attachment to them almost the same as to relations. He should have the means of cultivating the hopes and rewarding the care of a faithful servant, and of softening the regrets of a friend who has watched at his side, not to speak of the woman who, but for the omission of a ceremony, would be called his widow, and the orphans whom all the world but the legislator regard as his children.

Again, if to enrich the public treasury you deprive a man of the power of leaving his property to his friends, do you not force him to spend it all upon himself? If he has no control over his capital from the moment of his death, he will be tempted to convert his property into a life annuity. It is to encourage him to be a spendthrift, and almost to make a law against economy.

These reasons are, doubtless, more weighty than any consideration of gain to the public treasury. We ought to leave the proprietor who has no near relations the right of disposing of at least half his property by will, while the other half is reserved for the public; and to be contented with less would, perhaps, in this case, be a means of getting more. Besides, it is a matter of very great importance not to attack the principle which allows every one to dispose of his property after death; and not to create a class of proprietors who will regard themselves as inferior to others, on account of the legal incapacity attached to one-half of their fortune.

All that has been said of alienations between the living, applies also to testaments. On most of those points we shall be instructed by the conformity between contracts and testaments, and sometimes by contrast.

The same causes of nullity which apply to alienations between the living apply to testaments, except that in the place of *concealment* on the part of the receiver, it is necessary to substitute *erroneous supposition* on the part of the testator. For example, I leave a certain legacy to Titius, who is married to my daughter, believing that marriage to be lawful, and not knowing the bad faith of Titius, who, before marrying my daughter, had contracted another marriage, still subsisting.

Testaments are exposed to an unfortunate dilemma. Do we admit their validity when made upon a death-bed? The testator is exposed to coercion and to fraud. Do we exact formalities incompatible with this indulgence? We deprive the dying man of his power over the conduct of others, at the very moment when he needs it most. Barbarous heirs may torment him, in order to hasten or make sure of the advantage of a will executed in form. A dying man, who has no power to give or to take away, is no longer to be feared. A great many details will be necessary to reduce all these opposite dangers to their lowest amount.

CHAPTER V.

Rights to Services. Methods of acquiring them.

After *things*, *services* remain to be distributed, a kind of property sometimes confounded with things, and sometimes appearing under a distinct form.

There are as many kinds of services as there are ways in which man can be useful to man, either in procuring him some good, or preserving him from some evil.

In that exchange of services which constitute social intercourse some services are free, and others are compulsive. Those which are exacted by the laws constitute rights and obligations. If I have a *right* to the services of another, that other is in a state of *obligation* with respect to me; these two terms are correlative.

At first, all services were free. It was only by degrees that laws intervened to convert the more important into positive rights. It was thus that the institution of marriage changed into an obligation legally binding the hitherto voluntary connection between husband and wife, father and child. In the same way, the law, in certain states, has converted into an obligation the maintenance of the poor,—a duty which yet remains, among the greater part of nations, entirely voluntary. These *political* duties, compared to duties purely *social*, are like inclosures in a vast common, where a particular kind of cultivation is carried on with precautions which insure success. The same plant might grow on the common, and might even be protected by certain conventions; but it would always be exposed to more hazards than in the particular inclosure traced by the law, and protected by the public force.

Yet, whatever the legislator may do, there is a great number of services upon which he has no hold. It is not possible to order them, because it is not possible to define them, or because constraint would change their nature, and make them an evil. If it were attempted to enforce them by law, an apparatus of police and of penalties would be necessary, which would spread terror through society. Besides, the law could not act against the actual obstacles opposed to it; it could not put dormant powers into activity; it could not create that energy, that superabundance of zeal, which surmounts difficulties, and goes a thousand times further than commands.

The imperfection of law, in this respect, is corrected by a kind of supplementary law; that is, by the moral or social code—a code which is not written, which exists only in opinion, in manners, and in habits, and which begins where the legislative code finishes. The duties which it prescribes, the services which it imposes, under the names of equity, patriotism, courage, humanity, generosity, honour, and disinterestedness, do not directly borrow the aid of the laws, but derive their force from other sanctions, founded upon punishments and rewards. As the duties of this secondary code have not the imprint of the law, their fulfilment has more *éclat;* it is more meritorious; and a superior degree of honour attached to their performance happily makes up for their deficiency in positive force. After this digression upon morals, let us return to legislation.

The kind of service which is most important consists in giving up some good in favour of another.

The kind of good which plays the greatest part in civilized society is money,—a representative of value which is almost universal. It thus happens that the consideration of *services* is often confounded with that of *things*.

There are cases where the service is exacted for the benefit of him who commands; such is the state of a master in reference to his servant.

There are cases in which the service is exacted for the advantage of him who obeys; such is the condition of the ward in reference to his guardian.

These two correlative states are the foundation of all the others. The rights which belong to them are the elements of which all the others are composed. The father ought to be, in some respects, the guardian, in others the master of the child; the husband ought to be, in some respects, the guardian, in others the master of the wife. These states are capable of a constant and indefinite duration, and form domestic society. The rights which ought to be attached to them are discussed in subsequent chapters.

The public services of the magistrate and the citizen constitute other classes of obligations, of which the establishment belongs to the constitutional code.

But beside these constant relations, there are transient and occasional relations, in which the law may exact the services of one individual in favour of another.

The means of acquiring rights to services—that is, the causes which determine the legislator to create obligations—may be referred to three heads:—1st, *Superior need;* 2nd, *Anterior service;* 3rd, *Pact* or *Agreement.*

I. Superior Need.—That is, *a need of the service greater than the inconvenience of rendering it.*

Every individual has, as a constant occupation, the care of his own happiness—an occupation not less lawful than necessary; for suppose this principle could be reversed, and that the love of others should take an ascendancy over the love of self, what a ridiculous, what a fatal confusion would be the consequence! However, there are many occasions when we can make a considerable addition to the well-being of others by a slight and almost imperceptible sacrifice. In such circumstances, to do what depends upon us to prevent the evil about to fall upon another, is a service which the law may exact; and the omission of this service, in cases where the law might see fit to exact it, would form a sort of offence, which might be called *negative,* to distinguish it from *positive offences,* which consist in being the active and instrumental cause of evil.

But to make efforts, however slight, in the service of another, may be an evil; to be obliged to make such efforts certainly is one, for all restraint is evil. Therefore, to justify exacting from *you* a service in favour of *me*, the evil of not receiving the service ought to be so great, and the evil of rendering it so small, that there can be no room for hesitation as to the expediency of producing the one, for the sake of avoiding the other. There are no means of fixing precise limits; all must depend on the circumstances in which the individuals interested are placed, and we must leave to the judge the power of deciding upon individual cases as they occur.

The good Samaritan, by relieving the wounded traveller, saved his life. It was a noble action, a virtuous deed—nay, a moral duty. Can such actions be made a legal duty? Can we ordain them by a general law? No; not unless we limit that law by exceptions more or less vague. It would be very necessary to establish in such a law a dispensation in favour of the surgeon waited for by many wounded men in great need of his services—of the officer who hastens to his post to repel the enemy—of the father who is rushing to the succour of his child.

This principle of superior need is the foundation of many obligations. The duties required of a father to his children may be burdensome; but that evil is nothing when compared to the evil of the children being abandoned. The duty of defending the state may be more burdensome yet; but unless the state is defended, it cannot exist. If the taxes are not paid, the government is dissolved. If the public functions are not exercised, a career is opened to every disorder and to every crime.

The obligation of rendering the service ought to fall upon a particular individual, by reason of his peculiar position, which gives him, more than any other person, the power or the inclination to perform it. It is for this reason that in selecting guardians for orphan children, the choice falls upon relations or friends, to whom the duty must be less burdensome than to a stranger.

II. ANTERIOR SERVICE.—*A service rendered,—in consideration of which there is exacted from him who received the benefit a compensation, an equivalent in favour of him who conferred it.*

This case is more simple; it is only necessary to ascertain the value of a benefit already received, and to assign a compensation for it. The judge will not need so much latitude of discretion.

A surgeon has bestowed his services upon a sick man who had lost his senses, and who was not in a condition to ask for assistance. A depositary, though not requested to do so, has employed his labour, or has made pecuniary advances for the preservation of a deposit. A man has exposed himself in a fire to save valuable property, or to rescue persons in danger. The effects of a passenger have been thrown overboard to lighten the ship, and to preserve the rest of the cargo. In all these cases, and in a thousand others which might be cited, the laws ought to insure a recompense equivalent to the value of the service.

This title to indemnity is founded upon the best reasons. Grant it, and he by whom it is furnished will still be a gainer; refuse it, and you leave him who has done the service in a condition of loss.

Such a regulation is less for the benefit of him who receives the compensation, than for the benefit of those who need the service. It is a promise of indemnity made beforehand to every man who may have the power of rendering a burdensome service, in order that a prudent regard to his own personal interest may not come into opposition with his benevolence. Who can say how many evils might be prevented by such a precaution? In how many cases may not the duty of prudence restrain the wishes of benevolence? Is it not wise for the legislator, as far as possible, to reconcile these motives? It is said that ingratitude was punished at Athens as an infidelity injurious to the commerce of benefits. I do not propose to punish ingratitude; but as far as possible to prevent it. If the man to whom you have rendered a service is ungrateful,—no matter; the law does not count upon virtue; it assures you a compensation, and in important cases it will elevate that compensation to the level of reward.

Reward! that is the true means of obtaining services. In

comparison, punishment is but a feeble instrument. To punish an omission of service we must first be sure that the individual had the power to render it, and that he has no excuse for not having done so. All this requires a process of investigation, difficult and doubtful. Besides, if men act from the fear of punishment, nothing will be done except what is absolutely necessary to avoid it; but the hope of reward develops an unknown strength; it triumphs over real obstacles, and brings forth prodigies of zeal and ardour in cases where threats would produce only an unwilling submission.

Three precautions must be observed in arranging the interests of the two parties. First,—to prevent a hypocritical generosity from converting itself into tyranny, and exacting the price of a service which would not have been accepted had it not been supposed disinterested. Secondly,—not to authorize a mercenary zeal to snatch rewards for services which the person obliged might have rendered to himself, or have obtained elsewhere at a less cost. Thirdly,—not to suffer a man to be overwhelmed by a crowd of helpers, who cannot be fully indemnified without counterbalancing by an equivalent loss the whole advantage of the service.

Anterior service justifies many classes of obligations. On this is founded the right of fathers over their children. When in the order of nature the strength of ripening age has succeeded to the feebleness of infancy, the need of receiving ceases, and the duty of restitution begins. Upon this also is founded the right of the wife to the continuance of the union after the period when time has effaced the attractions which were its first motive.

Establishments at the public expense for those who have served the state rest upon the same principle,—reward for past services as a means of creating future ones.

III. PACT OR AGREEMENT.—*The intervention of a promise between two persons, with the understanding that a legal obligation attaches to it.*

Everything that has been said of *consent*, in relation to the distribution of property, applies to consent as respects the interchange of services. There are the same reasons for sanctioning this interchange of services as for sanctioning the interchange of property. Both rest on the same fundamental axiom, *that every alienation imports an advantage.* Bargains are not made except from the motive of utility.

The same reasons which annul consent in the one case, annul it in the other—Concealment; fraud; coercion; subornation; erroneous idea of legal obligation; erroneous idea of value; incapacity; pernicious tendency of the bargain, though without fault in the contracting parties.

We need not enlarge upon those subsequent causes which produce the dissolution of agreements:—1st, *Accomplishment;* 2nd, *Compensation;* 3rd, *Express or tacit remission;* 4th, *Lapse of time;* 5th, *Physical impossibility;* 6th, *Intervention of a superior inconvenience.* In all these cases, the reasons which caused the agreement to be sanctioned exist no longer; but the two latter relate only to the literal or specific accomplishment of the bargain, and may still leave room for compensation. If in a mutual bargain one of the parties only has fulfilled his part, or if his part be the more nearly performed, a compensation from the other will be necessary to re-establish the equilibrium.

It is enough to point out the principles without dwelling on the details. Particular arrangements must vary according to circumstances. However, if we establish firmly a small number of rules, these particular arrangements will not interfere with each other, and will all be arranged in the same spirit. These rules are so very simple that they need no development.

1st. Avoid producing disappointment.

2nd. When a portion of that evil is inevitable, diminish it as much as possible by dividing the loss among the parties interested in proportion to their means.

3rd. Take care in the distribution to throw the greater part of the loss upon him who, by attention, might have prevented the evil, so as to punish his negligence.

4th. Avoid especially producing an accidental evil greater than disappointment.

General Observation.—It is thus that the whole theory of obligations may be made to rest upon the basis of utility. We have built the whole of this vast edifice upon three principles—*superior need, anterior service, pact* or *agreement.* Who would have believed that to arrive at principles so simple and so familiar, it would have been necessary to open a new road? Consult those masters of the science, Grotius, Puffendorf, Burlamaque, Vatel, Montesquieu himself, Locke, Rousseau, and the crowd of commentators. When they wish to lay open the origin of obligations, they tell you of a natural right, of a law anterior to man, of the Divine law, of conscience, of a social contract, of a tacit contract, of a *quasi* contract, &c., &c. I know that these terms are not incompatible with the true principle, because all of them, by explanations more or less forced, may be made to signify good and evil. But this oblique and roundabout process involves uncertainty and embarrassment, and leads to interminable disputes.

They have not perceived that the pact, the contract of which they tell us, strictly speaking, is not a reason in itself; and that it wants a basis, an original and independent reason, on which to rest. The pact serves to prove the existence of a mutual advantage on the part of the contractors. It is this reason of utility which gives the contract all its force; thereby it is that the cases are distinguished in which a contract ought to be confirmed, as well as those in which it ought to be annulled. If a contract were a reason of itself, it ought always to have the same effect. If a pernicious tendency makes it void, it must be a useful tendency which makes it valid.

CHAPTER VI.

Community of Goods, or Tenancy in common. Its Inconveniences.

There is no arrangement more contrary to the principle of utility than community of goods; especially that kind of indeterminate community where the whole belongs to each of the partners.

1st. It is the source of never-ending discord. Instead of being a state of satisfaction and enjoyment for all interested, it is a state of discontent and disappointment.

2nd. This undivided property always loses a great part of its value for all the partners. Subject on the one hand to all kinds of depredations, because it is not under the protection of individual interest, on the other it receives no repairs or improvements. Shall I risk an expense of which the burden will be certain, and which will fall entirely upon me, while the benefit of it will be precarious and divided?

3rd. The apparent equality of this arrangement only serves to cover a real inequality. The strong abuse their strength with impunity; and the rich grow richer, at the expense of the poor. The community of goods calls to mind that sort of monster which is sometimes seen to exist,—beasts joined together back to back; in such cases, the stronger always carries off the weaker.

The question is not here of the community of goods between husband and wife. Called to live together, to cultivate their interests together, and to feel a mutual concern for the interests of their children, they ought to enjoy in common a fortune often acquired, and always kept by common cares. Besides, if their wills conflict, the dispute will not be lasting; the law confers upon the husband the right to decide.

Nor is the question here of common property among partners in trade. That tenancy in common is confined merely to acquisition; it has nothing to do with enjoyment. Now, as concerns acquisition, the partners have but one and the same interest. When the gains are to be enjoyed, they are divided, and each partner becomes independent of the others. Besides, associates in commerce are always few in number; they select each other, and separate at will. It is precisely the contrary with joint proprietors of land.

In England, one of the greatest and best established improvements is the division of commons. In passing through the lands which have undergone that happy change, we are enchanted as by the sight of a new colony. Harvests, flocks, smiling habitations, have succeeded to the dull sterility of a desert. Happy conquests of peaceful industry! Noble aggrandizement, which inspires no alarms, and provokes no enemies! But who would believe that in a country where agriculture is so highly estimated, millions of acres of productive land are still abandoned to the wild state of common tenancy? A short time since the government, desirous of knowing the true condition of its territory, caused an examination to be made in every county, which has brought to light a truth so interesting and so calculated to produce important consequences.*

The inconveniences of tenancy in common, except in accidental cases, do not apply to the case of *servitudes*,—that is, to rights of partial property exercised over immoveables, such as a right of passage, or a right to draw water. These rights are in general limited; the value lost by the subject property is not equal to the value acquired by the property to which the right attaches; or, in other terms, the inconvenience to the former is not so great as the conveniency to the latter.

In England, land which, being *freehold*, is worth thirty times the annual rent, being *copyhold*, is worth but two-thirds as much. The reason is, that in the latter case a lord of the manor possesses certain rights which establish a kind of common tenancy between him and the principal proprietor. But it is not to be supposed that what is lost by the copyholder is gained by the lord; for the greater part of it falls into the hands of agents and attorneys, and is consumed in useless formalities and minute vexations. These are the remnants of the feudal system.

"It is a fine spectacle," says Montesquieu, "that of the feudal laws,"—and afterwards he compares them to an ancient and

* There are circumstances which justify exceptions to general rules. The citizens of the small Swiss cantons, for example, possess the greater part of their lands, to wit, the High Alps, in common. It may be that this arrangement is the only one convenient for pasturages which are practicable only a part of the year. It may be, too, that this method of holding their lands forms the necessary basis of a constitution purely democratic, well adapted to the condition of a little community, shut up in an inclosure of mountains.

majestic oak. Let us rather compare them to that fatal tree whose sap is poisonous, and whose shade is destructive. That unfortunate system has produced in modern laws a confusion and complexity from which it is very difficult to deliver them; for being everywhere interlaced with property, it needs much management to get rid of feudal absurdities, without shaking the security of property itself.

CHAPTER VII.

Distribution of Loss.

THINGS make one branch of the objects of acquisition; *services* the other. After having treated of the different methods of acquiring and alienating these two objects, the analogy between gain and loss would seem to indicate, as the next point of inquiry, the different methods of distributing the losses to which possessions are exposed.

This task will not detain us long. Has a thing been destroyed, damaged, or lost? If the proprietor is known, the loss falls upon him; if he is not known, it falls upon nobody. It is, in fact, no loss. The question whether the loss shall be transferred to some other person than the proprietor,—that is, whether in any case a *satisfaction* shall be allowed him,—is a matter which will be discussed in that part of this work which treats of the Penal Code. I shall confine myself here to a single example, which will serve to indicate principles.

When the seller and buyer of an article of merchandise are at a distance apart, the article must pass through a greater or less number of intermediate hands. This transport is by land, by sea, or by internal navigation; the merchandise may be destroyed, damaged, or lost; perhaps it does not arrive at its destination, or it does not come there in the state in which it ought to be. Upon whom shall the loss fall—the buyer or the seller? I say the seller, reserving his claim against the intermediate agents. The seller, by care, may contribute to the safety of the merchandise;

he can choose the moment and the manner of sending it, and take the precautions on which, in case of loss, the acquisition of evidence depends. All this would be easier to a merchant, who makes a business of selling, than to an individual who buys. It is only by accident that the care of such a buyer can contribute in any way to the safe arrival of the goods. The *reason* of this decision is a superior preventive power; it is founded upon the *principle* of security.

Particular situations may show the necessity of establishing exceptions to this general rule. For a yet stronger reason, individuals may except themselves from it by agreements made between themselves. I only indicate principles. This is not the place for their application.

PART THIRD.

RIGHTS AND OBLIGATIONS ATTACHED TO SEVERAL PRIVATE CONDITIONS.

INTRODUCTION.

WE now proceed to consider more in detail the rights and obligations which the law ought to attach to the different states which compose the domestic or private condition. These states may be resolved into four: those of master and servant; guardian and ward; father and child; husband and wife.

If we followed the historical or natural order of these relations, the last in the catalogue would become the first. But, to avoid repetitions, it is better to begin with the simplest. The rights and obligations of a father and a husband are composed of the rights and obligations of a master and a guardian; the two former states are the elements of the two latter.

CHAPTER I.

Master and Servant.

ASIDE from the question of slavery, there is not much to be said as to the condition of *master*, and the correlative conditions created by the different kinds of *servants*. All these conditions are a matter of contract. It belongs to the parties interested to arrange them according to their own convenience.

The condition of *master,* to which the condition of apprentice corresponds, is a mixed condition. The master of an apprentice is at the same time a master and a guardian: a guardian as respects the art he teaches, a master as regards the profit he derives.

The work which the apprentice does, after the value of his labour is worth more than the expense of maintenance and instruction, is the salary or reward of the master for his anterior expenses.

This compensation ought naturally to be greater or less according to the difficulty of the art. Some arts may be learned in seven days; it is possible that some others may require seven years. Competition will best regulate the price of these mutual services, as of all other objects of commerce; and here, as elsewhere, industry should find its just reward.

But the greater part of governments have not adopted this system of liberty. They have desired to introduce what they call order into employments; that is, out of a mere passion for regulating, they have substituted an artificial for a natural arrangement. Intermeddling in this way with a business which they do not understand, they have been led by a false notion of uniformity to apply the same rule to things which have no resemblance. Thus the ministers of Elizabeth fixed the same term of seven years as the period of apprenticeship for the simplest as well as for the most difficult arts.

This mania for regulation conceals itself under the pretence of a desire to perfect the arts, to prevent workmen from being unskilful, or to guard the credit and honour of the national manufactures. But there is a simple and natural means of accomplishing these objects. It is, to leave everybody a perfect liberty of choosing the good and rejecting the bad, of being governed in their preferences by merit; and to excite the emulation of artists by the freedom of competition. But no; the public must be supposed incapable of judging, and the work must be regarded as good if the workman has wrought at the trade a certain number of years.

An artist must not be asked if he understands his business, but whether he has served a regular apprenticeship. For, if the work is to be judged by its merits, we may as well allow every one to work at his own risk. According to that system, some would be masters who had never been apprentices, and others would be apprentices all their lives.

CHAPTER II.

Of Slavery.

When servitude becomes a condition, and when the obligation to continue in that condition, with respect to a certain master, or to others who may derive a title from him, embraces the entire life of the servant, that condition is *slavery*.

Slavery is susceptible of many modifications, according to the fixed amount, more or less exact, of the services which may be demanded, and according to the coercive means, the use of which is permitted. There was a great difference in the state of a slave at Athens and at Lacedæmon; there is more yet between that of a Russian serf and a negro in the colonies. But whatever may be the limits or the means of authority, if the obligation of serving is unlimited in point of time, I still call it *slavery*. To draw a line of separation between servitude and liberty, we must start from some point; and that above assumed seems to be the most salient and the easiest to fix.

This distinction drawn from *perpetuity* is so much the more essential, because, wherever such perpetuity is found, it weakens, it enervates, it renders extremely precarious the wisest precautions for mitigating the exercise of authority. A power, not limited as regards time, can hardly be limited as regards anything else. If we consider, on the one side, the facility with which the master may aggravate the yoke, little by little, how he can exact with rigour the services that are due, extend his pretensions under different pretexts, and spy out occasions to torment an insolent servant, who dares refuse to render services which he does not owe; if we consider, on the other side, how difficult it is for slaves to demand or to obtain legal protection, how much more vexatious their domestic situation becomes after a public breach with their master, and how they will be driven to captivate him by an unlimited submission, rather than to irritate him by refusals,—we shall soon see that the project of limiting slavery by law is much easier to form than to execute; that a fixed amount of services is a very feeble means of softening the lot of slavery; that under the best laws for that purpose only the most crying infractions will be punished, while the ordinary course of domestic rigours will outbrave every tribunal. I do not say that on this account slaves ought to be abandoned to the absolute power of a master, and that the protection of laws should not be extended to them, because that protection is insufficient. But it is necessary to show the evil inherent in the very nature of the thing; to wit, the impossibility of submitting to a legal restraint the authority of a master over his slaves, so as to prevent him, if so disposed, from abusing his power.

That slavery is agreeable to the masters, does not admit of a doubt; since nothing is wanting but will on their part to bring it to an instant termination. That it is disagreeable to the slaves, is a fact not less certain, since they are never kept in that condition but by constraint. No one who is free wishes to become a slave, and there is no slave who does not wish to be free.

It is absurd to reason on the happiness of men, except from their own desires, and their own sensations. It is absurd to attempt showing, by calculations, that a man ought to be happy, when he is actually miserable; and that a condition into which no one wishes to enter, and from which everybody wishes to escape, is a condition good in itself, and adapted to human nature. I can well believe that the difference between liberty and servitude is not so great as it appears to ardent and prejudiced minds. The habit of evil, and, for a stronger reason, the ignorance of anything better, take away much of the interval which separates two conditions, at the first glance, so opposite. But these reasonings of probability upon the happiness of slaves are quite superfluous, since we have complete proof that this condition is never embraced by choice, and that, on the contrary, it is always an object of aversion.

Slavery has been compared to the condition of a schoolboy prolonged through life; and it is added, that a great many people think the time passed at school the happiest part of their existence.

The parallel is just only in one point. The circumstance which is common to these two states is subjection; but subjection is very far from being the circumstance which makes the happiness of a schoolboy. What makes him happy is, a freshness of mind which gives to all impressions the charm of novelty, lively and boisterous pleasures with companions of the same age, contrasted with the solitude and seriousness of the paternal dwelling. And after all, how many schoolboys are there who are not anxious to see their pupilage ended? Which of them desires to be a schoolboy for life?

Be this as it may, if slavery were established in such a proportion that there was one slave for one master, possibly I might hesitate before pronouncing upon the balance between the advantage of the one and the disadvantage of the other. It might be possible, all things considered, that the sum of good in this arrangement would be almost equal to the sum of evil. But things cannot be so arranged. Where slavery is once established, it presently becomes the lot of the greater number. A master counts his slaves, like his flocks, by hundreds, thousands, tens of thousands. The advantages are on the side of one, the disadvantages on the side of a multitude. Though the evil of servitude were not great in itself, the extent of that evil would be sufficient to render it very considerable. Generally speaking, and aside from every other consideration, there is no room at all for hesitating between the loss which emancipation would bring upon the masters, and the gain which it would confer upon the slaves.

Another very strong argument against slavery is drawn from its influence upon the wealth and power of nations. A freeman produces more than a slave. If the slaves of a master were set at liberty, that master would, doubtless, lose a part of his property; but the slaves taken together would not only possess all that he loses, but more too. Now happiness necessarily increases with abundance; and the public power increases in the same proportion.

Two circumstances combine to diminish the produce of slaves: the absence of the stimulus of reward, and the insecurity of their condition.

It is easy to see that the fear of chastisement is not well adapted to extract from a labourer all the industry of which he is capable, all the values he can furnish. Fear rather leads him to conceal his power than to show it; rather to sink beneath his true level than to rise above it.

He will bring a punishment upon himself by works of supererogation; by displaying his ability he will only cause the standard of his ordinary duty to be raised. Not only the slave produces less; he consumes more,—not in the way of enjoyment, but by waste, pillage, and bad economy. What does he care for interests not his own? All the labour he can save himself is a pure gain; what he suffers to perish is a loss only to his master. Why should he invent new means to do more, or to do better? To improve, one must think; and thinking is a trouble not taken without a motive. The man who is sunk into a mere labouring animal never rises above a blind routine; and generations succeed each other without any progress.

It is true that a master who understands his own interest will not dispute with his slaves the little profits which their industry may occasionally procure. He knows their prosperity to be his own, and that to offer them the inducement of an immediate reward is the surest way to animate them to labour. But this precarious favour, dependent upon the uncertain disposition of a master, does not inspire that confidence which carries one's views to the future, which shows in daily economy the foundation of future wealth, and which extends the care of fortune to posterity. Slaves clearly perceive that, if richer, they would be exposed to extortion, if not upon the part of their master, at least from overseers and other subalterns in authority, more greedy and more to be dreaded than the master himself. For the greater part of slaves there is no to-morrow. Joys instantly to be realized alone have power to tempt them. They are gluttonous, idle, dissolute, without reckoning the other vices which spring from their condition. Those who have any foresight hide their little treasures. The sad feeling of insecurity, inseparable from their condition, nourishes all the faults destructive of industry, and all the habits most fatal to society, and that too without compensation and without remedy. This is not an empty theory. It is an actual result, at all times, in all places.

But we are told that, in respect to labour, the free day labourer in Europe is nearly upon the same footing with the slave. He who is paid by the piece has recompense as a motive, and every effort has its reward; but he who is paid by the day has no motive but pain,—let him do much or little, he receives the price of a day's work ; so that, in fact, there is no reward for exertion. If he does less than ordinary workmen he may be dismissed from his employment, as a slave, in the like case, would be beaten. Both are excited only by fear, and have no interest in the produce of their labour.

To this reasoning there are three replies :—

1st. It is not true that the day labourer has not the motive of reward. The more skilful and the more industrious are better paid than others. Those who distinguish themselves are more constantly employed, and always have the choice of the most lucrative engagements. This is a real reward attendant upon their exertions.

2nd. If the only motives of the free workmen were, in fact, of the penal kind, still we should have more hold on him than on a slave. The free workman has his honour like the rest of us. In a free country there is a shame attached to the reputation of being idle and incapable; in this respect, the eyes of his comrades are an addition to those of his employer, and this punishment of honour is inflicted upon an infinity of occasions, by judges who have no interest to soften it. Free labourers exercise in this way a reciprocal inspection, and are sustained by emulation. This motive has much less force upon a slave. The treatment to which slaves are subjected renders them little sensible to a pain so delicate as that of honour; and as the injustice of labouring without compensation, for the sole benefit of another, cannot escape them, slaves are not ashamed to avow to each other a repugnance to labour, in which they all agree.

3rd. That which presents itself to a day labourer as a gain, is a sure gain; all that he can acquire belongs to himself, and nobody has any right to touch it; but, as we have seen above, a slave cannot enjoy any real security. Exceptions to this remark may be cited. Such a Russian lord, for example, has industrious slaves who possess many thousand roubles, and who enjoy their property in the same way as their master enjoys his. But these are particular cases which do not change the ordinary rule. Such particular and unusual incidents are of no importance in judging of the ordinary effects of a general arrangement.

In this short exposition of the inconveniences of servitude there has been no attempt to move the feelings, no appeal to the imagination, no endeavour to cast odium upon masters by generalizing particular abuses of power. There has been an omission of all reference to those terrible means of rigour and constraint, common in these domestic governments without law, without procedure, without appeal, without publicity, and almost without restraint; for, as we have already seen, the master is never responsible, except in extraordinary cases. Everything which touches the feelings is easily accused of exaggeration; and in this case the evidence of simple reason is so strong, that it needs no suspicious colouring. The owners of slaves, whom personal interest has not divested of common sense and of common humanity, will readily assent to the advantages of liberty over servitude, and would themselves desire that slavery were abolished, if that abolition could take place without overturning their rank and fortunes, and without any shock to their personal security. The injustice and the calamities which have accompanied precipitate attempts, form the greatest objection to projects of emancipation.

This operation could not take place suddenly, except by a violent revolution, which, by displacing all men, by destroying all property, by putting all persons into situations to which they had not been educated, would produce evils a thousand times greater than all the immediate good which could be expected from it.*

Instead of rendering emancipation burdensome to the master, it ought, as far as possible, to be rendered advantageous to him; and the first means which naturally offers itself to this end, is to fix a price at which every slave shall have the right to purchase his freedom. Unfortunately, there is a strong objection to this means. From the moment of its adoption, the interest of the master is in opposition to that of his slaves. He will attempt to prevent them from acquiring the sum necessary to their ransom, To leave them in ignorance and to keep them in poverty, to cut their wings as fast as they grow—such will be his policy. But this danger arises only from fixing the price. The liberty of redeeming themselves at such prices as may be agreed upon has no inconvenience. The interest of the slave would induce him to do his best, in order that he might have a greater price to offer. The interest of the master would induce him to suffer the slave to grow rich as fast as possible, in order to draw from him a heavier ransom.

A second means consists in limiting the power to dispose of slaves by will, so that where there is no successor in the direct line, emancipation shall be a right. The hope of inheritance is always very feeble in distant successors, and no such hope would exist after the law was once known. There could be no injustice where there was no disappointment.

We might go a little further. At each change of the proprietorship, even in successions the nearest, a small sacrifice of pro-

* Recent experience in the West Indies seems to contradict this theory; so does the case of the Polish lordships, cited in the last paragraph of the chapter.—*Translator.*

perty might be made to liberty, by the liberation, for example, of a tenth part of the slaves. Such a loss would not present itself to the heir as of any determinate amount. The defalcation of a tenth part of the inheritance would scarcely be perceptible. At the moment of succeeding to the estate it would be less a loss than a slight privation of gain. As respects nephews, who have an additional hope of succession on the side of their fathers, the tax in favour of liberty might be still greater.

This offering to liberty ought to be determined by lot. Choice, under pretext of selecting the most worthy, would be a source of intrigues and abuse. It would be more fruitful in discontent and jealousy than in happiness. The lot is impartial; it gives to all an equal chance of happiness; even those whom it does not favour it allows to participate in the charm of hope, and the fear of being deprived of this chance for certain specified offences would be an additional pledge for the fidelity of the slaves.*

The emancipation ought to take place by families rather than individually. A father enslaved, and a son free; a father free, and a son enslaved; what a disagreeable,—what a shocking contrast! what a source of domestic chagrin!

There might be other means of accelerating an object so desirable; but they can only be discovered by studying the particular circumstances of each country.

These bonds of slavery, which the legislator cannot cut at a single blow, time dissolves little by little; and the march of liberty, though slow, is not the less sure. The whole progress of the human mind, of civilization, of morals, of public wealth, and of commerce, brings on, little by little, the restoration of individual

* This means might tempt the slaves to employ murder to accelerate their liberty—a very serious objection to this lottery. We may observe, however, that its uncertainty would lessen the danger. There would be less temptation to commit a crime, the fruits of which might go entirely to others. But the temptation may be wholly got rid of, if it were provided that this partial emancipation should not apply to cases where the master was poisoned or assassinated, either by his slaves or by some one unknown. In this way, this means of liberation would become a safeguard to the master.

liberty. England and France have been what Russia, Poland, and a part of Germany now are.

Proprietors ought not to be alarmed at this change. Those who own the land have a natural power over those who can live only by their labour. The apprehension that freemen, at liberty to go where they choose, would abandon their native soil, and leave the earth uncultivated, is a fear absolutely chimerical, especially when the emancipation goes on gradually. Because it is seen that the slave runs aways when he can, it is concluded that, were he free, still he would run away. The opposite conclusion would be much more just. The motive for flight exists no longer, and the motives for remaining retain all their force.

We have seen in Poland some proprietors, enlightened as to their true interest, or animated by a love of glory, carry into effect, throughout vast lordships, a total and simultaneous emancipation. Did this generosity ruin them? Just the contrary: the farmer, having an interest in his own labour, has soon put himself into a condition to pay more than the slave; and the domains cultivated by the hands of freemen receive every year an addition to their value.

CHAPTER III.

Guardian and Ward.

The feebleness of infancy demands a continual protection. Everything must be done for an imperfect being, which, as yet, does nothing for itself. The complete development of its physical powers takes many years; that of its intellectual faculties is still slower. At a certain age it has already strength and passions, without experience enough to regulate them. Too sensitive to present impulses, too negligent of the future, such a being must be kept under an authority more immediate than that of the laws; it must be governed by punishments and rewards, which act, not at distant intervals, but continually, and which can adapt themselves to all the details of conduct during the process of education.

In order that a condition of life, or a profession, may be chosen for a child, he must of necessity be submitted to a particular authority. This choice is founded upon personal circumstances; upon the expectations, the talents, the inclinations of the pupil; upon his facility for adopting one business rather than another; in one word, upon probabilities of success. It is a question too complicated to be left to the decision of a public magistrate; it must be determined specially for every case; and such a determination would demand a knowledge of details, which the magistrate could not possess.

This power of protection and of government, over individuals thought incapable to protect and to govern themselves, constitutes *wardship*,—a kind of domestic magistracy, founded upon the manifest need of those who are submitted to it, and which ought to include all the powers necessary to the fulfilment of its object, and nothing more.

The powers necessary to education are those of determining the ward's method of life, and of fixing his domicile, with those means of reprimand and of correction, without which this authority would not be efficacious. The severity of these means may be the more easily limited, inasmuch as their application is more immediate, more certain, and more varied, and because domestic government possesses an inexhaustible fund of rewards; for at an age when nothing is acquired and everything is bestowed, there is no concession which may not take the form of remuneration.

As to the subsistence of the ward, it can be derived from three sources only: either from property he possesses in his own right, from a gratuitous gift, or from his own labour.

If the ward has property of his own, it is administered in his name and for his advantage by the guardian; and all that the guardian does in that particular, according to the prescribed forms, is ratified by the law.

If the ward have no property, he is supported either at the expense of the guardian—as in the case most common of all, when the wardship is exercised by the father or mother of the child;

or at the expense of some charitable establishment; or finally, by his own labour, as when, for example, he is bound an apprentice in such a way that the period of non-value shall be made up to his master by the profitable labour of a subsequent period.

Wardship being a charge purely burdensome, it is made to fall upon those persons who have the greatest inclination to sustain it, and the greatest facility for doing so. This is eminently the case with the father and mother. Natural affection disposes them to this duty more strongly than the law; yet the law which imposes it upon them is not useless. It is because instances occur in which children are abandoned by their parents, that this abandonment has been made an offence.

If the father, when dying, names a guardian for his child, it is to be presumed that he knew better than any one else who had the means and the inclination thus to supply his place. His choice therefore should be confirmed, unless there are very strong reasons to the contrary.

If the father has made no provision for the wardship, the obligation ought to fall upon some relation whose interest would induce him to preserve the family property, and whose honour and affection would be a security for the happiness and education of the child. In default of relatives, some friend of the orphan should be chosen who would voluntarily undertake the office, or some public officer appointed for that special purpose.

Some attention should be paid to those circumstances which ought to release particular individuals from the duty of wardship, such as advanced age, a numerous family, infirmities, or reasons of prudence and delicacy—such, for example, as a complication of interests.

Particular precautions against the abuse of this power are to be found among the penal laws. An abuse of authority as respects the person of the child belongs to the class of personal injuries; illicit gains at the expense of the ward's fortune fall into the class of fraudulent acquisitions. The only thing to be considered is the particular *circumstance* of the offence, namely, *the violation of confidence*. But though this renders the offence more odious, it is not always a reason for augmenting the punishment; on the contrary, as we shall see elsewhere, it is often a reason for diminishing it; the position of the delinquent being such that the discovery of the offence is easier, the reparation easier, and the alarm not so great. In the case of seduction, the character of guardian is an aggravation of the crime.

As regards general precautions, the wardship has often been divided; the administration of the property has been given to the nearest heir, who in quality of heir had the greatest interest in its good management; and the care of the person to some other relative more interested in the welfare of the child.

Some legislators have taken further precautions, such as forbidding guardians to buy the goods of their wards; or permitting wards to re-assume property sold by their guardians within so many years after their majority. The first of these two means does not appear liable to great inconveniences; the second cannot but affect the interest of the ward; for it diminishes the price of his property, in the same proportion that its value is diminished in the hands of the purchaser, on account of the precariousness of his possession,—a precariousness which prevents him from making any improvements; for in the end they might turn to his disadvantage by furnishing the former owner an additional motive to reclaim the possession. These two means appear useless if the sale of the property is required to be public, and under the inspection of a magistrate.

The most simple means of protection is to allow anybody to act as the friend of the ward in legal processes against his guardian, whether for mismanagement of the property, for negligence, or for violence. The law thus puts those who are too feeble to protect themselves under the protection of every man generous enough to undertake the charge.

Wardship being a state of dependence, is an evil which ought to cease as soon as there is no danger that its cessation will produce a greater evil. But what should be the age of emancipation? As to that matter, we must be guided by general presumptions. The English law, which has fixed upon the age of twenty-one years, seems much more reasonable than the Roman law, which has appointed the age of twenty-five for that purpose, and which has been followed throughout almost the whole of Europe. At twenty-one the faculties of man are developed; he has a perception of his strength; he yields to counsel what he refuses to authority; and can no longer bear to be kept in leading-strings. So strong is this feeling, that the prolongation of the domestic power often produces a state of irritation and ill-nature equally uncomfortable for all concerned. But there are individuals who seem incapable of arriving at maturity, or who are much slower than others in reaching it. Cases of that nature may be easily provided for by prolonging the guardianship whenever occasion for it occurs.

CHAPTER IV.

Father and Child.

It has been already mentioned that a father is, in some respects, the master, in others the guardian of the child.

In his character of master, he will have the right to impose services upon his children, and to employ their labour for his own advantage, till the age at which the law establishes their independence. This right given to the father is an indemnity for the pains and expenses of the children's education. It is well that the father should have an interest and a pleasure in the education of his children. The advantage which he finds in bringing them up is a good thing for both parties. In his quality of guardian he has all the rights and all the obligations which have been mentioned under that title.

Under the first relation the advantage of the father is considered; under the second, that of the child. These two relations are easily reconciled in the person of the father, on account of his natural affection, which leads him much rather to make sacrifices on account of his children, than to avail himself of his rights for his own advantage.

It would seem, at the first glance, that the legislator need not interfere between fathers and children; that he might trust to the tenderness of the parent and the gratitude of the child. But this superficial view would be deceptive. It is absolutely necessary, on one side, to limit the paternal power, and, on the other, to maintain filial respect by legal enactments.

As a general rule, we ought to confer no power by the exercise of which the child would lose more than the father would gain.

This rule has not been followed in Prussia, where, in imitation of the Romans, there has been given to the father the right to prevent his son from marrying without any limitation of age.

As respects the paternal authority, political writers have fallen into opposite excesses. Some have wished to make it despotic, as among the Romans; others have wished to annihilate it. Some philosophers have thought that children should not be delivered up to the caprice and ignorance of parents, but that the state ought to raise them in common; and they cite, in support of this scheme, Sparta, Crete, and the ancient Persians. It is not recollected that this education never existed, except for a small class of citizens; for in those states the mass of the population was composed of slaves.

In this artificial arrangement there would be the difficulty of dividing the expense, and of enabling the parents to support the burden of education without deriving any advantage from it;—a burden which would weigh the heavier upon parents little influenced by motives of tenderness for children who had become almost strangers to them. What would be a still greater inconvenience,—these children would not be seasonably formed for that diversity of pursuits which they would be called to follow. The choice of a business depends upon so many circumstances, that it belongs only to parents to fix upon it; no one else can so well judge, either what is proper for the children, what they expect, or for what their talents and inclinations are adapted. Besides, this system, which counts for nothing the reciprocal affection of fathers and children, would have a most fatal effect in destroying the family spirit, in weakening the conjugal union, in depriving fathers and mothers of the pleasure which they derive from seeing a new generation growing up around them. Would they feel the same zeal for the future happiness of children who would no longer be theirs? Would they cherish an affection which they had no hope would ever be returned? Would industry, no longer animated by the spur of paternal love, have the same ardour? Would not domestic enjoyments take a turn less advantageous to general prosperity?

As a last reason, I shall add, that the natural arrangement, which leaves the choice, the mode, and the burden of education to the parents, may be compared to a series of experiments for perfecting the general system. Everything is advanced and developed by the emulation of individuals, and by differences of ideas and of genius; in a word, by the variety of particular impulses. But let the whole be cast into a single mould; let instruction everywhere take the form of legal authority; errors will be perpetuated, and there will be no further progress. This perhaps is saying too much in relation to an idea so chimerical; but this notion of Plato's has seduced, in our day, some celebrated authors; and an error which has misled Rousseau and Helvetius will be likely to find other defenders.

CHAPTER V.

Of Marriage.

Inde casas postquam, ac pelles, ignemque pararunt,
Et mulier conjuncta viro, concessit in unum,
Castaque privatæ veneris connubia leata,
Cognita sunt, prolemque ex se videre creatam,
Tunc genus humanum primum molescere cœpit.

LUCRETIUS, v. 1109.

When huts, and skins, and fire they had prepared,
And woman joined to man, became as one,
And chaste connubial joys of private love
Were known, and offspring from themselves they saw,
Then first the human race began to soften.

UNDER whatever point of view the institution of marriage is considered, nothing can be more striking than the utility of that noble contract, the tie of society, and the basis of civilization.

Marriage, considered as a contract, has drawn woman from the severest and most humiliating servitude; it has distributed the mass of the community into distinct families; it has created a domestic magistracy; it has formed citizens; it has extended the views of men to the future, through affection for the rising generation; it has multiplied social sympathies. To perceive all its benefits, it is only necessary to imagine for a moment what men would be without that institution.

The questions relating to this contract may be reduced to seven. 1st. Between what persons shall it be permitted? 2nd. What shall be its duration? 3rd. What its conditions? 4th. At what age may it be contracted? 5th. At whose choice? 6th. Between how many persons? 7th. With what formalities?

Section I.

Between what Persons shall Marriage be permitted?

If we are guided upon this question by historical facts, we shall encounter great embarrassment, or rather, it will be impossible to deduce any single fixed rule from so many contradictory usages. There will not be wanting respectable examples, to authorize unions which we regard as most criminal, nor for prohibiting many which we esteem quite innocent. Every people pretend to follow in this respect what they call the law of nature; and they look with a sort of horror upon everything not conformed to the matrimonial laws of their own country. Let us suppose ourselves ignorant of all these local institutions; let us consult only the principle of utility, for the purpose of discovering among what persons it is fit to allow, or to prohibit, this union.

If we examine the interior of a family, composed of persons who differ among themselves in age, sex, and relative duties, there will be immediately presented to our minds strong reasons for prohibiting certain alliances among several individuals of it.

There is a reason which weighs directly even against the connection of marriage. A father, a grandfather, or an uncle holding the place of a father, might abuse their power by compelling a young girl to contract an alliance with them which would be odious to her. The more necessary the authority of these relatives is, the less temptation should they have to abuse it.

This inconvenience, however, extends but to a small number of the cases called incestuous, and is not the weightiest. It is the danger of dissolute manners, that is, the evil which would result from a transient commerce without marriage, that affords the true reasons for proscribing certain alliances.

If there were not an insurmountable barrier between near relatives called to live together in the greatest intimacy, this contact, continual opportunities, friendship itself and its innocent caresses, might kindle fatal passions. The family—that retreat where repose ought to be found in the bosom of order, and where the movements of the soul, agitated by the scenes of the world, ought to grow calm—would itself become a prey to all the inquietudes of rivalry and to all the furies of passion. Suspicions would banish confidence—the tenderest sentiments of the heart would be quenched—eternal enmities or vengeance, of which the bare idea is fearful, would take their place. The belief in the chastity of young girls, that powerful attraction to marriage, would have no foundation to rest upon; and the most dangerous snares would be spread for youth in the very asylum where it could least escape them.

These inconveniences may be arranged under four heads:—

1st. *Evil of Rivalry.*—The danger resulting from a real or suspected rivalry between a married person and certain relatives or connections.

2nd. *Prevention of Marriage.*—The danger of depriving girls of the chance of forming a permanent and advantageous establishment in the way of marriage, by diminishing the confidence of those who might desire to marry them.

3rd. *Relaxation of Domestic Discipline.*—The danger of inverting the nature of the relations between those who ought to command and those who ought to obey; or, at least, of weakening that tutelary authority which, for the interest of minors, ought to be exercised over them by the heads of the family or those who hold their place.

4th. *Physical Injury.*—Those dangers to the health and strength which might result from premature indulgences.

Table of Prohibited Alliances.

A man shall not marry,—

1. The wife or widow of his father, or of any other progenitor. *Inconveniences* 1, 3, 4.
2. Any descendant. *Inconveniences* 2, 3, 4.
3. His aunt. *Inconveniences* 2, 3, 4.
4. The wife or widow of his uncle. *Inconveniences* 1, 3, 4.
5. His niece. *Inconveniences* 2, 3, 4.
6. His sister. *Inconveniences* 2, 4.
7. Any descendant of his wife. *Inconveniences* 1, 2, 3, 4.
8. His wife's mother. *Inconvenience* 1.
9. The wife or widow of any descendant. *Inconvenience* 1.
10. The daughter of his father's wife by a former husband, or of his mother's husband by a former wife. *Inconveniences* 2, 4.

In a code of laws there would be necessary a corresponding table of alliances forbidden to the woman: here it would be a useless repetition.

Shall a man be allowed to marry the sister of his deceased wife?

There are reasons for and against it. The reason against it is the danger of rivalry between the sisters; the reason for it is the advantage of the children. If their mother dies, what an advantage to them to have their own aunt for a stepmother! What more likely to diminish the natural hostility of that connection than so near a relationship? This last reason seems to be the weightier; but to obviate the danger of rivalry, the wife ought to have the legal power of forbidding the house to her sister. If the wife does not choose to have her own sister in the house, what lawful motive can the husband have for desiring it?

Shall a man be allowed to marry his brother's widow? There

are reasons for and against it, as before. The reason against it is still the danger of rivalry; the reason for it is likewise the advantage of the children. But both these reasons seem to have very little weight.

My brother has no more authority over my wife than a stranger, and cannot see her but with my permission. The danger of rivalry on his part seems as small as on that of any other person. The reason *against* is reduced almost to nothing. On the other hand, children have little to fear from a father-in-law. If a stepmother is not the enemy of the children-in-law, it is very remarkable; but a stepfather is commonly their friend, their second guardian. The differences in the condition of the two sexes, the legal subjection of the one, the legal empire of the other, expose them to opposite weaknesses, which produce opposite effects. The uncle is already the natural friend of his nephews and his nieces. They have nothing to gain in that respect by his becoming the husband of their mother. If they find an enemy in a stepfather who is a stranger, the protection of their uncle is always a resource. If they find a friend in such a stepfather, they have acquired an additional protector, whom they would not have had if their uncle had married their mother. The reasons for and the reasons against having little force on either side, it would seem that the good of liberty ought to incline the balance in favour of permitting such marriages.

Instead of the reasons which I have given for prohibiting alliances within a certain degree of relationship, ordinary morals decide peremptorily upon all these points of legislation, without taking the trouble to examine any of them. "Nature," it is said, "is repugnant to such alliances; therefore they are forbidden."

This argument alone never can furnish a satisfactory reason for prohibiting any action whatever. If the repugnance be real the law is useless. Why forbid what nobody wishes to do? If, in fact, there be no repugnance, the reason is at an end; vulgar morality would have nothing more to say in favour of prohibiting the acts in question, since its whole argument, founded upon natural disgust, is overturned by the contrary supposition. If everything is to be referred to nature—that is, the bent of desire, we must equally conform to her decisions, whatever they may be. If those alliances must be forbidden to which she is repugnant, those with which she is pleased must be permitted. Nature which hates, merits no more regard than nature which loves and desires.

It is very rare that the passion of love is developed within the circle of individuals to whom marriage ought to be forbidden. There needs to give birth to that sentiment a certain degree of surprise, a sudden effect of novelty. It is this which the poets have happily expressed by the ingenious allegory of the arrows, quiver, and blinded eyes of Love. Individuals accustomed to see each other and to know each other, from an age which is neither capable of conceiving the desire nor of inspiring it, will see each other with the same eyes to the end of life; and this inclination finds no determinate epoch whence to begin. Their affections have taken another course, like a river which has dug its bed, and which does not change it.

Nature, then, agrees sufficiently well with the principle of utility. However, it will not do to trust to nature alone. There are circumstances in which the inclination may spring up, and in which an alliance will become an object of desire if it is not prohibited by the laws, and branded by public opinion.

Under the Greek dynasty of Egyptian sovereigns, the heir of the throne commonly married one of his own sisters. It was, apparently, to escape the danger of an alliance either with a subject or a foreign family. In that rank, such marriages might be exempt from the inconveniences that would attend them in private life. Royal opulence would admit a separation and a seclusion, which could not be maintained in the dwelling of a citizen.

Policy has produced some similar examples in modern times. In our day the kingdom of Portugal has introduced a practice not far distant from that of Egypt; a reigning queen has had a nephew and a subject for her husband. But to escape the blot of incest, kings and the great can address themselves to an experienced chemist, who changes at his pleasure the colour of certain actions. Protestants, to whom this laboratory is closed, have no power to marry their aunts. The Lutherans, however, have given the example of a similar extension of privileges.

The inconvenience of these alliances is not for the persons who contract them. The evil is wholly in the example. A permission granted to some makes others feel the prohibition as a tyranny. When the yoke is not the same for all, it weighs the heavier upon those who wear it.

It has been said that these intermarriages of the same blood cause the species to degenerate, and that the necessity of crossing the races is as great among men as among other animals. There might be some force in this objection if it were likely that alliances among relations, if not prohibited by law, would become the most common. But it is enough to show the futility of bad reasons; indeed it would be too much,—were it not an essential service to a good cause, to put aside the false and feeble arguments by which it is attempted to sustain it. Some well-intentioned men are of opinion that no support to good morals, not even a false one, ought to be taken away. This error is the same as that of those devotees who have thought to serve religion by pious frauds. Instead of fortifying it they have weakened it, by exposing it to the derision of its adversaries. When a depraved mind has refuted a false argument, it claims that refutation as a triumph over morality itself.

Section II.

For what time? Considerations on Divorce.

If the law did not prescribe any particular duration to this contract, if individuals were allowed to form this engagement like any other, for a longer or shorter term, what under the auspices of liberty would be the most common arrangement? Would it be very different from the order now established?

The end of the man in this contract might be only the gratification of a transient passion, and that passion satisfied, he would have had all the advantage of the union without any of its inconveniences. It is not the same with the woman; the engagement has for her very durable and very burdensome consequences. After the troubles of pregnancy, after the pains of child-birth, she is charged with the cares of maternity. Thus a union which would give the man nothing but pleasures, would be for the woman the beginning of sufferings, and would lead her to inevitable destruction, if she had not secured beforehand for herself, and for the germ which she nourishes in her bosom, the care and the protection of a husband. "I give myself up to you," she says, "but you shall be my guardian in my state of weakness, and you shall provide for the fruit of our love." Here is the beginning of a partnership, which would prolong itself through many years, though there were but one child; but successive births form successive ties; as time advances the engagement is prolonged; the bounds first assigned to it presently disappear, and meanwhile there is opened a new course of reciprocal pleasures and duties.

When the mother can expect no more children, when the father has made provision for the support of the youngest of the family, can we suppose that the union will be severed? After a cohabitation of so many years, will the parties think of separating? Will not habit have entwined their hearts by a thousand and a thousand ties, which death only can sever? Will not the children form a new centre of union? Will they not create a new fund of pleasures and of hopes? Will they not render the father and mother necessary to each other, by the cares and the charms of a common affection which no one else can share with them? It seems, then, that the ordinary course of the conjugal union would be for life; and if it is natural to suppose in the woman prudence enough thus to secure her dearest interests, can we expect less of a father, or a guardian, whose experience is more mature?

The woman has yet an additional interest in the indefinite duration of the union. Time, pregnancy, nursing, cohabitation itself, all conspire to diminish the effect of her charms; and she must expect that her beauty will decline at an age when the energy of the man is still increasing. She knows that, having worn out her youth with one husband, she will hardly find another; while the man will experience no such difficulty. Accordingly, foresight will dictate to her this new clause in the agreement: "If I give myself up to you, you shall not be free to leave me without my consent." The man, in his turn, demands the same promise; and thus on both sides is completed a lawful contract, founded upon the happiness of the parties.

It seems, then, that marriage for life is the most natural marriage, the best adapted to the wants and the circumstances of families, and, in general, the most favourable to individuals. If there were no laws to ordain it,—that is, no laws except those which sanction contracts in general,—this arrangement would always be the most common, because it is best adapted to the reciprocal interests of the parties. Love on the part of the man, love and foresight on the part of the woman; the enlightened prudence and affection of parents,—all conspire to imprint the character of perpetuity upon this alliance.

But what shall we think if the woman adds this clause: "We shall not be at liberty to separate, though hereafter we come to hate each other as now we love?" Such a condition would seem an act of folly; it has something about it contradictory and absurd which shocks at the first glance; everybody would agree in regarding such a promise as rash, and in thinking that humanity requires it to be omitted.

But it is not the woman who asks, it is not the man who invokes this absurd and cruel clause; it is the law, which imposes it on both, as a condition which cannot be avoided. The law comes in between the contractors; it takes them by surprise in the midst of youthful transports, in those moments which open all the perspective of happiness; and it says to them, "You form this connection in the hope of enjoyment; but I warn you, you are entering a prison of which the gate will never open. I shall be inexorable to the cries of your grief, and though you wound each other with your chains, I cannot suffer them ever to be loosened."

To believe in the perfection of the object beloved, to believe in the eternity of a passion felt and inspired, these are illusions which we may well pardon in two children blinded by love. But ancient lawyers, and legislators grey with age, do not yield themselves up to such chimeras. If they believe in this eternity of passion, why do they take away a power which nobody would use? But no; they foresee inconstancy, they foresee hatred; they foresee that the most violent love may be succeeded by more violent antipathy; and with the cold-blooded indifference of careless unconcern, they pronounce the eternity of the marriage vow, even though the sentiments in which it originated shall be followed by feelings entirely the reverse. If there were a law which forbade the taking a partner, a guardian, a manager, a companion, except on the condition of always keeping him, what tyranny, what madness it would be called! Yet a husband is a companion, a guardian, a manager, a partner, and more yet; and still, in the greater part of civilized countries, a husband cannot be had except for life.

To live under the perpetual authority of a man you hate, is of itself a state of slavery; but to be compelled to submit to his embraces, is a misfortune too great even for slavery itself. Is it said that the yoke is mutual? That only doubles the misfortune.

Since marriage presents to the generality of men the only means of satisfying fully and peaceably the imperious desires of love, to turn them from it is to deprive them of its pleasures, and is to do an evil of no small magnitude. Now what more terrible bugbear than the indissolubility of this contract? Whether it be a marriage, a service, a country, a condition of any kind, the prohibition to go out of it must operate as a prohibition to enter in.

It is enough just to indicate another observation, well founded, but common. As marriages are more rare, infidelity to the marriage bed is more frequent; the more seducers, the more seductions.

When death is the only deliverer, what horrible temptations, what crimes may result from a position so fatal! The examples which remain unknown, are perhaps more numerous than those which come to light. What most commonly takes place upon these occasions is *negative offence*. How easy is crime, even to unperverted hearts, where nothing but inaction is needed to accomplish it! Expose a detested wife and a beloved mistress to a common peril; will efforts as generous and as sincere be made for the one as for the other?

It must not be dissembled that there are objections against the dissolubility of marriages; which I now proceed to state, and to answer.

First Objection.—If divorce were allowed, neither party would regard their lot as irrevocably fixed. The husband would look round to find some woman who pleased him better; the wife, in like manner, would be employed upon comparisons and projects to procure a better husband. There would result a perpetual and mutual insecurity in this important state, on which every plan of life depends.

Answer.—1st. This same inconvenience exists in part, under other names, during an indissoluble marriage, whenever, according to the supposition, affection is extinguished. In that case, it is not a new wife that is sought for, but a mistress; it is not a second husband, but a lover. The strict duties of marriage, and its prohibitions so easily eluded, rather serve to produce inconstancy than to prevent it. It is well known that prohibition and constraint are a stimulus to the passions. Is it not a truth of experience, that even obstacles, by occupying the imagination, and by recalling the mind to the same object, serve only to increase the desire of surmounting them? The rule of liberty would produce fewer stray fancies than the law of conjugal captivity. Render marriages dissoluble, and there would be more apparent separations, but fewer real ones.

2nd. We should not confine ourselves to a consideration of the evil of the thing; we must look also at its advantages. Both parties knowing what they might lose, would cultivate those means of pleasing from which their mutual affection originated.

They would take more pains to study and to humour each other's disposition. They would perceive the necessity of making some sacrifices of inclination and self-love. In one word, care, attention, complaisance, would be prolonged after marriage; and what is now done only to gain affection, would then be practised to preserve it.

3rd. Young persons about to be married would not be so often sacrificed by the avarice and the cupidity of their parents. It would be necessary to give some attention to inclinations before forming a union which repugnance might break. That real suitability upon which happiness depends,—correspondence of age, of education, and of taste,—would then enter into the calculations even of prudence. It would no longer be possible to marry property without marrying the owner of it. Before forming an establishment, some attention would be paid to secure its durability.

Second Objection.—Each party, regarding the connection as transitory, would espouse with indifference the interests, especially the pecuniary interests, of the other. Hence, profusion, negligence, and bad economy of every kind.

Answer.—There is the same danger in partnerships of commerce, yet the evil is very rarely felt. A dissoluble marriage has one tie which such partnerships have not,—the strongest, the most durable of all moral ties,—an affection for their common children, which cements the affection of the married couple. We see this bad economy, attendant upon an indissoluble marriage, much oftener than on a partnership of commerce. Why? It is the effect of indifference and disgust, which produces in married people who are tired of each other a continual need of separation, and of something to distract their attention. The moral tie of the children is dissolved. Their education, the care of their future happiness, is hardly a secondary object; the charm of common interest vanishes; each, engaged in a separate pursuit of pleasure, cares little what may happen to the other. This principle of disunion introduces a thousand kinds of negligence and disorder into their affairs, and the ruin of their fortune is very often a consequence of the estrangement of their hearts. Under the reign of liberty, this evil would not exist. Before disuniting their interests, disgust would have separated their persons.

Facility of divorce tends rather to prevent prodigality than to produce it. Each would be careful of giving so all-sufficient a ground of discontent to an associate, whose esteem it would be necessary to conciliate. Economy estimated at all its worth by the interested prudence of both parties would always be so great a merit in their eyes, that it would cover a multitude of faults, and many wrongs would be forgiven for its sake. Moreover, it would be very evident that, in case of a divorce, that party who had gained the reputation of misconduct and prodigality, would have much less chance of forming a new and advantageous connection.

Third Objection.—The dissolubility of marriage would produce in the stronger party a disposition to maltreat the feebler, in order to force consent to a divorce.

Answer.—This objection is solid; it merits the greatest attention on the part of the legislator. Fortunately, a single precaution will be sufficient to diminish the danger. In case of bad treatment the party ill-treated should alone be set at liberty. Thenceforth, the more desirous a husband might be of a divorce, for the sake of a subsequent marriage, the more fearful he would be of ill conduct towards his wife, lest such actions might be construed as violence intended to force her consent. Gross and brutal means being prohibited, attractive means would be his only resource for persuading her to a separation. He would tempt her, if he had the means, by the offer of an independent provision; or he would find another husband for her as the price of his ransom.

Fourth Objection.—What would become of the children after the law had dissolved the union between their father and mother.

Answer.—What would become of them if death had dissolved it? In the case of divorce the disadvantage to which they are subjected is not so great. The children may continue to live with that parent whose cares are most necessary to them; for the law consulting their interest will confide the boys to the father and the girls to the mother. The great danger of children after the decease of a parent is, that of passing under the control of a stepfather or of a stepmother, who may look upon them with hostile eyes. Girls are especially exposed to the most vexatious treatment under the habitual despotism of a second mother. In the case of divorce this danger does not exist. The boys will have their father to educate them—the girls will have their mother. Their education will suffer less than it would have done from domestic discords and hatred. If the interests of the children would justify the prohibition of second marriages in case of divorce, for a much stronger reason might the same prohibition be justified in the case of death.

The dissolution of a marriage is an act sufficiently important to be submitted to formalities which would have the effect more or less to counteract the operation of caprice, and to leave the parties time for reflection. The intervention of a magistrate is necessary, not only to establish the fact that there has been no violence on the part of the husband to force the wife's consent, but also to interpose a delay, longer or shorter, between demanding and obtaining the divorce.

This is one of those questions upon which opinions will always be divided. Every person is inclined to approve or to condemn divorce according to the good or the evil which he may have seen to result from certain particular cases, or according to his own personal interest.

In England a marriage can be dissolved only when the adultery of the wife is proved. But it is necessary to pass through many tribunals, and, as an Act of Parliament on this subject costs at least five hundred pounds sterling, divorce is accessible only to a very limited class.

In Scotland the adultery of the husband is enough to found a divorce upon. In this respect the law exhibits a certain degree of facility; yet it is not destitute of rigour. While it dissolves the marriage it prohibits the guilty party from contracting another with the accomplice of his offence.

In Sweden divorce is allowed for adultery on either side, which there amounts to the same thing as permitting it by mutual consent; for the husband suffers himself to he accused of adultery, and the marriage is dissolved.

In Denmark it is the same, provided collusion cannot be proved.

Under the code Frederic the parties can separate at pleasure, and marry again after a year's solitude. It would seem that some part of this interval would be better employed in delaying the divorce.

At Geneva adultery is a ground of divorce; but it may also take place for mere incompatibility of character. A woman, by leaving her husband's house and retiring among her friends or relations, gives him occasion to ask a divorce, which demand, if persisted in, always has its legal effect. Divorce is rare. It is proclaimed in all the churches; and that proclamation is a sort of punishment or public censure always dreaded.

After marriage, in France, was made dissoluble at the pleasure of the parties, in two years there took place at Paris, out of all the marriages in that city, between five and six hundred divorces. But it is very difficult to judge of the real effects of an institution so new.

Divorces are not common in those countries where they have been a long time permitted. The same reasons which prevent legislators from permitting them deter individuals from availing themselves of the permission. The government which prohibits them decides, by so doing, that it understands the interests of individuals better than they do themselves. If such a law has any effect at all it must be a bad one.

In all civilized countries the woman who has experienced cruelties and bad treatment on the part of her husband, has obtained from the tribunals what is called a *separation;* but this is not attended by a liberty to either party of marrying again. The ascetic principle, hostile to pleasure, has only consented to the assuagement of suffering. The outraged woman and her tyrant undergo the same lot; but this apparent equality covers an inequality too real. Opinion leaves a great freedom to the man, while it imposes the strictest restraints upon the woman.

Section III.

On what Conditions?

The only question here is, to discover those general conditions of marriage which, according to the principles of utility, suit the greatest number best; for it ought to be left to the persons interested to fix upon the particular stipulations of their contract; or in other words, the conditions ought to be left to their will, with some general exceptions.

First Condition. *The wife shall be subject to the will of the husband, reserving an appeal to the courts of justice.* There may at any moment arise a contradiction between the wills of two persons who pass their lives together. The good of peace requires that a pre-eminence should be established which may prevent or end these contests. Bnt why should the man govern? Because he is the stronger. In his hands the power maintains itself. Give the authority to the woman, and every moment a revolt would break out on the part of her husband. This reason is not the only one. It is probable that the man, by his kind of life, has acquired more experience, more aptitude for affairs, more steadiness of mind. In these respects there are exceptions; but there are exceptions to every general rule.

I have said, *reserving an appeal to the courts of justice.* For it is not our object to make the man a tyrant, and to reduce to a passive state of slavery the sex, which by its feebleness and its tenderness, most needs the protection of the laws. The interests of women have been too often sacrificed. By the Roman law the rules of marriage are a code of violence; the man receives the lion's share. But those, on the other hand, who out of some vague notion of justice and generosity wish to give to the woman an absolute equality, only spread for her a dangerous snare. To absolve her by law, as far as possible, from the necessity of pleasing her husband, would operate to weaken her empire instead of strengthening it.

Man, assured of his prerogative, is not disturbed by the inquietudes of jealousy, and enjoys it while he yields it. Substitute for this arrangement, a rivalry of powers; the pride of the stronger would be continually wounded, it would convert him into a dangerous antagonist; and looking more at what was taken from him than at what was left, he would turn all his efforts towards re-establishing his pre-eminence.

Second Condition. *The control of the affairs of the family shall rest with the man alone.* This is the natural and immediate consequence of his authority. Besides, it is commonly upon his labour that the support of the family depends.

Third Condition. *Property shall be enjoyed in common.* The reasons are, first, the good of equality; second, the benefit of giving both parties the same interest in the domestic prosperity. But this condition is necessarily modified by the fundamental rule which submits the wife to the power of the husband. Differences in the mode of life and in the nature of property will require a great many details; but this is not the place to give them.

Fourth Condition. *The wife shall observe conjugal fidelity.* The reasons why adultery should be made an offence will be given in the Penal Code.

Fifth Condition. *The husband shall observe the same conjugal fidelity.* The reasons for punishing adultery on the man's part, are far less cogent. Still they are strong enough to justify this legal condition. They will be explained in the Penal Code.

SECTION IV.

At what Age.

At what age shall marriage be permitted? It ought never to be allowed before the age at which the contracting parties are supposed to know the extent of the engagement; and this requisition ought to be still more strict in countries where the marriage is indissoluble. What precautions are not necessary to prevent a rash engagement in a case in which repentance will be useless? Surely, in such a case, this right of contracting a marriage ought not to be allowed at an age earlier than that at which the individual is entrusted with the management of his property. It is absurd that a man should be able to dispose of himself for life, at an age when he cannot sell a piece of land of the value of ten crowns.

Section V.

At whose Choice.

On whom shall the choice of a husband or a wife depend? This question presents an apparent, or rather a real absurdity; as though such a choice could possibly belong to any other than the parties interested.

The law should never trust this power to fathers. They lack two things essential to its exercise: the knowledge requisite for such a choice, and a will directed to the true end. Parents and children neither see nor feel alike. They have not the same interest. Love is the motive of the young; and for that, old men care but little. In general, fortune is a trifling consideration with the children; it absorbs all the father's thoughts. The son wishes to be happy; the father wishes him to seem so. The son is ready to sacrifice every interest to that of love; the father wishes that interest to be subordinate to every other.

For a father to receive into his family a son-in-law or a daughter-in-law whom he dislikes, is a vexatious circumstance; but is it not more cruel that the child should be deprived of a companion who would make him happy? Is the pain of the father equal to that of the child? Compare the probable duration of the father's life with that of the son, and consider if you ought to sacrifice that which is beginning to that which is ending. Such is the objection to the mere right of preventing a marriage. How much stronger would it be if a pitiless tyrant might abuse the tenderness and the timidity of his daughter, and force her to marry a husband whom she hated?

The attachments of children depend very much upon their fathers and mothers. This is partly true of the sons, and almost wholly so of the daughters. If the parents neglect to use this right, if they do not apply themselves to direct the inclinations of their children, if they abandon to chance the choice of their acquaintances, whom ought they to blame for the imprudences of youth?

But in taking from the parents the power to restrain and to compel, there is no need to take from them the power of moderating and retarding. The marriageable age may be divided into two epochs. During the first, the want of consent on the part of the parents should be enough to prevent the marriage; during the second, they might still have the power of retarding for some months the celebration of the contract. This time might be allowed the parents to try what they could do in the way of advice.

There exists a very singular custom in a country of Europe celebrated for the wisdom of its institutions. The consent of the father is necessary to a minor, unless the lovers can run a hundred leagues before being caught. But if they are so lucky as to arrive in a certain village, and to procure at the moment some passer-by to pronounce a nuptial benediction, without any questions asked or answered, the marriage is valid and the father is ousted of his authority. Has this privilege been left in existence for the encouragement of fortune-hunters. Or is there a secret desire of weakening the paternal power and of favouring what are elsewhere called *mis-alliances?*

Section VI.

How many Parties to the Contract?

Between how many persons may this contract of marriage subsist at the same time? In other terms, ought polygamy to be tolerated? Polygamy is simple or complex. Simple polygamy is *polygyny*, multiplicity of wives, or *polyandia*, multiplicity of husbands.

Is polygyny useful or hurtful? All that anybody has been able to say in its favour relates to certain particular cases, to certain transient circumstances—as when a man by his wife's sickness is deprived of the pleasures of marriage, or when by his employment he is obliged to divide his time between two houses.

That polygyny might sometimes be agreeable to a man, is likely; but it never would be so to the women. For every man favoured by it, the interests of two women would be sacrificed.

1st. The effect of such a license would aggravate the inequality of conditions. Superiority of wealth has too great an ascendancy already, and such an institution would increase it. A rich man negotiating with a poor girl would avail himself of his position to secure the right to give her a rival. Each of his wives would find herself reduced to half a husband, when she might have made happy another man, who in consequence of this unjust arrangement is deprived of a companion.

2nd. Where would be the peace of families? The jealousies of rival wives would spread among their children. They would form two opposite parties, two little armies, each having at its head a protectress equally powerful, at least so far as rights were concerned. What a scene of contentions! what fury! what animosity! From the enfeeblement of paternal ties would result a like enfeeblement of filial respect. Each son would see in his father the protector of his enemy; all his acts of kindness or of severity, interpreted by opposite prejudices, would be attributed to unjust sentiments of favour or of hatred. The education of the children would be wretched in the midst of these hostile passions, under a system of favour or oppression which would spoil some by rigour and others by indulgence. In the East polygamy may be consistent with peace; but it is slavery that prevents discord, one abuse palliates another, all are tranquil under the same yoke.

There would result from polygyny an increase of the husband's authority. What zeal to satisfy him! What delight at anticipating a rival in an act pleasing to the husband! Would this be an evil or a good? Those persons who, out of a mean opinion of women, think they cannot be too submissive, find polygyny admirable. Those who think that the ascendancy of the sex is favourable to refinement of manners, that it augments all the pleasures of society, that the mild and persuasive authority of women is salutary in the family, must esteem polygyny a great evil.

It is not necessary seriously to discuss either polyandia, or complex polygamy. Too much has been said even on polygyny, were it not necessary to point out the true basis upon which manners rest.

Section VII.

With what Formalities.

The formalities of the marriage contract ought to have two objects in view:—1st. To establish the fact of the free consent of the parties, and of the lawfulness of their union. 2nd. To make known the marriage, and to secure proofs of its celebration. It is proper, besides, to explain to the contracting parties the legal rights which they respectively acquire, and the legal obligations they assume.

Most nations have made this act very solemn; and, without doubt, ceremonies which strike the imagination serve to impress upon the mind the force and dignity of the contract.

In Scotland, the law far too accommodating, exacts no formality whatever. A mutual declaration of marriage, in the presence of a witness, is enough to render the contract valid; and therefore it is that English minors, impatient of restraint, hasten to relieve themselves by an off-hand marriage at a village on the Scotch frontier, called *Gretna Green.*

In establishing the forms of marriage there are two dangers to be avoided:—1st. That of rendering them so embarrassing as to prevent marriage, when there is wanting neither freedom of consent nor capacity to contract. 2nd. That of giving to the persons who are required to be present at the formalities the power of abusing that right, and of employing it to some bad end.

In many countries one must watch a long time in the vestibule of the temple before arriving at the altar. Under the name of an *affiance* the chains of marriage are worn without its enjoyments. For what serves this preliminary, except to multiply embarrassment, and to spread snares? The code Frederic is loaded, in this respect, with useless restraints. The English law, on the other hand, is remarkable for its simplicity and clearness. By the English law the parties know what they are about; they are married, or they are not married; there is no intermediate condition.

The Theory of Legislation

Introduced by **James E. Crimmins,**
Huron University College, Ontario

Volume One
Introduction
Bibliography
The Theory of Legislation
Principles of Legislation
Principles of the Civil Code

Volume Two
The Theory of Legislation
Principles of the Penal Code
Appendix 'Preliminary Discourse. By M. Dumont'
Index

Printed in England by Antony Rowe Ltd, Chippenham

THE THEORY OF LEGISLATION

Introduced by
James E. Crimmins
Huron University College, Ontario

Volume 2

THOEMMES CONTINUUM

THE THEORY OF LEGISLATION

II

Jeremy Bentham

Translated from the French of Étienne Dumont by
Richard Hildreth

With an Introduction, Bibliography and Index by
James E. Crimmins

THOEMMES CONTINUUM

This edition published by Thoemmes Press, 2004

Thoemmes Press
11 Great George Street
Bristol BS1 5RR, England

http://www.thoemmes.com

The Theory of Legislation
2 Volumes : ISBN 1 84371 121 4

British Library Cataloguing-in-Publication Data
A CIP record of this title is available from the British Library

Publisher's Note

The Publisher has gone to great lengths to ensure the quality of this reprint but points out that some imperfections in the original book may be apparent.

This book is printed on acid-free paper, sewn, and cased in a durable cloth.

PRINCIPLES OF THE PENAL CODE.

PART FIRST.

OF OFFENCES.

INTRODUCTION.

The object of this first part is to describe offences, to classify them, and to point out the circumstances by which they are aggravated or extenuated. It is a treatise upon diseases, which of necessity precedes the inquiry as to cures.

The common nomenclature of offences is not only incomplete, it is deceptive. Unless we begin by reforming it, we never shall be able to dispel the obscurity in which the science of penal legislation is involved.

CHAPTER I.

Classification of Offences.

What is meant by an offence? The sense of this word varies according to the subject under discussion. If the question relates to a system of laws already established, *offences* are whatever the legislator has prohibited, whether for good or for bad reasons. If the question relates to a theoretical research for the discovery of the best possible laws, according to the principle of utility, we give the name of *offence* to every act which we think ought to be prohibited by reason of some evil which it produces or tends to produce. Such is the only sense of this word throughout this treatise.

The most general classification of offences may be derived from the classes of persons who suffer by them. They may be divided into the four following kinds:—

1st. *Private Offences.*—Those which are injurious to such or such assignable individuals,* other than the delinquent himself.

2nd. *Reflective Offences, or Offences against One's Self.*—Those by which the delinquent injures nobody but himself; or, if he injures others, it is only in consequence of the injury done to himself.

3rd. *Semi-public Offences.*—Those which affect a portion of the community, a district, a particular corporation, a religious sect, a commercial company, or any association of individuals united by some common interest, but forming a circle inferior in extent to that of the community.

It is never a present evil nor a past evil that constitutes a semi-public offence. If the evil were present or past, the individuals who suffer, or who have suffered, would be assignable. It would then be an offence of the first class, a private offence. In semi-public offences the point is a future evil,—a danger which threatens, but which as yet attacks no particular individual.

4th. *Public Offences.*—Those which produce some common danger to all the members of the state, or to an indefinite number of non-assignable individuals, although it does not appear that any one in particular is more likely to suffer than any other.†

* An *assignable* individual is such or such an individual in particular, to the exclusion of every other; as Peter, Paul, or William.

† The fewer individuals there are in a district or a corporation, the more probable it is that the parties injured will be assignable; so that it is sometimes difficult to determine whether a given offence is private or semi-public. The more considerable the district or corporation is, the nearer do the offences which affect them approach to public offences. These three classes are consequently liable to be confounded more or less with each other. But this inconvenience is inevitable in all the ideal divisions which we are obliged to establish for the sake of order and perspicuity.

CHAPTER II.

Sub-division of Offences.

SUB-DIVISION OF PRIVATE OFFENCES.—Since the happiness of an individual flows from four sources, the offences which may attack it can be arranged under four divisions :—

1st. Offences against the person.

2nd. Offences against property.

3rd. Offences against reputation.

4th. Offences against the condition; that is, against domestic or civil relations, such as the relation of father and child, husband and wife, master and servant, citizen and magistrate, &c.

Offences which are injurious in more respects than one may be designated by compound terms; as offences against the person and property, offences against the person and reputation, &c.

SUB-DIVISION OF REFLECTIVE OFFENCES.—Offences against one's self are, properly speaking, vices and imprudences. It is useful to classify them, not in order to subject them to legislative severity, but rather to remind the legislator, by a single word, that such or such an action is beyond his sphere.

The sub-division of these offences is exactly the same as that of offences of the first class; we are vulnerable by our own hand in as many points as by the hand of another. We can injure ourselves in our person, our property, our reputation, our civil and domestic condition.

SUB-DIVISION OF SEMI-PUBLIC OFFENCES.—The greater part of these offences consist in the violation of those laws of which the object is to protect the inhabitants of a district against the different physical calamities to which they may be exposed. Such are laws for preventing the spread of contagious diseases, for preserving dykes and causeways, for restraining the ravages of hurtful animals, for guarding against famine. The offences which tend to produce calamities of this sort form the first kind of semi-public offences.

Those semi-public offences which may be consummated without the intervention of a natural scourge, such as threats against a certain class of persons, calumnies, libels which touch the honour of some sect or company, insults to some object of religion, thefts of property belonging to societies, the destruction of the ornaments of a city, these and others like them form a second kind of semi-public offences. The first sort are founded upon some *calamity;* the second sort arise from *pure malice.*

Sub-division of Public Offences.—Public offences may be arranged under nine divisions.

1st. *Offences against External Security.*—Those which tend to expose the nation to the attacks of a foreign enemy; such as every act which provokes or encourages hostile invasion.

2nd and 3rd. *Offences against Justice and the Police.*—It is difficult to draw the line which separates these two branches of administration. Their functions have the same object—that of maintaining the internal peace of the state. Justice regards in particular offences already committed; her power does not display itself till after the discovery of some act hostile to the security of the citizens. Police applies itself to the prevention both of offences and calamities; its expedients are, not punishments, but precautions; it foresees evils, and provides against wants.

Offences against justice and police are those which have a tendency to thwart or to misdirect the operations of these two magistracies.

4th. *Offences against the Public Force.*—Those which have a tendency to thwart or misdirect the operations of the military force destined to protect the state, both against external enemies and against such internal adversaries as the government cannot subdue except by an armed force.

5th. *Offences against the Public Treasure.*—Those which tend to diminish the revenue, and to disturb or divert the employment of funds destined to the service of the state.

6th. *Offences against Population.*—Those which tend to a diminution of the numbers of the community.

7th. *Offences against National Wealth.*—Those which tend to diminish the quantity or the value of the property belonging to the individual members of the community.

8th. *Offences against the Sovereignty.*—It is the more difficult to give a clear idea of these offences because there are many states in which it would be almost impossible to resolve the question of fact—Where does the supreme power reside? The following is the simplest explication. We ordinarily give the collective name of government to the whole assemblage of persons charged with the different political functions. There is commonly in states *a person* or *a body of persons* who assign and distribute to the members of the government their several departments, their several functions and prerogatives, and who have authority over them and over the whole. The person or the collection of persons which exercise this supreme power is called the *sovereign.* Offences against the sovereignty are those which tend to thwart or to misdirect the operations of the sovereign, thus having a direct tendency to thwart or misdirect the operations of the different parts of the government.

9th. *Offences against Religion.*—Governments cannot possess either an universal knowledge of what passes in secret nor an inevitable power which leaves the guilty no means of escape. To supply these imperfections of human power it has been thought necessary to inculcate a belief in supernatural power. I speak generally of all religious systems, and not of any one in particular. To this superior power is attributed a disposition to maintain the laws of society, and to punish or to reward, at some future time, such acts as may have escaped punishment or may have failed to be rewarded among men. *Religion* is represented as an allegorical personage charged with preserving and strengthening among mankind a fear of this supreme judge. It follows that to diminish or to pervert the influence of religion is to diminish or to pervert, in the same proportion, the service which the state receives from it, whether that service is exercised in repressing crime or encouraging virtue. Whatever tends to thwart or to misdirect the operations of this power is an offence against religion.*

CHAPTER III.

Some other Divisions.

The divisions of which we are about to speak may all be resolved into the fundamental divisions already given; but they are sometimes employed for the sake of brevity, and to mark some particular circumstance in the nature of offences.

1st. *Complex Offences*, in opposition to *Simple Offences.*—An offence which makes a joint attack upon the person and reputation, or upon the reputation and property, is a complex offence. A public offence may include a private offence. For example, a perjury which saves a criminal from punishment is a simple offence against justice; a perjury which saves a criminal and at the same time causes the punishment to fall upon a person who is innocent includes a public and a private offence. It is a complex offence.

2nd. *Principle and Accessory Offences.*—The principal offence is that which produces the evil in question; accessory offences are acts which have a greater or less preparatory force towards the production of the principal offence. In the crime of counterfeiting the true principal offence is the act of issuing the false money, for thence comes his loss who receives it. The act of fabricating the false money in this point of view is only an accessory offence.

3rd. *Positive and Negative Offences.*—Positive offence is the result of an act intended to produce that end. Negative offence results from a neglect to act, from not doing what one is bound to do.

* The question here relates to the utility of religion in a political point of view, not to its truth. I say *offences against religion*, the abstract entity, not *offences against God*, the Existent Being. For how can a sinful mortal offend an impassive *Being*, or affect his happiness? Under what class could this imaginary offence be arranged? Would it be an offence against his person, his property, his reputation, or his condition?

With respect to defamation, Horace has well distinguished these two modifications of the offence:—

> ——— *Absentem qui rodit amicum,*
> *Qui non defendit, alio culpante . . . . hic niger est.*

> ——— Who blames an absent friend,—
> Another blaming, who does not defend him,
> They both are black.

Great offences are generally of the positive kind. The gravest of the negative kind belong to the class of public offences. If the shepherd allows himself to sleep, the flock will suffer.

There are many cases of negative offence, which, in a perfect system, might and ought to be placed by the side of positive offences. To induce a man to go with a lighted candle in his hand into a room which we know to be full of loose gunpowder, and so to cause his death, is a positive act of homicide; while seeing him go of his own accord, and suffering him to do it, without warning him of the danger, is a negative offence to be ranged under the same head.*

4th. *Imaginary Offences.*—These are acts which produce no real evil, but which prejudice, mistake, or the ascetic principle, have caused to be regarded as offences. They vary with time and place. They originate and end, they rise and they decay, with the false opinions which serve as their foundation. Such at Rome was the offence for which vestal virgins were buried alive. Such are heresy and sorcery, which have caused so many thousand innocent victims to perish in the flames.

To give an idea of these imaginary offences it is not necessary to prepare a catalogue of them; it will be enough to indicate some principal groups. We say to the legislator, "The evil attributed to such actions is imaginary; it will be better not to prohibit them by law." Such is our advice;—to the legislator, however, not to the citizen. We do not say,—"because they are imaginary, it will be well to commit them in spite of public opinion and the laws."

* It is proper to observe, however, that negative offences do not inspire the same degree of alarm, and that they are very difficult to prove.

Imaginary offences are, 1st. Offences against laws which impose religious belief, or religious practices. 2nd. Offences which consist in making innocent bargains, bargains forbidden by the laws for false reasons; usury, for example. 3rd. The offence of an artist or other person emigrating from his native country. 4th. Offences which consist in the violation of prohibitive rules of which the effect is to fetter one class of citizens for the benefit of another, such as a prohibition to export wool, intended to favour the manufacturer at the expense of the farmer.

We shall see hereafter that so far as the public is concerned, offences which originate in the sexual appetite, when there is neither violence, fraud, nor interference with the rights of others, and also offences against one's self, may be arranged under this head.

CHAPTER IV.

Evil of the Second Order.

The alarm which different offences inspire is susceptible of many degrees, from disquiet up to terror.

But does not the more or less of alarm depend on the imagination, the temperament, age, sex, position, experience? Can we calculate beforehand effects which vary with so many causes? Has alarm so regular a progress that its degrees can be measured s

Though that which is subject to the imagination, a faculty so changeable and so fantastic, cannot be reduced to rigorous precision, yet the general alarm produced by different offences, follows proportions sufficiently constant, and capable of being determined. Alarm is greater or less, according to the following circumstances.*

1st. The greatness of the evil of the first order.

2nd. The intention of the delinquent.

3rd. The position which has furnished him an opportunity to commit the offence.

* All these circumstances, except the first and last, have this in common, that they render the repetition of the offence more probable.

4th. His motive.

5th. The greater or less facility of preventing like offences.

6th. The greater or less facility of concealing them, and of escaping punishment.

7th. The character of the delinquent. To this head belong relapses.

8th. The condition of the individual injured, by virtue of which those in a like condition may or may not feel the impression of fear.

It is in the examination of these circumstances that we shall find the solution of the most interesting problems of penal jurisprudence.

CHAPTER V.

Evil of the first Order.

THE evil of the first order resulting from an offence may be estimated according to the following rules:—

1st. The evil of a complex offence will be greater than that of either of the simple offences into which it can be resolved.

A perjury, of which the effect shall be to cause the punishment of an innocent person, will produce more evil than a perjury which procures the discharge of a guilty one. In the former case there is a private offence combined with the public offence; in the latter case there is only a public offence.

2nd. The evil of a demi-public or public offence, which evil propagates itself, will be greater than the evil of a private offence of the same kind. It is a greater evil to carry a pestilence into a whole continent, than into some small island with few inhabitants, and little frequented. It is this tendency to spread, in which consists the particular enormity of arson and inundation.

3rd. The evil of a demi-public or public offence, which, instead of multiplying itself, tends constantly to subdivision, will be less than that of a private offence of the same denomination. If the public treasury be robbed, the evil of the first order will be less than in the case of an equal robbery committed upon an individual; for the evil which the individual has suffered can be made up by granting him at the public expense an indemnity equivalent to his loss. This being done, things will be brought to the same state as if the theft, instead of being committed upon Paul or Peter, had been directed against the public treasury.*

Offences against property are the only ones susceptible of this repartition; and the evil of these offences is diminished in proportion as it is distributed among a greater number, and as the individual sufferers are richer.

4th. The total evil of an offence is increased, if there result from it a consequential evil to the same individual. If in consequence of an imprisonment, or a wound, you have lost a place, a marriage, a lucrative business, it is plain that these losses are a net addition to the primitive evil.

5th. The total evil of an offence is increased, if there result from it a derivative evil, which falls upon some other person. If in consequence of a wrong done to you, your wife or your children feel the miseries of want, this is an incontestable addition to the primitive evil.

Besides these rules, which enable us to estimate the evil of the first order, we must take the aggravations into account; that is, the particular circumstances which augment the evil. We shall presently exhibit a complete table of them, founded upon the following principles:—

1st. Augmentation of evil resulting from an extraordinary portion of physical pain, not of the essence of the offence. *Addition of Physical pain.*

2nd. Augmentation of evil by a circumstance which, to the essential evil of the offence, adds the accessary evil of terror. *Addition of terror.*

3rd. Augmentation of evil from some extraordinary circumstances of ignominy. *Addition of disgrace.*

* But though, in a case like this, the evil of the first order is less, it is not so with the evil of the second order—that is, the alarm. But this will be considered in its proper place.

4th. Augmentation of evil from the irreparable nature of the damage. *Irreparable damage.*

5th. Augmentation of evil arising from the extraordinary sensibility of the individual injured. *Aggravation of suffering.*

These rules are absolutely necessary. We must be able to calculate the evil of the first order, because in proportion to its apparent or real value, alarm will be greater or less. The evil of the second order is only a reflection of the evil of the first order. Other circumstances, however, modify the alarm.

CHAPTER VI.

Of Intention.

WHETHER a man commits an offence knowingly and willingly or unwillingly and undesignedly, the immediate evil is exactly the same. But the alarm which results is very different. We regard him who has done an evil with *knowledge and design*, as a bad and dangerous man. He who has done an evil without designing and without knowing it, is looked upon as a man to be feared only by reason of his inadvertence or his ignorance.

The security felt by the public, notwithstanding the commission of an offence, when the act was unintentional, is not surprising. Observe the circumstances of the act. The delinquent had no design to put himself in opposition to the law. He has either committed the offence because he lacked a motive to abstain from it, or it resulted from an unfortunate concourse of circumstances; it is an isolated and fortuitous fact, which has no tendency to produce a repetition of itself. But an offence intentionally committed is a permanent cause of evil. We see in what the delinquent has done what he wishes to do, and what he is able to do again. His past conduct is a prognostic of his future conduct. Beside the idea of a villain saddens and frightens us. It recalls to our minds that dangerous and mischievous class which surrounds us with secret snares, and carries on its conspiracies in silence.

The people, guided by a just instinct, almost always say of an unintentional offender that he is more deserving of pity than of blame. In fact, a man of no more than ordinary sensibility cannot but experience the most lively regrets at evils of which he is the innocent cause. He needs consolation rather than punishment. He is even less to be feared than any other man; his regrets for the past furnish a particular security for the future.

Beside, an offence committed without intention holds out the hope of indemnity. When a delinquent expects to encounter punishment, he takes precautions to cover himself against the law; an innocent man acts openly, and will not think of refusing a legal reparation.

Such is the general principle. Its application is a matter of considerable difficulty. To become well acquainted with all the characteristics of intention, it is necessary to examine all the different possible states of mind at the moment of action, as respects design and knowledge; and how numerous are the possible modifications of the understanding and the will!

An archer shoots an arrow on which is written, "For Philip's left eye;" the arrow strikes Philip's left eye. Here is an intention corresponding exactly to the fact.

A jealous husband surprises his rival, and to perpetuate his vengeance, mutilates him. The operation produces death. In this case the intention to kill was not full and absolute.

A hunter sees a deer and a man close together. He really thinks that he cannot shoot at the deer without danger to the man. However, he shoots; and the man is killed. In such a case the killing was voluntary, but the intention to kill was only indirect.

As to the relation of the understanding to the different circumstances of an action, it may be in three states: *knowledge, ignorance, misinformation.* You may know that a beverage is a poison; you may know nothing about it; you may think it can do only a trifling injury, or that it is, in certain cases, a remedy.

Such are the preliminaries for settling the question of intention. I shall not attempt at present to enter further into this difficult subject.

CHAPTER VII.

Position of the Delinquent; its Effect upon Alarm.

There are offences which anybody may commit; there are others dependent upon a particular position which furnishes the delinquent an occasion for the offence.

This latter circumstance tends, in general, to diminish the alarm by contracting its sphere.

A larceny produces a general alarm. An act of peculation committed by a guardian upon his ward produces hardly any.

Whatever might be the alarm caused by the extortions of an officer of the police, a contribution levied by robbers upon the highway produces terror infinitely greater. Why? Because everybody sees that an extortioner in place, however rapacious, still has some restraints and some limits. He must have occasions and pretexts to abuse his power; while robbers on the highway threaten all the world, at all times, and are not at all controlled by public opinion.

This circumstance has the same sort of influence upon other kinds of offences, such as seduction and adultery. You cannot seduce the first woman you meet, as you might rob her. Such an enterprise requires an intimate acquaintance, a certain correspondency of rank and fortune—in one word, the advantage of a particular position.

Of two homicides, one committed to secure an inheritance, the other as a means of robbery; the first evinces a more atrocious character, but the second excites the greater alarm. The man who feels confident of the good disposition of his heirs experiences no sensible terror at the first event; but what security can he have against robbers? The villain who commits a murder to make sure of an inheritance is not likely to change into a highway assassin. He will hazard a danger for the sake of an estate which he would not risk for a few crowns.

This same observation may be extended to all offences which imply a violation of deposit, an abuse of confidence, or a misuse of power, whether public or private. They cause less alarm in proportion as the situation of the delinquent is more peculiar, the number of persons in similar situations smaller, and the sphere of the offence more limited.

However, there is one *important exception*. If the delinquent is clothed with great powers; if he envelopes in his sphere of action a great number of persons; his situation, though peculiar, increases the circuit of alarm instead of diminishing it. Let a judge undertake to rob, to kill, to tyrannize; let a military officer make it his business to plunder, to vex, to shed blood; the alarm they will excite, being proportioned to the extent of their powers, may surpass that of the most atrocious robberies.

In these elevated positions, alarm may be created even without offence. A simple mistake without bad intention may cause the most lively terror. Is an innocent man condemned to death by an honest but ignorant judge? The moment this mistake is known the public confidence is wounded, the shock is everywhere felt, and inquietude reaches the highest point.

Fortunately, this kind of alarm may be arrested at once, by the displacement of incompetent officer.

CHAPTER VIII.

The Influence of Motives upon the greatness of Alarm.

If the offence in question proceeds from a particular motive, rare, and belonging to a class of motives small in number, the alarm will have little extent. If it proceeds from a motive common, frequent, and powerful, the alarm will have a greater extent, because a greater number of persons will feel themselves to be in danger.

Compare the results of an assassination committed by a robber, with those of an assassination committed for revenge. In the first case, the danger is regarded as almost universal; the second is a crime which terrifies those only who have enemies, and enemies whose hatred has reached an uncommon pitch of atrocity. An offence which grows out of a party quarrel causes a greater alarm than the same offence when produced by private hostility.

Towards the middle of the last century, there existed in Denmark and a part of Germany, a religious sect whose principles were more frightful than the blackest passions. According to these fanatics, not good actions, but repentance, was the surest means of gaining heaven; and the efficacy of repentance would be the greater the more it absorbed all the faculties. Now, the more atrocious was the crime, the greater certainty there was of giving to remorse an expiatory force sufficiently energetic. Upon the strength of this logic, a madman sought to merit salvation and a hanging, by the murder of an infant child. If this sect had been able to maintain itself, the human race would have come to an end.*

Motives are commonly spoken of as *good* or *bad*. This is an error. Every motive, in the final analysis, is the perspective of a pleasure to be procured, or of a pain to be avoided. Now the same motive, which in certain cases leads to the performance of an action esteemed good, or indifferent, may lead in other cases to an action reputed to be bad. A beggar steals a loaf; another person buys one; a third works, that he may get the means to buy. The motive which actuates all three, is one and the same, to wit, the physical pain of hunger. A pious man founds a hospital for the poor, another goes on a pilgrimage to Mecca, a third assassinates a prince whom he thinks to be a heretic; their motive may be exactly the same,—the desire of conciliating the Divine favour, according to the different opinions which they have formed

* I have somewhere read that the great Frederic, when the first instance of this fanaticism made its appearance in Prussia, ordered the assassin to be shut up in a madhouse. He thought putting him to death would be rather a reward than a punishment. This was enough to put a stop to the crime.

of it. A geometrician lives in an austere retreat, and gives himself up to the profoundest labours; a man of the world ruins himself and a multitude of creditors by excessive expenditures; a prince undertakes a conquest, and sacrifices myriads of men to his projects; an intrepid warrior rouses the courage of a beaten people, and triumphs over an usurper;—all these men may be animated by a motive exactly the same, the love of reputation.

In this way, we might examine all motives, and we should perceive that each of them may give birth to actions the most laudable, or the most criminal. Motives then ought not to be regarded as exclusively good or bad.

However, in considering the whole catalogue of motives, that is, the whole catalogue of pleasures and pains, we may classify them according to the tendency which they seem to have to unite or to disunite the interests of the individual and of the community. Upon this plan, motives may be distinguished into four classes,—the *purely social motive*, benevolence; *semi-social motives*, the love of reputation, the desire of friendship, religion; *anti-social motives*, antipathy in all its branches; *personal motives*, pleasures of sense, love of power, pecuniary interest, the desire of self-preservation.

The personal motives are the most eminently useful, the only ones whose action can never be suspended, because nature has intrusted to them the preservation of individuals. They are the great wheels of society; but their movements must be regulated, moderated, and maintained in a right direction, by motives drawn from the two first classes.

It must not be forgotten that even the anti-social motives—necessary, to a certain degree, for the defence of the individual—may, and often do, produce useful actions, actions absolutely necessary to the existence of society; for example, the denouncement and prosecution of criminals.

Another classification of motives may be made, by considering their more common tendency to produce good or bad effects. The social and demi-social motives may be called *tutelary motives;* the anti-social and personal may be denominated *seductive motives.* These denominations must not be taken in a rigorous sense, but they are not without justice and truth; for whenever there is a conflict of motives acting in opposite directions, it is found that the social and demi-social motives generally operate in conformity with utility, while the anti-social and personal motives are those which tend the other way.

Without entering into a deeper investigation of motives, let us stop at that point in which the legislator is interested. To judge an action it is necessary to look first to its effects abstracted from everything else. The effects being well ascertained, we may in certain cases ascend to the motive, in order to discover its influence on the greatness of the alarm, but without giving any attention to the good or bad quality which its common name implies.* For the most approved motive cannot transform a pernicious action into an action useful or indifferent; nor can a motive the most reprobated transform a useful action into a bad one. All that the motive can do is to raise or lower the moral quality of the action. A good action prompted by a *tutelary* motive becomes better; a bad action founded on a *seductive* motive is so much the worse. Let us apply this theory to practice. A motive belonging to the seductive class is no offence in itself, but it may form a means of *aggravation*. A motive of the tutelary class will not have the effect to justify or to excuse, but it may serve to diminish

* What I mean by the *common names of motives* are those names which carry with them an idea of approbation or disapprobation. A neuter name is that which expresses the motive without any association of blame or praise; for example, *pecuniary interest*, *love of power*, *desire of friendship or favour*, *whether of God or man*, *curiosity*, *love of reputation*, *pain from the infliction of an injury*, *desire of self-preservation*. But these motives have common names, as avarice, cupidity, ambition, vanity, vengeance, animosity, &c. When a motive bears a name of reprobation, it seems contradictory to maintain that any good can result from it; if it bears a name of favour it seems equally contradictory to suppose it can result in evil. Almost all moral disputations rest upon this foundation of ambiguity. To cut them up by the roots, it is only necessary to give neuter names to motives. We can then go on with the examination of their effects, without being disconcerted by the common association of ideas.

the necessity of a punishment; in other words, it forms a ground of *extenuation*.

Let us recollect that there is no room for considering the motive except when it is manifest and palpable. It would often be very difficult to discover the true or dominant motive, when the action might be equally produced by different motives, or where motives of several sorts might have co-operated in its production. In the interpretation of these doubtful cases it is necessary to distrust the malignity of the human heart, and that general disposition to exhibit a brilliant sagacity at the expense of good nature. We involuntarily deceive even ourselves as to what puts us into action. In relation even to our own motives we are wilfully blind, and are always ready to break into a passion against the oculist who desires to remove the cataract of ignorance and prejudice.

CHAPTER IX.

Facility or Difficulty of Preventing Offences. Their Influence on Alarm.

THE mind sets itself at once to examine the means of attack and the means of defence, and according as the offence is judged more or less easy to be consummated, our inquietude is greater or less. This is one of the reasons which raises the evil of an act of robbery so far above that of a theft. Force can effect many things which would be beyond the reach of stratagem. Robbery directed against a dwelling-house is more alarming than robbery on the highway; that done by night is more terrifying than that done in the day-time; that which is combined with arson than that which is limited to ordinary means.

On the other hand, the greater facility we see in repelling an offence, the less alarming it appears to us. The alarm cannot be very great when the offence cannot be perpetrated except with the consent of him who suffers by it. It is easy to apply this principle to cases of fraudulent acquisition, seduction, duels, and to offences against one's self, particularly suicide.

The rigour of laws against domestic theft has doubtless originated in the difficulty of guarding against it. But the aggravation which results from that circumstance is not equal to the effect of another circumstance which tends to diminish the alarm, to wit, the peculiarity of position necessary to furnish occasion for the theft. The domestic thief once known is no longer dangerous. He needs my consent to plunder me; I must introduce him into my house and give him my confidence. When it is so easy to guard against him, he can inspire only a very feeble alarm.*

CHAPTER X.

Effect produced upon Alarm by greater or less Facilities for Secrecy.

The alarm is greater when by the nature or the circumstances of the offence it is more difficult to discover it or to find out its author. If the delinquent remains unknown, his success is an encouragement to him and to others; there seems no limit to the impunity of similar offences, and the injured party loses the hope of indemnity.

There are offences which admit particular precautions adapted to secrecy, such as a disguise, the choice of the night as the time of action, and anonymous, threatening, extorsive letters.

There are also distinct offences which are committed to render the discovery of other offences more difficult. Persons are imprisoned, abducted, or murdered for the sake of suppressing their testimony.

In cases where by the nature of the offence the author must be known, the alarm is considerably diminished. Thus a personal injury, resulting from some momentary transport of passion, excited by the presence of an enemy, inspires less alarm than a

* The principal reason against severity of punishment in this case is, that it gives masters a repugnance to prosecute, and of course favours impunity.

theft which affects concealment, although the evil of the first order may be greater in the former case than in the latter.

CHAPTER XI.

Effect of the Delinquent's Character upon Alarm.

The character of the delinquent will be presumed from the nature of the offence, especially from the magnitude of the evil of the first order, which is the most apparent part of it. Other presumptions will be furnished by circumstances and details attending the perpetration of the offence.

The character of a man will appear more or less dangerous, according as the tutelary motives appear to have more or less empire over him, as compared with the seductive motives.

There are two reasons why character ought to exert an influence upon the choice and the quantity of the punishment; first, because it augments or diminishes the alarm; secondly, because it furnishes an index of sensibility. There is no need of employing such strong means to restrain a character, weak, but good at bottom, as would be necessary in case of an opposite temperament.

The grounds of aggravation which may be derived from this source are as follows :—

1st. The less an injured party is capable of defending himself, the stronger ought to be the natural sentiment of compassion. The law of honour, coming to the support of this instinct of pity, makes it an imperious duty to be tender with the feeble, and to spare those who cannot resist. The first index of a dangerous character is *oppression of the weak.*

2nd. If weakness alone ought to excite compassion, the sight of suffering ought to act in that direction with a yet stronger force. A refusal to succour misfortune forms of itself a presumption little favourable to character. But what shall we think of him who selects the moment of distress to add new anxieties to an afflicted spirit, to render a disgrace more bitter by a new affront, or to complete the plunder of suffering poverty? The second index of a dangerous character is *aggravation of distress.*

3rd. It is an essential branch of moral police, that those who have been able to form superior habits of reflection, those in whom greater wisdom and experience can be presumed, should obtain the regard and the respect of those who have not been able, in the same degree, to acquire habits of reflection, and the advantages of education. This kind of superiority is commonly met with among the most distinguished citizens, in comparison with the less elevated, among the old men and the more aged of the same rank, and in certain professions consecrated to public instruction. There have been formed among the mass of the people sentiments of deference and of respect, relative to these distinctions: and this respect, which is of the greatest use in repressing without effort the seductive passions, is one of the most solid foundations of morals and of laws. The third index of a dangerous character is *disrespect towards superiors.*

4th. When the motives which have led to crime are comparatively light and trifling, it is evident that the sentiments of honour and benevolence have very little force. If that man is esteemed dangerous who is pushed by an imperious desire of vengeance to transgress the laws of humanity, what shall be thought of him who gives himself up to acts of cruelty out of a mere motive of curiosity, imitation, or amusement? The fourth index of a dangerous character is *gratuitous cruelty.*

5th. Time is particularly favourable to the development of the tutelary motives. At the first assault of a passion, as at the first blast of a storm, the sentiments of virtue may bend for a moment; but if the heart is not perverted, reflection presently restores their former force, and leads them back in triumph. If a considerable space of time has elapsed between the project of a crime and its accomplishment, it is an unequivocal proof of a ripe and settled wickedness. The fifth index of a dangerous character is *premeditation.*

6th. The number of accomplices is another mark of depravity. This concert supposes reflection, and a sustained and continuous plan. Besides, the union of several against one is the double mark of cruelty and of cowardice. The sixth index of a dangerous character is *conspiracy*.

To these grounds of aggravation may be added two others less easy to classify—*falsehood*, and *violation of confidence*.

Falsehood impresses a deep and degrading blot upon the character, which even brilliant qualities cannot efface. In this respect public opinion is just. Truth is one of the first wants of man; it is one of the elements of our existence; it is as necessary to us as the light of day. Every instant of our lives we are obliged to form judgments and to regulate our conduct according to facts, and it is only a small number of these facts which we can ascertain from our own observation. There results an absolute necessity of trusting to the reports of others. If there is in these reports a mixture of falsehood, so far our judgments are erroneous, our motives wrong, our expectations misplaced. We live in restless distrust, and we do not know upon what to put dependence. In one word, falsehood includes the principle of every evil, because in its progress it brings on at last the dissolution of human society.

The importance of truth is so great, that the least violation of its laws, even in frivolous matters, is always attended with a certain degree of danger. The slightest deviation from it is an attack upon the respect we owe to it. It is a first transgression which facilitates a second, and familiarizes the odious idea of falsehood. If the evil of falsehood is so great in things which are themselves of no consequence, what must it be upon those more important occasions, when it serves in itself as the instrument of crime?

Falsehood is a circumstance sometimes essential to the nature of an offence, and sometimes simply accessory. It is necessarily involved in perjury, and in fraudulent acquisition under all its modifications. In other offences it is collateral and accidental. It is only in relation to these latter offences that it can furnish a separate ground of aggravation.

Violation of Confidence has reference to a particular position, to an intrusted power which imposes upon the delinquent some strict obligation which he has violated. It may be considered sometimes as the principal offence and sometimes as an accessory offence. It is not necessary to enter here into details.

There is one general remark which may be made upon all these grounds of aggravation. Though they all furnish indications unfavourable to the character of the delinquent, that is no reason for a proportionate augmentation of punishment. It will be sufficient to modify it in a certain way analogous to the attending aggravation, and so as to excite in the minds of the citizens a salutary antipathy against the aggravating circumstance. But this will become more clear when we treat of the means of rendering punishments characteristic.*

Let us now pass to the *extenuations*, which may be derived from the same source of character, and which should have an effect to diminish punishment. I give this name to circumstances which furnish a favourable indication with respect to the cha-

* We may here propose a question interesting to the moralist and the legislator:—If an individual indulges in actions which the public opinion condemns, but which, according to the principles of utility, it ought not to condemn, can we deduce from this circumstance an indication unfavourable to his character?

I answer, that a virtuous man, though he submits in general to the tribunal of public opinion, may still vindicate his independence in particular cases, in which he thinks the judgment of that tribunal contrary to reason and his own happiness; or where it demands a sacrifice painful to him, and of no real use to anybody. Take a Jew at Lisbon for example; he dissembles, he violates the laws, he braves an opinion which has all the force of popular sanction in its favour, and is he therefore the worst of men? Shall he be thought capable of all crimes? Would he calumniate, rob, and commit perjury if he had a hope of doing it with impunity? No: a Jew in Portugal is no more given to these offences than elsewhere.—Let a monk permit himself secretly to violate some of the absurd and painful observances of his convent, does it follow that he is a false and dangerous man, ready to violate his word upon a point where probity is involved? This conclusion would be quite unfounded. Simple good sense, enlightened by self-interest, is often able to explode a general error, without leading on that account to a contempt of essential laws.

racter of the delinquent, and which tend in consequence to lessen the alarm. They may be reduced to nine:—

1st. Absence of bad intention.
2nd. Self-preservation.
3rd. Provocation.
4th. Preservation of some near friend.
5th. Transgression of the limit of self-defence.
6th. Submission to menaces.
7th. Submission to authority.
8th. Drunkenness.
9th. Childhood.

It is a point common to these circumstances, except the two last, that the offence does not originate in the will of the delinquent. The primary cause is the act of another, the will of another, or some physical accident. Aside from that event, the offender would not have dreamed of the offence; he would have remained entirely innocent; and, even though he should not be punished, his future conduct would still be as good as if he had not committed the offence.

Each of the circumstances above enumerated demands details and explanations; but I shall confine myself here to the observation that the judge must be allowed a great latitude in appreciating the validity and extent of these different grounds of extenuation.

Does the question relate to a provocation? A provocation, to deserve indulgence, must be recent; it must have been received in the course of the same quarrel. But what constitutes the same quarrel? What ought to be looked upon as a recent injury? It is necessary to trace lines of demarcation. *Let not the sun go down upon your wrath,* is the precept of Scripture. Sleep ought to calm the transport of the passions, the fever of the senses, and prepare the mind for the influence of the tutelary motives. In the case of homicide, this natural period might serve to distinguish what is premeditated and what is the effect of sudden passion.

In the case of drunkenness it is necessary to examine if the intention to commit the offence did not exist beforehand, if the drunkenness were not feigned, and if it were not designed to create energy for the perpetration. Repetition ought, perhaps, to annihilate this excuse. He who knows by experience that wine renders him dangerous, does not merit indulgence for the excesses into which it may lead him.

The English law does not admit any plea of extenuation in the case of drunkenness. That would be, it is said, to excuse one offence by another. This reasoning seems to be hardhearted and superficial; it springs from the ascetic principle,—that austere and hypocritical doctrine which those of a certain profession think themselves obliged to maintain, but which is scouted by all the rest of the world.

As to childhood, we do not here speak of that tender age which is not responsible for its actions, and at which punishments would produce no effect. Infancy of that sort is not an extenuation; for in fact there is no offence. Such a child is not a moral agent. What good would be done by punishing judicially, for the crime of arson, an infant four years old?

Within what limits ought this ground of extenuation to be restricted? A limit sufficiently reasonable seems to be the epoch at which enough of mental maturity is presumed to release a person from pupilage, and to render him master of himself. Before that period he is not thought to have sufficient understanding to be intrusted with the management of his own affairs. Why should the law despair before it allows him to hope?

It is not intended that the ordinary punishment ought necessarily to be diminished in the case of every offence committed before the age of majority. That diminution ought to depend upon all the circumstances of the case. What is intended is, that after that epoch is passed, punishment shall no longer be liable to diminution under the plea of childhood.

Infamous punishments are those which ought principally to be remitted under this plea. He who has no hope of recovering his reputation will hardly recover his virtue.

When I speak of the age of majority, I do not mean the Roman majority, fixed at twenty-five years; because it is an injustice and a folly to retard so long the liberty of men, and to retain them in the leading-strings of infancy after the full development of their faculties. It is the English rule of twenty-one years which I have in view. We have seen Great Britain governed for years by a minister who managed, with great reputation, the infinitely complicated system of its finances, long before the age at which, in the rest of Europe, he would not have been capable of selling an acre of land.

CHAPTER XII.

Cases in which there is no Alarm.

THERE is no alarm whatever in those cases in which the only persons exposed to danger are incapable of fear.

This circumstance explains the insensibility of many nations on the subject of infanticide, that is, homicide committed on the person of a new-born infant, with the consent of the parents. I say with their *consent*, for otherwise the alarm would be almost the same as if the sufferer were an adult. As the susceptibility to fear is less on the part of infants, the more readily is paternal tenderness alarmed on their account.

I do not justify these nations. It is a striking additional mark of their barbarity that they have given to the father the right of destroying the infant without the consent of the mother, who, after all the dangers of maternity, is deprived of her reward, and reduced by this unworthy servitude to the same state with the inferior animals whose fecundity is a burden to us.

Infanticide, such as I have described it, ought not to be punished as a principal offence, since it produces no evil either of the first or of the second order. But it ought to be punished as an introduction to crimes, and as furnishing a proof against the character of those who commit it.

It is not possible to fortify too strongly the sentiments of respect for humanity, or to inspire too much repugnance against everything that conduces to cruel habits. This offence ought, then, to be punished by branding it with disgrace. It is commonly the fear of shame which is its cause; it needs a greater shame to repress it. But at the same time the occasions for punishing it ought to be made very rare, by requiring for a conviction of it proofs difficult to be collected.

The laws against this offence, under pretence of humanity, are a most manifest violation of it. Compare the offence with the punishment. The offence is what is improperly called the death of an infant, who has ceased to be, before knowing what existence is,—a result of a nature not to give the slightest inquietude to the most timid imagination; and which can cause no regrets but to the very person who, through a sentiment of shame and pity, has refused to prolong a life begun under the auspices of misery. And what is the punishment?—the barbarous infliction of an ignominious death upon an unhappy mother, whose very offence proves her excessive sensibility; upon a woman guided by despair, who, in hardening her heart against the softest instinct of nature, has harmed no one but herself! She is devoted to infamy because she has dreaded shame too much, and the souls of her surviving friends are poisoned with grief and disgrace! And if the legislator was himself the first cause of the evil, if he may justly be considered as the real murderer of these innocents, how still more odious does his rigour appear! It is he alone who, by severity against a weakness well entitled to indulgence, has excited that combat of tenderness and shame, which tears the mother's heart, and makes her the destroyer of her child.

CHAPTER XIII.

Cases in which there is greater Danger than Alarm.

Though there is a general correspondency between *danger* and *alarm*, there are cases in which the proportion is not exact; the danger may be much greater than the alarm.

This is the case with all mixed offences which include a private evil, and at the same time a danger, whence results their character of public offences.

It might happen that a prince was robbed by faithless agents, and the public oppressed by subaltern vexations. The accomplices in these disorders, forming a powerful phalanx, might permit nothing but mercenary praises to reach the throne, and truth might be esteemed the greatest of crimes. Timidity, under the mask of prudence, would soon become the leading trait in the national character. If, during this universal abjection, a virtuous citizen, daring to denounce the guilty, should become the victim of his zeal, his destruction would excite little alarm; his magnanimity would appear only an act of madness; and the citizens, promising themselves not to imitate his example, would be unmoved by a misfortune in their power to shun. But alarm thus subsiding gives place to a greater evil:—the danger of impunity to all public crimes; the cessation of all voluntary services to justice; a profound indifference for everything not personal to one's self.

It is said that in some of the Italian states, those who have given testimony against robbers or brigands, exposed to the vengeance of their accomplices, are obliged to seek in flight a security which the law does not afford. It is more dangerous to lend aid to justice than to take arms against it; a witness runs more risks than an assassin. The alarm which results from this state of things is not great, because all can avoid exposure to the evil; but in proportion as alarm diminishes, danger is augmented.

CHAPTER XIV.

Grounds of Justification.

I PROCEED to speak of some circumstances which, in connection with an offence, operate to take away its injurious quality. We may give to these circumstances the common name of *means of justification*, or, for shortness, *justifications*.

General justifications, which apply to nearly all offences, may be reduced to the following heads:—

1st. Consent.
2nd. Repulsion of a greater evil.
3rd. Medical practice.
4th. Self-defence.
5th. Political power.
6th. Domestic power.

How do these circumstances furnish justifications? We shall see that sometimes they import proof of the absence of evil; and sometimes they evince that the evil has been compensated—that is, that a good more than equivalent has resulted from it. The question here relates to the evil of the first order; for in all these cases there is no evil of the second order. I confine myself to some general observations.

1st. *Consent.* Meaning the consent of the person who suffers the evil, if there is an evil. What more natural than to presume that there is in fact no evil, or that it is perfectly compensated, where there is such a consent? We therefore admit the general rule of the lawyers, that *he who consents suffers no injury.* This rule is founded upon two very simple propositions: one, that every person is the best judge of his own interest; the other, that no man will consent to what he thinks hurtful to himself.

This rule admits many exceptions of which the reason is palpable;—such as coercion, fraud, concealment, a consent out of date or revoked, madness, drunkenness, childhood.

2nd. *Repulsion of a greater Evil.*—This is the case in which evil is done to prevent a greater evil. It is to this ground of justification that we must refer the extreme measures which may become necessary on occasions of contagious diseases, sieges, famines, tempests, shipwrecks.

But the more serious a remedy of this nature is, the more evident ought its necessity to be. The welfare of the state has served as a pretext for all crimes. To give validity to this means of justification, three essential points must be established—the *certainty* of the evil to be avoided; the *absolute inapplicability* of any means less costly; the *certain efficacy* of the means employed.

It is hence that the justification of tyrannicide must be derived, were tyrannicide justifiable; but it is not; for it is not necessary to assassinate a hated tyrant, it is enough to desert him, and he is lost. James II. was abandoned by everybody, and the revolution was completed without the effusion of blood. Nero himself saw his power overthrown by a simple decree of the senate, and the death he was obliged to inflict with his own hand was a more terrible lesson for tyrants than if it had been dealt by the dagger of a Brutus. Greece boasts its Timoleon; but we may see in the perpetual convulsions by which she was agitated how ill this doctrine of tyrannicide accomplished its object. It only served to irritate suspicious tyrants, and to render them ferocious in proportion to their cowardice. When the blow failed the vengeance was frightful. If it succeeded in popular states, factions immediately regained all their violence, and the victorious party inflicted all the evils it had feared; in monarchies, the terrified successor harboured a profound resentment; and if he became oppressive, he disguised his tyranny under the plausible pretext of providing for his own security.

It is said that the penetrating eye of Sylla discovered more than a single Marius, in a voluptuous youth yet famous only for his debaucheries. He saw the fires of the most ardent ambition concealed under the most effeminate softness of manners, and he regarded those dissolute pleasures only as a cover to the project of enslaving his country. Would these suspicions have authorized him to put Cæsar to death? Is it a fact, then, that an assassin only need turn prophet, to justify a murder? May an impostor, who pretends to a supernatural insight into futurity, immolate all his enemies for crimes not yet committed? Under pretence of avoiding an evil, this would be to produce the greatest of all evils, the annihilation of general security.

3rd. *Medical Practice.*—This ground of justification is only a subdivision of the preceding. An individual is made to suffer for his own good. A man is seized with an apoplexy. Shall we wait for his consent to bleed him? There cannot be a doubt as to the propriety of using the lancet, because it is very certain that it is not the patient's wish to die.

The case is very different if a man, master of his faculties, and able to consent, thinks proper to refuse it. Shall we give his friends or physicians the right to force an operation which he declines? This would be to substitute a certain evil for a danger almost imaginary. Distrust and terror would watch by the sick man's bed. If a physician, through humanity, goes beyond his right, and the experiment turns out unfavourably, he ought to be exposed to the rigour of the laws, and his intention, at most, should only serve as an extenuation of his offence.

4th. *Self-defence.*—This, too, is a modification of the second ground of justification. In fact, it is only the repulsion of a greater evil, since even the death of an unjust aggressor is a less evil for society than the suffering of an innocent person. This right of defence is absolutely necessary. The vigilance of magistrates can never make up for the vigilance of each individual in his own behalf. The fear of the law can never restrain bad men so effectually as the fear of the sum total of individual resistance. Take away this right, and you become, in so doing, the accomplice of all bad men.

This ground of justification has its limits. Overt acts must not be employed except to defend the person or the property. To answer a verbal injury by a corporal injury, would not be self-defence; it would be vengeance. Voluntarily to do an irreparable evil, merely to avoid one which might be repaired, would be passing the legitimate bounds of self-defence.

But can we defend nobody but ourselves? Ought we not to have the right of protecting our fellows against an unjust aggression? Surely it is a noble movement of the heart, that indignation which kindles at the sight of the feeble injured by the strong. It is a noble movement which makes us forget our own danger at the first cry of distress. The law ought to beware how it enfeebles this generous alliance between courage and humanity. Let him rather be honoured and rewarded who performs the function of the magistrate in favour of the oppressed. It concerns the public safety that every honest man should consider himself as the natural protector of every other. In this case there is no evil of the second order; on the contrary, all the effects of the second order are good.

5th and 6th. *Political and Domestic Power*.—The exercise of lawful power implies the necessity of doing evil to repress evil. Lawful power may be divided into political and domestic. The magistrate and the father, or he who stands in the father's place, cannot maintain their authority, the one in the state, and the other in the family, unless they are armed with coercive means against disobedience. The evil which they inflict is called punishment or chastisement. The whole object of these acts is the good of the great or little society which they govern; and it is hardly necessary to say that this exercise of lawful authority is a complete ground of justification, since no one would choose to be a magistrate or a father, if he were not secure in the exercise of his power.

PART SECOND.

POLITICAL REMEDIES AGAINST THE EVIL OF OFFENCES.

CHAPTER I.

Subject of this Part.

HAVING considered offences as *diseases* of the body politic, we are led by analogy to regard as *remedies* the means of prevention or redress.

These remedies may be arranged in four classes:—

1st. Preventive Remedies.
2nd. Suppressive Remedies.
3rd. Satisfactory Remedies.
4th. Penal Remedies, or Punishments.

Preventive Remedies are means which tend to prevent offences. They are of two kinds: direct means, which have an immediate application to such or such an offence in particular; indirect means, which consist in general precautions against an entire class of offences.

Suppressive Remedies are means which tend to put a stop to an offence already begun, an offence in progress, but not completed, and so to prevent the evil, or at least a part of it.

Satisfactory Remedies consist of reparations or indemnities, secured to those who have suffered from offences.

Penal Remedies or *Punishments* are also useful; for after a stop has been put to the evil, after the party injured has been indemnified, it still remains to prevent like offences, whether on the part of the same offender or of others. There are two ways of arriving at that end; one to correct the will, the other to take away the physical power. To take away the inclination to repeat the act, is reformation; to take away the power, is incapacitation. A remedy which operates by fear is called a punishment, whether or not it produces a physical incapacity depends upon its nature.

The principal end of punishments is to prevent like offences. What is past is but one act; the future is infinite. The offence already committed concerns only a single individual; similar offences may affect all. In many cases it is impossible to redress the evil that is done; but it is always possible to take away the will to repeat it; for however great may be the advantage of the offence, the evil of the punishment may be always made to outweigh it.

These four kinds of remedies sometimes require as many separate operations; sometimes the same operation suffices for the whole.

In this part I shall treat of direct preventive remedies, suppressive remedies, and satisfactory remedies; the third part will treat of punishments; in the fourth part will be considered the indirect means of preventing offences.

CHAPTER II.

Direct means of preventing Offences.

Before an offence is committed, it may give warning of its approach in many ways; it passes through a train of preparations which often allow it to be arrested before it reaches its catastrophe.

This part of police may be exercised either through functions assigned to all individuals alike, or by special powers intrusted to authorized persons.

The powers given to all the citizens for their protection are those which are exercised before justice takes cognizance of the matter, and which may be called, on that account, *ante-judicial* means. Such is the right to oppose open force to the execution of an apprehended offence; to seize a suspected person; to guard him; to carry him before a magistrate; to call in aid; to sequester into responsible hands articles believed to be stolen, or those the destruction of which it is desired to prevent; to summon the bystanders as witnesses; to require the passers-by to assist in carrying before the magistrates those who are suspected of bad designs.

The obligation of lending themselves to this service may be imposed upon all the citizens, and its fulfilment should be strictly required, as one of the most important duties of society. It will even be proper to establish rewards for those who may have aided to prevent an offence, or who have assisted to deliver the guilty into the hands of justice.

Is it said that these powers may be abused, and that unprincipled people may employ them to obtain assistance in an act of mere outrage? This danger is imaginary. The affectation of order and publicity would be quite unsuited to such views, and would too manifestly expose to punishment. There is not much danger in granting rights which cannot be exercised but at the risk of suffering the legal consequences in case of their misapplication. To refuse justice the aid which it might receive from these means would be to suffer an irreparable evil, through fear of an evil which carries with it its own redress.

Besides those powers which ought to appertain to every citizen, there are others, which should be confined to the magistrate, and which may be very useful in preventing apprehended offences.

1st. *Admonition.*—This is a simple intimation, given, however, by a judge, warning the suspected individual that he is watched, and recalling him to his duty by a respectable authority.

2nd. *Threats.*—This is the same means reinforced by a menace of the law. In the first case, it is the persuasive voice of a father; in the second, it is a magistrate whose severe rebuke intimidates.

3rd. *Exacting a Promise to keep away from a certain place.*—This means, applicable to the prevention of many offences, is particularly so to quarrels, to personal injuries, and to seditious plots.

4th. *Partial Banishment.*—A prohibition to the suspected person to go into the presence of the threatened party; to be found in the neighbourhood of his house; or in any other place adapted to become the theatre of the apprehended offence.

5th. *Security.*—The obligation to furnish sureties, who are bound to forfeit a certain sum in case the required limits be passed over.

6th. The establishment of *guards* or *watchmen* for the protection of the person or property in danger.

7th. *Seizure* of arms or other implements designed to assist in the execution of the apprehended offence.

Besides these general means, there are others which may be specially applied to certain offences; but I shall not enter here into these details of police and administration. The choice of these means, the occasion and the manner of applying them, depend upon a great number of circumstances; they are besides sufficiently simple, and almost always indicated by the nature of the case. If the question relates to a defamatory writing, it should be seized before publication; if it relates to things to be eaten or drunk, or to medicines of a dangerous nature, they ought to be destroyed before being put to use. Judicial visits and inspections are proper means to prevent frauds, clandestine acts, and offences of contraband.

This kind of cases seldom admits of precise rules. Something must be left to the discretion of public officers and judges. But the legislator ought to give such instructions as will prevent arbitrary abuses.

These instructions should rest upon the following maxims. The more rigorous is the means, the more scrupulous we ought to be as to its use. Greater liberties may be taken in proportion to the magnitude of the apprehended offence, and its apparent probability; in proportion as the delinquent appears more or less dangerous, and as he has more means of accomplishing his evil intentions. There is one limit which ought never to be passed. Never use a preventive means of a nature to do more evil than the offence to be prevented.

CHAPTER III.

Of Chronic Offences.

Before treating of suppressive remedies, that is, of the means of stopping the progress of offences, we must first discover what are the offences whose progress can be stopped; for there are some which do not admit of this measure: and those which do, do not all admit it in the same manner.

The capability of being stopped supposes that the offence has a sufficient duration to admit the intervention of justice; but all offences do not have such duration. Some have a transient, others a permanent effect. Homicide and violation cannot be repaired. Theft may last only a moment, or if the thing stolen has been consumed or destroyed, it may last for ever.

It is necessary to distinguish the circumstances according to which offences have a greater or less duration, because they have an influence on the suppressive means which may be applied to them.

1st. An offence acquires duration by the simple continuation of an act capable of ceasing at each instant without ceasing to have been an offence. The detention of a person, the abstraction of a thing, are offences of this kind.

2nd. Wherever the design of committing an offence is regarded as an offence in itself, it is clear that the continuance of the offence will be co-extensive with the continuance of the design. This class of chronic offences is a sub-division of the former.

3rd. The greater part of negative offences, those which consist in omissions, have a certain duration. Not to provide for the support of a child, not to pay one's debts, not to appear at the summons of a court, not to make known one's accomplices, not to put a person in the enjoyment of a right that belongs to him—all these appertain to this class.

4th. There are material works of which the continuance is a prolonged offence, such as a manufacture injurious to the health of a neighbourhood, a building which obstructs a road, a dam which interrupts the course of a river.

5th. Productions of the mind, through the intervention of printing, may have the same effect. Such are libels, pretended histories, alarming prophecies, obscene pictures—in one word, everything which presents to the citizens, under the durable signs of language, ideas which ought not to be presented.

6th. A series of repeated actions may have in their collectiveness a character of unity, in virtue of which he who commits them is said to have contracted a habit. Such are the fabrication of false money, forbidden processes in a manufacture, and contraband in general.

7th. There is a degree of duration in certain offences which, though distinct in themselves, yet, taken together, assume a character of unity, because one is the occasion of the other. A man commits a theft in a garden—he beats the owner who hastens to oppose him—he pursues him into his house, insults his family, spoils his furniture, kills a favourite dog, and continues his depredations. Thus is formed an indefinite series of offences, the duration of which may give time for the intervention of justice.

8th. There is a certain duration in the proceedings of a number of offenders who, with or without consent, pursue the same object. Thus from a confused medley of acts of destruction, threats, verbal injuries, personal injuries, insulting cries, and provoking shouts, is formed that sad and fearful composition called a tumult, a rising, an insurrection—forerunners of rebellion and civil war.

Chronic offences are apt to lead to a catastrophe. A projected offence ends in an executed offence. Simple corporal injuries have a tendency towards irreparable corporal injuries and homicide. There is no offence of which imprisonment may not be the forerunner. It may be used for getting rid of a marriage tie which proves to be inconvenient, or to carry out a scheme of seduction; to suppress testimony, to extort a secret, to prevent a claim of property; to force the prisoner to aid in some criminal enterprise—in one word, imprisonment may always have some particular catastrophe according to the object of the offender.

In the course of a criminal undertaking the end may change with the means. A thief surprised in the act, through fear of punishment, or enraged by the loss of his plunder, may become an assassin.

The foresight of the magistrate ought to picture in every case the probable catastrophe of the offence, and prevent it by a prompt and well-directed interference. In determining the punishment, reference must be had to the intentions of the offender; in applying preventive and suppressive remedies, we must take into account all the probable consequences, both those intended and those which the offender overlooks or does not foresee.

CHAPTER IV.

Suppressive Remedies for Chronic Offences.

The different kinds of chronic offences demand different suppressive remedies. These suppressive means are the same as the preventive means of which we have given a catalogue. The difference is in the time and the application.

There are cases in which the preventive means to be used correspond so visibly to the nature of the offence that they scarcely need to be indicated. It is very plain that wrongful imprisonment demands release, and that theft requires restitution. The only difficulty is to know where the person or thing detained can be found.

There are other offences, such as seditious meetings, and some negative offences, particularly the non-payment of debts, which require more complicated means to suppress them. We shall have occasion to examine these cases under their proper head.

The evil of dangerous writings is an evil very difficult to suppress. They lie hid, they multiply, they revive with more vigour after the most notable attempts to destroy them. When treating of indirect means of prevention, we shall show how this evil may be most effectually met.

The magistrate must be allowed more latitude in the employment of suppressive than in the use of preventive means. The reason is plain. When the question is to suppress, there is an actual offence, and consequently a punishment fixed for it. Too much is not risked to stop it, provided we do not go further than we must go to punish it. But while the point merely is to prevent an offence, we cannot be too scrupulous how we act. Perhaps no such offence is intended; perhaps we are deceived in the person to whom we attribute the intention; perhaps the person suspected is acting in good faith, and instead of committing the offence he will stop of himself. Each, *perhaps*, demands a procedure milder and more moderate in proportion as the apprehended offence is more problematical.

The offences of illegal detention and deportation are of such a nature as to demand some particular means for preventing and suppressing them. These means may be reduced to the following precautions:—

1st. To require a register of the houses of all kinds in which individuals are detained in spite of themselves, such as prisons, hospitals for the insane or for idiots, and private institutions for persons thus disordered.

2nd. To have a second register containing the causes of detention, and not to permit a person of unsound mind to be detained till after a juridical consultation of physicians. These two registers, kept in the tribunals of each district, should be publicly exposed, or at least left open to be consulted by everybody.

3rd. To establish some signal, such as shall be as much as possible in the power of a person forcibly carried away, which shall be a sufficient authority to any passer-by to call the ravishers to account, to accompany them if they declare an intention to carry the prisoner before a magistrate, and to compel them to go if they evince a different intention.

4th. Granting to all the right to obtain authority to search every house in which they suspect a person to be forcibly detained.

CHAPTER V.

Observations upon Martial Law.

In England, in the case of seditious disturbances, it is not the fashion to begin by a military assassination. Warning precedes the punishment; martial law is proclaimed, and the soldier cannot act till the magistrate has spoken.

The intention of this rule is excellent; but what shall we say of its execution? The magistrate is obliged to go into the midst of the tumult; he must pronounce a long drawling formula, which nobody understands; and bad luck to those who are on the spot an hour after!—they are declared guilty of a capital offence. This statute, dangerous for the innocent and difficult to be executed against the guilty, is a mixture of weakness and violence.

In such a moment of disorder, the magistrate ought to announce his presence by some extraordinary signal. The *red flag*, so famous in the French revolution, had a great effect upon the imagination. In the midst of cries, the ordinary means of language do not answer. The multitude cannot hear; it is necessary to speak to their eyes. An harangue supposes attention and silence; but visible signs have a rapid and powerful operation. They say at once all they have to say; they have but one sense, and that unequivocal; a studied disturbance, a concerted uproar, cannot prevent their effect.

Besides, words lose their influence through a multitude of unforeseen circumstances. If the orator is personally odious, from his mouth even the language of justice is hateful. If his character, his air, or the style of his oratory, have in them anything ridiculous, this ridicule extends to his official acts. Here is an additional reason for speaking to the eyes by respectable symbols, not subject to like caprices.

But, as it may be necessary to join words to signs, a speaking trumpet is an essential accompaniment. The singularity even of that instrument would give to the orders of justice more dignity and *éclat;* it would banish every idea of familiar conversation, and convey the notion of not hearing a man, the mere individual magistrate, but the privileged minister, the herald of the law.

This means of being heard afar has long been used at sea. There, distance and the noise of winds and waves early made evident the insufficiency of the human voice. The poets have often compared a tumultuous people to a stormy ocean. Does this analogy belong exclusively to the agreeable arts? It would be of much more importance in the hands of justice.

The orders should be in few words; nothing which is of the nature of ordinary discourse or discussion. Let it not be *by command of the king.* Speak in the name of justice. The chief magistrate may be an object of hatred, just or unjust; perhaps that very hatred is the cause of the tumult. To call up his image would be to inflame passions instead of allaying them. If not odious already, such a procedure would expose him to become so. Every favour, everything which bears the character of pure beneficence, ought to be presented as the personal act of the father of his people. All rigorous proceedings,—those of severe benevolence,—ought to be attributed to nobody. Let the hand that acts be veiled. Throw the responsibility upon some creature of reason, some animated abstraction; such as *Justice,* daughter of necessity and mother of peace, whom men ought to fear, but whom they cannot hate, and who ought always to possess their supremest homage.

CHAPTER VI.

Nature of Satisfaction.

Satisfaction is a good received, in consideration of a damage suffered. If the question relate to an offence, satisfaction is an equivalent given to the party injured on account of the damage he has sustained.

Satisfaction is *complete*, whenever the good conferred is equal to the amount of evil suffered; so that if the injury should be repeated and the same reparation should follow, the event would appear indifferent to the injured party. If something is wanting to raise the value of the good to an equality with the evil, the satisfaction is partial and imperfect.

Satisfaction has two aspects or two branches, the past and the future. Satisfaction for the past is what is called *indemnity;* satisfaction for the future consists in putting a stop to the evil of the offence. If the evil ceases of itself, nature has performed the functions of justice, and in this respect the tribunals have nothing more to do.

If a sum of money has been stolen, from the moment it is restored to the owner the satisfaction for the future is complete. It only remains to indemnify him for the past, for the temporary loss which he experienced while the offence continued.

But if the question is of a thing spoiled or destroyed, satisfaction for the future can only take place by giving to the party injured a similar or equivalent article. Satisfaction for the past would consist in an indemnity for the temporary privation.

CHAPTER VII.

Reasons on which the necessity of Satisfaction is founded.

Satisfaction is necessary to put a stop to the evil of the first order, to re-establish things in the state in which they were before the offence was committed, and to restore the sufferer to the condition in which he would have been if the law had not been violated.

Satisfaction is yet more necessary to put a stop to the evil of the second order. Punishment alone is not sufficient for that purpose. It tends, without doubt, to diminish the number of offenders; but this number, though diminished, can never be considered as nothing. Examples of the commission of offences, as they are more or less known, excite more or less of apprehension. Every observer sees in them the chance of suffering in his turn. If it be desired to dissipate this sentiment of fear, it is necessary that the offence should be as constantly followed by satisfaction as by punishment. If it were followed by punishment without satisfaction, as many offenders as were punished, so many proofs there would be of the inefficacy of punishment; and consequently so much alarm weighing upon society.

But here needs to be made an essential observation. To take away the alarm, it is enough that the satisfaction is complete in the eyes of observers, although not complete to the persons interested. How can we determine whether the satisfaction is complete for him who receives it? The balance, in the hands of passion, would always incline to the side of interest; to the greedy it would be impossible to give enough; the vindictive never would think his adversary sufficiently humbled. We must suppose, then, an impartial observer, and regard that satisfaction as sufficient which he would estimate as equivalent to the evil endured.

CHAPTER VIII.

The different Kinds of Satisfaction.

We may distinguish six kinds:—

1st. *Pecuniary Satisfaction.*—As money is a pledge for the greater part of pleasures, it is an efficacious compensation for a multitude of evils. But it is not always in the offender's power to pay it, nor always proper that the offended party should receive it. To offer a man, whose honour has been outraged, a compensation in money for the insult is a new affront.

2nd. *Restitution in Nature.*—This satisfaction consists either in returning the thing taken away or in giving a thing similar or equivalent to that taken away or destroyed.

3rd. *Attestatory Satisfaction.*—If the evil results from a falsehood, a statement false in point of fact, satisfaction is complete by a legal attestation of the truth.

4th. *Honorary Satisfaction.*—An operation which has for its end either to maintain or to re-establish in favour of an individual a portion of honour, of which the offence had deprived him, or threatened to deprive him.

5th. *Vindictive Satisfaction.*—Everything which implies a manifest pain to the offender implies a pleasure of vengeance to the party injured.

6th. *Substitutive Satisfaction,* or satisfaction at the expense of a third party; when a person not a party to the offence is held responsible in his fortune for the person who committed it.

To determine our choice as to the kind of satisfaction, three things must be considered,—the *ease* of furnishing it; the *nature* of the evil to be compensated; and the probable *sentiments* of the party injured. These different heads will presently be taken up, and more fully considered.

CHAPTER IX.

The Quantity of Satisfaction.

As much as the satisfaction fails of being complete, to the same degree the evil remains without a remedy.

We may fix, by two rules, what is necessary to prevent a deficit in this respect.

1st. *Follow the evil of the offence in all its ramifications, and among all parties to it, and proportion the satisfaction accordingly.*

If the question relates to irreparable corporal injuries, two things must be considered; a means of enjoyment and a means of subsistence taken away for ever. There cannot be a compensation of the same nature, but there ought to be applied to the evil a perpetual periodical remedy.

If the question relates to a homicide, it is proper to consider the loss experienced by the heirs of the deceased, and to make it up by a gratification paid at once, or periodically for a longer or shorter term.

If the question relates to an offence against property, we shall see, under the head of Pecuniary Satisfaction, what is required to put the reparation on a level with the offence.

2nd. *In doubtful cases, the balance ought to incline in his favour who has suffered the injury, rather than in favour of him who committed it.*

All accidents ought to be at the risk of the offender. All satisfaction ought rather to be superabundant than defective. If superabundant, the excess being in the nature of a punishment, cannot but serve to prevent like offences. If defective, that deficit always leaves a certain degree of alarm; and in vindictive offences, all the unsatisfied evil is a matter of triumph to the offender.

Laws are everywhere very imperfect upon this point. On the side of punishments there has been little fear of excess; on the side of satisfaction, a deficit has caused little concern. Punishment, which, if it goes beyond the limit of necessity, is a pure evil, has been scattered with a prodigal hand. Satisfaction, which is purely a good, has been dealt out with the most evident parsimony.

CHAPTER X.

The certainty of Satisfaction.

Certainty of satisfaction is an essential branch of security; and in proportion as this certainty is wanting, in the same proportion security is diminished.

What shall be thought of those laws which, to the natural causes of uncertainty, add other factitious and voluntary causes? To obviate this defect the following rules are necessary:—

1st. *The obligation to satisfy ought not to be extinguished by the death of the injured party. The satisfaction due to the deceased is due to his heirs.*

To make the right of receiving satisfaction dependent upon the life of an individual, is to take away from that right a part of its value. It is like reducing a perpetual annuity into an annuity for life. Satisfaction is not to be obtained except by a process which may last a long time. If the claimant is an aged or infirm person, the value of his right fluctuates with his health; if the claimant is on his death-bed, his right is worth nothing.

Moreover, if you diminish on one side the certainty of satisfaction, you increase on the other the hope of impunity. You show in perspective to the offender a time when he may hope quietly to enjoy the fruit of his offence. You give him a motive to retard, by a thousand impediments, the judgment of the court, and even to hasten the death of the injured party. At all events you put out of the protection of the law those persons who have the greatest need of it,—the dying and the sick.

It is true that, although the obligation of satisfaction be extinguished by the death of the injured party, the offender may still be subjected to another punishment; but what other punishment can be so fit and proper?

2nd. *The right of the injured party ought not to be extinguished by the death of the offender, the author of the wrong. The satisfaction due from him is due from his heirs.*

To determine otherwise would be to diminish the value of the right, and to encourage offences. A man conscious that death was near, might commit an injustice with no other object except to advance the fortune of his children,—a case more common than is generally supposed.

Is it said that if satisfaction be given to the injured party, after the death of the delinquent, it is only by an equivalent suffering imposed upon his heirs? But there is a great difference between the two cases. The expectation of the injured party is a clear, precise, decided expectation, firm in proportion to his confidence in the protection of the laws. The expectation of the heir is but a vague hope. The object of it is not the entire succession, but a certain, unknown, net produce, after all lawful deductions. That which the deceased might have spent in pleasures he has spent upon injustice.

CHAPTER XI.

Pecuniary Satisfaction.

There are cases in which pecuniary satisfaction is demanded by the very nature of the offence; there are other cases in which it is the only satisfaction that circumstances permit.

It should be employed by preference, upon occasions where it promises to have the greatest effect.

Pecuniary satisfaction is at its highest point of propriety in cases where the damage experienced by the injured party, and the advantage obtained by the delinquent, are alike of a pecuniary nature; as in theft, peculation, and extortion. The remedy and the evil are homogeneous; the compensation may be exactly measured by the loss, and the punishment by the profit of the offence.

This kind of satisfaction is not so well founded when there is a pecuniary loss upon one side, without any pecuniary profit upon the other; as in the case of offences committed through hostility, negligence, or accident.

It has still less foundation in those cases in which it is not possible to value in money either the evil of the party injured, or the advantage of the offender; as in case of injuries to honour.

The more a means of satisfaction is incommeasurable with the injury, the more a means of punishment is incommeasurable with the advantage of the offence, the more likely are both to fail of their end.

The old Roman law, which appointed a fixed sum of money as the damages for a blow, was no protection to honour. The reparation having no common measure with the outrage, its effect was precarious, whether as a satisfaction or a punishment.

There is still in existence an English law, which is a true relic of barbarous times. A daughter is considered as the servant of her father; if she is seduced, the father cannot obtain any other satisfaction than a sum of money, the price of the domestic services which he is supposed to have lost by the pregnancy of his daughter.

As respects injuries to the person, a pecuniary indemnity may be proper or not, according to the respective wealth of the parties.

In regulating a pecuniary satisfaction, the two branches of the past and the future must not be forgotten. Satisfaction for the future consists merely in putting a stop to the evil; satisfaction for the past consists in an indemnity for the wrong endured. To receive a sum due, is a satisfaction for the future; to receive the accrued interest upon that sum, is a satisfaction for the past.

Interest ought to begin from the happening of the evil to be compensated; from the moment, for example, when the debt became due; when the thing in question was taken, damaged, or destroyed; or when the service to which one had a right was refused.

This interest, granted as a satisfaction, ought to be higher than the ordinary rate of commerce; at least, whenever there is a suspicion of bad faith. Such an excess is very necessary. If the interest did not exceed the customary rate, there would be cases when the satisfaction would be incomplete, and other cases in which a profit would result to the offender,—the pecuniary profit, for example, of obtaining a forced loan at the ordinary interest; a pleasure of vengeance or hostility, if the offender has wished to keep the injured party in need, and to enjoy his distress.

For the same reason, compound interest should be allowed; that is, every time a payment of interest became due, that interest should be added to the principal, and should become a part of it. The capitalist, at each payment, might have converted his interest into capital, or have drawn an equivalent advantage from it. If this part of the damage is left without satisfaction, there will be a loss to the innocent party, and a gain to the delinquent.

The expense of satisfaction ought to be shared among the offenders in proportion to their wealth, or, according to circumstances, in proportion to their respective degrees of criminality. For, in fact, the obligation to satisfy is a punishment; and it would be in the highest degree unequal if co-delinquents of unequal wealth were mulcted in the same sum.

CHAPTER XII.

Restitution in Nature.

Restitution in nature is chiefly important in the case of property which possesses a value of affection.*

But it is due in every case. The law ought to assure me everything which is mine, without forcing me to accept equivalents, even though I have no particular objection to them. Without restitution in nature, security is incomplete. How can we be secure as to the whole, when we are secure of nothing in particular?

A thing taken away, either in good or bad faith, may have passed into the hands of a stranger who holds it in good faith. Shall it be restored to the former owner, or be kept by the new one? The rule is simple. The thing ought to remain with the person who may be supposed to have the greatest affection for it. This superior degree of affection may be easily estimated, from the relations of the two parties to the thing in question, from the time they have possessed it, from the services they have drawn from it, from the cares and expense it has cost them. These indications commonly unite in favour of the original owner.†

The preference is also due to him in doubtful cases, and for these reasons:—1st. The new owner may have been an accomplice in the fraudulent acquisition, though it may be impossible

* Such as immoveables in general, also family relics, portraits, the handiwork of a dear friend, domestic animals, antiquities, curiosities, pictures, manuscripts, instruments of music,—in fine, everything which is unique, or which appears to be so.

† When the thing or animal in question is of the kind which produces its like, we may ascertain, by the same considerations, on which side is likely to be the superiority of affection as respects its fruits or offspring, as wine of a particular vineyard, the colt of a favourite horse, &c. It may well be that the claims of the former owner are not so strong in this case as in the other. The new possessor is only owner at second hand of the thing or animal that produces, but he is the first owner of the things produced.

to get proofs of it. This suspicion is not unjust; formed by the law and not by man, bearing upon the class and not upon the individual, it does not impeach anybody's honour. 2nd. If the new owner was not an accomplice, he may have been guilty of negligence or rashness, either by omitting ordinary precautions to verify the title of the seller, or by putting an undue confidence in proofs of little weight. 3rd. When the question relates to grave offences, such as robbery, the preference ought to be given to the former possessor, in order to strengthen the motives which induce him to prosecute. 4th. If the spoliation has been an act of malice, to leave the thing in the possession of anybody except the injured party, would be to leave the offender a gainer by the offence.

A purchase of such articles at a low price ought always to be followed by restitution at the price paid. If this circumstance does not prove the purchaser to be an accomplice, it always carries with it a strong presumption of bad faith. The purchaser cannot have overlooked the probability of a wrongful possession on the part of the seller; for it is the danger of carrying them to an open market which causes the low price of stolen goods.

When the possessor, though esteemed innocent, is obliged, on account of the bad faith of the seller, to restore the thing to the original owner, there ought to be awarded to him a pecuniary equivalent, to be fixed by the magistrate.

The expenses of preservation, and, for a stronger reason, the costs of improvements, and other extraordinary outlays, ought to be liberally allowed to him who restores the property. This is not only a means of favouring general wealth, it is for the interest even of the original proprietor, though the indemnity be paid at his expense. According as this indemnity is granted or refused, the improvement of the thing is favoured or prevented.

Neither the original owner nor the subsequent possessor ought to gain at the expense of the other. The losing party ought to be allowed a claim of indemnity, first against the offender, and in his default, upon the subsidiary fund of which we shall presently speak.

When an identical restitution is impossible, there ought to be substituted for it, as far as may be, the restitution of a similar thing. Suppose two rare medals of the same coinage. The owner of one of them has seized upon the other, and spoiled or lost it, by negligence or design. In such a case the best satisfaction is to give *his* medal to the injured party.

In offences of this kind pecuniary satisfaction is liable to prove insufficient or useless. A value of affection is seldom appreciated by third persons. It needs a very enlightened benevolence, and philosophy very uncommon, to sympathize with tastes different from our own. The Dutch florist, who sells tulip bulbs for their weight in gold, laughs at the antiquary who pays a great price for a rusty lamp.*

Legislators and judges have too often thought like the vulgar. They have applied gross rules to cases which required a nice discernment. There are cases in which the offer of money is not a satisfaction, but an insult. Shall a lover take money as the price of his mistress's portrait, of which a rival has robbed him?

Mere restitution in nature leaves a deficiency of satisfaction proportioned to the amount of enjoyment lost during the continuance of the offence. An example will show how this amount is to be estimated. Suppose a statue illegally taken away. This statue put up at auction would have brought a hundred pounds sterling, according to the estimate of experts. A year elapses

* Some years since a canary-bird was the subject of a lawsuit before one of the Parliaments of France. A journalist, who gave an account of it, amused himself at the expense of the parties, and regarded the whole affair as very ridiculous. I cannot agree with him. Is it not the imagination which gives a value to the objects esteemed most precious? As laws are made only out of deference to the universal sentiments of men, can they show too much anxiety to guard everything which makes a part of human happiness? Should they not acknowledge and protect the sensibility which attaches us to creatures we have raised and familiarized, and who in their turn are attached to us? This lawsuit, so frivolous in the eyes of the journalist, was but too serious a matter, since one of the parties had sacrificed to it, to say nothing of money, his probity and his honour. Can an object rated so highly be considered a trifle?

between the robbery and the restitution; interest is at five per cent. Put down under the head of satisfaction for the past, ordinary interest, five pounds; additional for penal interest (*see* ch. xi.), say two pounds ten shillings; total, seven pounds ten shillings.

In fixing the damages we must not forget the deterioration, whether accidental or necessary, which the thing may have undergone in the interval between the commission of the offence and the restitution. The statue would not have deteriorated,—at least, not necessarily; but a horse of the same price must of course have diminished in value. A collection of tables of natural deterioration, year by year, according to the nature of the several articles, is one of the things which the library of justice requires.

CHAPTER XIII.

Attestatory Satisfaction.

This means of satisfaction is particularly adapted to offences of falsehood whence there is liable to result an opinion prejudicial to an individual; but the weight of which, its extent, and even its existence, cannot be established by evidence. While the error exists, it is a constant source of actual or probable evil; there is but one means of arresting it, and that is to make its falsehood evident.

This is the proper place for enumerating the principal offences of falsehood.

1st. *Simple Mental Injuries, consisting in the spread of False Alarms.*—For example, stories of apparitions, ghosts, vampires, sorcerers, diabolical possessions; false reports of a nature to strike some individual with fear or sadness, pretended deaths; stories of the bad conduct of near relations, of conjugal infidelities, of losses of property; falsehoods adapted to alarm a class more or less numerous, as reports of contagious diseases, invasions, conspiracies, conflagrations, &c.

2nd. *Offences against Reputation*, of which there are many kinds:

defamation by the positive statement of particular injurious facts; *diminution of reputation,* which consists in weakening what cannot be destroyed—concealing from the public, for example, a circumstance which would add to the *éclat* of a celebrated action; *interception of reputation,* which consists in preventing the performance of an action honourable to the individual in question, or in taking from him the occasion of distinguishing himself by causing an enterprise to be regarded as impossible or finished already; *usurpation of reputation,* of which all plagiarisms, whether of authors or artists, are examples.

3rd. *Fraudulent Acquisition.*—Examples: false reports to affect the rate of exchange or the price of stocks.

4th. *Disturbance in the Enjoyment of Domestic and Civil Rights.*—Examples: denying to a husband, a wife, or a child their legal titles to that condition; or setting up a false claim of that nature; or aiding in a like falsity in regard to any privilege or civil condition.

5th. *Preventing Acquisition.*—Preventing a man from buying or selling by false reports as to the value of the thing or his right to dispose of it. Preventing a person from acquiring a certain condition, such as marriage, by false reports which make him postpone it or give it over.

In all these cases the arm of justice is powerless; forcible means are null or imperfect. The only efficacious remedy is an authentic declaration which destroys the falsehood. To dissipate error, to publish the truth—how respectable a function, how worthy of the highest tribunals!

What should be the form of attestatory satisfaction? It may vary with the means of publicity; it may consist in printing and publishing the judgment at the expense of the offender, in handbills distributed under the direction of the injured party, or publications in the national and foreign newspapers.

The idea of this satisfaction, so simple and so useful, is drawn from French jurisprudence. When a man had been calumniated, the parliaments almost always ordered that the sentence which re-established his reputation should be printed and circulated at the expense of the calumniator.

But why force the offender to declare that he has been guilty of false charges, and to acknowledge publicly the honour of the party interested? This form is objectionable in several respects. It is wrong to compel a man to the expression of certain sentiments which perhaps he does not entertain, and to risk the judicial command of a falsehood. It is wrong to enfeeble the reparation by an act of constraint; for what does a compulsory retraction prove, except the weakness or the fear of him who utters it?

The offender may be the organ of his own condemnation, if it be thought fit so to augment the punishment; but he may be so without swerving from the exactest truth, provided the formula prescribed to him includes only the opinion of the court as being the opinion of the court, not his own. "The court has decided that I have alleged a falsehood; the court has adjudged that I have departed from the character of an honest man; the court are of opinion that in all this business my opponent has conducted himself like a man of honour." This is all that concerns the public or the injured party. This is triumph enough for truth, humiliation enough for the offender. What is gained by forcing him to say, "I have alleged a falsehood; I have departed from the character of an honest man; my opponent has comported like a man of honour?" This declaration, stronger than the former in appearance, is much less so in reality. The fear which dictates such avowals does not change the actual sentiments of the speaker; and when the mouth pronounces them before a numerous audience, all feel and understand that the heart makes no assent.

Where the question is of a fact, the court is less likely to be deceived; and a direct avowal of falsehood, exacted in his own name from the guilty party, will almost always be conformable to his intimate opinion; but when the question relates to an opinion —to wit, that of the offender—a disavowal which is commanded will almost always be contrary to his interior conviction. In such contests impartial people will condemn an individual ten times for once that he condemns himself.

Even if he is calm enough to give himself up to reflection, the triumph of his opponent is before his eyes, he is himself the instrument of it, and the irritation of wounded pride must increase his prejudices. He may have been deceived, and you compel him to accuse himself of falsehood; you place him in a cruel position, where, the honester he is, the more he will suffer—that is, he will be more severely punished in proportion as he deserves it less.

How many scoundrels by the decision of a court would make themselves be declared men of honour and probity by the very persons who best knew the contrary! Besides, what signifies such a general declaration? Because a particular imputation is false or doubtful, does it follow that a man's character is above all imputation? Because a person has been once slandered, is his reputation therefore above all blame? Let one of these patents of honour be once granted to a man in bad estimation, and at once a contradiction appears between public opinion and the sentence of the judges; their authority is weakened, and they are no longer recurred to for a remedy which, by being badly administered, has lost its efficacy.

With respect to promises less reserve is necessary. It is enough if the engagement includes nothing contrary to honour or to probity. For example, a promise ought not to be extorted from a man to serve against his country or his party; but a promise not to fight may be extorted, because such an undertaking on his part produces no loss to his party or his country; for he would not have been able to serve them if, instead of being set at liberty upon his promise, he had been put to death or kept in irons.

CHAPTER XIV.

Honorary Satisfaction.

We have seen what remedy can be provided for those offences against reputation of which falsehood is the instrument. But there are others more dangerous; hatred has surer means of striking a deadly blow at honour. It does not always lurk under a timid calumny; it makes an open attack; not, however, by those violent means which put the person in danger. Humiliation is its end. An act, the least painful in itself, is often the most so in its consequences; a greater evil to the person would be a less injury to the honour; for when we would make a man an object of contempt, we should avoid exciting in his favour a sentiment of pity which will produce an antipathy against his adversary. Hatred has exhausted all its refinements upon this kind of offences. They must be opposed by those particular remedies to which we give the name of *honorary satisfaction*.

To perceive the necessity of this course, it is necessary to examine the nature and tendency of these offences; the causes of their importance, the remedy hitherto applied to them by the usage of duelling, and the imperfection of that remedy. These inquiries, which relate to all that is most delicate in the human heart, have been almost entirely neglected by those who have made laws; and yet they are the first foundation of all good legislation upon the subject of honour.

In the actual state of manners among the most civilized nations, the ordinary and natural effect of these offences is to take from the offended person a more or less considerable portion of his honour; that is, he no longer enjoys the same esteem among his fellows; he loses a proportional part of the pleasures, services, and good offices of every kind, which are the fruits of that esteem; and he finds himself exposed to the disagreeable consequences of their contempt.

Now, as the evil, at least the essential part of it, consists in this change in the sentiments of men it is they who ought to be considered as its immediate authors. The nominal offender has inflicted but a trifling wound, which, left to itself, would soon close up. It is other men who pour a poison into it, which makes it dangerous, and often incurable.

At the first view, the rigour of public opinion against an insulted person seems a piece of revolting injustice. Does a man stronger or more daring abuse his superiority to maltreat, in a certain manner, a person whose feebleness ought to be his protection? All the world, as if by a concerted movement, instead of being angry with the oppressor, arrange themselves upon his side, and heap upon his victim a succession of cowardly sarcasms and neglects, often more bitter than death itself. At the signal of some worthless wretch, the public eagerly dashes upon the innocent object of his malice, like a ferocious dog, which only waits his master's order. Thus it is that a scoundrel, who desires to inflict upon some worthy man the torments of disgrace, employs those who are called men of the world, men of honour, as the executioners of his tyrannical injustice; and, as the contempt with which the injury is attended is in proportion to the injury itself, this domination of ruffians is the more inexcusable, as its abuses are the more atrocious.

Whether an insult be deserved or not, is a question which nobody deigns to ask; deserved or not, it furnishes a triumph not only to its insolent author, but to everybody else who chooses to assist in aggravating it. People take honour to themselves for trading on the fallen; an affront received separates a man from his equals; and, like a social excommunication, renders him impure in their eyes. Thus the real evil—the ignominy—is more the work of other men than of the first offender; he has but pointed out the game, they have torn it to pieces; he orders the punishment, they are the executioners.

For example, let a man go so far as publicly to spit in another's face. In itself, what is this evil?—a drop of water, forgotten as soon as felt. But this drop of water turns into a corrosive poison which torments the sufferer through his whole life. What works the change? Public opinion, that opinion which distributes at pleasure honour and shame. The cruel enemy who inflicted it knew well that this affront would be the forerunner and the signal for a torrent of contempt.

A brute, a vile wretch, can at pleasure dishonour a virtuous man! He can fill with chagrin and distress the termination of the most respectable career! And how does he enjoy this fatal power? He enjoys it, because an irresistible corruption has subjugated the first and the purest of tribunals, that of the popular sanction. In consequence of this deplorable state of things, all the citizens depend individually for their honour upon the worst man among them, and are collectively subject to his orders, to execute his decrees of proscription against each individual in particular.

Such is the charge which may be brought against public opinion; and these imputations are not without foundation. Men, admirers of power, are often guilty of injustice towards the feeble; but when we probe to the bottom the effects of this kind of offences, we perceive that they produce an evil independently of opinion, and that the sentiments of the public upon affronts received and endured, are not in general so contrary to reason as at first sight they appear to be; I say in general, because there are a great number of cases in which public opinion is quite without excuse.

To perceive all the evil which may result from these offences, it is necessary to put all remedies out of view; it is necessary to suppose there are none. Upon this supposition, these offences may be repeated at will; an unlimited career is opened to insolence; the person insulted to-day may be insulted to-morrow, the next day, every day, and every hour; each new affront facilitates another, and renders more probable a succession of injuries of the same kind. Now, under the notion of a *corporal insult* is comprehended every act offensive to the person which can be inflicted without causing a lasting physical evil, every act which produces a disagreeable sensation, inquietude, or pain. But an act of this sort, which if single would be scarcely sensible, may produce, by force of repetition, a very painful degree of uneasiness, or even intolerable torture. I have read somewhere that water, falling drop by drop upon the crown of the naked head, is one of the most cruel tortures ever invented. *Gutta cavat lapidem*, dropping water hollows the rock, says the Latin proverb. Thus, the individual exposed by his relative weakness to suffer vexations of this sort at the will of his persecutor, and destitute, as we have supposed, of all legal protection, would be reduced to a most miserable situation. Nothing more is needed to establish on one side absolute despotism, and on the other complete servitude.

But such a one is not the slave of a single person only; he is the slave of everybody who has a mind to play the despot. He is the sport of the first comer, who, knowing his weakness, may be tempted to abuse it. Like a Spartan helot, he is dependent upon all the world, always fearing and always suffering, an object of general ridicule, and of a contempt not even softened by compassion; in one word, lower than any slave, because the misfortunes of a slave spring from a compulsatory condition entitled to pity; while *his* degradation grows out of the baseness of his character.

These little vexations, these insults, have, for another reason, a sort of pre-eminence in tyranny over violent attacks. Those acts of wrath sufficient to quench at once the hostility of the offender, and even to give an immediate feeling of repentance, offer to view a termination of sufferings; but a humbling and malignant insult, far from exhausting the hatred which produces it, appears rather to serve as an incentive; so that it presents itself to the imagination as the forerunner of a succession of injuries, the more alarming because indefinite.

What is here said of corporal insults may be applied to threats, since it is to their threatening quality alone that corporal insults owe all their consequence.

Outrages in words are not altogether of the same character. They are only a kind of vague defamation, an employment of injurious terms of indeterminate signification, and of which the meaning varies much, according to the condition of persons.* What is signified by these verbal assaults is this, that the person assailed is thought worthy of public contempt; but on what particular account is not specified. The probable evil which may result is the renewal of similar reproaches. We may fear, too, lest a profession of contempt publicly made may invite other men to join in it. It is, in fact, an invitation which many will

* We must carefully distinguish outrageous words of special defamation from those which have no particular object. The former can be refuted; they furnish room for attestatory satisfaction. The latter, being vague and indefinite, do not offer the same hold.

be ready to accept. The pride of censure, the pleasure of triumphing at another's expense, the spirit of imitation, the inclination to believe all strong assertions, give weight to these sorts of injuries. But they seem to owe their principal importance to the negligence of the laws, and to the usage of duelling,—that subsidiary remedy, by which the popular sanction has attempted to supply the silence of the laws.

It is not surprising that legislators, fearing to give too much importance to trifles, have left in a state of almost universal abandonment that part of security which consists in a freedom from the petty acts of vexation above enumerated. The physical evil, so natural a measure of the importance of an offence, is almost nothing; and the distant consequences quite escaped the inexperience of those by whom laws were first established.

Duelling offered itself to fill this gap. This is not the place to inquire into its origin, or to examine its variations and apparent absurdities. It is enough that duelling exists; that in fact it assumes the form of a remedy, and serves to restrain that enormity of disorder which otherwise would result from the negligence of the laws.

This usage once established, produces the following consequences.

The first effect of duelling is to put a stop, in a great measure, to the evil of those offences to which it applies—that is, to the shame which results from insult. The offended party is no longer in that miserable condition, exposed by his weakness to the outrages of the insolent, and the contempt of all. He is delivered from a state of continual fear. The blot upon his honour is effaced; and if the duel has followed immediately upon the affront, there is no blot; it has no time to fix itself; for dishonour does not consist in receiving an insult, but in submitting to it.

The second effect of duelling is, that it acts as a punishment, and tends to prevent the reproduction of like offences. Every new example is a promulgation of the penal laws of honour, a notification that offensive acts cannot be indulged in, without exposure to the consequences of a private combat—that is, according to the event of the duel, to the danger of different degrees of bodily suffering, or to death itself. Thus the brave man, impelled by the silence of the law to expose himself in order to punish an insult, upholds the general security, while labouring for his own.

But considered as a *punishment*, the duel is extremely defective.

1st. It is not a means of which everybody can avail themselves. There are numerous classes who cannot participate in the protection which it affords, such as women, children, old men, the sick, and those who lack courage to purchase exemption from shame at the risk of so great a danger. Besides, by an absurdity in the point of honour worthy of its feudal origin, the upper classes have not admitted their inferiors to the equality of the duel; the peasant outraged by a gentleman cannot obtain this satisfaction. The insult in this case may have less serious effects, but still it is an insult, and an evil without a remedy. In all these respects the duel, considered as a punishment, is *inefficacious.*

2nd. Often it is no punishment whatever, because opinion attaches a reward to it, which may appear, in many eyes, superior to all its dangers. This reward is the honour attributed to the proof of courage,—an honour which has often an attractive power superior to the force of all opposing motives. The time has been when it was essential to the character of a gallant gentleman to have fought at least one duel. A turn of the eye, an inattention, a preference, a suspicion of rivalry, anything was cause enough with men who only wanted a pretext, and who found themselves a thousand times paid for the danger by obtaining the applauses of both sexes, by each of which bravery, for different reasons, is equally admired. Punishment, being thus amalgamated with reward, has no longer a truly penal character, and becomes still more *inefficacious.*

3rd. The duel, considered as a punishment, is also defective by excess, or, according to the proper expression, which will be elsewhere explained, it is too *expensive.* Sometimes, indeed, it amounts to nothing; but it may be capital. Between these extremes of all and nothing there is a hazard of all the intermediate degrees,—wounds, scars, mutilations, limbs crippled or lost. It is plain that if a satisfaction for insults were to be chosen, the preference should be given to a punishment less uncertain and less hazardous, which can neither extend to the life of the offender, nor be entirely powerless.

There is still another singularity in the penal justice which appertains to a duel. Costly to the aggressor, it is no less so to the injured party. The offended person cannot claim a right to punish the offender but by exposing himself to the same punishment, and even with a manifest disadvantage; for the chance is naturally in favour of him who has the choice of his antagonist. This punishment, then, is at once *expensive* and *misdirected.*

4th. Another particular inconvenience of this jurisprudence of duelling consists in this: it aggravates the evil of the offence in every case in which a challenge is not sent, except for some known impossibility of sending it. If the offended party does not send a challenge, he is forced to betray two capital defects of character,—want of courage, and want of honour: want of that virtue which protects society, and without which it cannot be maintained, and want of sensibility to the love of reputation, one of the great foundations of morality. It thus happens that the offended party finds himself, by the law of duelling, in a worse situation than if there were no such law; for if he refuses this austere remedy it changes into a poison, the infection of which he cannot escape.

5th. If in certain cases the duel, in quality of punishment, is not so inefficacious as it appears to be, it is only because an innocent person has exposed himself to a punishment which is in fact a pure evil. Such is the case of persons who by reason of some infirmity of sex, age, or state of health, cannot employ this means of defence. In their condition of personal feebleness they have no resource, except chance grants them a protector, who has at the same time the power and the will to risk his person, and to fight in their place. It is thus that a husband, a lover, a brother, may take upon themselves to punish an injury to a wife, a mistress, and a sister; and if in such a case the duel becomes efficacious as a protection, it is only by hazarding the security of a third person, who finds himself burdened with a quarrel with which he has no personal connection, and with the origin of which he had nothing to do.

It is certain that duelling, considered as a branch of penal justice, is an absurd and monstrous means; but absurd and monstrous as it is, it cannot be denied that it answers well its principal object, *it entirely effaces the blot which an insult imprints upon the honour.* Vulgar moralists, by condemning public opinion upon this point, only confirm the fact. Now, whether this result of duelling is legitimate or not, no matter; it exists, and has its cause. It is essential that the legislator should look into it; so interesting a phenomenon should not remain without investigation.

An affront makes him who is the object of it be looked upon as degraded by his own feebleness and cowardice. Always placed between insult and disgrace, he can no longer stand on an equal footing with other men, nor pretend to the same attentions. But if, after an insult, I present myself to my adversary, and consent to risk my life against his, by that act I emerge from the humiliation into which I had sunk. If I fall, at least I am delivered from the public contempt and the insolent dominion of my enemy. If he falls, I am freed from humiliation, and the guilty is punished. If he is only wounded, it is a sufficient lesson for him and for those who might be tempted to imitate his conduct. Am I wounded, or is neither hurt?—still the combat is not useless; it always produces its effect. My enemy perceives that he cannot renew his insults but at the peril of his life; I am not a passive being who may be outraged with impunity; my courage protects me, nearly as the law would do, if it visited such offences by a capital or afflictive punishment.

But if, when this means of satisfaction is open to me, I patiently endure an insult, I render myself contemptible in the eyes of the public, because such conduct betrays timidity, and timidity is one of the greatest imperfections in the character of a man. A poltroon has always been an object of contempt.

But ought this want of courage to be classed among the vices? Is the opinion which degrades poltroonery a hurtful or a useful prejudice?

It can hardly be doubted that this opinion is conformable to the general interest, if we consider that the first passion of every man is the desire of his own preservation, and that courage is more or less a factitious quality, a social virtue which owes its birth and growth to public esteem more than to every other cause. A momentary ardour may be kindled by anger, but a courage, tranquil and sustained, is only formed and ripened under the happy influences of honour. The contempt, then, which is felt for poltroonery is not a useless sentiment; the suffering which it brings upon poltroons is not a pain wholly thrown away. The existence of the body politic depends upon the courage of the individuals who compose it. The external security of a state against its rivals depends upon the courage of its soldiers; the internal security of a state against those very soldiers depends upon the courage of the mass of citizens. In one word, courage is the public soul, the tutelary genius, the sacred palladium by which alone we can be protected against all the miseries of servitude, remain in the condition of men, or escape falling beneath the very brutes. Now the more honourable courage is, the greater will be the number of courageous men; the more poltroonery is despised the fewer poltroons.

This is not all. Where duels are in vogue, he who, being in a condition to fight, puts up with an insult, not only betrays timidity; he revolts against the popular sanction which has made it a law to fight, and shows himself, on an essential point, indifferent to reputation. But the popular sanction is the most active and the most faithful minister of the principle of utility, the most powerful and the least dangerous ally of the political sanction. The laws of the popular sanction, as a general rule, are in accordance with the laws of utility. The more sensitive a man is upon the point of reputation, the more likely he is to be virtuously inclined; the less sensitive he is on that point, the more readily does he yield to the seduction of all the vices.

The result of this discussion is, that in the state of abandonment in which the laws have hitherto left the honour of the citizens, he who endures an insult without recurring to the satisfaction which public opinion prescribes, is thereby reduced to a humiliating dependence, and exposed to receive an indefinite series of affronts. He exhibits a want of that sentiment of courage on which the general security depends; and a lack of sensibility to reputation, that sensibility which is the protector of all the virtues and a defence against all the vices.

Upon examining the progress of public opinion in relation to insults, it appears to me that, generally speaking, it has been good and useful; and the successive changes which the practice of duelling has undergone have made it more and more conformable to the principle of utility. The public would be wrong, or rather its folly would be palpable, if, being spectator of an insult, it immediately directed a decree of infamy against the insulted party; but that it does not do. This decree of infamy is issued only in case the person insulted shows himself a rebel to the law of honour, and signs with his own hand the judgment of degradation.

To speak generally, then, the public has some reasons for this system of honour.* The real blunder is on the part of the laws. 1st. In having suffered, in respect to insults, that anarchy and want of all legal redress which has caused the strange and unlucky

* Does the public know what reason there is in its opinion? Is it guided by the principle of utility, or by a mere spirit of imitation, and a blind instinct? Does the duellist act from an enlightened view of his own and the general interest? This is a question more curious than useful; but the following observation may help to resolve it. It is one thing to be determined by the presence of certain motives, and another thing to perceive the influence of those motives. There is no action, no judgment, without a motive, as there is no effect without a cause. But to ascertain the influence which a motive exercises upon us, we must know how to turn the mind inward upon itself and to anatomize thought. The mind must be divided into two parts, of which one is employed in observing the other,—a difficult operation, so seldom practised that few are capable of it.

remedy of duelling to be resorted to; 2nd, In having set itself in opposition to duelling, a remedy imperfect and objectionable, but the only remedy against insults in the power of the sufferers; 3rd, In having opposed it by disproportioned and inefficacious means.

CHAPTER XV.

Remedies for Offences against Honour.

We will begin with the means of satisfaction for offended honour; and will afterwards point out the reasons which justify those means.

Offences against honour may be divided into three classes:—verbal outrages, corporal insults, insulting threats. The punishment, if rendered analogous to the offence, may be made to operate at the same time as a means of satisfaction to the party injured.

List of these punishments:—

1st. Simple admonition.

2nd. The offender obliged to read aloud his own sentence.

3rd. The offender on his knees before the injured party.

4th. An apology pronounced by him.

5th. Emblematical dresses (in certain particular cases).

6th. Emblematical masks.

7th. The witnesses of the insult called in to be witnesses of the reparation.

8th. The persons whose good opinion is most important to the offender called to be present at the execution of the sentence.

9th. Publicity of the judgment.

10th. Banishment, longer or shorter, either from the presence of the injured party or from that of his friends. For an insult given in a public place—as a market, a theatre, or a church—banishment from those places.

11th. For a corporal insult, a retort of the same kind, inflicted by the injured party, or, if he prefer it, by the hand of the executioner.

12th. For an insult to a woman, the man to be dressed in women's clothes, and the retort to be inflicted by the hand of a woman.

Many of these means are new, and some of them will appear singular; but new means are necessary, since experience has shown the insufficiency of the old ones; and as to their apparent singularity, that very thing adapts them to their end, for it enables them, by analogy to the insult, to transfer to the offender the contempt he desired to fix upon the innocent sufferer. These means are varied and numerous to meet the number and variety of this sort of offences, to correspond to the gravity of cases, and to furnish reparations adapted to the different social distinctions; for it is not fit to treat in the same way an insult to a subaltern and to a magistrate, to an ecclesiastic and to a soldier, to a youth and to an old man. All this theatrical play, apologies, attitudes, emblems, forms solemn or grotesque, according to the difference of cases—in one word, these public satisfactions turned into spectacles, would furnish to the injured party immediate pleasures, and pleasures of recollection, which would well compensate the mortification of the insult.

Since the injury is wrought by artificial means, artificial means should aid in the reparation; otherwise it would fail to strike the imagination in the same way, and would not be complete. The offender has availed himself of a certain form of insult to turn the public contempt upon his adversary; it is necessary to employ an analogous form of infliction in order to turn this contempt back upon him. Opinion causes the disease, opinion must cure it. The wounds inflicted by the spear of Telephus could only be healed by the touch of the same weapon. This is a symbol of the operations of justice in matters of honour. An affront has done the evil, an affront must work the cure.

Let us follow out the effect of a satisfaction of this kind. The injured man, reduced to an intolerable state of inferiority in respect to his aggressor, can no longer frequent with security his old places of resort, and he discovers in the future only a perspective of injuries. But immediately after the legal reparation he regains what he had lost; he walks securely with upraised head, and even acquires a positive superiority over his adversary. How is this change produced? It is because he appears no longer a feeble and miserable being whom any one may tread under foot; the power of the magistrate has become his; no one will be tempted to repeat an insult so signally punished. His oppressor, who for a moment seemed so high, has fallen from his car of triumph; the punishment to which he has been subjected in the sight of so many witnesses proves that he is no longer to be feared; and nothing of his violence remains except the recollection of his chastisement. What more can the insulted party desire? What more could he do if he had the strength of a giant?

If legislators had always fitly applied this system of satisfactions, duelling never would have come into existence, for it always has been, and now is, only a supplement to the insufficiency of the laws. In proportion as this void of legislation is filled by regulations adapted to the protection of honour, we shall see the usage of duels diminished; and it would cease at once if a system of honorary satisfactions were introduced, conformed to public opinion, and faithfully administered. In former times duels served as a means of decision in a great number of cases in which it would be the height of absurdity to employ them now. A suitor who should send a challenge to his antagonist to prove a title, or to establish a right, would be thought a fool; but in the twelfth century that means was constantly employed for those purposes. Whence the change? It comes from that change in jurisprudence which has gradually taken place. Justice growing more enlightened, and directing itself by better rules and forms, has offered means of redress preferable to the duel.* The same cause will continue to produce the same effects. As soon as the law shall offer a certain remedy against offences that wound the honour, no one will be tempted to recur to an equivocal and dangerous means. Who loves pain and death? Nobody. Such a sentiment is equally a stranger to the heart of the hero and to the soul of the coward. It is the silence of the

* In France, the duel in civil cases was abolished by Philip-le-Bel, in 1305. He had rendered the Parliament stationary at Paris, and had done much for the establishment of judicial order.

laws, it is the forgetfulness of justice, which drives the wise man to this sole, sad resource of self-protection.

To give to honorary satisfaction all the extent and force of which it is susceptible, the definition of offences against honour ought to have latitude enough to embrace them all. Follow public opinion, step by step; be its faithful interpreter. All which opinion regards as an assault upon honour, let the laws so regard. Is a word, a gesture, a look sufficient in the public eye to constitute an insult?—that word, that gesture, that look, in the view of justice, should constitute an offence. The intent to injure is an injury. Everything intended to testify contempt for a man, or to draw contempt upon him, is an insult, and ought to have its reparation.

Is it said that these insulting signs, doubtful in their nature, fugitive and often imaginary, would be difficult to ascertain, and that persons easily offended, seeing an insult where there was none, might subject the innocent to undue punishment?

This danger amounts to nothing; for it is quite easy to trace the line of separation between real and imaginary injuries. This may be accomplished by allowing the plaintiff to question the defendant as to his intention—"Did you design by such a word or action to testify contempt for such a person?" If the defendant denies the intention, his answer, true or false, is enough to purge the honour of him who has been, or who thinks himself offended. For even if the injury were quite unequivocal, to deny it is to have recourse to falsehood; it is the avowal of a fault, it is the betrayal of fear or weakness; in one word, it is an act of inferiority, it is to humble one's self before an adversary.

In arranging the catalogue of offences which have the character of insult, there are some necessary exceptions. Care must be taken not to involve in a decree of proscription useful acts of public censure, an exercise of the power of the popular sanction. There must be reserved to friends and to superiors the authority of correction and reprimand; it is necessary to protect the liberty of history, and the liberty of criticism.

CHAPTER XVI.

Vindictive Satisfaction.

This subject does not require many particular rules. Every kind of satisfaction, as it is a punishment to the offender, naturally produces a pleasure of vengeance to the injured party.

That pleasure is a gain; it calls to mind Samson's riddle—it is the sweet coming out of the terrible, it is honey dropping from the lion's mouth. Produced without expense, a clear gain resulting from an operation necessary on other accounts, it is an enjoyment to be cultivated, like any other; for the pleasure of vengeance, abstractly considered, is, like every other pleasure, a good in itself. It is innocent while restrained within the limits of the law; it only becomes criminal at the moment when it breaks those limits. It is not vengeance which is to be regarded as the most malignant and dangerous passion of the human heart; it is antipathy, it is intolerance—the hatreds of pride, of prejudice, of religion, of politics. The enmity which is dangerous is not that which is well founded, but that which springs up without any substantial cause.

Useful to the individual, this motive is also useful to the public; indeed, it is necessary. It is this vindictive satisfaction which sets the tongues of witnesses in motion; it is this which animates the accuser and engages him in the public service, in spite of the embarrassments, the expenses, the enmities to which it exposes him; it is this, too, which surmounts the public pity in the punishment of criminals. Take away this resource, and the power of the laws will be very limited; or, at all events, the tribunals will not obtain assistance, except for money—a means not only burdensome to society, but exposed to other very serious objections.

Common moralists, always duped by words, are not able to comprehend this truth. The spirit of vengeance is odious; all satisfaction drawn from that source is faulty; forgiveness of injuries is the first of virtues. No doubt those implacable characters which no satisfaction can soften are odious, and ought to be so. Forgetfulness of injuries is a virtue necessary to humanity; but it becomes a virtue only after justice has done its work, when it has furnished or denied a satisfaction. Before that, to forget injuries is to invite their repetition; it is not being the friend, it is being the enemy of society. What more can crime desire than an arrangement by which offences shall be always pardoned?

What ought to be done to afford this vindictive satisfaction? Everything which justice requires for the sake of satisfactions of other kinds and for the punishment of the offence, but nothing more. The least excess consecrated to the sole object of vengeance would be a pure evil. Inflict the proper punishment, and let the injured party derive from it such a degree of satisfaction as comports with his situation, and of which his nature is susceptible.

But though nothing should be added to the severity of punishment with this particular end in view, the punishment may be modified for the accomplishment of this end, according to what may be supposed to be the sentiments of the injured party, from his position or from the nature of the offence. The preceding chapter contains some examples of this sort; others will be given when treating of the choice of punishments.

CHAPTER XVII.

Substitutive Satisfaction; or, Satisfaction at the charge of a Third Party.

In ordinary cases, the expense of satisfaction ought to fall upon the author of the evil; because, falling in that way, it tends in quality of punishment to prevent the evil—that is, to diminish the frequency of the offence. Where it falls upon another person, it has no such tendency.

Where this reason does not exist, with regard to the first respondent, the law of responsibility must be modified in consequence; or, in other terms, a third person must be called in to pay, instead of the author of the damage, when he cannot himself furnish the satisfaction, and when such an obligation imposed upon a third person tends to prevent the offence.

This may happen in the following cases:—1st. The responsibility of a master for his servant. 2nd. The responsibility of a guardian for his ward. 3rd. The responsibility of a father for his children. 4th. The responsibility of a mother for her children, in her character of guardian. 5th. The responsibility of a husband for his wife. 6th. The responsibility of an innocent person who profits by the offence.

I. Responsibility of a Master.—This responsibility is founded upon two reasons, the one of security, the other of equality. This obligation imposed upon the master acts like a punishment, and diminishes the chance of like mishaps. He is interested to know the character, and to watch over the conduct of those for whom he is responsible. By making him accountable for neglect of this duty, the law appoints him a police inspector and a domestic magistrate.

Besides, the condition of a master almost necessarily supposes a certain fortune, the quality of being an injured party supposes nothing of that sort. Since an inevitable evil lies between two parties, it is best to throw the weight of it upon him who has most means of sustaining it.

This responsibility may have some inconveniences, but if it did not exist there would be more and worse ones. If a master wished to occasion a trespass upon the lands of his neighbour, to expose him to some accident, to inflict a piece of vengeance upon him, to make him live in continual inquietude, he would only need choose some vicious domestics, to whom he might hint the service of his passions and his hatreds, and that without commanding anything, without being an accomplice, and without affording any evidence of participation; always ready to sustain or to disavow, he would make them the instruments of his designs, and would run no risks himself.* By showing them a little more than ordinary confidence, by taking advantage of their

* There are many ways of injuring another without any trace of participation. I have been told by a French lawyer, that when the Parliaments wished to save a culprit, they selected with design some

attachment, their devotedness, their servile vanity, there is nothing he could not attain by general instigations without exposing himself to the danger of commanding anything in particular, and he would enjoy with impunity the evil which he had done by their hands. "Unfortunate that I am," cried Henry II., one day, when wearied with the haughtiness of an insolent prelate. "What! so many servants who boast their zeal, and not one who dares to avenge me!" The murder of Becket was the fruit of this imprudent or criminal apostrophe.

What, in the master's case, diminishes in a great degree the danger of his responsibility, is the responsibility of the servant. The real author of the evil, as far as circumstances permit, ought to be the first to support its troublesome consequences; he ought to be charged with the burden of satisfaction according to his capacity; so that a negligent or vicious servant may not coolly say, while doing the damage, "It is my master's affair, not mine."

Besides, the responsibility of the master is not always the same; it must vary according to circumstances, which must be examined with attention.

The first thing to be considered is the degree of connection subsisting between the master and the servant. If the question is of a day-labourer, or a man engaged by the year; of a workman who lodges abroad, or in the house; of an apprentice or a slave; it is clear that the closer the connection is the greater should be the responsibility. A foreman is less dependent upon his employer than a lackey upon his master.

The second thing to be considered is the nature of the work upon which the servant is employed. The presumptions against the master will be weaker in those cases in which his interest is most exposed to suffer by the negligence of his servants, and stronger in the contrary cases. In the first case the master already has a sufficient motive to be watchful; in the second he may not have that motive, and the law should supply it.

unskilful person to report the cause, hoping that his blunders would leave some loop-hole for annulling the sentence! Chicane so artful is almost entitled to the epithet of genius.

Third. The master is peculiarly responsible when the mischief has happened by occasion, or in the act of his service: because it is to be presumed that he directed it, or at least that he foresaw what has happened; and because he can easier watch his servants at those times than while they are at liberty.

There is a case which seems to reduce to a low degree, if it does not altogether annihilate, the strongest reason for the master's responsibility: viz., when the evil is caused by a grave offence, accompanied consequently by a proportionate punishment. If a man of mine, for example, having a personal quarrel with my neighbour, sets his barn on fire, ought I to be responsible for a damage which I could not prevent? If the fellow did not fear being hung, would he fear a dismissal from my service?

Such are the presumptions which serve as a basis to responsibility; presumption of negligence on the part of the master; presumption of his superiority in wealth. But it is not to be forgotten that presumptions are nothing when belied by facts. For example, an accident has happened by the overturn of a vehicle. Nothing is known of the injured party. It is presumed that he stands in need of an indemnity from the owner of the vehicle, who offers himself to the imagination as being well able to support the loss. But what becomes of this presumption, when it is known that this owner is a poor farmer, and the injured party an opulent landlord; that the first would be ruined if obliged to pay an indemnity, hardly of the slightest consequence to the other? Presumptions ought to guide, but not to govern us. The legislator ought to consult them in establishing general rules; he should leave it to the magistrate to modify their application according to individual cases.

The general rule would establish the responsibility of the master; but the magistrate, according to circumstances, might change this arrangement, and make the weight of the loss fall upon the true author of the evil.

The greatest abuse which can result from leaving to the magistrate the utmost latitude in this distribution will be to produce, in certain cases, the same inconvenience which must necessarily result from a general and inflexible rule. Should the magistrate on one occasion favour the author of the evil, and the master on another? He who suffers wrong will suffer no more from this partiality than he might have suffered from the inflexibility of the law.

In our systems of law, no attention has been given to these modifications. The entire burden of the loss has been thrown sometimes upon the servant who has caused the damage, and sometimes upon the master; whence it follows that sometimes security and sometimes equality have been neglected, both of which ought alternately to have the preference, according to the nature of the case.

II. Responsibility of a Guardian.—The ward is not an advantage to the guardian; in general he is a burden. If the ward has sufficient means to furnish satisfaction, it is not necessary that another should pay for his acts. If he has no means of his own, the wardship is too heavy a burden in itself to be loaded with factitious responsibility. All that security requires is to attach to the negligence of the guardian, proved or even presumed, an amend more or less weighty, according to the nature of the proofs, but such as never to exceed the amount required for satisfaction.

III. Responsibility of a Father.—If a master ought to be responsible for the faults of his servants, for a much stronger reason a father ought to be so for those of his children. If a master can and ought to watch over those who depend upon him, it is a duty more pressing upon a father, and much easier to be fulfilled. He not only exercises over his children the authority of a domestic magistrate, but he has all the ascendancy of affection. He is not only the guardian of their physical existence, he has it in his power to be the controller of their feelings. If a master may abstain from employing, or may dismiss upon discovery, a servant who evinces dangerous dispositions, a father, who can fashion at his pleasure the character and habits of his children, is justly thought to be the author of all the dispositions which they manifest. If they are depraved, it is almost always the effect of his negligence or of his vices; and he ought to bear the consequences of an evil which he might have prevented.

If, after a reason so weighty, there needs yet another argument, it may be said that children, saving the rights which their quality of sensitive beings confers upon them, are a part of the father's property, and ought so to be regarded. He who enjoys the advantages of the possession, ought to support its inconveniences. The good is more than a compensation for the evil. It would be strange if the loss or depredations occasioned by children should be borne by an individual who knows nothing of them, except by their heedlessness or their malice, rather than by him who finds in them the greatest source of his happiness, and who indemnifies himself by a thousand hopes for the actual cares of their education.

But this responsibility has a natural limit. The majority of a son, or the marriage of a daughter, putting an end to the father's authority, puts an end also to his legal responsibility. He ought not to be answerable for actions which he no longer has the power to prevent.

To perpetuate for life the father's responsibility, on the plea that he is the author of the vicious dispositions of his children, would be unjust and cruel; for in the first place it is not true that all the vices of an adult are attributable to the defects of his education. Diverse causes of corruption, after the epoch of independence, may triumph over the most virtuous education. Besides, the condition of a father is sufficiently unfortunate when the bad dispositions of a son arrived at man's estate break out into offences. What he has already suffered in his family, the anguish he feels from the misconduct or dishonour of a son, is a kind of punishment which nature inflicts upon him, and which the law need not aggravate. It would be pouring poison upon his wounds, and that without any hope of repairing the past, or providing against the future. Those who have attempted to justify such barbarous jurisprudence by the example of China, have not recollected that the authority of a father, ending in that country only with his life, it is but just that his responsibility should continue as long as his power.

IV. Responsibility of the Mother.—The obligation of the mother is naturally regulated by her rights, on which her means of control depend. If the father is alive, the mother's responsibility, like her power, remains absorbed as it were in that of her husband. If he is dead, and she has taken the reins of domestic government into her own hands, she becomes responsible for those who are subject to her authority.

V. Responsibility of a Husband.—This case is as simple as the preceding. The obligation of a husband depends upon his rights. As the administration of the property belongs to him alone, unless the husband were answerable, the injured party would be without remedy. This reasoning supposes the order of things generally established; that order so necessary to the peace of families, to the education of children, to the maintenance of manners,—that order so ancient and universal, which subjects the wife to the power of the husband. As he is her chief and her guardian, he is answerable for her in the eye of the law. He is even charged with a responsibility still more delicate before the tribunal of opinion; but that is a matter which does not appertain to the present subject.

VI. Responsibility of an innocent Person.—It often happens that a person, without having had any share in an offence, derives from it a certain and perceptible profit. Is it not proper that this person should be called upon to indemnify the injured party, if the offender cannot be found, or cannot furnish an indemnity?

Such a procedure would be conformable to the principles which we have laid down, namely,—first, regard for *security:* for there might be an aiding and abetting, though there might be no proof of it; next, the care of *equality:* since it is better for one person merely to be deprived of a gain, than for another to be left to suffer a loss.

Examples will make this clearer. By means of a breach made in a dike, he who was in possession of the benefit of irrigation has been deprived of it, and it has been bestowed upon another. He who comes into the enjoyment of this unexpected advantage ought to share a part at least of his gain with the person who has experienced the loss.

A tenant for life, whose property passes by settlement to a stranger, is killed, and leaves a family in want. The residuary proprietor, who realizes in consequence a premature possession, ought to make some allowance to the children of the deceased.

A benefice is vacated, because the possessor has been killed; if he leaves a wife and children in poverty, the successor owes them an indemnity proportionate to their need and to his gain.

CHAPTER XVIII.

Subsidiary Satisfaction at the Public Expense.

The best fund whence satisfaction can be drawn is the property of the delinquent,—since it then performs, as we have seen, with superior convenience the functions both of satisfaction and of punishment.

But if the offender is without property, ought the injured person to remain without satisfaction? No; for, according to the reasons already laid down, satisfaction is almost as necessary as punishment. It ought to be furnished out of the public treasury, because it is an object of public good, and the security of all is interested in it. This obligation of the public to furnish satisfaction is founded upon a reason which has the evidence of an axiom. A pecuniary charge divided among the mass of individuals is nothing to each contributor, in comparison with what it would be to an individual or a small number.

If *insurance* is useful in enterprises of commerce, it is not less so in the great social enterprise in which the associates find themselves united as partners, in consequence of a train of chances, without knowledge or choice on their part, without the power of separation, or of securing themselves by any prudential means from a multitude of snares which they mutually spread for each other. The calamities which spring from offences are evils not less real than those which result from accidents of nature. If the owner of a house sleeps sounder because it is insured against fire, his sleep will be sounder yet if he is also insured against robbery. Putting out of sight the abuses to which it is liable, it seems impossible to give too much extension to a means so ingenious, which renders real losses so slight, and which gives so much security against eventual evils.

But all kinds of *insurances* are exposed to great abuse from fraud or negligence; fraud on the part of those who feign or exaggerate losses for the sake of obtaining indemnities not due; negligence on the part of the assurers in not taking necessary precautions, or on the part of the assured, who use less diligence in protecting themselves against losses which are certain to be made up.

In a system of satisfactions at the public expense we have, then, to fear—

1st. A secret connivance between a party pretending to be injured and the author of a pretended offence to obtain an indemnity not due.

2nd. Too great security on the part of individuals, who, not having the same consequences to fear, will no longer make the same efforts for the prevention of offences.

This second danger is little to be dreaded. Nobody will neglect an actual possession certain and present in the hope of recovering, in case of loss, an equivalent for the thing lost, even a perfect equivalent; and when we consider that an indemnity cannot be obtained without trouble and expense, that there is a temporary privation, that the vexations of a claim and its pursuit are to be encountered, and the disagreeable part of an accuser to be played; and that, after all, under the best system of procedure, success is always doubtful;—these things considered, it is plain that every man will still have motives enough to watch over his property, and not to encourage offences by negligence.

On the side of fraud the danger is much greater. It can only be prevented by detailed precautions, which will be explained elsewhere. It will here suffice to point out, as examples, two opposite cases, one in which the utility of the remedy surpasses the danger of abuse, the other in which the danger of abuse is greater than the utility of the remedy.

Whenever the damage is occasioned by an offence of which the punishment is severe, and the author of which must be juridically ascertained, and also the fact of an offence committed, fraud is very difficult. The only method an impostor, who pretends to be injured, can employ to procure an accomplice, is to give him a part of the profits of the fraud; but, provided there has not been a neglect of the clearest principles of proportion between offences and punishments, the punishment which such an accomplice must encounter would be more than equivalent to the total profit of the fraud.

Observe, that the offender must be judicially convicted before the satisfaction is granted; without that precaution the public treasure would be exposed to pillage. Nothing would be more common than stories of imaginary robberies, of pretended thefts committed by unknown persons who had taken to flight, in a manner the most secret, and in nights the darkest. But when it is necessary to bring the offenders into court, a secret understanding is not easy. This is not a part which can be readily filled; for, besides the certainty of punishment for the alleged offence encountered by the person who charges himself with it, in case the imposture be discovered, there will be still a particular and additional punishment to be shared by both accomplices; and if it be recollected how difficult it is to fabricate a probable history of an offence absolutely imaginary, it is likely that these kinds of frauds will be very rare, if they ever happen at all.

The danger most to be apprehended is the exaggeration of a loss resulting from a real offence. But then it is necessary that the offence be susceptible of such sort of falsehood,—a case sufficiently rare.

It would seem, then, that it may be regarded as a general maxim, that in all cases in which the punishment of the offence is severe, there is no occasion for apprehending that an imaginary offender will charge himself with the offence for the sake of a doubtful gain.

But, for the opposite reason, when the damage results from an offence of which the punishment is slight or nothing, if the public treasure were responsible in such cases, the danger of abuse would be at its highest point. Insolvency is an example of this sort. Who so poor that he would not be trusted, if the public were his security? What treasure would suffice to pay the creditors, whose debtors were really deficient, and how easy it would be to get up false debts?

Not only would such an indemnity be liable to abuse, it would be unreasonable; for, in the transactions of commerce, the risk of loss makes a part of the price of merchandise and of the interest of money. Let the merchant be sure of losing nothing, and he would sell cheaper; so that, to demand an indemnity from the public for a loss thus made up for beforehand, would be asking to be paid twice over.

There are still other cases in which satisfaction ought to be a public charge.

1st. The case of physical calamities, such as inundations and fires. Aids furnished by the state to sufferers in that way are not solely founded on the principle that an evil divided among many becomes light; they rest also upon this other principle—that the state, as protector of the national wealth, is interested to prevent the deterioration of its domain, and to re-establish the means of reproduction in places which have suffered. Such were the liberalities, so called, of the great Frederic towards provinces desolated by some scourge; they were acts of prudence and conservation.

2nd. Losses and misfortunes in consequence of hostilities. Those who have been exposed to the invasions of a public enemy have so much the clearer right to a public indemnity, since they may be considered as having sustained a shock which threatened all the citizens, and as having been by their situation the most exposed points of the public defence.

3rd. Evils resulting from unintentional mistakes of the ministers of justice. An error of justice is always of itself a subject of lamentation; but that such an error, when known, should not be repaired by proportional indemnities, is an overthrow of social order. Ought not the public to follow the same rules of equity which it imposes upon individuals? Is it not an odious thing that the government should exert its power to exact severely all that is due to it, and should avail itself of the same means to refuse the payment of its own debts? But this obligation is so evident, that no attempt to demonstrate it can make it clearer.

4th. Responsibility of a community for a high-handed offence committed in a public part of its territory. It is not properly the public which is responsible in this case; it is the district or the province which should be taxed for the reparation of an offence resulting from negligence of police.

In cases of competition, the interests of an individual ought to take precedence of those of the treasury. What is due to an injured party under the title of satisfaction ought to be paid in preference to what is due to the public by way of fine. This is not the decision of vulgar jurisprudence, but it is the decision of reason. The loss to an individual is an evil that is felt; the gain to the public is a good felt by nobody. What the offender pays in quality of fine is a punishment, and nothing more; what he pays in quality of satisfaction is also a punishment, and a severer one; it is, beside, a satisfaction to the injured party, and so far a good. What I pay to the state, a creature of reason with which I have no quarrel, affects me only with the sort of chagrin I should feel if I dropped the same money into a well; what I pay to my adversary, the satisfaction which I am forced to make, at my own expense, to him I wished to injure, is a degree of humiliation which gives to punishment its most appropriate character.

PART THIRD.

PUNISHMENTS.

CHAPTER I.

Punishments which ought not to be inflicted.

THE cases in which punishment ought not to be inflicted may be reduced to four heads: when punishment would be—1st, Misapplied; 2nd, Inefficacious; 3rd, Superfluous; 4th, Too expensive.

I. PUNISHMENTS MISAPPLIED.—Punishments are misapplied wherever there is no real offence, no evil of the first order or of the second order; or where the evil is more than compensated by an attendant good, as in the exercise of political or domestic authority, in the repulsion of a weightier evil, in self-defence, &c.

If the idea of what constitutes a real offence has been clearly apprehended, it will be easy to distinguish real from imaginary offences—from those acts, innocent in themselves, which have been arranged among offences by prejudice, antipathy, mistakes of government, the ascetic principle, in the same way that several wholesome kinds of food are considered among certain nations as poisonous or unclean. Heresy and witchcraft are offences of this class.

II. INEFFICACIOUS PUNISHMENTS.—I call those punishments *inefficacious* which have no power to produce an effect upon the will, and which, in consequence, have no tendency towards the prevention of like acts.

Punishments are inefficacious when directed against individuals who could not know the law, who have acted without intention, who have done the evil innocently, under an erroneous supposition, or by irresistible constraint. Children, imbeciles, idiots, though they may be influenced, to a certain extent, by rewards and threats, have not a sufficient idea of futurity to be restrained by punishments. In their case laws have no efficacy.

If a man is determined to act by a fear superior to that of the heaviest legal punishment, or by the hope of a preponderant good, it is plain that the law can have little influence over him. We have seen laws against duelling disregarded, because men of honour are more afraid of shame than of punishment. Punishments directed against religious opinions generally fail to be effectual, because the idea of everlasting reward triumphs over the fear of death. According as these opinions have more or less influence, punishment, in such cases, is more or less efficacious.

III. Superfluous Punishments.—Punishments are superfluous in cases where the same end may be obtained by means more mild —instruction, example, invitations, delays, rewards. A man spreads abroad pernicious opinions: shall the magistrate therefore seize the sword and punish him? No; if it is the interest of one individual to give currency to bad maxims, it is the interest of a thousand others to refute him.

IV. Punishments too Expensive.—If the evil of the punishment exceeds the evil of the offence, the legislator will produce more suffering than he prevents. He will purchase exemption from a lesser evil at the expense of a greater evil.

Two tables should be kept in view—one representing the evil of offences, the other the evil of punishments.

The following evils are produced by every penal law:—1st. *Evil of coercion.* It imposes a privation more or less painful according to the degree of pleasure which the thing forbidden has the power of conferring. 2nd. *The sufferings caused by the punishment,* whenever it is actually carried into execution. 3rd. *Evil of apprehension* suffered by those who have violated the law, or who fear a prosecution in consequence. 4th. *Evil of false prosecutions.* This inconvenience appertains to all penal laws, but particularly to laws which are obscure and to imaginary offences. A general antipathy often produces a frightful disposition to prosecute and to condemn upon suspicions or appearances. 5th. *Derivative evil* suffered by the parents or friends of those who are exposed to the rigour of the law.

Such is the table of evils or of *expenses* which the legislator ought to consider every time he establishes a punishment.

It is from this source that the principal reason is drawn for general amnesties, in case of those complicated offences which spring from a spirit of party. In such cases it may happen that the law envelopes a great multitude, sometimes half the total number of citizens, and perhaps more than half. Will you punish all the guilty? Will you only decimate them? In either case the evil of the punishment is greater than the evil of the offence.

If a delinquent is loved by the people, so that his punishment will cause national discontent; if he is protected by a foreign power whose good-will it is necessary to conciliate; if he is able to render the nation some extraordinary service;—in these particular cases the grant of pardon is founded upon a calculation of prudence. It is apprehended that punishment of the offence will cost society too dear.

CHAPTER II.

Adsit
Regula, peccatis quæ pœnas irroget æquas:
Ne scutica dignum, horribile sectere flagello.
HOR. l. i. Sat. iii.

Let's have a rule
Which deals to crimes an equal punishment:
Nor tortures with the horrid lash for faults
Worthy a birchen twig.

Proportion between Offences and Punishments.

MONTESQUIEU perceived the necessity of a proportion between offences and punishments. Beccaria insists upon its importance.

But they rather recommend than explain it; they do not tell in what that proportion consists. Let us endeavour to supply this defect, and to give the principal rules of this moral arithmetic.

First Rule.—*The evil of the punishment must be made to exceed the advantage of the offence.*

The Anglo-Saxon laws, which established a price for the lives of men, two hundred shillings for the murder of a peasant, six times as much for that of a noble, and thirty-six times as much for that of the king, notwithstanding this show of pecuniary proportion, were evidently deficient in moral proportion. The punishment might appear as nothing compared to the advantage of the offence.

The same error is committed whenever a punishment is decreed which can only reach a certain point, while the advantage of the offence may go much beyond.

Some celebrated authors have attempted to establish a contrary maxim. They say that punishment ought to be diminished in proportion to the strength of temptation; that temptation diminishes the fault; and that the more potent seduction is, the less evidence we have of the offender's depravity.

This may be true; but it does not contravene the rule above laid down: for to prevent an offence, it is necessary that the repressive motive should be stronger than the seductive motive. The punishment must be more an object of dread than the offence is an object of desire. An insufficient punishment is a greater evil than an excess of rigour; for an insufficient punishment is an evil wholly thrown away. No good results from it, either to the public, who are left exposed to like offences, nor to the offender, whom it makes no better. What would be said of a surgeon, who, to spare a sick man a degree of pain, should leave the cure unfinished? Would it be a piece of enlightened humanity to add to the pains of the disorder the torment of a useless operation?

Second Rule.—*The more deficient in certainty a punishment is, the severer it should be.*

No man engages in a career of crime, except in the hope of impunity. If punishment consisted merely in taking from the guilty the fruits of his offence, and if that punishment were inevitable, no offence would ever be committed; for what man is so foolish as to run the risk of committing an offence with certainty of nothing but the shame of an unsuccessful attempt? In all cases of offence there is a calculation of the chances for and against; and it is necessary to give a much greater weight to the punishment, in order to counterbalance the chances of impunity.

It is true, then, that the more certain punishment is, the less severe it need be. Such is the advantage that results from simplicity of laws, and a good method of procedure.

For the same reason it is desirable that punishment should follow offence as closely as possible; for its impression upon the minds of men is weakened by distance, and, besides, distance adds to the uncertainty of punishment, by affording new chances of escape.

THIRD RULE.—*Where two offences are in conjunction, the greater offence ought to be subjected to severer punishment, in order that the delinquent may have a motive to stop at the lesser.*

Two offences may be said to be in conjunction when a man has the power and the will to commit both of them. A highwayman may content himself with robbing, or he may begin with murder, and finish with robbery. The murder should be punished more severely than the robbery, in order to deter him from the greater offence.

This rule would be perfectly carried out if it could be so ordered that for each portion of evil committed there should be a corresponding portion of punishment. Let a man who has stolen ten crowns be punished as severely as if he had stolen twenty, and he will be a fool to take the less sum in preference to the greater. Equal punishment for unequal offences is often a motive for committing the greater offence.

FOURTH RULE.—*The greater an offence is, the greater reason there is to hazard a severe punishment for the chance of preventing it.*

We must not forget that the infliction of punishment is a certain expense for the purchase of an uncertain advantage. To apply great punishments to small offences is to pay very dearly for the chance of escaping a slight evil.

The English law which condemned women to be burnt for passing counterfeit coin, was a direct invasion of this rule of proportion. If burning were a punishment ever to be adopted, it ought to be confined to the single case of incendiary homicides.

FIFTH RULE.—*The same punishment for the same offence ought not to be inflicted upon all delinquents. It is necessary to pay some regard to the circumstances which affect sensibility.*

The same nominal punishments are not the same real punishments. Age, sex, rank, fortune, and many other circumstances, ought to modify the punishments inflicted for the same offence. If the offence is a corporal injury, the same pecuniary punishment would be a trifle to the rich, and oppressive to the poor. The same punishment which would brand with ignominy a man of a certain rank, would not produce even the slightest stain in case the offender belonged to an inferior class. The same imprisonment would be ruin to a man of business, death to an infirm old man, and eternal disgrace to a woman, while it would be next to nothing to an individual placed under other circumstances.

Let it be observed, however, that the proportion between punishments and offences ought not to be so mathematically followed up as to render the laws subtle, complicated, and obscure. Brevity and simplicity are a superior good. Something of exact proportion may also be sacrificed to render the punishment more striking, more fit to inspire the people with a sentiment of aversion for those vices which prepare the way for crimes.

CHAPTER III.

Of Prescription as regards Punishment.

OUGHT punishment to be limited in point of time?—in other words, if the delinquent is successful for a given period in evading the law, ought he to escape punishment? Shall the law in such a case no longer take cognizance of the offence? This is a question still contested. There must always be much that is arbitrary, both in the choice of offences which shall have the privilege of this pardon, and in the number of years after which the privilege shall begin.

Pardon can be safely allowed for offences of rashness and negligence, offences resulting from a fault exempt from bad intention. The very accident which makes such offenders puts them on their guard, and thenceforth they are little to be feared. For such individuals pardon is a good; and in such cases it is an evil to nobody.

Prescription may also be extended to offences not completed, to attempts that have failed. The delinquent, during the interval, has undergone the punishment in part,—for to fear it is to feel it. Besides, he has abstained from like offences, he has reformed, he has become a useful member of society. He has recovered his moral health without the employment of that bitter medicine which the law had prepared for him.

But when the question relates to more serious offences, for example, the fraudulent acquisition of a large sum of money. polygamy, a rape, a robbery, it would be odious and fatal to allow wickedness, after a certain time, a triumph over innocence. No treaty should be had with malefactors of that character. Let the avenging sword remain always hanging above their heads. The sight of a criminal in the peaceful enjoyment of the fruit of his crime, protected by the laws he has violated, is a consolation to evil doers, an object of grief to men of virtue, a public insult to justice and to morals.

To perceive all the absurdity of an impunity acquired by lapse of time, it is only necessary to imagine the law to be expressed in terms like these: "But if the murderer, the robber, the fraudulent acquirer of another's goods, shall succeed for twenty years in eluding the vigilance of the tribunals, his address shall be rewarded, his security shall be re-established, and the fruit of his crimes shall become his lawful possession."

CHAPTER IV.

Mistaken Punishments, or Punishments misapplied.

Punishment ought to bear directly upon the individual who is to be subjected to its influence. If you desire to influence Titius, it is upon Titius that the punishment ought to act. If a punishment destined to influence Titius falls upon any one else than Titius himself, it is quite clear that such a punishment is misapplied.

But a punishment directed against those who are dear to a man is a punishment to that man; for he participates in the sufferings of those to whom he is attached by sympathy, and a hold can be got upon him by means of his affections. This doctrine is true, but is it good? Is it conformable to the principle of utility?

To ask if a punishment of sympathy acts with as much force as a direct punishment, is to ask if, in general, attachments to others are as strong as the love of one's self.

If self-love is the stronger sentiment, it follows that recourse should not be had to punishments of sympathy till we have exhausted all the direct sufferings of which human nature is capable. No torture is so cruel that it ought not to be employed before punishing the wife for the acts of the husband, or children for the offences of their father.

In punishments misapplied, four principal faults are perceptible:—

1st. What shall be thought of a punishment which must often fail for want of objects on which to act? If to inflict suffering upon Titius you set about finding the persons who are dear to him, you have no other guide than the domestic relations; you are conducted by that thread to his father and his mother, his wife and his children. The most cruel tyranny has attempted to go no further. But there are many men who have no father nor mother, no wife nor child. It is necessary, then, to apply to this class of men a direct punishment; but the same direct punishment that answers in their case, will it not answer in every case?

2nd. And does not this punishment suppose sentiments which may not exist? If Titius does not concern himself about his wife and children, if he has contracted a dislike to them, at the very least he will be indifferent to their sufferings, and this part of his punishment will not affect him.

3rd. But what makes this system so frightful is the profusion, the multiplication of evils involved in it. Consider the chain of domestic connections, calculate the number of descendants that a man may have; the punishment is communicated from one to the other; it spreads step by step like a contagion; it envelops a crowd of individuals. To produce a direct pain equivalent to one, it is necessary to create a pain indirect and misapplied, equivalent to ten, to twenty, to thirty, to a hundred, to a thousand.

4th. Punishment thus turned aside from its natural course, has not even the advantage of conforming to the public sentiment of sympathy and antipathy. When the offender has paid his personal debt to justice, the public vengeance is satisfied, and demands nothing more. If you pursue him beyond the scaffold, and extend the punishment to an innocent and unhappy family, the public pity presently revives; an indistinct sentiment pronounces the laws unjust; humanity declares against you; and every day enlists new partisans on the side of your victim. Respect for the government, and confidence in it, is lessened in every heart; and all that is gained by this policy is a reputation of ignorance with the wise, and of barbarity with the multitude.

The ties that bind men together are so complicated that it is not possible completely to separate the lot of the innocent from the lot of the guilty. The evil designed by the law for a single individual bursts its bounds, and extends itself along all those connecting ties of common sensibility which result from the affections, from honour, and mutual interests. A whole family is in suffering and in tears for the offence of one. But this evil inherent in the nature of things, this evil which all the wisdom and all the benevolence of the legislator cannot entirely prevent, is no reproach to him, and does not constitute a misapplication of punishment. If the father is compelled to undergo a punishment for his offence, that punishment must, in the nature of things, be a disadvantage to his children; it cannot be avoided; but if after the death of a guilty father the paternal succession is ravished from the innocent children, it is a voluntary act of the legislator, who himself turns the punishment aside from its legitimate channel.

The legislator, in this respect, has two duties to fulfil. In the first place he ought to avoid punishments misapplied in their primitive application. The innocent son of the greatest criminal ought to receive from the law as complete a protection as the most illustrious citizen. In the second place, it is necessary to reduce to its least term that portion of misapplied suffering which falls upon the innocent, in consequence of a direct punishment inflicted on the guilty. If a rebel, for example, is condemned to perpetual imprisonment, or to death, everything has been done against him which should be done. A total confiscation of his property, to the prejudice of his heirs, or at least of his wife and children, would be a tyrannical and odious act. The rights of an unfortunate family smitten in its head are on that account only the more sacred. A national treasure composed of such spoils is like those impure exhalations which carry in their bosom the germs of disease.

It will be sufficient to give a simple enumeration of the most common cases in which legislators have misapplied punishments, by making them bear upon the innocent for the sake of an oblique effect upon the guilty.

1st. *Confiscation.*—A remnant of barbarity which still exists throughout almost all Europe. It is applied to many offences, especially to crimes of state.* This punishment is the more

* Confiscation, for offences of state, ought hardly to be looked upon as a judicial punishment; for in civil wars, generally speaking, as both parties act in good faith, there can be no criminality. Confiscation is a measure purely hostile. To leave their fortunes untouched, would be

odious, since it cannot be employed till the danger is past; and the more imprudent, since it prolongs animosities and a spirit of revenge, of which the remembrance ought to be effaced as soon as possible.

2nd. *Corruption of Blood.*—A cruel fiction of the lawyers to disguise the injustice of confiscation. The innocent grandson cannot inherit from the innocent grandfather, because his rights are corrupted and destroyed in passing through the blood of a guilty father. This corruption of blood is a fantastic idea; but there is a corruption too real in the understandings and the hearts of those who dishonour themselves by such sophisms.

3rd. *Loss of Privileges, whereby an entire Corporation is punished for the Misbehaviour of a part of its Members.*—In England the city of London is exempted, by a particular Act, from such an infliction; but what city, what corporation ought to be subject to it, provided its privileges are not contrary to the interest of the state?

4th. *Disastrous Lot of Bastards.*—The incapacity to inherit is not here referred to. The loss of that right is no more a legal punishment in case of bastardy than in the case of younger sons; and endless contests might result, if heirs could be brought forward, whose birth had not the attestation of publicity. But the incapacity to fulfil certain trusts, the privation of many public rights, to which they are subjected in several states of Europe, is a true punishment, which falls upon innocent children for a fault of imprudence committed by their parents.

5th. *Infamy attached to the Relatives of Persons who have committed serious Offences.*—This is not the place to consider what appertains merely to public opinion. Opinion in this respect has taken the character of antipathy only in consequence of mistakes of the law, which in many cases has branded the families of criminals. This kind of injustice, little by little, is passing away.

leaving munitions of war in the hands of the enemy. But a precaution adapted to a state of war, to which recourse should be had only in extreme cases, ought to cease, or be softened as much as possible, as soon as the danger ceases to exist.

CHAPTER V.

Of requiring Security for good Behaviour.

To require security for good behaviour, is to demand of a person, who is suspected of designing to commit some unlawful act, that he procure some other person, who will consent to undergo a certain penalty, provided the apprehended offence is committed.

At first view, this appears contrary to the principles above laid down, since it exposes the innocent to be punished for the guilty. It ought, then, to be justified by an advantage more than equivalent to that evil. This advantage is the great probability of preventing an offence, and of protecting the general security by individual responsibility.

The great influence which it exercises over the conduct of the suspected individual constitutes the chief merit of this procedure. He reflects that generous friends have given him a decisive proof of confidence or attachment in risking their fortunes and their quiet to protect his liberty and his honour. They are hostages who have voluntarily surrendered themselves on his account. Shall he be vile enough to turn their kindness against themselves? Shall he quench every sentiment of gratitude? Shall he publicly declare himself a traitor to friendship, and condemn himself to solitary remorse? But suppose him imprudent, fickle, or vicious, and not capable of restraining himself, still the security required of him is not useless. Those who thus are responsible for him, being interested in his actions, are guardians given him by the law; their vigilance will make up for his neglect, their eyes will closely watch his proceedings. Beside their personal interest in making themselves be listened to, they have the strongest title to be heard, from the service they have rendered, and from the right which they ought always to have to withdraw their security, and to leave the suspected to his fate. Such is the operation of this means in preventing offences.

It serves in another way to diminish the alarm, because it furnishes a favourable indication of the character or the resources of the suspected individual. It is a kind of contract of assurance. You demand, for example, the imprisonment of a man who has attempted to do you a certain injury. One of his friends presents himself, and disputes the necessity of so rigorous a means. "I ought to know him better than you do, and I assure you that you have nothing to fear from him. This penalty, which I consent to pay in case I am mistaken, is a proof of my belief and my sincerity."

Such are the advantages of demanding security for good behaviour. It may produce an evil; but that evil must be compared with its benefits, and especially with the vigorous measures which it would be necessary to employ against suspected persons if this procedure were not resorted to. Whenever an evil results to him who becomes security, that evil, having been voluntarily incurred, produces no danger and no alarm. If, through an imprudent zeal, he has become security with his eyes shut, the consequences concern him alone. None are alarmed lest the same evil should befall them. But in the greater number of cases this engagement results from a feeling of security. He who becomes bound for another knows better than anybody else the character and situation of the person for whom he engages; he is well aware of the risk he runs, and he does not assume it except with the opinion that he can do so with safety.

Let us now consider in what cases it is proper to employ this means.

1st. It is useful for the prevention of offences apprehended from quarrels of hostility or honour, especially duels. In general this class of delinquents cannot be suspected of a want of sensibility to public esteem; it is honour which puts them in hostile array. But honour does not command vengeance more positively than it forbids ingratitude, and especially that black ingratitude which punishes the benefactor by means of his very benefit.

2nd. It is extremely well adapted to prevent abuses of confidence, offences which violate the duties of a trust. Nobody is compelled to undertake such and such employments; it is fit that these employments should not be intrusted except to men who have, in riches or reputation, wherewith to furnish a sufficient guarantee for their good behaviour. At the same time, the security which is exacted, being attached to the office, cannot be offensive to anybody.

3rd. This means may have a peculiar utility in certain situations of political affairs, in case of enterprises against the state where many delinquents are concerned. Such men, often rather misled than perverse, nourish exalted sentiments of affection and honour, and in the midst of their revolt against society almost always preserve intimate relations with each other. When such a conspiracy is discovered, the conspirators most suspected should be compelled to give security for their conduct. This means, at first sight so feeble, is very efficacious—not only because the principals, seeing themselves watched, take the alarm; but because the sentiment of honour of which we have spoken furnishes a real or plausible motive, a motive founded upon justice and gratitude, for renouncing the enterprise.

4th. When sureties are required to prevent the escape of an accused person, there is the advantage of restraint upon the partiality of the judge. Without this condition a corrupt magistrate, or one of too easy temper, under pretext of a provisional enlargement, might withdraw an accused criminal from corporal or even pecuniary punishment, and change a severe penalty into simple banishment. This abuse becomes impossible when the judge cannot set the accused at liberty except upon sufficient security.

Only a single word is necessary as to the penalty to which the sureties should be subjected. That penalty should be pecuniary, and never anything else. Any afflictive punishment would be revolting, and would not furnish an indemnity.

It is true that a pecuniary punishment may bring on the imprisonment of the sureties, in case they are not able to pay their bonds. But if they were insolvent when they became sureties, they have deceived the court. If their insolvency is posterior to their suretyship, on the occurrence of that event they ought to have withdrawn their security by an application to the court. However, as in the case of other insolvencies, attention must be paid to circumstances; fraud must be distinguished from misfortune. If the suretyship was the cause of insolvency, in that case particular indulgence is needed.

CHAPTER VI.

The Choice of Punishments.

In order that a punishment may adapt itself to the rules of proportion above laid down, it should have the following qualities:—

1st. *It ought to be susceptible of more or less*, or *divisible*, in order to conform itself to variations in the gravity of offences. Chronic punishments, such as imprisonment and banishment, possess this quality in an eminent degree. They are divisible into portions of any requisite magnitude. It is the same with pecuniary punishments.

2nd. *Equal to Itself.*—It ought, to a certain extent, to be the same for all individuals guilty of the same offence, being made to correspond to their different measures of sensibility. This demands attention to age, sex, condition, fortune, individual habits, and many other circumstances; otherwise the same nominal punishment, being often found too severe for some persons, too mild for others, will overshoot the mark, or will fail to reach it. A fine fixed by law will never be a punishment equal to itself, on account of differences of fortune. Banishment has the same inconvenience; too severe for one, to another it is nothing.

3rd. *Commeasurable.*—If a man has two offences before his eyes, the law ought to give him a motive to abstain from the greater. He will have that motive, if he can see that the greater offence will draw upon him a greater punishment. It ought, then, to be in his power to compare these punishments, to measure their different degrees.

There are two methods of fulfilling this object. 1st. By adding to a given punishment another quantity of punishment of the same kind; for example, to five years' imprisonment for such an offence, two years' additional for such an aggravation. 2nd. By adding a punishment of a different kind; for example, to five years' imprisonment for such an offence, public ignominy for such an aggravation.

4th. *Analogous to the Offence.*—The punishment will more easily engrave itself on the memory, it will present itself more strongly to the imagination, if it has a resemblance, an analogy to the offence, a common character with it. The *lex talionis* is admirable in this respect—*An eye for an eye, a tooth for a tooth.* The most imperfect understanding is capable of connecting these ideas. But these sort of punishments are rarely practicable, and in most cases would be too expensive.

There are other means of analogy. Search out, for example, the motives of offences, and generally you will recognise the dominant passion of the offender, and you may punish him, according to the proverbial saying, with the instrument of his sin. Offences of cupidity will best be punished by pecuniary fines, when the wealth of the offender admits it; offences of insolence, by humiliation; offences of idleness, by compulsory labour, or forced rest.

5th. *Exemplary.*—A real punishment which should not be apparent would be lost upon the public. The great art consists in augmenting the apparent punishment without augmenting the real punishment. This may be accomplished, either in the selection of the punishments themselves, or by accompanying their execution with striking solemnities.

The *auto-da-fé* would be one of the most useful inventions of jurisprudence, if instead of being an act of faith it were an act of justice. What is it but a public execution, a solemn tragedy which the legislator presents to the assembled people; a tragedy truly important, truly pathetic by the sad reality of its catastrophe, and by the greatness of its object! The preparations, the scenery, the ornaments, cannot be too studied, since upon them the effect principally depends. The tribunal, the scaffold, the dresses of the officers of justice, the habiliments of the criminals, the religious service, the procession, all the accompaniments, ought to bear a grave and mournful character. Why should not the executioners be covered with a mourning crape? The terror of the scene would be increased by it, and at the same time these useful servants of the state would be concealed from the unjust hatred of the people. Were it possible to keep up the illusion, all might pass in effigy. The reality of punishment is only necessary to maintain the appearance of it.

6th. *Economical.*—That is, punishments should have only that degree of severity absolutely necessary to answer their end. All beyond is not only so much superfluous evil, but produces a multitude of inconveniences, which intercept the ends of justice.

Pecuniary punishments are highly economical, since all the evil felt by him who pays turns into an advantage for him who receives.

7th. *Remissible or Revokable.*—It is necessary that the damage inflicted should not be absolutely irreparable, since unfortunately cases may occur in which the infliction may be subsequently discovered to have been without lawful cause. As long as testimony is susceptible of imperfection, as long as appearances may be deceitful, as long as men have no certain criterion whereby to distinguish truth from falsehood, one of the most important precautions which mutual security requires is, not to admit of punishments absolutely irreparable, except upon the clearest evidence of their necessity. Have we not seen all the appearances of crime accumulated upon the head of a culprit whose innocence was demonstrated, when nothing remained but to lament over the mistake of an arrogant precipitation? Weak and inconsistent that we are! We judge like fallible creatures; we punish as if we could not be deceived!

To these important qualities of punishment three others may be added, of less extensive utility, but to be aimed at when it is possible to procure them without detracting from the great object of example.

1st. It is a great merit in a punishment to contribute to the *reformation of the offender*, not only through fear of being punished again, but by a change in his character and habits. This end may be attained by studying the motive which produced the offence, and by applying a punishment which tends to weaken that motive. A house of correction, to fulfil this object, ought to admit a separation of the delinquents, in order that different means of treatment may be adapted to the diversity of their moral condition.

2nd. *Taking away the power of doing Injury.*—It is much easier to obtain this end than the preceding. Mutilations and perpetual imprisonment possess this quality. But the spirit of this maxim leads to an excessive rigour. It is this which has rendered the punishment of death so frequent.

If there are cases in which it is possible to deprive the offender of the power of doing injury only by taking away his life, it is upon very extraordinary occasions; for example, in civil wars, where the name of a leader, as long as he lives, is enough to inflame the passions of a multitude. And, even in such cases, death inflicted upon actions of a character so equivocal ought rather to be looked upon as an act of hostility than as a punishment.

3rd. *To furnish an indemnity to the injured party* is another useful quality in a punishment. It is a means of accomplishing two objects at once,—punishing an offence, and repairing it: removing the evil of the first order, and putting a stop to alarm. This is a characteristic advantage of pecuniary punishments.

I conclude this chapter by a general observation of the highest importance. *The legislator, in the choice of punishments, ought carefully to avoid such as shock established prejudices.* If there has been formed in the minds of the people a decided aversion to a given kind of punishment, though it has all the other requisite qualities, it ought not to be admitted into the penal code, because it would do more harm than good. In the first place, it is an evil to inspire the public with a painful feeling by the establishment of an unpopular punishment. It is no longer the guilty alone who are punished. It is the most innocent and tender-hearted persons upon whom is inflicted a punishment very real, though it has no particular name, by wounding their sensibility, braving their opinion, and presenting to them the image of violence and of tyranny. What can be expected from conduct so injudicious? The legislator, by despising public sentiment, imperceptibly turns it against himself. He loses the voluntary assistance which individuals lend to the execution of the law when they are content with it; the people, instead of being his assistants, are his enemies. Some endeavour to facilitate the escape of the guilty; others feel a scruple at denouncing them; witnesses hesitate to testify; there is formed insensibly a fatal prejudice, which attaches a kind of shame and of reproach to the service of the law. This general discontent may go further; it sometimes bursts out into open resistance to the officers of justice, or to the execution of sentences. A success against authority is regarded by the people as a victory; and the unpunished delinquent triumphs over the weakness of the laws.

What renders punishments unpopular is almost always their bad selection. The more the penal code is conformed to the rules we have laid down, the more it will secure the enlightened esteem of the wise, and an approbation of feeling on the part of the multitude. Such punishments will be thought just and moderate. Everybody will be struck with their propriety, their analogy to offences, and with that scale of gradation by which aggravation of punishment is made to correspond to aggravation of offence, and mildness of punishment to smallness of offence. This kind of merit, founded upon domestic and familiar notions, is level to the comprehension of every mind. Nothing is more fit to give the idea of a paternal government, to inspire confidence, to make public opinion act in concert with authority. When the people are on the side of the laws, the chances of escape are reduced to their lowest term.

CHAPTER VII.

The Kinds of Punishments.

There is no punishment which, taken separately, unites all the requisite qualities. To attain that end, it is necessary to have a choice among many punishments, to vary them, and to make several of them enter into the same infliction. Medicine has no panacea. Different means must be recurred to, according to the nature of disorders and the temperament of the patient. The art of medicine consists in studying all remedies, in combining them and in putting them into operation according to circumstances.

The catalogue of punishments is the same with that of offences. The same evil done by authority of the law, or in violation of the law, will constitute a punishment, or an offence. The nature of the evil is the same, but how different the effect! The offence spreads alarm; the punishment re-establishes security. Offence is the enemy of all; punishment is the common protector. Offence, for the advantage of a single person, produces a universal evil; punishment, by the sufferings of an individual, produces a general good. Suspend punishment, the world becomes a scene of robbery, and society is dissolved. Re-establish it, and the passions grow calm, order is restored, and the weakness of each individual is sustained by the protection of the public force.

The whole matter of punishment may be distributed under the following heads:—

1st. *Capital Punishments.*—Such as put an immediate end to the life of the offender.

2nd. *Afflictive Punishments.*—Such as consist in corporal sufferings, but which produce only a temporary effect, as flagellation, compulsory fasting, &c.

3rd. *Indelible Punishments.*—Such as produce a permanent effect upon the body, as branding and amputation.

4th. *Ignominious Punishments.*—Their principal aim is to expose the offender to the contempt of the spectators, and to make him be looked upon as unworthy the society of his old friends. The *amende honorable* is an example.

5th. *Penitential Punishments.*—Destined to awaken the sentiment of shame, and to expose to a certain degree of censure. They are not severe or public enough to bring on infamy, nor to make the offender be looked upon as unworthy the society of his former companions. It is, in fact, such chastisements as these that a father has the power to inflict upon his children, and which the most tender father would feel no scruple at inflicting upon the child he most loved.

6th. *Chronic Punishments.*—Their principal rigour consists in their duration, so that they would be almost nothing if it were not for that circumstance. Banishment and imprisonment are examples. They may be perpetual or temporary.

7th. *Punishments simply restrictive.*—Those which, without participating in any of the preceding characters, consist in some restraint, some restriction, in being prevented from doing what one would desire; for example, the prohibition to exercise a certain profession, the prohibition to frequent a certain place.

8th. *Punishments simply compulsive.*—Those which oblige a man to do a thing from which he would wish to be exempted; for example, the obligation to present one's self at certain times before an officer of justice. This punishment consists not in the thing itself, but in the inconvenience of the constraint.

9th. *Pecuniary Punishments.*—They consist in depriving the delinquent of a sum of money, or of some article of actual property.

10th. *Punishments quasi pecuniary.*—They consist in depriving the offender of a kind of property in the services of individuals, —pure and simple services, or services combined with some pecuniary profit.

11th. *Characteristic Punishments.*—Punishments which, by means of some analogy, present to the imagination a lively idea of the offence. These punishments do not properly form a separate class; they are distributed among all the others, ignominious, penitential, afflictive, &c. A characteristic punishment is a manner of inflicting one of the preceding punishments with some circumstance which has relation to the nature of the offence. Suppose a counterfeiter, instead of being punished with death, were condemned to some other punishments, and, among other things, to be branded indelibly. If the word *counterfeiter* were branded on his forehead, and upon each cheek the impress of *a piece of current money*, this punishment, recalling the offence by a sensible image, would be eminently characteristic.

In a house of correction, the delinquents, according to the diversity of their offences, should be obliged to wear emblematical dresses, or other exterior marks of some striking analogy. Thus the notion of their offence would become inseparable from them; their mere presence would be like a new proclamation of the law; and the hope of escaping this shame, by resuming a common dress, would be a powerful attraction to engage them to good conduct.

CHAPTER VIII.

Et quoniam variant morbi, variabimus artes;
Mille mali species, mille salutis erunt.

And as diseases vary, aids must vary;
A thousand kinds of ill, a thousand cures.

Justification of Variety in Punishments.

We have already seen that the choice of punishments is the result of a multitude of considerations, that they ought to be susceptible of more or less, equal to themselves, commeasurable, analogous to the offence, exemplary, economical, reformative, popular, &c.

We have seen that a single punishment never can have all these qualities, that it is necessary to combine them, to vary them, to assort them, in order to find the composition which we need.

If a code founded upon these principles were only a project, it might be regarded as a fine speculation impossible to be realized. Cold and indifferent men who are always armed with a despairing incredulity wherever the happiness of mankind is concerned, would not want that common reproach of impracticability, so convenient to idleness and so flattering to self-love. But the work is done, the plan is executed; a penal code has been constructed upon these principles, and that code, in which all these rules are scrupulously adhered to, has no quality more remarkable than its clearness, its simplicity, its precision.* All penal legislation hitherto known, without having accomplished a moiety of the object, is infinitely more complicated, more vague, more difficult to comprehend.

It has been necessary to seek out a great variety of punishments, to adapt them to each offence, and to invent new means of rendering them exemplary and characteristic. But the same persons who will agree to the general proposition that these two qualities are essential will perhaps be constantly revolting against their application. Punishments naturally excite antipathy, and even horror, when considered separately from offences. Besides, opinions upon a matter submitted to sentiment and imagination are so floating and capricious, that the same punishment which would excite the indignation of one as too severe, would be blamed by another as too mild and quite inefficacious.

I wish here only to anticipate an objection. A penal system ought not to be thought cruel because it includes a great variety of punishments. The multiplicity and the variety of punishments prove the industry and the cares of the legislator. To have but one or two kinds of punishment is an effect of ignorance of principles, and of a barbarous contempt of proportion. I might mention states in which despotism is all-powerful and civilization but little advanced, where it may be said that but one kind of punishment is known. The more we study the nature of offences and of motives, the more we examine the diversity of characters and circumstances, the more we shall feel the necessity of employing different means to counteract them.

* This refers to the penal division of that *Universal Code,* to the construction of which Bentham devoted the greater part of his life. It has not been published, and, indeed, was never finished to the satisfaction of the author.—*Translator.*

Offences, those interior enemies of society, which carry on against it an obstinate and varied war, display all the instincts of mischievous animals: some employ violence; others have recourse to stratagem—they know how to assume an infinity of shapes and everywhere keep up a secret correspondence. If they have been combated without being conquered, if the revolt continues to subsist, it must be principally ascribed to the defect of legal tactics and of the instruments hitherto employed to suppress them. Certainly, there needs as much talent, calculation, and prudence to defend society as to attack it, and to prevent offences as to commit them.

To determine whether a penal code is rigorous, observe how it punishes the most common offences, those against property. The laws everywhere have been too severe upon this point, because, punishments being ill-chosen and misapplied, it has been attempted to compensate by rigour what was wanting in justice. It is necessary to be less prodigal of punishment as respects offences which attack property, in order to deal it with more severity upon offences which attack the person. The first are susceptible of indemnity; the others do not admit it, at least not in kind. The evil of offences against property may be reduced to a trifle by means of insurances; while all the treasure of Potosi cannot recall to life one murdered person, or calm the terrors spread by such a crime. But the question is not whether a penal code be more or less severe; that is a wrong view of the subject. The only question is, whether the severity of the code be necessary or not.

It is cruel to expose even the guilty to useless sufferings; and such is the consequence of punishments too severe. But is it not more cruel still to leave the innocent to suffer? Such is the result of punishments too mild to be efficient.

We may conclude that variety in punishments is one of the perfections of a penal code, and that the more repugnant to a sensitive heart is the search for these means, the more necessary is it that the legislator should be so penetrated with humanity as to gain this victory over himself. Was Sangrado, whose only physic consisted in bleeding, more humane than Boerhaave, who consulted all nature to discover new remedies?*

* The ideas suggested in this chapter are expanded at much greater length, and sustained by additional arguments, in the *Theory of Punishments*, which is one of the works of Bentham, compiled and published by Dumont. Notwithstanding all the reasonings of Bentham upon the subject of diversity of punishment, I am constrained, by his own principles, to adopt the opinion that *imprisonment*, variously modified, is the only punishment which the legislator need employ,—with the exception of those *satisfactions*, pecuniary and honorary, which ought to form a part of every code, and which in a certain sense may be regarded as punishments.

Imprisonment combines all the qualities enumerated by Bentham as desirable in a punishment. 1. It is peculiarly *susceptible of more or less.* 2. It may easily be made *equal to itself*—that is, uniform in its severity as respects the punishment of different offenders guilty of the same offence. 3. It is *commeasurable* in a high degree. 4. It is *exemplary*, inasmuch as a gaol is a constant warning to offenders. 5. It is *economical*, or may easily be made so by proper arrangements, and that too in more senses than one; for while it is considered as a punishment both by the offender and the public, instead of inflicting any injury on the offender, in many cases it may be made to confer upon him a high degree of benefit, both physical and moral; and as respects the pecuniary expense to the public, every gaol, mere houses of detention excepted, might be made, and ought to be made, to support itself. 6. It is *remissible*, and quite as revocable as any other punishment. 7. It also may be regarded as *analogous to the offence*, since every offence consists in an abuse of liberty and power, and is properly punished by a restraint of liberty and power.

It also possesses in a high degree two of the other qualities esteemed by Bentham as important, though less so than those above mentioned. 1. It has a *tendency to reform the offender*, by removing him from the temptations of liberty, and giving virtuous motives an opportunity to regain an ascendancy. 2. It takes away, so long as it lasts, which may be for a long time, *the power of doing injury.*

It is a point of the highest importance that severity of punishment should be proportioned to magnitude of offences, and that according to a scale simple, and easily to be understood. Variety of kinds in punishment seems to be inconsistent with this essential object, for by what common measure shall we calculate them?—how many lashes are equivalent to how many days of imprisonment? This is a matter of fancy upon which no two men will agree.

CHAPTER IX.

Examination of some Common Punishments.

Afflictive Punishments.—These are not good for all offences, because they cannot exist in a slight degree, or at least only in case of persons in a state of the lowest degradation. Every corporal punishment publicly inflicted is infamous. Inflicted in private, it is less infamous, but it is not exemplary.

The most common afflictive punishment is whipping. In its ordinary application, this punishment has the inconvenience of not being equal to itself; it varies from the slightest pain to the most atrocious torture, and may even result in death. Everything depends upon the kind of lash, the force of the application, and the temperament of the individual. The legislator who orders this punishment knows not what he does; the judge is nearly as ignorant; its execution will always be in the highest degree arbitrary and uncertain. In England, whipping is usual for such thefts as juries, by a humane perjury, declare to be below the value of a shilling. This punishment is a revenue to the executioner. If the delinquent suffers, it is only because he has no money wherewith to purchase the impunity of a mock infliction.

Indelible Punishments.—Indelible afflictive punishments, taken separately, are not capable of graduation. The mildest of them has a very high degree of severity. Some, such as branding, only disfigure the person; others take away the use of some limb; others consist in mutilations, as the loss of the nose,

Imprisonment, moreover, has the decided advantage of not inflaming the vindictive feelings or giving the sanction of the law to revolting cruelties. Who can doubt that barbarous punishments tend to barbarize the people which inflicts them?

I might suggest many other considerations in favour of adopting imprisonment as the only kind of punishment, did the limits of a note permit it. It must be confessed, however, that imprisonment has been fitted to serve for that purpose only by reason of those vast improvements lately introduced into prison discipline, of which Bentham, next to *Howard*, deserves the credit. See the treatise entitled *Panoptique*, compiled by Dumont from the writings of Bentham.—*Translator.*

the ears, the feet, or the hands. Mutilation of the organs which are necessary for labour ought not to be inflicted upon common offences, such as those which spring from want, as theft, smuggling, &c. What can the offenders do after being maimed? If the state maintains them the punishment becomes too expensive; if they are left to themselves, it is the same as condemning them to despair and death. Penal mutilations have two inconveniences; they are irremissible, and they are apt to be confounded with natural accidents. There is no apparent difference between him who has had an arm cut off for a crime, and him who has lost an arm in the service of his country. An artificial and evident brand ought always to be added, to be the certificate of offence and the safeguard of misfortune. These punishments might be suppressed altogether; and if used at all, it should only be for some very rare offences, where they have the recommendation of analogy.

Indelible brands are a powerful means of which a bad use has been made. Among offenders convicted of theft, or of furtive concealment, many have only yielded to a transient temptation, and might return to virtue if the nature of the punishment had not corrupted them. In such cases there should be no indelible brand, no infamous punishment. That would be to take away the hope of re-establishing their reputation, and redeeming a moment of error. If an indelible brand is stamped upon counterfeiters, for example, it is a sign which excites distrust of their honesty, but which does not deprive them of the means of livelihood. Despised as rogues, they will still be employed as ingenious workmen. But if a man is branded for a first theft, what will become of him? Who will employ him? What would it avail him to be honest? He is compelled to be a knave.

An indelible brand is only useful to mark a dangerous offender, who will cease to be dangerous provided he is known, or to secure the execution of another punishment. When the offence is infamous, branding ought to accompany perpetual imprisonment, to prevent the flight of the prisoner. It binds him like a chain, for it makes the prison his asylum, and he would be worse off out of it than in it. To make these marks permanent and distinguishable, they should be imprinted by coloured powders pricked into the skin, and not with a hot iron.

Ignominious Punishments.—Infamy is one of the most salutary ingredients in penal pharmacy: but ideas upon this subject are very confused, and the means employed very imperfect. According to the notion of the lawyers, it would seem that infamy was a homogeneous thing, indivisible, an absolute and invariable quantity. If it were so, the employment of this punishment would be almost always impolitic and unjust; for it is equally applied to very unequal offences, and to some offences which ought not to be visited with it at all. Infamy, well managed, is very susceptible of graduation. It is, in a moral view, what defilement is in a physical. It is one thing to have a spot on one's clothes, and quite another to be covered with mud.

Loss of honour is another phrase in common use, but not less deceptive. It includes two false suppositions: one, that honour is a good of which all men possess a certain share; the other, that it is entirely in the power of the law, and can be taken away at pleasure. The term *dishonour*, which differs from infamy in not excluding the idea of more or less, would be more appropriate.

Infamy, as it is commonly employed, bears rather upon the criminal than the crime. If it bore upon the offence, its effect would be more certain, more durable, and more efficacious. It might then be proportioned to the nature of the case. But in order to attain that end it is necessary that a particular kind of dishonour should be found for every kind of offence.

All this cannot be effected, except by a new apparatus of justice; inscriptions, emblems, dresses, pictural representations; signs which speak to the eyes, which strike the imagination through the senses, which form associations not to be effaced. It is thus that public indignation, which is but too apt to be directed against the laws and the judges, may be concentrated upon the offender and the offence. The legislator should not disdain to borrow from the theatre imposing shows and representations. To surround the criminal with symbols of his offence would not be, as some may incline to represent it, a vain display of power, a ridiculous parody: it would be an instructive exhibition which would announce the moral objects of punishment, and would render justice more respectable by showing it, even in the sad function of punishment, aiming rather to impress a great lesson than to satisfy a spirit of vengeance.

The *pillory*, used in England, is of all punishments the most unequal and unmanageable. The delinquent is abandoned to the caprice of individuals, and this singular infliction is sometimes a triumph, and sometimes it is death. An author was condemned to it, some years since, for what is called a *libel*. The platform upon which he was placed became a kind of lyceum; and the whole time passed away in compliments between him and the spectators. In 1760, a bookseller was put in the pillory for having sold some impious or seditious work. A subscription was opened for him, while he was still standing in it, and soon amounted to upwards of a hundred guineas. What an affront to the law! Lately, a man condemned to the same punishment for a lascivious offence, was murdered by the populace under the eyes of the police, who did not even attempt to defend him. Mr. Burke had the spirit to denounce this abuse in the House of Commons. "The man who undergoes a punishment," he said, "is still under the protection of the law, and ought not to be abandoned as a prey to ferocity." The orator was applauded, but the abuse remains; yet a simple iron grating to inclose the criminal would prevent all such acts of barbarity.

Chronic Punishments.—Chronic punishments, such as banishment and imprisonment, are adapted to many offences; but they demand a particular attention to the circumstances which affect individual sensibility. Banishment would be an infliction in the highest degree unequal if it were decreed without exception. Its severity depends upon the condition and the fortune of those who undergo it. Some have no reason to be attached to their country; others would be overwhelmed with despair at the idea of leaving their property and their home. Some have families, others have no such ties. One would be deprived of every resource if compelled to leave his country, to another banishment would be a lucky escape from his creditors. Age and sex make a great difference. Much latitude must be allowed to the judge, who can be directed only by general instructions.

The English, before the independence of America, were in the habit of transporting to the colonies a numerous class of offenders. For some this transportation was slavery, for others a party of pleasure. A rogue, who had a mind to travel, was a fool if he did not commit some offence to insure himself an outfit and a free passage. The more industrious of the convicts gained property and a home in the colonies. Those who knew nothing, except how to steal, not being able to exercise their art with any success in a country of which they did not know even the geography, soon ended their career on the gallows. Once condemned and transported, their lot was unknown. Though they died of disease or famine, nobody cared. Thus the whole effect of example was lost, and the principal end of punishment was wholly neglected. The transportation to Botany Bay, which is now in use, answers its end no better. It has all the faults which a punishment can have, and none of the qualities which it ought to have.

If an establishment in a distant country were offered to the citizens, on condition of attaining it by a violation of the laws, what absurdity! what madness! But transportation must present itself to many wretches as an advantageous offer, of which they can take advantage only by committing an offence. Thus the law, instead of counterbalancing the temptation, adds, in many cases, to its force.

As to *imprisonment*, it is impossible to give any opinion with respect to that punishment, until all that concerns the structure and the internal government of prisons has been determined with the greatest exactitude. Prisons, with the exception of a small number, include every imaginable means of infecting both body and mind. Consider merely the state of forced idleness to which the prisoners are reduced, and this punishment is excessively expensive. Want of exercise enervates and enfeebles their faculties, and deprives their organs of suppleness and elasticity; despoiled, at the same time, of their characters and of their habits of labour, they are no sooner out of prison than starvation drives them to commit offences. Subject to the subaltern despotism of men who for the most part are depraved by the constant spectacle of crime and the habit of tyranny, these wretches may be delivered up to a thousand unknown sufferings, which aggravate them against society, and which harden them to the sense of punishment. In a moral point of view, an ordinary prison is a school in which wickedness is taught by surer means than can ever be employed for the inculcation of virtue. Weariness, revenge, and want preside over these academies of crime. All the inmates raise themselves to the level of the worst; the most ferocious inspires the others with his ferocity; the most cunning teaches his cunning to all the rest; the most debauched inculcates his licentiousness. All possible defilements of the heart and the imagination become the solace of their despair. United by a common interest, they assist each other in throwing off the yoke of shame. Upon the ruins of social honour is built a new honour, composed of falsehood, fearlessness under disgrace, forgetfulness of the future, and hostility to mankind; and thus it is that unfortunates, who might have been restored to virtue and to happiness, reach the heroic point of wickedness, the sublimity of crime.

A convict, after having finished his term of imprisonment, ought not to be restored to society without precautions and without trial. Suddenly to transfer him from a state of surveillance and captivity to unlimited freedom, to abandon him to all the temptations of isolation and want, and to desires pricked on by long privation, is a piece of carelessness and inhumanity which ought at length to attract the attention of legislators. At London, when the hulks in the Thames are emptied, the malefactors at that jubilee of crime rush into the city like wolves, who after a long fast have succeeded in entering a sheep-fold; and until all these plunderers have been apprehended for new offences, there is no security upon the highways, no safety in the streets of the metropolis.

Pecuniary Punishments.—These inflictions have the triple advantage of being susceptible of graduation, of fulfilling the end of punishment, and of serving as an indemnity to the injured party. But it must be recollected that a pecuniary punishment, if the sum is fixed, is in the highest degree unequal. This consideration, so obviously true, has been neglected by all legislators. Fines have been determined without any regard to the profit of the offence; to its evil, or to the wealth of the offender. Everybody recollects the story of that insolent young Roman, who amused himself by lashing all the passers-by, while a slave of his at the same time offered them a coin, fixed by the laws of the Twelve Tables, as the fine for that offence.

Pecuniary punishments should always be regulated by the fortune of the offender. The relative amount of the fine should be fixed, not its absolute amount; for such an offence, such a part of the offender's fortune; with such modifications, however, as would meet the difficulties liable to attend a literal execution of this rule.

Punishments simply Restrictive.—There is nothing in penal legislation more ingenious than *banishment from the presence of the injured party.* This punishment is suggested by the old French law, and some traces of it may be found in the Danish code. With some improvements, it would offer an excellent remedy for offences growing out of individual hostilities, from which the public in general has nothing to fear. This punishment affords a triumph to the oppressed over the oppressor, and re-establishes, in the mildest manner, the preponderance of injured innocence over insolent force. Besides, it prevents the renewal of quarrels, and takes away from the aggressor the power of doing harm. But to put in operation a means so closely connected with honour, requires a scrupulous attention to the condition of individuals.

Capital Punishments.—The more attention one gives to the punishment of death, the more he will be inclined to adopt the opinion of Beccaria,—that it ought to be disused. This subject is so ably discussed in his book, that to treat it after him is a work that may well be dispensed with. Those who wish to see, at a single glance, all that can be said for and against it, have only to turn back to the chapter containing the table of qualities desirable in a punishment.

Whence originated the prodigal fury with which the punishment of death has been inflicted? It is the effect of resentment which at first inclines to the greatest rigour; and of an imbecility of soul, which finds in the rapid destruction of convicts the great advantage of having no further occasion to concern one's self about them.

Death! always death! It requires neither the meditations of genius nor resistance to the passions. It is only to yield one's self to them, and we are carried at once to that fatal term.

Is it said that death is necessary to take from an assassin the power of reiterating his offence? For the same reason, then, we ought to destroy the frantic and the mad, from whom society has everything to fear. If we can guard against these, why not against assassins? Is it said that death is the only punishment which can outweigh certain temptations to commit homicide? These temptations can only arise from hostility or cupidity; and do not these passions, from their very nature, dread humiliation, want, and captivity more than death?

I should astonish the reader were I to expose to him the penal code of a nation celebrated for its humanity and its enlightenment. We should expect to find in it the most exact proportion between offences and punishments; but, in fact, that proportion is continually outraged or forgotten, and the punishment of death is lavished upon the most trifling offences. The mildness of the national character is in contradiction to the laws, and, as might be expected, it is that which triumphs; the laws are eluded; pardons are multiplied; offences are overlooked; testimony is excluded; and juries, to avoid an excess of severity, often fall into excess of indulgence. Thence results a system of penal law, incoherent, contradictory, uniting violence to weakness, dependent on the humour of a judge, varying from circuit to circuit, sometimes sanguinary, sometimes null.

English law-makers have not yet adopted imprisonment joined to labour—a sort of punishment good in so many respects. Instead of compulsive occupation, they reduce their prisoners to complete idleness. Is this by design? No; it is doubtless by habit. Things have been found upon that footing; it has been disapproved, but has not been changed. There needs pecuniary advances, vigilance, and sustained attention, to combine imprisonment with labour; none of these are needed to shut up a man, and leave him to himself.

CHAPTER X.

Of the pardoning Power.

What punishment lacks in certainty must be made up in severity. The less certain a punishment is, the severer it must be; the more certain it is, the less it need be severe.

What shall be said of a power created for the very purpose of making punishment uncertain? Such, however, is the direct consequence of a power to pardon.

In the species, as in the individual, the age of passion precedes that of reason. Anger and vengeance have dictated the earliest penal laws. When these barbarous enactments, founded upon caprices and antipathies, begin to shock an enlightened public, the power of pardoning offers a safeguard against the sanguinary rigour of the laws, and becomes, so to speak, a comparative good; and nobody inquires whether this pretended remedy is not, in fact, a new evil.

How many eulogiums have been bestowed upon clemency! It has been repeated a thousand times that it is the first virtue of a sovereign. Doubtless, if the crime be only an attack upon the sovereign's self-love; if the question be of a satire upon him or his favourites; the moderation of a prince is meritorious, the pardon which he grants is a triumph over himself. But when the question is of an offence against society, a pardon is not an act of clemency; it is a mere piece of partiality.

In cases where punishment would do more evil than good, as after seditions, conspiracies, and public disorders, the power of pardoning is not only useful, it is necessary. These cases being foreseen and pointed out in a good legislative system, pardon applied to them is not a violation, it is an execution of the law. But pardons without motive, effects of the favour or the facility of a prince, impeach either the laws or the government: the laws, of cruelty to individuals; or the government, of cruelty to the public. Reason, justice, and humanity must be wanting somewhere; for reason is never in contradiction with itself; justice cannot destroy with one hand what it has done with the other; humanity cannot require that punishment should be established for the protection of innocence, and that pardons should be granted for the encouragement of crime.

The power of pardoning, it has been said, is the noblest prerogative of sovereignty. But may not that prerogative sometimes turn to the disadvantage of him by whom it is exercised? If, instead of gaining for the prince a more constant affection on the part of his subjects, it exposes him to caprices of judgment, to clamours, and to libels; if he can neither yield to solicitations without being suspected of feebleness, nor show himself inexorable without being accused of severity, where then is the splendour of this dangerous right? It would seem that a just and humane prince must often dread the exposure to this combat between public and private virtues.

Homicide ought, at least, to make an exception. He who has the right to pardon that offence is master of the life of every citizen.*

* To prevent the abuse of this power, it would suffice to require that its exercise should be accompanied by an exposition of motives. Where capital punishments are in use, it would be better to preserve the power of pardoning, even without restrictions, than to abolish it entirely.

To sum up. If the laws are too severe, the power of pardoning is a necessary corrective; but that corrective is itself an evil. Make good laws, and there will be no need of a magic wand which has the power to annul them. If the punishment is necessary, it ought not to be remitted; if it is not necessary, the convict should not be sentenced to undergo it.

PART FOURTH.

INDIRECT MEANS OF PREVENTING OFFENCES.

INTRODUCTION.

In all the sciences there are branches which have been cultivated more tardily than others, because they demand a longer series of observations and meditations more profound. It is thus that mathematics have their transcendental or higher branch—that is, a new science, as it were, above ordinary science.

The same distinction, to a certain extent, may be applied to the art of legislation. What means shall be adopted to prevent injurious actions? The first answer, which presents itself to everybody, is this: "Forbid those actions; punish them." This method of combatting offences being the most simple and the first adopted, every other method of arriving at the same end is, so to speak, a refinement of the art, and its transcendental branch.

That branch consists in devising a course of legislative acts adapted to *prevent* offences—in acting principally upon the inclinations of men, in order to turn them from evil and to impress upon them the direction most useful to themselves and to others.

The first method—that of combatting offences by punishments—constitutes *direct legislation.*

The second method—that of combatting offences by *preventive means*—constitutes a branch of legislation which may be called *indirect.*

The sovereign acts *directly* against offences when he prohibits them individually under special penalties. He acts *indirectly* when he takes precautions to prevent them.

By direct legislation the evil is attacked in front. Indirect legislation attacks it obliquely. In the first case, the legislator declares open war against the enemy, points him out, pursues him, meets him foot to foot, and carries his defences sword in hand. In the second case, he does not announce his whole design; he works underground, he procures intelligence, he seeks to prevent hostile enterprises, and to keep still in his alliance those who may have formed secret intentions against him.

Speculative writers upon politics have had glimpses of this art; but in speaking of this second branch of legislation they do not evince any clear idea of it. The first branch has been a long time reduced to system, the good part of it as well as the bad. The second branch has never been thoroughly examined; nobody has undertaken to treat it with method, to arrange it, to classify it—in one word, to master it in its whole extent. It is yet a new subject.

Writers who have composed political romances tolerate direct legislation as a necessary evil; it is a choice of evils to which they submit, but as to which they never express a very lively interest. But when they come to speak about the means of preventing offences, of rendering men better, of perfecting morals, their imagination grows warm, their hopes are excited; one would suppose they were about to produce the great secret, and that the human race was going to receive a new form. It is because we have a more magnificent idea of objects in proportion as they are less familiar, and because the imagination has a loftier flight amid vague projects which have never been subjected to the limits of analysis. *Major e longinquo reverentia*—the greater distance, the greater reverence—this is a saying as applicable to ideas as to persons. A detailed examination will reduce all these indefinite hopes to the just dimensions of the possible; and if in the process we lose fictitious treasures, we shall be well indemnified by the certainty of what remains.

To distinguish exactly what appertains to these two branches, it is necessary to begin by forming a just idea of direct legislation. It proceeds, or ought to proceed, in this way:—

1st. The choice of acts to be erected into offences.

2nd. The description of each offence, as murder, theft, peculation, &c.

3rd. An exposition of the reasons for attributing to these acts the quality of offences—reasons which ought to be deduced from the single principle of utility, and consequently to be consistent with themselves.

4th. The assigning of a competent punishment for each offence.

5th. An exposition of the reasons which justify these punishments.

The penal system, though it be made as perfect as possible, is defective in several respects:—1st. The evil must exist before the remedy can be applied. The remedy consists in the application of punishment, and punishment cannot be applied till offence is committed. Every new instance of punishment inflicted is an additional proof that punishment lacks efficacy and leaves behind it a certain degree of danger and alarm. 2nd. Punishment itself is an evil, though necessary to prevent greater evils. Penal justice, in the whole course of its operation, can only be a series of evils—evils arising from the threats and constraint of the law, evils arising from the prosecution of the accused before it is possible to distinguish innocence from guilt, evils growing out of the infliction of judicial sentences, evils from the unavoidable consequences which result to the innocent. 3rd. The penal system is not able to reach many injurious actions, which escape justice either by their frequency, the facility of concealing them, by the difficulty of defining them, or finally by some vicious turn of public opinion by which they are favoured. Penal law can operate only within certain limits, and its power extends only to palpable acts, susceptible of manifest proof.

This imperfection of the penal system has caused new expedients to be sought for to supply its deficiencies. These expedients have for their object the prevention of offences, either by preventing the acquisition of the *knowledge* necessary to their commission or by taking away the *power* or the *will* to commit them. The most numerous class of these means relates to the art of directing the inclinations by weakening the seductive motives which excite to evil, and by strengthening the tutelary motives which impel to good.

Indirect means, then, are those which, without having the character of punishments, act upon man physically or morally, to dispose him to obey the laws, to shield him from temptations, to govern him by his inclinations and his knowledge.

These indirect means not only have a great advantage on the side of mildness, but they succeed in a multitude of cases in which direct means will not answer. All modern historians have remarked how much the abuses of the Catholic Church have diminished since the establishment of the Protestant religion. What popes and councils could not do by their decrees a fortunate rivalry has accomplished without difficulty; and scandals which would afford to hostile sects a matter of triumph have been carefully avoided. The indirect means of free competition among religions has more power to restrain and reform the clergy than all positive laws.

Let us take another example from political economy. Attempts have been made to reduce by law the price of merchandise, and particularly the interest of money. It is true that high prices are an evil only in comparison with some good of which they prevent the enjoyment; but such an evil as they are, there is reason for seeking to diminish it. To effect that purpose, a multitude of restrictive laws have been devised, a fixed tariff of prices, a legal rate of interest. And what has been the consequence? These regulations have always been eluded; punishments have been multiplied; and the evil, instead of being diminished, has become greater. The only efficacious means is an *indirect* one, which few governments have had the wisdom to employ. To grant all merchants and capitalists a free right of competition, to intrust to them the business of making war upon each other, of underbidding each other, and of attracting purchasers by the offer of more advantageous terms—such is this means. Free competition amounts to the same thing as the grant of a reward to him who furnishes merchandise of the best kind at the lowest price. This immediate and natural reward, which a multitude of competitors flatter themselves with the hope of obtaining, acts with more efficacy than a distant punishment which every one expects to escape.

Before entering upon the exposition of these indirect means, it should be observed that the classification here employed is, to a certain extent, arbitrary, and that several of them may be properly arranged under different heads. To distinguish them invariably, one from the other, would require us to enter upon a metaphysical analysis, very subtle and very fatiguing. It is enough for the present purpose that all indirect means may be placed under one or the other of the heads proposed, and that the attention of the legislator is directed to the principal sources whence they may be derived.

There is one more preliminary remark of essential importance. Among the variety of means about to be explained, there is none which is recommended as especially fit for any particular government, and still less for all government in general. The special advantage of each measure, considered by itself, will be indicated under its proper head; but each may have relative inconveniences, which it is impossible to determine without knowing the circumstances of the particular case. It ought to be well understood that the object here proposed is not to advise the adoption of such or such a measure, but simply to bring it into view, and to recommend it to the attention of those whose province it is to judge of its applicability.

CHAPTER I.

Means of taking away the Physical Power to do Harm.

When the will, the knowledge, and the power necessary to the performance of an act concur, that act is of necessity performed. *Inclination, knowledge, power,*—these, then, are the three points at which it is necessary to apply the influence of law, in order to determine the conduct of men. These three words contain in the abstract the sum and substance of all that can be done by legislation, direct or indirect.

I begin with *power*, because means in this respect are more simple and more limited, and because, in those cases in which we can succeed in taking away the power to do harm, we have accomplished everything. Success is certain.

Power may be distinguished into two kinds: 1st. *Internal* power, that which depends upon the intrinsic faculties of the individual; 2nd. *External* power, that which depends upon persons and things external to the individual, but the aid of which he must have, in order to act.

As to internal power, that which depends upon the faculties of the individual, it is scarcely possible to deprive a man of it with advantage. The power of doing evil is inseparable from the power of doing good. With his hands cut off, a man cannot steal, but neither can he work.

Besides, these privative means are so severe that they cannot be employed except upon criminals already convicted. Imprisonment is the only one of them that can be justified, in certain cases, to prevent an apprehended offence.

The legislator will find greater resources for the prevention of offences by turning his attention to the material objects which aid their commission.

There are cases in which the power of doing harm may be taken away, by excluding what Tacitus calls *irritamenta malorum*, irritations to evil,—the subjects, the instruments of offence. In such cases, the policy of the legislator may be compared to that of a nurse; iron bars at the windows, grates around the fire, the care of keeping sharp and dangerous instruments from the hands of children, are means of the same kind as the prohibition to sell and to make tools for the fabrication of false money, venerific drugs, arms easy to be concealed, dice, or other instruments of prohibited games, and the prohibition to make or to have certain nets for the chase, or other instruments for trapping wild game.

Mahomet, not trusting to the restraining power of reason, wished to take away from men the power of abusing strong drinks; and if we consider the climate of warm countries, where wine renders men furious rather than stupid, we shall find perhaps that the total prohibition is a milder method of procedure than a permission which produces a numerous class of offences, and consequently of punishments.

Imposts upon spirituous liquors fulfil, in part, the same end. In proportion as the price is raised above the capacity of the most numerous class to purchase, they are deprived of the means of giving themselves up to intemperance.

Sumptuary laws, inasmuch as they prohibit the introduction of certain articles which are objects of jealousy to the legislator, may be referred to this head. It is this which has rendered so famous the legislation of Sparta; the precious metals were banished; strangers were excluded; travelling was not permitted.

At Geneva there was a prohibition to wear diamonds, and the number of horses which an individual might keep was limited.*

There might be mentioned under this head many English statutes relative to the sale of spirituous liquors. It is prohibited to expose them to sale in the open air. A licence must be obtained, and paid for, &c. The prohibition to open certain places of amusement upon Sunday appertains to this head.

To the same class belong the measures adopted to destroy libels, seditious writings, obscene figures exposed in the streets, and to prevent the printing and publication of works thought to have a pernicious tendency.

The ancient police laws of Paris forbade a servant to wear a sword, or even to carry a cane or staff. This perhaps was a simple distinction of rank; perhaps it was a measure of security.

Where a particular class of the people is oppressed by the sovereign power, prudence requires that they should be forbidden

* To cite these usages is not to propose them as models. They are cited to show under what class such laws ought to be arranged.

to carry arms. The greater injury becomes a justification for the smaller injury. The Philistines obliged the Jews to come to them every time they wanted to sharpen their axes and scythes. In China the fabrication and the sale of arms is reserved exclusively to the Tartar-Chinese.

By a statute of George III., all persons, except traders, are forbidden to keep in their houses more than fifty pounds weight of gunpowder, and traders are not allowed to have more than two hundred pounds weight on hand at one time. The reason assigned is the danger of explosions. In the statutes relating to high roads and turnpikes, the number of carriage horses is limited to eight, with an exception in favour of certain transportations, and of artillery and munitions of war, for the service of the king. The reason assigned is the preservation of the roads.

Whether any of these measures, and others of the same sort, have a political object behind the reasons assigned for them, that is what I do not pretend to say; but it is certain that such expedients may operate to take away the means of revolt, and to diminish facilities for smuggling.

Among the expedients of this sort, I know none more happy or more simple than that commonly used in England to render difficult the theft of bank-notes. When it is necessary to send them by a messenger or the post, they are cut into two parts, which are sent separately. The theft of half a bank-note would be useless, and the difficulty of stealing the two parts, one after the other, is so great that the offence is almost impossible.

There are professions for the exercise of which proofs of capacity are required. There are others which the laws render incompatible with each other. In England many offices of justice are incompatible with the profession of an attorney; it is feared that the right hand might be secretly labouring for the left.

Persons who contract with the administration for the supply of commissary stores, and the provisioning of the fleet, cannot have a seat in parliament. These persons may be defaulters, and be subject to parliamentary investigation; it is not proper, therefore, that they should be members. But there are stronger reasons yet for this exclusion, derived from the danger of increasing ministerial influence.

CHAPTER II.

Prohibition of acquiring Knowledge which may be turned to a bad purpose.

I MENTION this kind of policy only to condemn it. It has produced the censorship of the press; it has produced the inquisition; and wherever it is employed it will always produce the brutalization of mankind.

I propose here to show,—1st, that the diffusion of knowledge is not injurious on the whole, the offences of refinement being less fatal than those of ignorance; 2nd, that the most advantageous method of combatting the evil which may result from a limited degree of knowledge is to augment its quantity.

In the first place, the diffusion of knowledge is not injurious on the whole. Some writers have thought, or seemed to think, that the less men know the better off they will be: that the less enlightened they are, the less acquaintance they will have with the objects that serve as motives to evil, or as means of committing it. It is not surprising that fanatics have entertained this opinion, since there is a natural and constant rivalry between the knowledge of things real, useful, and intelligible, and the knowledge of things unintelligible, imaginary, and useless. But these notions about the dangers of knowledge are sufficiently common among the mass of mankind. The age of gold,—that is, the age of ignorance,—is spoken of with regret. To put in a clear light the error upon which these notions rest, there needs a more precise method of estimating the evil of an offence than any hitherto employed.

It is not astonishing that offences of refinement are more odious than offences of ignorance,—that is, of brutal violence. In determining the greatness of offences, the principle of antipathy has been more followed than the principle of utility. Antipathy gives more attention to the apparent depravity of character indicated by the offence than to anything else. This, in the eyes of passion, is the *salient point* of the action, in comparison with which the strict examination of utility always appears too cool. Now, the more knowledge and refinement an offence indicates, the more proof there is of reflection on the part of the offender, and of depravity in his moral disposition. But the evil of an offence, the sole object which the principle of utility regards, is not determined by depravity of character alone; it depends immediately upon the sufferings of the persons who are affected by the offence, and upon the alarm which it excites in the community; and, in the sum of evil, the depravity which the culprit manifests is not an essential circumstance, but merely an aggravation.

The greatest offences are those for which the smallest degree of knowledge is sufficient; the most ignorant individual always knows enough to commit them. Inundation is a graver crime than house-firing; house-firing than homicide; homicide than robbery; robbery than pilfering. This proposition may be demonstrated by an arithmetical process, by an inventory of the items of evil in each case, by a comparison of the greatness of each individual suffering, and of the number of individuals who are made to suffer. But how much knowledge is required to enable a man to commit these offences? The most atrocious of all demands only a degree of intelligence possessed by the most barbarous, the most savage of men.

Robbery is worse than seduction or adultery; but robbery is most frequent in times of barbarism, seduction and adultery in those of refinement.

The dissemination of knowledge has not increased the number of offences, nor even the facility of committing them; it has only diversified the means of their perpetration. And how? By gradually substituting less injurious means in the place of those which are more injurious.

Is a new method of theft invented? The inventor profits for a time by his discovery; but presently his secret is found out, and people are on their guard. It then becomes necessary to have recourse to some new means, which has its turn, like the first, and passes by in the same way. All this is still but theft, not so bad as highway robbery, which itself is not so bad as plundering committed by armed bands.* Why? Because the confidence every one has in his own prudence and his own sagacity prevents him from being so much alarmed by theft as by robbery.

Let it be granted, however, that bad men abuse everything; that the more they know, the more means they have of doing evil; what follows?

If the good and the bad composed two distinct races, like the white and black, the one might be enlightened and the other kept in ignorance. But since it is impossible to discriminate between them, and especially when we consider the frequent alternation of good and evil in the same individual, all must be subjected to the same rule. General light, or general darkness; there is no middle course.

However, the very evil complained of carries with it its own cure. Knowledge cannot give advantage to the bad, except so far as they have the exclusive possession of it. A snare which is known ceases to be a snare. The most ignorant tribes have known how to poison the tips of their arrows; but it is only nations well instructed who have become acquainted with all poisons, and have known how to oppose them by antidotes.

All men have the capacity to commit offences; but only enlightened men are able to discover laws which can prevent them. The more ignorant a man is, the more he is inclined to separate his private interest from the interest of his fellows. The more

* That is, on the supposition that the damage of the offence is the same; for there is a point of view in which theft is worse than robbery, since one may possess himself of a greater sum of money by fraud than by robbing on the highway.

For proofs of the superiority of modern manners over ancient times, see *Hume's Essay on Population*. For proofs of their superiority over the manners of the Middle Ages, see *Voltaire's General History; Hume's History of England; Robertson's Introduction to Charles V.; Barrington's Observations upon English Statutes*; and *Chastellux*, in his *Treatise upon Public Happiness*, a work happily conceived but not well executed.

enlightened he is, the more clearly will he perceive the connection between his private interest and the interest of the whole.

Look through history; the most barbarous ages present an assemblage of all offences, offences of cunning as well as offences of violence. Barbarism, though it has some vices peculiar to itself, seems not to exclude vices of any kind. At what epoch were false titles and forged grants most multiplied? When the clergy alone knew how to read; when, through the superiority of their knowledge, they regarded men almost as we regard horses, animals which we could not subdue to the bit, if their intellectual faculties were equal to ours. Why was recourse had, during the same period, to judicial duels, to trials by fire and water, and to all those strange means called *judgments of God?* Because, during that infancy of reason, there were no principles known by which to distinguish truth from falsehood.

Compare the results in states in which the publication of ideas has been restrained, and in those where freedom of thought and of speech has been permitted. You have, on the one side, Spain, Portugal, Italy; on the other, England, Holland, North America. Where is the most happiness? Where the best morals? Where the most crimes? Where is society most agreeable and most secure?

Too many praises have been lavished upon institutions, the founders of which made knowledge a monopoly. Such were the priests in ancient Egypt, the Brahmins of Hindostan, the Jesuits in Paraguay. If their conduct merits praise, it is only in relation to the interests of those persons who have administered these forms of government, not as regards the interest of those who have been subject to them. It may be admitted that the people have been quiet and docile under these theocracies; but have they been happy? It is not credible that they have been, unless an abject servitude, vain terrors, useless obligations, macerations, painful observances, saddening opinions, are no obstacles to happiness.

These governments have not so much attained their end by maintaining natural ignorance, as by spreading prejudices, and propagating errors. The chiefs themselves have always ended by becoming the victims of this narrow and pusillanimous policy. States retained in a constant inferiority, by institutions opposed to every kind of progress, become the prey of nations who have acquired a relative superiority. States grown old in an infancy, which has been prolonged by their tutors, that they might the more easily govern, have always offered an easy conquest; and once subjected, have passed with little or no resistance from one master to another.

But it is said we do not pretend to keep men in ignorance; all governments perceive the necessity of knowledge; what they are afraid of is the liberty of the press. They do not oppose the publication of scientific treatises; but is it not reasonable that they should oppose the spread of immoral or seditious writings, the evil effects of which cannot be prevented if they are once allowed to circulate? Punishing a guilty author may act as a preventive to those who might incline to imitate him; but to prevent the publication of bad books by the institution of the censorship, is to check the evil at its source.

The liberty of the press has its inconveniences; nevertheless, the evils which result from it are not to be compared to those of a censorship.

Where will you find that rare genius, that superior intelligence, that mortal, accessible to all truths, and inaccessible to any passion, to whom can be intrusted this supreme dictatorship over all the productions of the human mind? Do you suppose that a Locke, a Leibnitz, or a Newton, would have had the presumption to undertake it? And what is this power which you are forced to confer upon inferior men? It is a power which by a singular necessity combines in its exercise all the causes of partiality, and all the characteristics of injustice. What is a censor? He is an interested judge, a sole judge, an arbitrary judge, who proceeds in secret, condemns without a hearing, and decides without appeal. Secrecy of procedure, that greatest of abuses, is absolutely essential. If a book were publicly examined, it would be publishing the book, in order to know if it ought to be published.

As to the evil which results from a censorship, it is impossible to measure it, because it is impossible to tell where it ends. It is nothing less than the danger of stopping the whole progress of the human mind in all its paths. Every new and important truth must of necessity have many enemies, for the single reason that it is new and important. Is it to be presumed that the censor will belong to that class, infinitely the smaller, which elevates itself above established prejudices? And though he should have that uncommon strength of mind, will he have the courage to endanger himself on account of discoveries of which he will not share the glory? There is but one sure course for him to take; to proscribe everything which rises above common ideas, to draw his pen through everything elevated. He risks nothing by prohibition, but everything by permission. In doubtful cases, it will not be he that suffers; it will be Truth.

If the advance of the human mind had depended upon the good-will of those in authority, where should we be to-day? Religion, legislation, morals, the physical sciences, all would be in darkness. But it is not necessary to dwell upon so common an argument.

The true censorship is that of an enlightened public, which discountenances false and dangerous opinions, and encourages useful discoveries. In a free country, the audacity of a libel does not save it from general contempt; but by a contradiction easy to be explained, the indulgence of the public in this respect is always in proportion to the rigour of the government.

CHAPTER III.

Indirect Means of preventing the Wish to commit Offences.

We have seen that legislation can only operate by influencing the power, the knowledge, and the will. We have spoken of the indirect means of taking away the power to do injury; we have shown that the policy of preventing men from acquiring information, does more harm than good. All the indirect means, then, which we can use with advantage, must be employed in directing the inclinations of men, in putting into operation the rules of a logic hitherto but little known, *the logic of the will*—a logic which, as Horace has so well expressed it, seems often to be opposition to that of the *understanding* :—

Videa meliora
Proboque, et deteriora sequor.

I see the better
And approve it ; and the worse I follow.

The means about to be presented are of a nature to put a stop in many cases to this interior discord; to diminish that contrariety among motives, which often owes its existence to want of address on the part of the legislator, to an opposition which he has himself created between the natural sanction and the political sanction, between the moral sanction and the religious sanction. If he could make all these powers concur towards the same end, all the faculties of man would be in harmony, and the will to do evil would not exist. In cases where this end cannot be attained, it is necessary, at all events, that the force of the tutelary motives should exceed that of the seductive motives.

The indirect means by which the will can be influenced, may be illustrated under the form of political or moral problems, of which the solution may be shown by various examples:

Problem First.—To change the course of dangerous desires, and to direct the inclinations towards amusements conformable to the public interest.

Second.—To arrange so that a given desire may be satisfied without injury, or with the least possible injury.

Third.—To avoid furnishing encouragements to crime.

Fourth.—To increase responsibility in proportion as temptation increases.

Fifth.—To diminish the sensibility to temptation.

Sixth.—To strengthen the impression of punishments upon the imagination.

Seventh.—To facilitate knowledge of the fact of an offence.

Eighth.—To prevent an offence by giving to many persons an immediate interest to prevent it.

Ninth.—To facilitate the means of recognising and finding individuals.

Tenth.—To increase the difficulty of escape.

Eleventh.—To diminish the uncertainty of prosecutions and punishments.

Twelfth.—To prohibit accessory offences, in order prevent the principal offence.

After these means, of which the object is special, others more general will be pointed out, such as the culture of benevolence, the culture of honour, the employment of the impulse of religion, and the use to be made of the power of instruction, and of education.

CHAPTER IV.

To change the Course of Dangerous Desires, and to direct the Inclinations towards Amusements conformable to the Public Interest.

THE object of direct legislation is to combat pernicious desires, by prohibitions and punishments directed against the injurious acts to which those desires give birth. The object of indirect legislation is to counteract their influence by increasing the force, of less dangerous desires, capable of entering into rivalry with them.

There are two objects to be considered—What are the desires which it is an object to weaken? By what means can that end be obtained?

Pernicious desires are of three classes:—1st, Malevolent passions; 2nd, The appetite for strong drinks; 3rd, Idleness.

The means of weakening these desires may be reduced to three heads:—1st, To encourage honest inclinations; 2nd, To avoid forcing men into idleness; 3rd, To favour the consumption of non-inebriating liquors, in preference to those of an intoxicating quality.

Some persons may be surprised that the catalogue of vicious inclinations is so limited; but they should recollect that the human heart has no passions absolutely bad. There is none which does not stand in need of guidance; and at the same time none which ought to be eradicated. When the angel Gabriel prepared the prophet Mahomet for his divine mission, he plucked from his heart a black spot, which contained the seed of evil. Unfortunately, this operation cannot be practised upon the hearts of ordinary men. The seeds of good and the seeds of evil are inseparably mixed. The inclinations are governed by motives; but all pains and all pleasures are motives; pains to be avoided, pleasures to be pursued. Now, all these motives may produce all sort of effects, from the best to the worst. They are trees which bear wholesome fruits or poisons, according to exposure, according to the care of the gardener, according to the wind that blows, or the temperature of the day. The purest benevolence, confining itself too exclusively to a single subject, or mistaken in its means, may produce great evils. Attachment to one's self, though occasionally it becomes hurtful, is constantly necessary; and in spite of their deformity, the malevolent passions are at least useful as means of defence, as safeguards against the invasion of personal interest. We ought not, then, to attempt rooting out any affections of the human heart, since there is none which does not play its part in the system of utility. We should confine ourselves to the operation of these affections in detail, according to the direction which they take, and the effects which they are likely to produce. A useful balance may be established between these inclinations, by strengthening those which are apt to be too weak, and by weakening those which are too strong. It is thus that the cultivator directs the course of waters in such a manner that his grounds suffer neither from overflow nor from drought.

The passion for inebriating liquors is, properly speaking, the only one that can be extirpated without doing any injury; for the irascible passions, as I have said, are a necessary stimulant in cases when persons are obliged to protect themselves, and to repel the attacks of an enemy. The love of repose is not injurious in itself; indolence, however, is an evil, inasmuch as it favours the ascendancy of the hurtful passions. However, these three desires may be looked upon as equally in need of being repressed. It is hardly to be feared that we can have too great success against the inclination to idleness, or that the vindictive passions can be reduced below the point of utility.

The first expedient, as I have said, is to encourage innocent amusements. It is a branch of that science, so complicated and so ill-defined, which consists in advancing civilization. The state of barbarism differs from civilization by two characteristic traits :—1st, The force of the *irascible* appetites; 2nd, The small number of objects of enjoyment offered to the *concupiscent* appetites.*

The occupations of a savage after he has supplied himself with physical necessaries, the only ones he knows, are soon described. The pursuit of revenge; the pleasure of drunkenness if he has the means; sleep; or perfect indolence; such is the sum total of his resources. Each of these inclinations is favourable to the development and to the action of the other. Resentment finds easy access to a mind unoccupied; idleness leads to drunkenness; and drunkenness produces quarrels, which nourish and multiply resentments. The pleasures of love, not being mingled with the sentimental refinements which embellish and increase them, seem not to play a great part in the life of the savage, and go but a little way towards filling up the intervals of exertion.

Under a regular government the necessity of vengeance is suppressed by legal protection, and the pleasure of giving one's self up to it is counteracted by the fear of punishment; the power of indolence is enfeebled; but the love of strong liquors is not diminished. A nation of savages and a nation of hunters are convertible expressions. The life of the hunter, as well as that of the fisherman, provided they know how to preserve the game they take, affords long intervals of idleness; while in a civilized state, the mass of the community is composed of labourers and artisans, who have scarcely the leisure necessary for sleep and

* This distinction of the schoolmen is sufficiently complete. To the first class belong the pleasures of malevolence; to the second, all other pleasures.

relaxation. But the misfortune is, that the passion for strong drink can be satisfied in the midst of a most laborious life, and that it trenches upon the hours allotted to repose. In the lowest conditions poverty is a restraint upon it; but artisans, whose labour is better paid, can make great sacrifices to this fatal taste, and the opulent classes may devote all their time to it. Thus we see, in ages of barbarism, that the upper classes have divided their whole life between war; the chase, which is the image of war; the animal functions; and long repasts, of which drunkenness was the greatest attraction. Such is the whole history of a great proprietor, a great feudal lord of the Middle Ages. The privilege of this noble warrior, or of this noble hunter, extended into the midst of a more civilized society the occupations and the character of a savage.

This being so, every innocent amusement which human art can invent, is useful under a double point of view :—1st, For the very pleasure which results from it; 2nd, From its tendency to weaken the dangerous inclinations above described. By innocent amusements must be understood all those which cannot be proved to be injurious. Their introduction being favourable to the happiness of society, it is the duty of the legislator to encourage them, or, at least, to put no obstacle in their way. They will be enumerated here; first, those which are esteemed the most gross, and afterwards those which suppose more refinement.

1st. The introduction of a variety of aliments, and the progress of the art of gardening, applied to the production of nutritious vegetables.

2nd. The introduction of non-inebriating liquors, of which tea and coffee are the principal. These two articles, which superficial minds will be astonished to see figuring in a catalogue of moral objects, are so much the more useful, since they come into direct competition with inebriating liquors.

3rd. Progress in all that constitutes elegance, whether in dress, furniture, the embellishment of grounds, &c.

4th. The invention of plays and pastimes, whether athletic or sedentary, among which games of cards hold a distinguished rank. Games of hazard should alone be excluded. These tranquil sports have brought the sexes together, have diminished *ennui*, that malady peculiar to the human race, especially to the opulent class and to the old.

5th. The cultivation of music.

6th. Theatres, assemblies, public amusements.*

7th. The cultivation of the arts and sciences, and of literature.

When these different means of enjoyment are placed in opposition to the means necessary to provide for subsistence, they are called objects of luxury; but if their tendency be such as is above suggested, luxury, singular as it may appear, is rather a source of virtue than of vice.

This branch of policy has not been entirely neglected; but it has been cultivated rather with political than with moral views. The object has rather been to render the people tranquil and submissive to the government, than to render the citizens more united among themselves, more happy, more industrious, more virtuous.

The sports of the circus, among the Romans, formed one of the principal objects of the government's attention. It was not only a means of conciliating the affections of the people, but also of drawing off their thoughts from public affairs.

Cromwell, whose ascetic principles did not allow him this resource, had no other means to occupy the public mind but to engage the nation in foreign wars.

At Venice, a government excessively jealous of its authority showed the greatest indulgence to pleasures.

The processions and other religious *fêtes* of Catholic countries fulfil, in part, the same object as the games of the circus.

All these institutions have been considered by political writers

* "I heard M. d'Argenson say, that when he was Lieutenant of Police there were more irregularities and debaucheries committed in Paris, during the fifteen days of Lent, when the theatres were shut, than during four months of the season when they were open."—*Memoirs of Pollnitz*, vol. iii. p. 312.

as so many means of alleviating the yoke of power, of turning the public attention towards agreeable objects, and preventing it from being occupied with public affairs. This effect, though it was not the object of their establishment, has caused them to obtain more favour after being established.

Peter the Great made use of a higher and more generous policy. The manners of the Russians, their proneness to intoxication excepted, were rather Asiatic than European. Peter I., wishing to moderate their grossness, and to temper their ferocity, employed expedients perhaps a little too direct. He used all possible encouragements, and even had recourse to violence, in order to introduce European dress and European spectacles, assemblies and arts. To lead his subjects to imitate the other nations of Europe was, in other words, to civilize them. But he encountered the greatest resistance to all these innovations. Envy, jealousy, contempt, and a multitude of anti-social passions, opposed this assimilation with foreign rivals. These passions no longer recognised their objects, when visible marks of distinction were effaced. In taking from his subjects the exterior by which they were distinguished, he took from them, so to speak, the pretext and the aliment of a hateful rivalry. He associated them with the great republic of Europe; and they had everything to gain by that association.

The rigid observation of Sunday, such as prevails in Scotland, in England, and in some parts of Germany, is a violation of this policy. The Act of Parliament upon this subject, passed in 1781, seems more appropriate to the times of Cromwell than our own. It prohibits people from every kind of Sunday amusement, except sensual pleasures, drunkenness, and debauchery. It was in the name of good morals that a law so contrary to good morals was enacted. Sunday becomes by this kind of rigour an institution in honour of idleness, and profitable to all the vices.

Two suppositions are necessary to justify such a law: one, that amusements, innocent six days in the week, change their nature, and become mischievous on the seventh; the other, that idleness, the mother of all the vices, is the safeguard of religion.

I do not know what to make of these ideas; let the theologians expound them.*

If a revealed law is in contradiction to morality, it ought not to be listened to. We have more certain proofs of the political effects of an institution than we can have of the truth of a religious history, founded upon events out of the course of nature. In one case we have the testimony of our own senses; in the other case we must rely upon the testimony of others, a testimony transmitted from hand to hand, and weakened by every transmission, which alters more or less its primitive traits.

But this contradiction does not exist This rigorous observance of Sunday has no foundation in the Gospel; it is even contrary to its text, and its positive examples. The judicious Fenelon, whom no one will accuse of having misunderstood the spirit of Christian morality, rebuked the indiscreet severity of his curates, and was unwilling that the people of his diocese should be forbidden to indulge on Sundays, after the exercises of religion were over, in dances and rustic sports.

I find fault not with a day for the suspension of ordinary labours, nor with a day devoted in part to religious worship; but with the absurdity of converting into offences, during that day, the most necessary labours of the field, and the public exercise of the most harmless amusements.

To deprive the people one day in the week of pleasures acknowledged to be innocent, is to take away a portion of their happiness; for if happiness is not composed of pleasures, of what is it composed? How is it possible to justify the severity of the

* The chaplain of Newgate takes great care to have it inserted in the Biography of Malefactors, as their own confession, that the commencement of their career was the *violation* of the Sabbath. I believe he would be nearer the truth, if he said that they began their career by *observing* the Sabbath—observing it, that is, in a particular way. Not knowing what to do with their time and their money, what other resource have they but the tavern? Drunkenness renders them quarrelsome and stupid, destroys their health, their aptitude for labour, and their habits of economy, and throws them into bad company. Thus they are prepared to enter upon the career of crime.

legislator, who, without necessity, takes away from the labouring classes those little enjoyments which soften their hard lot, and who forces them into gloominess or vice, under pretext of religion?

There are two ways of doing injury to mankind: one, the introduction of pains; the other, the exclusion of pleasures. If one of these ways deserves to be condemned, how can the other be worthy of praise? Both are acts of tyranny; for in what does tyranny consist, if not in this? It is only effects which are here spoken of; no doubt good is intended; but it is easier to reason vaguely, than to go to the bottom of a matter; to float here and there between folly and wisdom, than to persevere in one or the other; to follow the current of prejudice, than to resist its torrent. However good the intention may be, it is certain that the tendency of this ascetic practice is hurtful and immoral.

Happy the people which is seen to elevate itself above gross and brutal vices, to cultivate elegance of manners, the pleasures of society, the embellishment of gardens, the fine arts, the sciences, public amusements, the exercises of the understanding! Religions which inspire gloom, governments which render men distrustful, and which keep them apart, contain the germ of the greatest vices, and the most injurious passions.

CHAPTER V.

To satisfy certain Desires without Injury, or with the least possible Injury.

Desires, both those of which we have spoken, and those of which we are about to speak, are susceptible of being satisfied in different ways, and upon different conditions, through all the degrees of the moral scale, from innocence up to the highest point of criminality. That these desires may be satisfied without injury, is the first object to be accomplished; but if this object is unattainable, the second object is to render their satisfaction less injurious to the community than would be the violation of a law. If even this second end is unattainable, it then becomes an object to arrange things in such a way that the individual, placed by his desires between two offences, may be inclined to choose that which is the least injurious. This last object seems humble; it is a kind of composition with vice; it is, as it were, haggling with it, and beating it down to the lowest possible rate.

Let us examine how these several points can be attained, in the case of three kinds of imperious desires:—1st, Vengeance; 2nd, Want; 3rd, The sexual passion.

Section I.

There are two means of satisfying the vindictive appetites without harm:—1st, To provide legal redress for every kind of personal injury; 2nd, To establish some competent satisfaction for injuries which affect the point of honour.

Failing these means, there is only one expedient to satisfy these vindictive appetites with the least harm, and that is, by showing indulgence to duelling.

1st. *To provide Legal Redress for all kinds of Injuries.*—The vices and the virtues of mankind depend very much upon the circumstances of society. Hospitality, it has been observed, is most practised where it is most necessary. It is the same with vengeance. In the state of nature the fear of private revenge is the only restraint upon force, the only safeguard against the violence of the passions. It corresponds to the fear of punishment in a state where laws are established. Every improvément in the administration of justice tends to diminish the force of the vindictive appetites, and to prevent acts of private animosity.

The principal interest in view, in cases of legal redress, is the interest of the injured party. But even the offender finds an advantage in this arrangement. Leave a man to revenge himself, and his vengeance knows no limits. Grant him what, upon a cool examination, you regard as a competent satisfaction, and at the same time forbid him to go further, and he will rather accept what you give him without risk or hazard than expose himself to the judgment of the law, by attempting to obtain by his own hand a greater satisfaction. This, then, is an accessory benefit which results from providing a legal redress. Reprisals are prevented. Covered with the buckler of justice, the transgressor, after his offence, finds himself in a state of comparative security, under the protection of the law.

It is sufficiently evident that the better provision there is for legal redress, the less powerful will be the motive which excites the injured party to procure it for himself. If every pain which a man is exposed to suffer by the conduct of another were instantly followed by what he regarded as an equivalent pleasure, the irascible appetite would not exist. This supposition is evidently exaggerated beyond anything that can possibly be accomplished. But, exaggerated as it is, it includes truth enough to show that every amelioration in this branch of justice tends to diminish the force of the vindictive passions.

Hume has observed, in speaking of the barbarous ages of English history, that the great difficulty was, to engage the injured party to receive satisfaction; and that the laws respecting satisfaction aimed as much at restraining resentment as at securing a certain indulgence to it.

More yet. Establish a legal punishment for an injury, and you give room for generosity; you create a virtue. To pardon an injury when the law offers a satisfaction, is to gain a kind of superiority over your enemy, by the obligation you impose upon him. Such a pardon cannot be attributed to weakness. The motive is above suspicion.

2nd. *To provide competent Redress for those particular Injuries which attack the Point of Honour.*—Injuries of this kind demand a more particular attention, inasmuch as they have a more marked tendency to provoke the vindictive passions. (See Chap. XIV.)

In this respect the laws of France have long been superior to those of other nations.

English jurisprudence is eminently defective upon this point. It does not recognise the existence of such a thing as honour. It has no means of measuring a corporal insult, except by the dimensions of the wound. It does not suspect that there is any other evil in the loss of reputation except the loss of money, which may be the consequence of it. It considers money as the remedy for all evils, the palliative for all affronts, the equivalent for all insults. He who has not received a pecuniary compensation has received nothing; he who has been paid in money can ask nothing more. There is no other reparation of any kind. But the grossness of barbarous ages ought not to be a reproach to the present generation. These laws were established before the feelings of honour were developed. Honour exists in the tribunal of public opinion, and its decrees are pronounced with a peculiar force.

Still, it cannot be doubted that the silence of the law has a bad effect. An Englishman cannot travel in France without remarking that the feeling of honour and the contempt for money descend, so to speak, much further among the inferior classes in France than in England. This difference is especially remarkable in the army. The sentiment of glory, the pride of disinterestedness, are everywhere to be found among the private soldiers; and they would think the brilliancy of a good action tarnished if they received a reward for it. A sword of honour is the highest recompense.

3rd. *To show Indulgence to Duelling.*—When offended persons will not be content with the satisfaction offered by the laws, it is necessary to show indulgence to duelling. Where the duel is established, poisoning and assassination are seldom heard of. The comparatively slight evil which results from that practice, is like a premium of insurance, by which a nation guarantees itself against the grave evil of those two crimes. The duel becomes a preservative of politeness and peace. The fear of being obliged to give or to receive a challenge extinguishes quarrels in the bud. The Greeks and Romans, we are told, attained a high pitch of glory without having known the duel. So much the worse for them; their sentiment of glory did not oppose itself either to poison or the dagger. In the political dissensions of Athens one half the citizens plotted the destruction of the other half. Observe what passes in England and in Ireland, and compare it with the dissensions of Greece and Rome. Clodius and Milo, according to our practice, would have fought a duel; according to the Roman practice, they formed mutual projects of assassination, and he who killed his adversary did but anticipate him.

In the island of Malta duelling had become a kind of rage, and almost a civil war. One of the grand masters made such severe laws against it, and caused them to be so rigorously executed, that duelling ceased; but it was only to give place to a crime which united cowardice to cruelty. Assassination, hitherto unknown among the knights, became so common that the duel was presently regretted, and finally it was expressly tolerated in a fixed place, and at certain hours. The result was such as was expected. An honourable career being opened to revenge, clandestine means resumed a character of infamy. Duels are less common in Italy than in France and England; poisonings and assassinations much more so.

In France the laws against duelling were severe; but means were found to elude them.

In England the laws confound duelling and murder; but juries do not confound them; they acquit, or, what amounts to the same thing, they bring in a verdict of manslaughter. The people are more correctly guided by good sense than the lawyers are by their science. Would it not be better that the remedy should be according to law, instead of being subversive of it?

Section II.

We come now to *indigence;* and here we have to consider both the interest of the poor themselves, and that of the community.

A man in need of the means of subsistence is pushed by the most irresistible motives to commit all the offences by which he can supply his wants. Where this stimulus exists it is useless to combat it by the fear of punishment. There are few punishments which can be greater than starvation; and, making allowance for uncertainty and distance, there are none which can appear so great. The only sure means of protection against the effects of indigence, consists in furnishing necessaries to those who are in need of them.

In this point of view the indigent may be distributed into four classes:—1st, The industrious poor, those who ask only to labour in order to live; 2nd, Idle mendicants, those who had rather trust to a precarious charity than live by work; 3rd, Suspected persons, those who have been arrested for some offence, but discharged for want of proof, and upon whose character a blot remains, which prevents them from finding employment; 4th, Convicts who have finished their term of imprisonment, and who have been set at liberty. These different classes ought not to be treated in the same way; and in establishments for the benefit of the poor, particular care ought to be taken to separate the suspected from the innocent. One rotten sheep, says the proverb, is enough to infect a whole flock.

All which the poor can be made to earn by their labour is not only a profit to the community, it is a gain to themselves. Not only is life to be sustained, but time is to be filled up. Humanity requires that occupations should be found for the deaf, the blind, the dumb, the maimed, the impotent, the infirm. The wages of idleness are never so sweet as the reward of industry.

If a man has been put upon trial for an alleged offence of indigence, though he should be acquitted, he ought to be required to give an account of his means of subsistence, at least for the last preceding six months. If they were honest, this inquiry can do him no harm; if they were not honest, he ought to suffer the consequences.

Women labour under particular disadvantages, as respects facility of finding occupation, especially those of a condition a little above ordinary labour. Men, having more activity, more liberty, perhaps more dexterity, have possessed themselves even of those employments the best fitted for the female sex, and which are almost indecent in the hands of a man. Men sell children's toys, keep fashionable shops, and make women's shoes, women's stays, and women's dresses. Men even perform the office of midwives. There is a reason to doubt whether the injustice of custom might not be redressed by the law, and whether women should not be put in possession of these means of subsistence to the exclusion of men. This would be an indirect means of preventing prostitution, by securing to women suitable occupations.

With respect to the treatment of the poor, no universal measure can be proposed. Local and national circumstances must control particular arrangements. In Scotland, with the exception of some large towns, the government does not concern itself with the care of the poor. In England, the tax on their account amounts to more than three millions sterling.* Still the condition of the poor is better in Scotland than in England. The object is better accomplished by custom than by law. In spite of the inconveniences of the English system it cannot be suddenly abandoned; otherwise half the poor would perish before the necessary habits of benevolence and frugality had taken root. In Scotland the influence of the clergy is very salutary. Having but a moderate salary and no tithes, the ministers are known and respected by their parishioners. In England, the clergy being rich and having tithes, the rector is often in a quarrel with his flock, and knows but little about them.

In Scotland, Ireland, and France, the poor are moderate in their wants. At Naples the climate saves the expense of fire, of lodging, and almost of dress. In the East Indies dress is hardly necessary except for decency. In Scotland, cleanliness excepted, domestic economy is good in all respects. In Holland it is as good as it can be. In England wants are greater than elsewhere, and economy is perhaps upon a worse footing than in any country in the world.

* It has since much increased, and in some years has exceeded eight millions.—*Translator.*

The surest means is not to wait for indigence, but to prevent it. The greatest service which can be rendered to the labouring classes is the establishment of banks, in which the poor may be induced, by the double attraction of security and profit, to deposit their little savings.

Section III.

We come now to that class of desires for which it is not easy to find any neuter name,—any name which does not present some accessory idea of blame or praise, but especially of blame. The reason is evident. The ascetics have never been able to satisfy themselves with degrading and criminating the desires to which nature has intrusted the perpetuity of the species. Poetry, on the other hand, has protested against these usurpations, and has delighted in embellishing the images of pleasure and of love,—a laudable object, when it has respected decency and morals. It may be observed, however, that these inclinations naturally have strength enough, and that there is no need of exciting them by exaggerated and seducing pictures.

As this desire is satisfied in marriage, not only without prejudice to society, but advantageously for it, the first object of the legislator in this respect ought to be to facilitate marriage: that is, to put no obstacle in its way not absolutely necessary.

In the same spirit divorce ought to be authorized, under suitable restrictions. Instead of a marriage broken in fact, and which subsists only in appearance, divorce naturally leads to a real marriage. *Separations*, permitted in countries where marriages are indissoluble, have the inconvenience either of condemning individuals to the privations of celibacy, or of leading them into illicit connections.

But if we are willing to speak upon this delicate subject in good faith, and with a frankness more modest in fact than any hypocritical reserve, we shall acknowledge at once that there is an age at which man has attained the development of his senses, though his faculties are not yet mature enough for the management of affairs or the government of a family. This is true, especially among the upper classes of society. Among the poor, the necessity of labour diverts the desires of love, and retards their development; a more frugal diet, and a simpler kind of life, keep the senses and the imagination longer quiet. Besides, the poor can hardly buy the favours of the other sex, except by the sacrifice of liberty.

In addition to the young, not yet marriageable in a moral point of view, how many men there are unable to burden themselves with the support and the cares of a family. On the one side, domestics, soldiers, sailors, living in a state of dependence, and often having no fixed dwelling; on the other, men of a more elevated rank, who are waiting for a fortune or an establishment; here is a very numerous class cut off from marriage, and reduced to a forced celibacy.

The first means which presents itself to diminish this evil is to legitimate contracts for a limited time. This means has great inconveniences; it is a fact, however, that concubinage actually exists in all societies where there is a great disproportion in fortunes. By prohibiting these arrangements they are not prevented; they are only rendered criminal, and made disgraceful. Those who dare to avow them proclaim their contempt for the laws and for morals; those who conceal them are exposed to suffer a pain of self-reproach in proportion to their moral sensibility.

According to the common way of thinking, the idea of virtue is associated with this contract when its duration is indefinite, and the idea of vice when its duration is limited. Legislators have followed this opinion; they have forbidden contracts for a year which they allow for life. The same action, criminal in the first case, is innocent in the second. What is to be thought of this difference? Can the duration of the engagement change the quality of an act which equally grows out of it, whether the engagement be for a longer or a shorter time?

But though marriage for a limited period be innocent in itself, it does not follow that it ought to be so honourable as a permanent marriage to the woman who contracts it. Indeed, she never would obtain the same respect with a woman married for life. The first idea which would present itself with respect to her would be—"If this woman had been as worthy as others, she would have been able to obtain conditions which others have obtained. This precarious arrangement is a sign of inferiority, either in rank or merit."

What good would result from authorizing this kind of contracts? It would save the law, by which they are now forbidden, from being broken and despised. It would preserve the women who enter into such contracts from a humiliation which, having degraded them in their own esteem, leads almost always to utter worthlessness. Besides, it would give publicity to the birth of children, and would secure for them a father's care.

In Germany, what are called *left-handed* marriages are generally established. The object is to reconcile domestic happiness with family pride. The woman acquires in this way some of the privileges of a wife; but neither she nor her children are entitled to the name or the rank of the husband. These marriages were forbidden by the *Code Frederic*. However, the king reserved the right of granting particular dispensations.

The idea now proposed is not at all conformable to common opinions; let it be observed, however, that it is proposed, not as good in itself, but as a means of alleviating an existing evil. In countries where manners are so simple and where fortunes are so equal that this expedient is not needed, it would be absurd to introduce it.

With the same apology, I shall proceed to speak of a yet graver disorder, of an evil which exists particularly in great cities, and which also springs from inequality of fortune, and from the combination of all those causes which produce celibacy. That evil is prostitution.

There are countries where the laws tolerate it; there are others, such as England, where it is strictly prohibited. But though prohibited, it is as common, and as publicly exercised, as can be imagined, because the government does not dare to suppress it, and because the public would not approve such a display of authority. Prostitution, thus nominally forbidden, is as common as if there were no law against it, and much more mischievous.

The infamy of prostitution is not solely the work of the law. There would always be a degree of shame attached to that condition, even though the political sanction remained neuter. The condition of a courtesan is a condition of dependence and servitude; her resources are precarious, and indigence and famine always threaten to overwhelm her. Her very name is associated with evils distressing to the imagination, for courtesans are unjustly considered as the causes of disorders of which they are only the victims. There is no need to say with what sentiments they are regarded by *honest* women. The most virtuous may lament their miseries, but all agree in despising them. Nobody, in their behalf, attempts defence or excuse. It is natural that they should be crushed by the weight of public opinion. They have never thought of forming a combination, which might counterbalance this public contempt; and, though they wished it, they could not effect it. If the interest of a common defence should unite them, they would soon be divided by rivalry and want. The person, as well as the name of a public woman, is an object of hatred and disdain to her fellows. This is perhaps the only employment publicly despised by the very persons who publicly profess it. Self-love, with the most singular inconsistency, seeks as it were to shake off the recollection of its own misfortunes; each unhappy creature strives to forget what she is, or to earn an exception for herself, by severity towards her fellows.

Kept mistresses are regarded as almost equally infamous with public women. The reason is plain; they do not yet belong to that class, but they are always on the eve of falling into it. Still, the longer a female has lived with the same man, the further is she removed from a state of degradation, and the nearer she approaches to the condition of a married woman. The longer the connection has endured, the more difficult it seems to break it, and the greater is its prospect of perpetuity.

The result of these observations is, that the remedy, as far as there can be one, is to be found in the evil itself. The more this condition is a natural object of contempt, the less it is necessary for the law to brand it. It carries along with it a natural punishment; a punishment already too severe, if we consider all the reasons for pitying this unhappy class, the victims of social inequality, and always so near to despair. How few of these women have embraced this profession knowingly and by choice! How few would go on, if they could quit it; if they could pass out of this circle of disgrace and misery; if they were not repelled from every business upon which they might attempt to enter! How many have been precipitated into it by the error of a moment; by the inexperience of youth; by the corruption of their parents; by the crime of a seducer; by an inexorable severity towards a first fault; almost all by destitution and misery! If opinion is tyrannical and unjust, ought the legislator to exasperate that injustice, ought he to convert himself into an instrument of tyranny?

And what is the effect of these laws? They only serve to increase the corruption of which these unhappy women are accused. They drive them into drunkenness in search of a momentary oblivion of misery; they render them insensible to the restraints of shame, by exhausting upon misfortune the disgrace which ought to be reserved for real crimes. Finally, they prevent those precautions which might alleviate the inconveniences of this disorder, were it tolerated by the laws. All these evils, which the laws so lavishly dispense, are a price which folly pays to obtain an imaginary good, which after all is not obtained, and never will be.

The Empress Queen of Hungary undertook to extirpate this evil, and laboured at it with a laudable perseverance worthy of a better cause. What followed? Corruption spread itself through public and private life; the marriage bed was violated; the seat of justice was corrupted. Adultery gained all that libertinage lost. Magistrates made traffic of connivance. Fraud, partiality, oppression, extortion spread themselves through the country; and the evil it was desired to abolish, driven to conceal itself, became so much the more dangerous.

Among the Greeks, this profession was permitted, and sometimes even encouraged; but the parents themselves were not allowed to traffic in the honour of their daughters. Among the Romans, during what are called the best times of the republic, the law was silent on this subject. The saying of Cato to a young man, whom he met coming out of a brothel, is a proof of it. Cato was not a person to encourage violations of the law.

In the metropolis of the Christian world, this vocation is freely exercised.* This fact was doubtless one reason for the excessive rigour of the Protestants.

At Venice, under the republic, the profession of a courtesan was publicly authorized.

In the capital of Holland, houses of this nature receive a license from the magistrate.

Retif of Brittany published an ingenious work, entitled *The Pornograph,* in which he proposed that government should establish an institution, subject to certain rules, for the reception and government of public women.

In some respects, the toleration of this evil in great cities is useful; its prohibition amounts to nothing, and has certain inconveniences besides.

The asylum at London for penitent prostitutes is a very excellent institution; but those who regard prostitution with absolute rigour, are not very consistent in approving of that charity. If it reforms some, it encourages others. Is not the hospital at Chelsea an encouragement to soldiers, and that at Greenwich to sailors?

It would be well to institute an establishment for selling annuities to these women, to begin at a certain age; and the arrangement should be adapted to the nature of this sad profession, in which the time of harvest is necessarily short, but of which the profits are sometimes considerable.

The spirit of economy is formed from small beginnings, and goes on always increasing. A sum too inconsiderable to offer a

* This has ceased to be the case, but it remains to be seen whether severity on this point will be an advantage to morals.

resource as actual capital, might furnish a considerable annuity, at a distant period.

Upon points of morals, as to which there are contested questions, it is well to consult the laws of different nations. It is a kind of mental travelling. In the course of such an exercise, we are able to disengage ourselves from local and national prejudices, by passing in review the usages of other communities.

CHAPTER VI.

To avoid furnishing Encouragements to Crime.

To say that government ought not to give rewards to crime, that it ought not to weaken the moral nor the religious sanction, in cases where they are useful, is a maxim which seems too simple to stand in need of proof. Yet it is often forgotten; and I might give striking examples of it; but the more obvious they are, the less need there is to point them out. It will be better to dwell upon those cases in which this maxim is more covertly violated.

I. Injurious Detention of Property.—If the law suffers a man who unjustly detains the property of another to gain by delay of restitution, the law becomes an accomplice in the wrong. The cases in which the English law is defective in this respect are innumerable. In many cases, a debtor has only to refuse payment till he dies, and he will escape the debt altogether; in many others, he can, by delay, escape the payment of interest; and he can always retain the amount for a longer or shorter period, and thus compel his creditor to submit to a forced loan, at the ordinary rate of interest.

A few simple regulations would suffice to cut off these temptations to injustice:—1st. So far as landed property is liable for debts, the death of either party should make no difference. 2nd. Interest should run from the moment the obligation commences. 3rd. The obligation should commence, not from the liquidation of damages, but from the moment of the damage. 4th. This interest should be higher than the ordinary rate. How happens it that means so simple have never been adopted? Those who ask this question do not know the power of habit, of indolence, of indifference to the public good; they are ignorant of the bigotry of lawyers, and of the strength of personal interest, and the professional spirit.

II. Unlawful Destruction.—When a man insures his property against some calamity, if the value insured exceeds the real value, it is his interest, in a certain sense, to bring on the calamitous event: to set fire to his house, if it is insured against fire; to sink his vessel, if it is insured against the dangers of the seas. The law, then, which authorizes these contracts, may be considered as furnishing a motive for the perpetration of these offences. Does it follow, then, that the law ought not to sanction them? Not at all; but only that it ought to command or suggest to the assurers precautions best adapted to the prevention of these abuses, without being so restrictive as to interfere with the business: such as preliminary inquiries; certificates of the real value of the property insured; in case of loss, the testimony of some respectable persons to the character and honesty of the party insured; in doubtful cases, an inspection of the property insured, &c.

III. Treason.—If the insurance of vessels belonging to a hostile nation is permitted, the state may be exposed to two dangers:—1st, The commerce of the hostile nation, which is one of the sources of its power, is facilitated; 2nd, The insurer, to protect himself against a loss, may give secret information to the enemy of movements made by the fleets and cruisers of his own nation. As regards the first of these inconveniences, it is not an evil, unless the enemy cannot obtain insurance elsewhere, or if he can employ his capital with the same profit in some other branch of industry. As to the second inconvenience, it is absolutely nothing, unless the insurer is led to give information to the enemy which otherwise money could not buy, and unless his facility of giving this information is so great as to transcend the infamy and the risk of treason.

On the other hand, the advantage to the nation that assures

is certain. In this kind of traffic, it has been found that the balance of profit, during a given time, is in favour of the assurers; that is, taking the losses and gains together, they receive more in premiums than they pay out in indemnities. It is then a lucrative branch of commerce, and may be considered as a tax levied upon the enemy.

IV. Peculation.—In making a bargain with architects and contractors, it is quite common to give them so much per cent. upon the amount of their expenditures. This mode of payment, which seems natural enough, opens the door to peculation, and to peculation of the most destructive kind; since, while the peculator makes a little profit, the employer must suffer a great loss. This danger is at its highest point in the case of public works, where nobody has a particular interest to prevent waste, and where many persons may find an interest in conniving at it.

One remedy would be to fix the expense by estimation, and to say to the contractor, "So far you shall have your per centage, but beyond that you shall have nothing. If you reduce the expense below the estimate, you shall still have the same profit."

V. Abuse of Public Trusts.—If a public man who has it in his power to contribute towards war or peace possesses an employment of which the emoluments are more considerable in war than in peace, he has an interest to exert his power for the prolongation of war. If these emoluments increase in proportion to the expense, he has an additional interest that the war should be conducted with the greatest possible prodigality. Exactly the opposite state of things should be aimed at.

VI. Offences of every kind.—When an individual makes a bet on the affirmative side of a future event, he has an interest in the happening of that event, proportioned to the amount of the bet. If the event is one of those things prohibited by law, he then has an interest to commit an offence. He is even stimulated by a double force, the one partaking of the nature of reward, the other of the nature of punishment; a reward to be received in case the event happens; a punishment to be experienced in the opposite case. It is as if he had been suborned by the promise of a sum of money on one side, and as if he had made an engagement under a formal penalty on the other.*

If, then, all kinds of bets, without distinction, were acknowledged to be valid, venality of every kind would receive the sanction of the laws, and liberty would be given to everybody to enlist accomplices for all sorts of offences. On the other side, if all bets, without restriction, were prohibited, insurances, so useful to commerce, and such a resource against a multitude of calamities, would not be lawful; for insurance is nothing but a sort of bet.

The middle course seems the best. In all cases in which bets may become instruments of mischief, without answering any useful object, prohibit them absolutely. In cases like insurance, in which they may be useful, admit them; but leave it to the judge to make necessary exceptions when it shall appear that they have been only a cover to subornation.

CHAPTER VII.

To increase Responsibility in proportion as Temptation increases.

This precaution relates principally to public employments. The more of fortune or honours those who exercise such employments have to lose, the stronger hold we have upon them. Their salary is a means of responsibility. In case of misconduct, the loss of this salary is a punishment which they cannot escape, though they may avoid every other. This means is specially useful in employments which relate to the handling of public money. If you cannot insure the honesty of a cashier in any other way, make his appointments rise something above the interest of the greatest sum which is intrusted to him. This excess of salary is like a premium paid for an insurance against his dishonesty.

* In the *Adventures of a Guinea*, there is a bet made between the wife of a clergyman and the wife of a minister, that the clergyman would not be an archbishop. It is easy to imagine which was the gainer.

He has more to lose in becoming a rogue than by remaining honest.

Birth, honours, family connections, religion, may become so many means of responsibility, so many pledges for the good conduct of individuals. There are cases in which legislators have not chosen to trust bachelors; they have regarded a wife and children as hostages given to one's country.

CHAPTER VIII.

To diminish the Sensibility to Temptation.

In the preceding chapter the question was to discover precautions against dishonesty; in this, the object is to avoid the diminution of probity through the exposure of honest men to the influence of seductive motives too strong for their virtue.

First, of salaries; for money, according to the manner of its application, may serve as a poison or an antidote.

Apart from any regard to the happiness of individuals, the interest of the public service requires that the persons employed in it should be above the pressure of want, especially in all those employments which afford an opportunity of acquisition by injurious means. The greatest abuses have been produced in Russia, throughout the whole administration, by the insufficiency of salaries. When men, under the pressure of want, abuse their power, become greedy extortioners and robbers, the blame ought to be shared between them and the government which has spread this snare for their honesty. Placed between the necessity of living, and the impossibility of living honestly, they are led to look upon extortion as a lawful supplement to their pay, tacitly authorized by those who employ them.

Will it be putting them beyond the reach of need to supply their physical wants? No. If there is not a certain proportion between the dignity with which a man is clothed, and his means of sustaining it, he is in a state of suffering and privation, because he cannot do what is expected of him, nor keep upon a level with that class with whom he is called to associate. In one word, wants increase with honours, and what is relatively necessary varies with condition. Place a man in an elevated rank, without giving him wherewith to maintain himself, and what is the consequence? His dignity will furnish motives to do evil, and his power will give him the means.

Charles II. being too much fettered by the economy of Parliament, sold himself to Louis XIV., who offered to supply his profusion. The hope of escaping the embarrassments into which he was plunged, drove him, like any other bankrupt, into criminal schemes. This miserable parsimony cost the English two wars, and a peace yet more fatal. It is not easy to tell what sum would have been sufficient to operate as an antiseptic upon a prince so corrupt; but this example is enough to show that the civil list of the English king, which appears exorbitant to vulgar calculators, tends in fact to promote the general security. Besides, by that intimate alliance which exists between riches and power, everything which augments the magnificence of dignity gives it additional force; the royal pomp, under this point of view, may be compared to those architectural ornaments, which serve also to support and strengthen the edifice.

This great rule of diminishing as much as possible the sensibility to temptation, has been remarkably violated in the Catholic church. To impose celibacy upon priests, and at the same time to intrust them with the most delicate functions in the examination of consciences, and the direction of families, is to place them in a violent situation, between the misery of observing a useless law, and the disgrace of violating it.

When Gregory VII., in a council held at Rome, established the rule that married clerks, or those having concubines, should no longer be permitted to say mass, they uttered cries of indignation, they accused him of heresy, and according to the historians of those times, they declared—"If he persists, we had rather renounce the priesthood than our wives; let him find angels to govern the churches."—(*Hist. of France*, by the Abbé Milot, vol. i. Reign of Henry I.) In our times the government of France desired to make the marriage of priests lawful; but by this time there were no men to be found among them; they were all angels.

CHAPTER IX.

To strengthen the Impression of Punishment upon the Imagination.

It is the real punishment which does all the evil; it is the apparent punishment which does all the good. We ought, then, as much as possible to diminish the former, and to augment the latter. Humanity, in this case, consists in the appearance of cruelty.

Speak to the eyes, if you wish to move the heart. The precept is as old as Horace, and the experience which dictated it was much older. Every one feels its force, and strives to take advantage of it; the comedian, the charlatan, the orator, the priest, all know how to turn it to their purpose. Render your punishments exemplary; give to the attendant ceremonies a sort of mournful pomp. Call to your aid all the imitative arts; and let the exhibitions of these important procedures be among the first to strike the eyes of childhood.

A scaffold spread with black, that livery of woe; the officers of justice in mourning; the executioner covered by a mask, which may serve to increase the terror of the beholders, and at the same time to conceal him from a misplaced indignation; emblems of his crime placed upon the head of the criminal, so that the witnesses of his sufferings may be informed of the offence that has produced them;—such are a part of the decorations proper to these tragedies of the law. Let all the persons in this terrible drama move in a solemn procession; let a grave and religious music prepare the hearts of the auditors for the important lesson they are going to receive. The judge should not think it beneath him to preside at this public scene, so that its sombre dignity may be consecrated by the minister of the law.

Instruction is not to be rejected, even though it come from an enemy. The Secret Tribunal, the Inquisition, the Star Chamber

—I consult them all; I examine every means; I consider all that has been done; I prize a diamond though it be picked from a dunghill. Because assassins use a pistol to commit murders, shall I not employ it in my own defence?

The emblematic robes of the inquisition may be usefully applied to criminal justice. An incendiary clothed in a robe of pictured flames, would offer to every eye the image of his crime, and the indignation of the spectator would be fixed by the image of the offence.

A system of punishments accompanied by emblems appropriate as far as possible to each offence, would have an additional advantage. It would furnish allusions to poetry, to eloquence, to dramatic authors, to ordinary conversation. The ideas thence derived would be re-echoed, if I may be allowed the expression, by a thousand objects, and would be scattered on all sides.

The Catholic priests have known how to derive from this source the greatest aids to the efficacy of their religious opinions. I remember having seen at Gravelines a striking exhibition. A priest showed the people a picture, which exhibited a multitude of wretches in the midst of flames, and one of them making signs for a drop of water, by showing his burning tongue. It was a day of public prayers for souls in purgatory. It is clear that such an exhibition was less fitted to inspire a horror of crime than a horror of poverty. The moral was, that one ought at all events to have the wherewithal to pay for a mass; for where money expiates every sin, the sin of poverty is the greatest, the only one without remedy.

The methods of punishment which prevail in England form a perfect contrast to everything that can inspire respect. A capital execution has no solemnity; the pillory is sometimes a scene of buffoonery, sometimes an exhibition of popular cruelty, a game of chance, in which the sufferer is exposed to the caprices of the multitude, and the accidents of the moment. The severity of a public whipping depends upon the money given to the executioner; branding in the hand, according to the understanding between the convict and the officer, is sometimes inflicted with a cold iron, and sometimes with a hot one; if it be done with a hot iron, the branding is often confined to a slice of bacon interposed between the branding-iron and the criminal's skin. To keep up the farce, while the meat is smoking and burning, the supposed sufferer puts forth loud cries of agony and pain. The spectators who understand the whole game, only laugh at this parody on the law.

It may perhaps be said,—for all questions have two sides,—that these real representations, these terrible scenes of penal justice, would spread fright among the people, and would make dangerous impressions. I do not think so. If they presented to the dishonest the idea of danger, to the honest they would offer only the idea of security. When eternal punishments are loudly threatened, when the flames of hell are frightfully decreed for kinds of offences indefinite and undefinable, the imagination may be so excited that madness is the consequence. We suppose, on the contrary, a manifest offence, a proved offence, an offence of which everybody can avoid the commission, so that the terror of punishment cannot be excited to a dangerous degree. However, we must avoid producing false and odious associations.

In the first edition of the *Code Theresa*, the portrait of the empress was surrounded with medallions representing gibbets, wheels, and other instruments of torture and punishment. What a blunder to offer the image of the sovereign with these hideous emblems, like the head of Medusa shaking her serpents! This scandalous frontispiece was suppressed; but a print was allowed to remain which represented all the instruments of torture—a picture of bad omen, which no one could look at without saying to himself, "Even though innocent, to these evils am I exposed!" But if an abridgment of the penal code were accompanied by pictures representing the characteristic punishments attached to each crime, it would be an imposing commentary, a sensible and speaking image of the law. The reader would say, "If I am guilty, this must I suffer!" In legislation, a single shade sometimes distinguishes good from evil.

CHAPTER X.

To facilitate Knowledge of the Fact of an Offence.

In penal cases there are two points as to which the judge must be certain before he can perform his office: the fact of an offence, and the person of the offender. These two points being known, his information is complete. In different cases there are different proportions of obscurity as to these two points; sometimes the first is most obscure, sometimes the second. Let us consider, in the first place, the fact of an offence, and the means which may facilitate its discovery.

I. *To require Proofs of Title to be in Writing.*—It is only by writing that testimony can be rendered permanent and authentic. Verbal transactions, unless they are of the most simple kind, will be subject to innumerable disputes. Mahomet himself has recommended to his followers to observe this precaution. It is almost the only passage of the Koran which has a glimmer of common sense.

II. *To enrol upon the face of Title Deeds the names of Witnesses.*—It is one thing to require witnesses to the execution of a deed; and another thing to require that their presence be noticed, attested, and registered upon the face of the deed. A third step is to add the circumstances which will enable the witnesses to be found if they are needed.

In the attestation of deeds, it will be useful to observe the following precautions:—1st. To prefer a large number of witnesses to a small number; this will diminish the danger of falsehood, and give a chance of finding some of them, if they are needed. 2nd. To prefer married persons to bachelors; heads of families to servants; persons who have a public character to individuals less distinguished; young or middle-aged men to the old and infirm; persons who are known to strangers. 3rd. When the deed is composed of many sheets, each sheet ought to be signed by the witnesses; if there are corrections and erasures, a separate list ought to be made of them, which list ought to be attested; the lines ought to be counted, and their number on each page marked. 4th. Let each witness add to his name in full his description, place of abode, age, &c. 5th. Let the time and place at which the deed is executed be minutely specified; the time, not only by the day, month, and year, but also by the hour; the place, by the district, parish, even the house, and the name of the present occupant. This circumstance is an excellent preventive against forgery. A man would hardly dare venture upon such an enterprise when he must be sure of so many details before fabricating a false date; and if he dared attempt it he would be much more easily discovered. 6th. All numbers ought to be written out in letters, especially dates and sums, except in matters of account, where it is sufficient to write the sum total in letters, and except also when the same date or sum often recur in the same deed. The reason of this precaution is, that figures, unless they are written very carefully, are apt to be taken one for another; and besides, it is easy to alter them, and the least alteration may have very considerable influence. A sum of hundreds is easily changed into a sum of thousands. 7th. The formalities to be observed in the execution of a deed ought to be printed upon the margin of the sheet of paper or parchment upon which it is written.

Should these formalities be left to the discretion of individuals, as a means of security required by prudence, or should they be regulated by law? Some of them should be required, and others should be optional; a latitude should be left to the judge in favour of those cases in which it is not possible to fulfil them. It may happen that a deed is to be made in a place where the prescribed kind of paper is not to be had, where a sufficient number of witnesses cannot be found, &c. In such cases, the deed may be declared valid provisionally, and until the requisite formalities can be fulfilled.

A greater latitude ought to be allowed in testaments than in deeds between the living. Death does not wait for an attorney, nor for witnesses; and making a will is a business which men are apt to procrastinate to a time when they have neither leisure nor capacity for precision and exactness. On the other hand, precautions are most requisite in this sort of deeds, because they are most exposed to forgery. In case of a deed between the living, the party to whom it is falsely ascribed may still be alive and able to contradict it; in case of a testament, there is no such chance.

Many details are necessary to explain the forms which ought to be established, and the exceptions which should be made. I shall only observe that I do not know of any formality, even the most simple, the omission of which ought to render a will absolutely invalid.

If instructions upon this subject were published by the government, even without being made necessary, everybody would be inclined to observe them, since, in case of deeds executed in good faith, every one desires to insure himself all possible securities. The omission of these formalities would then become a vehement suspicion of fraud, unless it could be clearly seen that it ought to be attributed either to ignorance, or to circumstances which rendered their observance impossible.

III. *To establish Registrations for the Authentication of Titles.*—Why ought deeds to be registered? What deeds ought to be registered? Ought the registry to be secret or public? Ought the registration to be optional, or should its omission be visited by a penalty?

Registers are useful:—1st, Against acts of forgery; 2nd, Against acts of falsification; 3rd, Against accidents, as the loss or destruction of originals; 4th, Against a double alienation of the same property to different purchasers.

For the first and last of these objects, a simple abstract might suffice; for the second, an exact copy would be needed; for the third, an extract would be sufficient, but an entire copy would be much better.

Against forgery, the registration would only be useful by being obligatory; the deed being null when not recorded, with a latitude for accidental cases. This advantage would result, that after the expiration of the time allowed for registration, the forgery of a deed which, according to its date, ought to be registered, would be of no avail. It amounts to limiting to a short period the time within which a fraud of this nature can be committed, with a possibility of success; and at a period so near that of the supposed act, proofs of the fraud could be easily obtained.

So, too, when the registration is intended to prevent double alienations, it should be obligatory, under pain of nullity. Without a clause to that effect, the registration would hardly take place, since neither party would have an interest in it. In fact, the seller has an interest the other way. If he is honest, he may have a repugnance to its being known that he has sold or encumbered his property; if he is a rogue, he may desire the opportunity of selling it twice over.

Testaments are the kind of deeds most apt to be forged. The surest protection against this fraud is to require them, under pain of nullity, to be registered during the life of the testator. It may be objected that this would put a dying man at the mercy of those who surround him in his last moments, since he would no longer have the power to reward or to punish; but this objection might be obviated by giving him the right to dispose of a tenth part of his property by a codicil.

What deeds ought to be registered?

All in which third persons are interested, and which are important enough to justify this precaution.

In what cases should the registry be secret or public?

Deeds between the living in which third persons are interested, hypothecations, and marriage settlements, ought to be public. Testaments ought to be inviolably secret during the life of the testator. Deeds, such as indentures of apprenticeship and marriage settlements, which do not affect lands, might be kept secret, with the reserve of communicating them to such persons as have a special title to examine their provisions.

The registry office might be divided into departments, secret and public, optional and obligatory. Optional registrations would be frequent if the price were moderate. It is an act of prudence to preserve copies against accidents, and where could copies be more securely lodged than in an office of this sort?

The necessity of registering mortgages of landed property would be a kind of restraint upon prodigality. A man could not borrow money upon his estate, to be spent upon mere pleasures, without some degree of shame. This consideration, so favourable to the measure, has been regarded as an objection against it, and, in fact, has prevented its adoption.

The law of many countries has adopted this system of registration to a greater or less extent. The French law seems to have hit upon a medium tolerably just.

In England the law varies. In the counties of Middlesex and York there are offices of registry, established in the reign of Queen Anne, of which the principal object is to prevent double alienations, and the good effects are such that the value of lands is higher in these countries than elsewhere. How does it happen that after so many years of an experience so decisive, this law has not yet been made general?

Ireland enjoys this benefit, but the registry is left to the free choice of individuals. It has been established in Scotland. There, testaments must be registered before the death of the testator. In the county of Middlesex, the registry is not obligatory till after the death of the testator.

IV. *Method of preventing Falsifications.*—There is an expedient which, in some respects, may take the place of registration. A particular sort of paper or parchment being required for the deed in question, those who sell it by retail may be forbidden to furnish it without endorsing upon it the day and the year of the sale, and the names of the seller and purchaser. The distribution of this paper might be limited to a certain number of persons, of whom a list should be kept. Their books would be true registers, and after their death might be deposited in an office. This precaution would prevent the forgery of deeds of any kind, pretending to be of a distant date.

It would be an additional restraint, if the paper were required to be of the same date with the deed. The date of the paper might be marked in its tissue, in the same way as the name of the maker. In that case, a paper-maker must be a party to every forgery.

V. *Institutions for the Registry of Events on which Titles depend.* —There is no need of dwelling upon the plain necessity of preserving evidence of births and interments. A prohibition to inter the dead without a previous inspection by a police officer, is a general precaution against assassinations. It is singular that in England, marriages, instead of being recorded, were for so long a time abandoned to the mere notoriety of a transient ceremony. The only reason that can be given is the simplicity of this contract, which is the same for all, except in particular dispositions relative to fortune. Fortunately, under the reign of William III., marriages, which serve as the foundation for so many titles, presented themselves as fit objects for a tax. It thus became necessary to have them registered. The tax has been suppressed, but the register remains. But even now the security of rights which depend upon these events is not so certain nor so universal as it ought to be. There is but one copy of the registration. The register of each parish ought to be transcribed in a more general office. In the Marriage Act of George II., either through intolerance or negligence, the advantage of registration was denied to Quakers and Jews.*

VI. *To put People on their Guard against Offences.*

1st. Against poisoning.

By giving instructions respecting the different substances which operate as poisons, with the means of detecting them, and the methods of preventing their effects. If these instructions were spread among the multitude without discrimination, they might do more harm than good. This is one of those peculiar cases in which knowledge is more dangerous than useful. The means of employing poisons are surer than the means of counteracting them. The middle course would be to limit the circulation of these instructions to the class of persons who could make a good use of

* A new Registry Act has lately been enacted by the British Parliament, which puts this matter on a better footing.—*Translator.*

them, and whose condition, character, and education furnished a guarantee against the danger of abuse; such are the parish clergy and the practitioners of medicine. With this view, the instructions ought to be in the Latin language, which these persons are supposed to understand.

But as regards those poisons which present themselves without being sought for, and which ignorance may administer innocently, the knowledge of them should be rendered as familiar as possible. There must be a strange depravity in the character of a people, if hemlock, which is so easily mistaken for parsley, and copper, which is so apt to be dissolved in vessels of which the tinning is worn, do not oftener operate as poisons by accident than by design. In these cases, however dangerous knowledge may be, there is more to hope than to fear from it.

2nd. Against false weights and measures.

By furnishing instructions relative to false weights and measures, and the methods of deception in the employment of true ones, such as scales with unequal arms, measures with double bottoms, &c. Such knowledge cannot be too widely diffused. Every shop ought to have a copy of these instructions pasted up in plain sight, as a pledge of fair dealing.

3rd. Against frauds in money.

By instructions to teach people to distinguish good money from bad. If a particular kind of false coin makes its appearance, the government ought to give notice of it in the most public manner. At Vienna, the officers of the mint always give notice of counterfeit coins the moment they appear; but the Austrian coinage is upon so good a footing that such attempts are rare.

4th. Against impostures of mendicants.

Some counterfeit diseases, although they are in perfect health; others inflict upon themselves some slight wound to aid them in counterfeiting the appearance of the most disgusting maladies; others get up false stories of fires and shipwrecks by which they pretend to have suffered; others borrow or steal children, whom they make the instruments of their trade. But these instructions ought to be accompanied by a preface, lest the knowledge of so many impostures should harden the heart, and make it indifferent to real miseries. In a country with a well-regulated police, an individual who displays the aspect of misery ought never to be neglected, nor left to himself; it should be the duty of the first person who meets him to consign him to the hands of public charity. Instructions of this kind would prove more amusing to the people than tracts of religious controversy.

5th. Against theft, pilfering, methods of obtaining by false pretences.

By furnishing instructions which explain all the arts employed by thieves and swindlers. There are many books upon this subject, the materials of which have been supplied by criminals who had repented, or who hoped to purchase pardon by their confessions. These compilations are miserable affairs; but useful extracts might be made from them. One of the best is the *Discoveries and Revelations of Poulter*, otherwise *Baxter*, of which sixteen editions were published in twenty-six years,—a fact which shows how wide a circulation might be obtained for an authentic book of this kind, authorized by the government. The tone which might be given to such a work would make it an excellent moral lesson, and at the same time a book of amusement.

6th. Against religious impostures.

By furnishing instructions respecting offences committed by the aid of a superstitious belief in the power and malice of spiritual agents. These offences are too numerous; but they are trifles in comparison with the legal persecutions which have derived their origin from the same source. There is hardly a nation in Christendom which cannot reproach itself with a multitude of bloody tragedies occasioned by the belief in witchcraft. Histories of offences committed by these means would furnish a very instructive subject for homilies which might be read in the churches; but as to the errors of governments and magistrates, it were needless to give to them a sad publicity. The opinions of so many respectable and honest judges who have been so miserably duped by superstitions of this sort would be more likely to confirm the people in error than to disabuse them of it. It is much to be desired that the witch of Endor could be got rid of. I do not know what evils this Jewish Canidia may have caused in Palestine, but she has produced frightful ones throughout Europe. The wisest theologians find great objections against that history, at least when taken in its literal and vulgar sense.

The English law has the honour of being the first expressly to reject from its penal code the pretended crime of witchcraft. In the *Code Theresa*, though compiled in 1773, that pretended offence makes a considerable figure.

VII. *To publish Tables of Prices as a Check to Mercantile Extortion.*—If the exaction of an exorbitant price cannot properly be treated as an offence, and be subjected to a punishment, it may at least be regarded as an evil which it will be useful to put a stop to, if it can be done without producing a greater evil. As direct punishments are not admissible for this object, indirect means must be employed. Fortunately this is a kind of offence of which the evil, instead of being augmented, is diminished by increasing the number of offenders; and it therefore should be the object of the law to increase the number as much as possible. Such an article is sold very dear; the profit made from it is exorbitant; spread abroad this information, and sellers will flock in from all sides, and, by the mere effect of competition, the price will fall.

Usury may be placed under the head of mercantile extortion. To lend money, is selling a sum of money in hand for a sum of money to be paid at a future day, at a time determined or undetermined, depending or not upon certain events, and reimbursable all at once, or in parts, &c. By forbidding usury, and making the transaction unlawful, and so increasing the risk, of course you augment the price.

VIII. *Publication of the Fees of Office.*—Almost always fees are allowed in the departments of government for services rendered; these fees are a part of the salaries of the officers. As an artisan sells his labour as dear as he can, so does a public officer.

Competition, and the facility of going to another market, restrain this disposition within its just limits as respects ordinary labour; but there is no competition in a public office; the right of selling this particular kind of labour becomes a monopoly in the hands of the officers. Leave the price to the discretion of the seller, and it will presently have no other limits except those which are prescribed by the wants of the purchaser. Fees of office ought to be strictly limited by law; otherwise, the extortions which will take place ought to be imputed less to the rapacity of the officers than to the negligence of the legislator.

IX. *Publication of Accounts in which the Nation is interested.*—When accounts are rendered at a fixed time, before a limited number of auditors, chosen perhaps by the influence of the accountant himself, and where nobody is called in specially to examine them, the greatest errors may pass without being seen, or without being corrected. But when accounts are published, neither witnesses, commentators, nor judges will be wanting.

Each item is examined. Was this article necessary? Was it really needed, or was it only a pretext for expense? Is the public served as cheaply as individuals? Has not some contractor obtained an advantage at the expense of the state? Has no secret advantage been granted to a favourite? Has nothing been given under false pretences? Have not manœuvres been used to prevent competition? Is not something kept back in the accounts? There are a hundred other questions of a similar kind, which never can be answered in a satisfactory manner, except by publication of the accounts. In a particular committee some may want integrity, and others may want knowledge; a mind slow in its operations passes over what it does not understand, for fear of betraying its want of quickness; a lively understanding will not subject itself to the study of details; each leaves to the rest the fatigues of examination. But all the deficiencies of a small body will be made up by the body of the people. In that heterogeneous and discordant mass, the worst principles have their use as well as the best; envy, hatred, malice, perform the task of public spirit; and these very passions, by reason of their activity and their perseverance, are the better adapted to scrutinize all parties, and to make the strictest and most exact examination.

There seem to be but two grounds of exception, one relating to the expense of publication, the other in regard to services of a kind which ought to remain secret. It would be useless to publish the accounts of a little parish, because the originals would be accessible to all those who wished to examine them; and if accounts of sums employed in secret service were published, you would no longer be able to obtain information of the designs of your enemies.

X. *Uniformity of Weights and Measures.*—Weights indicate the quantity of matter, measures the quantity of space. Their uses are:—1st, The satisfaction of individuals; 2nd, The termination of disputes; 3rd, The prevention of frauds.

To establish uniformity in this respect throughout a single state, has been the object of many sovereigns. To find a common and universal measure for all nations, has been an object of research for many philosophers, and at length the French government has taken it in hand. This is a service truly honourable; for what is there rarer or greater, than to see a government labouring at one of the foundations essential to the union of the human race!

A uniformity of weights and measures, under the same government, and among a people who have, in other respects, the same language, is a thing, the utility of which may be made apparent without any great depth of reasoning. A measure of which one does not know the value, is the same as no measure. If the measures of two cities differ either in name or quantity, the commerce of individuals is exposed to great mistakes or great difficulties. In this respect, these cities are strangers to each other. The nominal price of two articles may be the same, but if the measures are different the real prices are different. Constant attention is necessary, and distrust interrupts the course of business; errors slip into transactions where good faith was intended, and fraud conceals itself under deceptive names.

There are two means of introducing uniformity. The first is, to establish standard measures by public authority, to distribute them throughout the country, and to forbid the use of any other; the second is, to establish such standards, and to leave the care of their adoption to the public convenience. I do not know any example in which the first of these methods has been followed; the second was practised with success by the archduke Leopold in Tuscany.

In England, there are not less than thirty Acts of Parliament upon this subject, and a thousand more may be made in the same style, without success. 1st. The clauses which enforce conformity to the standard are not sufficiently binding. 2nd. There is no provision for the manufacture and distribution of standards; a few have been scattered here and there, and the thing has been left to chance.

A beginning should be made by furnishing each community with a legal standard; a penalty might be imposed upon every workman who made weights and measures not conformed to that standard; and finally, all contracts according to other weights and measures might be declared null and void. But this last means would not be necessary; the two first would suffice.

Between different nations, the want of uniformity in this respect cannot produce so many mistakes, because the mere difference of language puts every one upon his guard. However, there results from it much embarrassment to commerce; and fraud, favoured by mystery, often prevails over the ignorance of purchasers.

An inconvenience, less extensive, but not less important, is felt in medicine. If weights are not exactly the same, especially for substances where the smallest quantities are essential, the pharmacopœia of one country can hardly serve for another, and may expose practitioners to fatal errors. This is a considerable obstacle to the free communication of science; and the same inconvenience is felt in other arts, of which the success depends upon delicate proportions.

XI. *Establishment of Standards of Quality.*—It would be

necessary to go very much into details, to mention all that governments might do for the establishment of the fittest *criterions* of the quality and value of a multitude of objects, which are susceptible of different tests. The touch-stone is an imperfect test of the quality and value of mixed metallic compositions of gold and silver. The hydrometer is a certain test, since identity of quality and identity of specific gravity always go together.

Falsifications, the most important to be known, are those which may prove injurious to health, such as the mixture of chalk and burnt bones with flour, lead employed to remove the acidity of wine, or arsenic to refine it. Chemistry affords the means of discovering all these adulterations; but much knowledge is needed for its application.

The interference of governments with these matters should be limited to three points:—1st, To encourage the discovery of means of proof, in cases where they are wanting; 2nd, Spreading knowledge of these discoveries among the people; 3rd, Defining the duties of those officers of government to whom functions of this sort are intrusted.

XII. *To establish Brands or Marks attesting the quantity or quality of Articles which ought to conform to a certain Standard.*—These marks are declarations or certificates under an abridged form. In these documents, five points are to be considered:—1st, Their object; 2nd, The person whose attestation they bear; 3rd, The extent and the details of the information they contain; 4th, The distinctness and intelligibility of the mark; 5th, Its permanence and indestructibility.

The usefulness of these authentic attestations cannot be doubted. They are successfully employed for the following purposes:—

1st. To give certainty to the rights of property. We may trust to the prudence of individuals to make use of this precaution in what concerns themselves; but, as far as relates to public property, or to objects in deposit, it should be made an affair of the law. Thus, in England, everything that appertains to the royal marine bears a particular mark, which the mercantile marine is not allowed to use. In the royal arsenals the imprint of an arrow is made use of, and a peculiar thread is twisted into the tissue of the cordage, which individuals are not permitted to employ.

2nd. To assure the quantity and quality of mercantile articles for the benefit of purchasers. Thus, by the English statutes, marks are affixed to a great number of objects, as leather, bread, tin, silver ware, woollen clothes, stockings, and many other articles of trade.

3rd. To assure the payment of taxes. If the article subject to the tax has not the mark in question, it is a proof that the tax has not been paid. Examples are innumerable.

4th. To insure obedience to laws which prohibit importation.

CHAPTER XI.

To prevent Offences by giving to many Persons an Interest to prevent them.

I SHALL cite a particular example, which may be referred to the preceding head as well as to this; for an offence is prevented either by increasing the difficulty of concealing it, or by giving to many persons an immediate interest to prevent it.

The carriage of the mails in England had always been deficient in expedition and punctuality. The postmen loitered by the way, as their own convenience or profit required; the innkeepers never hastened their departure. All these delays were so many little offences,—that is, violations of established rules. What remedy could be applied? Watchfulness soon grew weary; penalties were gradually relaxed; informations, always odious or embarrassing, became rare; and abuses, suspended for a moment, presently regained their ordinary course.

A very simple means was hit upon, which required neither law, nor penalty, nor information, and which was all the better for not requiring them.

This means consisted in combining two establishments, which hitherto had been separate, the transportation of the mails and the carriage of travellers. The success of this project was complete; the celerity of the post was doubled; and travellers were better served. This is worth the trouble of being analyzed.

The travellers who accompany the postman are so many inspectors of his conduct; he cannot escape their observation; while he is excited by their praises, and by the reward he expects from them, he cannot be ignorant that if he loses time, these travellers will have good reason to complain, and that they can inform against him without odium, or the reputation of doing it for pay. Such are the advantages of this little combination! Witnesses to the least fault; the motive of reward substituted for that of punishment; economy of informations and prosecutions, the occasions of punishment rendered rare, and the two services, by their union, made more convenient, more prompt, and more economical!

I offer this happy idea of Mr. Palmer as a study in legislation. It is necessary to meditate upon what has been successfully accomplished in one kind, to learn how to conquer difficulties in another. By investigating the cause of success in particular cases, we may rise to general rules.

CHAPTER XII.

To facilitate the Means of recognising and finding Individuals.

The greater part of offences are committed only by reason of the great hope which the offenders entertain of remaining unknown. Everything which augments the facility of recognising men, and of finding them, adds to general security.

This is one of the reasons why very little is to be apprehended on the part of those who have a fixed abode, property, and a family. The danger is from those who, by their indigence, or their independence of all ties, may easily conceal their proceedings from the eye of justice.

Registers of the population, in which are inscribed the dwelling, age, sex, profession, and the marriage or celibacy of individuals, are the first materials of a good police.

The magistrate ought to be authorised to demand an account from every suspected person of his means of livelihood, and to send to a place of security those who cannot prove either industry or income.

There are two things to be observed on this subject. The rules of police ought not to be so minute and particular as to expose the citizens frequently to break them, nor should they be rendered vexatious by imposing numerous and troublesome restraints. Precautions, necessary at certain times of danger or trouble, ought not to be prolonged into a season of quiet, as the regimen proper for sickness ought not to be kept up after the health is restored. The second observation is, to avoid shocking the national spirit. One nation could not endure the police of another. In the capital of China every one is obliged to wear his name upon his dress. This measure will appear useful, indifferent, or tyrannical, according to the turn of national prejudices.

Characteristic dresses have a relation to this end. Those which distinguish the sexes are a means of police as mild as it is salutary. Those which serve to distinguish soldiers, sailors, and the clergy, have more than one object, but their chief end is subordination. In the English universities the pupils have a particular dress, which is no restraint, except when they wish to transgress some rule. In charity-schools the pupils are made to wear a uniform, and even a numbered ticket.

It is inconvenient that the surnames of individuals should be upon so irregular a footing. These distinctions, invented in the infancy of societies, to answer the wants of a hamlet, fulfil their object but imperfectly in a great nation. Many inconveniences arise from this confusion of names. The greatest of all is, that the testimony which depends upon a name is very vague; suspicion is cast upon a multitude of persons; and the danger of innocence may become the protection of guilt.

A new system of nomenclature might easily be devised, so that each individual in a nation should have a peculiar name, borne by no one but himself. In the actual state of things, the embarrassments of a change would, perhaps, exceed its advantages; but it might be well to prevent this disorder in a growing colony.

It is a common usage among English sailors to trace their family and baptismal name upon the wrist, in distinct and indelible characters. It is done that they may be recognised in case of shipwreck. If it were possible for such a practice to become universal, it would furnish a new aid to morals, a new power to the laws, an almost infallible precaution against a multitude of offences, especially all kinds of fraud, for the success of which a certain degree of confidence is necessary. Who are you? Who am I dealing with? There would be no room for prevarication in the answer to this important question.

This means, by reason of its very energy, would favour personal liberty, by permitting the rigours of procedure to be relaxed. Imprisonment, where it has no object except securing the person, would be less often necessary, if men were thus held as it were by an invisible chain.

Doubtless there are plausible objections. In the course of the French revolution, how many persons owed their safety to a disguise which an imprint of this nature would have rendered impossible! Public opinion in its actual state opposes an insurmountable obstacle to this institution; but patience and address may change opinion; especially were a beginning made by some great examples. If it were the custom to print marks upon the foreheads of the great, an idea of power and of honour would be associated with them. The women in the islands of the South Sea submit to a painful operation in printing certain figures upon the skin, to which an idea of beauty is attached. The imprint is made by a multitude of punctures which penetrate to the quick, and into which coloured powders are rubbed.

CHAPTER XIII.

To increase the Difficulty of Escape.

THESE means depend very much upon the geographical situation of a country, and upon natural and artificial barriers. In Russia, the sparseness of the population, the severity of the climate, the difficulty of communications, give a power to justice, of which it would hardly be thought capable in so extensive a country.

At Petersburg and Riga, passports cannot be obtained, unless the intention of departure has been several times advertised in the gazettes. This precaution against fraudulent debtors adds to the security of commerce.

Everything which increases the facility of transmitting and spreading intelligence, may be referred to this head.

CHAPTER XIV.

To diminish the Uncertainty of Prosecutions and Punishments.

I DO not intend to enter here upon the vast subject of procedure; that will be the subject, not of a chapter, but of a separate work. I confine myself to two or three general observations.

If an offence has been committed, it is for the interest of society that the magistrate to whose cognisance it belongs should be informed of it; and informed in such a manner as to be authorised to inflict a punishment. If it be alleged that an offence has been committed, it is the interest of society that the truth or falsehood of that allegation be subjected to proofs. Therefore the rules of testimony and the forms of procedure ought to be such as, on the one hand, to admit every true information, and on the other, to exclude every false information, that is, everything which is more likely to mislead than to enlighten.

Nature has placed before us a model of procedure. Consider what passes in the domestic tribunal; examine the conduct of the father of a family towards his children, his domestics, of which he is the head. We shall find there the original features of justice, which can no longer be recognised, after they have been disfigured by men incapable of discerning the truth, or interested to disguise it. A good judge is only a good father, acting upon a much larger scale. The means which are adapted to guide a father in the search after truth, ought equally to be good for a judge. It is this model of procedure upon which justice began, and from which it ought never to have departed.

It is true that a confidence may be felt in the father of a family which cannot be felt in a judge, because a judge has not the same motives of affection, and may be perverted by personal interest. But this only proves that in case of a judge, it is necessary to take precautions against partiality and corruption which are not needed in the domestic tribunal. It does not prove that the forms of procedure or the rules of testimony ought to be different.

The English law admits the following principles :—

1st. That no one ought to be a witness in his own case.

2nd. That no one should be received as his own accuser.

3rd. That the testimony of persons interested in a cause ought not to be taken.

4th. That hearsay evidence ought never to be admitted.

5th. That no one ought to be put on trial a second time for the same offence.

It is not my intention to discuss here these rules of testimony to which may be applied that description—*penitus toto divisos orbe Britannos*—Britain wholly separate from the rest of the world. In a treatise on procedure in general, a proper place will be found to inquire whether the English jurisprudence, superior in some respects to that of all nations, owes its superiority to to these maxims, or whether they are not the principal cause of that weakness in the executive power of justice whence there results in England an ineffective police and such frequency of offences.

All I shall say here is, that every precaution which is not absolutely necessary for the protection of innocence affords a dangerous lurking-place to crime. What maxims of procedure can be more dangerous than those which put justice in opposition to itself, and which establish a kind of incompatibility between its duties? When it is said, for example, that it is better that a hundred of the guilty should escape than that one innocent person should perish, a dilemma is supposed which does not exist; the security of innocence may be complete without favouring the impunity of crime; indeed, it can only be complete on that condition; for every culprit who escapes threatens the public security; and, so far from being a protection to innocence, such an escape exposes innocence to become the victim of a new offence. To acquit a criminal is to commit by his hands all the offences of which he is afterwards guilty.

The difficulty of proceeding against offences is a great cause of feebleness in the executive power of justice, and of impunity to crime. When the law is clear, when the judge is appealed to immediately after the supposed offence, the function of accuser is almost confounded with that of a witness. When the offence is committed under the eye of the judge, there are, so to speak, but two persons necessary in the drama—the judge and the delinquent. It is distance of time and place which separate the function of the witness from that of the judge. But it may happen that all the witnesses of the facts cannot be suddenly collected, or that the offence is not discovered till long after its commission, or that the accused alleges facts in his defence which it requires time to verify—all these causes may bring on delays. Delays give occasion to incidents which produce new delays. The process of justice becomes complicated, and, in order to follow out this chain of operations without confusion or negligence, it is necessary to intrust its management to a particular person. Hence results the function of an accuser. The accuser may either be one of the witnesses, or a person interested in the affair, or a public officer specially appointed for that purpose.

The judicial functions have often been divided, so that the judge who receives the testimony while it is recent, has not the right to decide; but is obliged to send the affair to another judge, who, unless the evidence were thus collected, would have no leisure to attend to it till the proofs were half effaced. There have been established, in most countries, a great number of useless formalities, and it has become necessary to create officers to attend to those formalities. The system of procedure is so complicated that it has become an abstruse science; he who wishes to prosecute an offence is obliged to put himself into the hands of an attorney, and the attorney himself cannot go on without the aid of another man of the law of a superior class, who directs him by his counsels, and who speaks for him.

To these disadvantages, two others must be added:—

1st. Legislators, by a strange piece of self-contradiction, have often closed all access to the tribunals against those who have the most need of their assistance, by subjecting proceedings at law to taxes, the effect of which is little considered.

2nd. There is a public disfavour attached to all those who lend their aid, in quality of accusers, to the execution of the laws,—a stupid and pernicious prejudice, which legislators have often had the weakness to encourage, without ever having made the slightest effort to subdue it.

It is easy to see the consequence of this accumulation of delays and discouragements. The laws are not executed. If a man could address the judge at once, and tell what he has seen, the expense to which this procedure would subject him would be but a trifle. In proportion to the number of intermediate steps which he is obliged to take his expenses are increased. When to this we add loss of time, vexations, and the uncertainty of succeeding, it is astonishing that men can be found bold enough to engage in such a pursuit. There are but few, and there would be still fewer if those who adventure in this lottery knew as well as the lawyers what it will cost, and how many chances there are of failure.

These difficulties would vanish by the mere institution of a public accuser, clothed with the character of a magistrate, who should conduct all prosecutions at the public expense. Informers who expected pay would require but a moderate compensation. A hundred gratuitous accusers would present themselves to one who would demand pay for his services.* Every law, being put into force, would manifest its good or bad effects; the wheat would be winnowed from the chaff. Good laws would be appreciated; bad laws would be repealed. Informers, animated by public spirit, and rejecting all pecuniary reward, would be heard with due respect and confidence; and delinquents could no longer escape the punishment of their offences by a bargain with the prosecutor.

It is true that in England, in all grave cases, the accuser is forbidden to make a compromise with the accused, without the permission of the court; but although this prohibition were universal, what possibility is there of its observance in cases where it is the interest of both parties to elude it?

CHAPTER XV.

To prohibit Accessory Offences in order to prevent the Principal Offence.

ACTS which are related to a pernicious event as causes may be considered in relation to the *principal offence*, as *accessory offences*.

The principal offence being well determined, there may be distinguished as many accessory offences as there are acts which may serve as preparations for the principal offence, and which manifest, on the part of those who perform them, an intention of committing it. Now, the more distinctly these preparatory acts are pointed out and prohibited, the more chances there are of

* The smallest expense of a prosecution in an English court of justice is twenty-eight pounds sterling,—a sum almost sufficient for the yearly subsistence of a common family. This sum comes out of the pocket of the prosecutor. Under such a system, it is almost a miracle that there are any prosecutions.

preventing the principal offence. If the offender is not stopped at the first step, he may be at the second, or the third. It is thus that a vigilant legislator, like a skilful general, takes care to reconnoitre all the exterior posts of the enemy, in order to interrupt his enterprises. Along all the defiles, and all the passes, he stretches a chain of works, diversified according to circumstances, but connected together in such a way that the enemy finds at each step new dangers and new obstacles.

If we consider the practice of legislators we shall find none who have laboured systematically upon this plan, and none who have not followed it to a certain extent.

Offences of the chase, for example, have been divided into many accessory offences, according to the nature of the game, or the kinds of nets or instruments necessary to take it. Smuggling has been attacked, by prohibiting many preparatory acts. Counterfeiting has been attacked in the same manner.

I shall give some other examples of what might be done in this way against homicide and other corporal injuries.

The prohibition to carry arms only useful for attack and easy to be concealed. It is said that an instrument is made in Holland in the form of a needle, which is shot through a tube, and which inflicts a mortal wound. The manufacture, the sale, the possession of these instruments ought to be forbidden, as accessary to murder.

Ought pocket-pistols, such as English highwaymen use, to be prohibited? The utility of such a prohibition is problematical. Of all methods of robbery, that which makes use of fire-arms is least dangerous to the person attacked. In such a case, the mere threat is usually sufficient to accomplish the object. The robber who began with shooting, would not only commit an act of useless cruelty, he would disarm himself; while by reserving his fire, he stands on the defensive. He who uses a club or a sword, has not the same motive to abstain from striking; and one blow becomes the motive for a second, in order to deprive the victim of power to pursue.

The prohibition to sell poisons demands a catalogue of poisonous substances. The sale of them cannot be absolutely prohibited;* all that can be done is, to regulate it, to subject it to precautions, to require that the seller should know the purchaser, that he has witnesses of the sale, that he enters it in a separate book; and still, some latitude must be left for unexpected cases. These rules, to be complete, demand many details. Would their advantages counterbalance the embarrassments they would produce? That depends upon the manners and habits of a people. If poisoning is a frequent offence, it will be necessary to take these indirect precautions. They would have been proper in ancient Rome.

Accessory offences may be distinguished into four classes.

The first class imply a formed intention to commit the principal offence. Offences of this kind are comprehended under the general name of attempts, preparations.

The second class do not imply a criminal intention actually formed, but place the individual in a situation in which there is reason to fear that he may presently conceive a criminal design. Such are gaming, prodigality, and idleness, when poverty is added to it. Cruelty towards animals is an incentive to cruelty towards men, &c.

Accessory offences of the third class do not imply any criminal intention, actual or probable, but only accidentally possible. Offences of this kind are created by those regulations of police intended to prevent calamities. When, for example, the sale of certain poisons or the sale of gunpowder is forbidden, the violation of these rules, separate from any criminal intention, is an offence of this third class.

The fourth class is composed of presumed offences, that is, of acts which are considered as proofs of an offence. They may be called *evidentiary offences;* acts injurious or otherwise in themselves, but furnishing a presumption of an offence committed. By an English statute, the concealment by the mother of the birth of an illegitimate child, is punished as murder, because such conduct is regarded as a sure proof of infanticide.

* Taken in a certain dose, every active medicine is a poison.

By another statute, it is a capital crime for men to meet together armed and disguised, because this is supposed to be a proof of a formed design to offer violent resistance to the officers of the customs. By another statute, it is an offence to have stolen goods in possession without being able to render a satisfactory account how they were obtained; because this circumstance is regarded as proof of participation in the theft. By another statute, it is an offence to obliterate the marks upon shipwrecked property, because such an act indicates intention of theft.

These offences, founded upon presumptions, suppose two things:—1st, Distrust of the system of procedure; 2nd, Distrust of the wisdom of the judge. The English legislature fearing that juries, too prone to lenity, would not see in these presumptions a certain proof of guilt, has thought fit to erect the Act which furnishes the presumption into a second offence, an offence distinct from every other. In those countries in which a perfect confidence is placed in the tribunals, these Acts may be arranged under their proper head, and be considered merely as presumptions, from which the court is to draw such inferences as the circumstances warrant.

In relation to accessory offences, it is essential to lay down three rules by way of *memento* to the legislator.

1st. Whenever a principal offence is created, all preparatory acts and simple attempts ought also to be prohibited, ordinarily under a less penalty than the principal offence. This rule is general, and the exceptions ought to be founded upon particular reasons.

2nd. To the description of the principal offence there ought to be appended a description of all accessory, preliminary, and concomitant offences which are susceptible of a specific description.

3rd. In the description of these accessory offences, care must be taken not to impose too many restraints, not to entrench too far upon individual liberty; not to expose innocence to danger by conclusions too precipitate. The description of an offence of this kind would be almost always dangerous, if it did not include a clause leaving power to the judge to estimate the degree of presumption to be derived from it. In that case, creating an accessory offence is pretty much the same thing as suggesting the fact in question to the judge, by way of instruction, as an indicative circumstance; but not authorizing him to draw any conclusion from it, if he see any special reason to regard the indication as inconclusive.

If the punishment of a preliminary offence, or of an offence begun but not finished, were the same with that of the principal or complete offence, without allowing anything for the possibility of repentance or a prudent stopping short, the delinquent perceiving that he had already incurred the whole danger by the simple attempt, would feel himself at liberty to consummate the offence without incurring any further risk.

CHAPTER XVI.

The Culture of Benevolence.

The sentiment of benevolence is distinct from the love of reputation. Each may act without the other. This sentiment may originate in an instinctive principle, the gift of nature; but, in a great measure, it is the produce of culture, the fruit of education. Where is the greater amount of benevolence to be found, among the English or the Iroquois, in the infancy of society or its maturity? If the sentiment of benevolence be susceptible of increase, and that it is cannot be doubted, that increase is to be obtained by the aid of another principle of the human heart, the love of reputation. When the moralist paints benevolence with the most amiable features, and selfishness, hardness of heart, in the most odious colours, at what does he aim? He seeks to unite to the purely social principle of benevolence, the demi-personal and demi-social principle of reputation. He seeks to combine them; to give them the same direction; to strengthen them one by the other. If his efforts are crowned with success, to which of these two principles ought he to ascribe the honour.

Neither to the one nor to the other exclusively, but to their reciprocal concourse; to the sentiment of benevolence as the immediate cause; to the love of reputation as the remote cause. He who yields with pleasure to the mild promptings of the social principle knows not, and does not desire to know, that it is a less noble principle to which his benevolence owes its impulse. Such is the disdainful delicacy of the better element of our nature; it is unwilling to owe its birth to anything but to itself; it blushes at every foreign association.

There are two objects for the legislator:—1st, To give new force to the sentiment of benevolence; 2nd, To regulate its application according to the principle of utility.

1st. The legislator who wishes to inspire a people with humanity ought himself to give the first example of it. Let him show the utmost respect, not only for the lives of men, but for all the circumstances which have an influence upon their sensibility. Sanguinary laws have a tendency to render men cruel, by fear, by imitation, and by fostering a spirit of revenge. Mild laws humanize the manners of a nation; the spirit of the government is reproduced among the citizens.

The legislator ought to forbid everything that serves as an incitement to cruelty. The barbarous gladiatorial shows introduced at Rome, in the latter times of the republic, contributed, without doubt, to inspire that ferocity of spirit which the Romans displayed in their civil wars. Will a people accustomed to despise human life in their sports respect it in the rage of passion?

It is proper, for the same reason, to forbid every kind of cruelty to animals, whether by way of amusement or for the gratification of gluttony. Cock-fights and bull-fights, the chase of the hare and the fox, fishing, and other amusements of the same kind, necessarily suppose a want of reflection or a want of humanity; since these sports inflict upon sensitive beings the most lively sufferings, and the most lingering and painful death that can be imagined. Men must be permitted to kill animals; but they should be forbidden to torment them. Artificial death may be rendered less painful than natural death by simple processes, well worth the trouble of being studied, and of becoming an object of police. Why should the law refuse its protection to any sensitive being? A time will come when humanity will spread its mantle over everything that breathes. The lot of slaves has begun to excite pity; we shall end by softening the lot of the animals which labour for us and supply our wants.

I do not know whether the Chinese legislators, in establishing their minute ceremonials, have had for their object the cultivation of benevolence, or only the maintenance of peace and subordination. In China, politeness is a kind of worship or ritual, the great object of education, and the principal science. The bodily movements of the Chinese, always regulated, always prescribed by etiquette, are almost as uniform as those of a regiment which goes through the manual exercise. This pantomime of benevolence may be destitute of reality, as a devotion loaded with minute observances may have little to do with morals. So much restraint does not seem to accord well with the human heart; and such demonstrations of respect do not confer any obligation, because they have no merit.

There are principles of antipathy, which are sometimes so interlaced with the political constitutions of states, that it is very difficult to extirpate them. There are hostile religions which excite their partisans to hate and to persecute each other; hereditary feuds between hostile families; privileges of rank which erect insurmountable barriers between the citizens; results of conquest, where the conquerors have not been able to mix and incorporate themselves with the conquered people; animosities founded upon ancient wrongs; the rule of factions which rise with a victory, and fall with a defeat. In this unfortunate condition of things, hearts are oftener united by hatred than by love. Men must be freed from fear and oppression, before they can be taught to love each other. The destruction of prejudices which make men hostile, is one of the greatest services that can be rendered to morals.

Mungo Park in his African travels, has represented the blacks in a most interesting point of view; their simplicity, the strength of their domestic affections, the picture of their innocent manners, has increased the public interest in their favour.

Satirical writers weaken this sentiment. After reading Voltaire, does one feel favourably disposed towards the Jews? If that author's benevolence had not been eclipsed by his prejudices, while exposing the degradations to which the Jews are subjected, he would have explained by that very fact the less favourable traits of their character, and would have exhibited the remedy by the side of the evil.

The most dangerous assaults upon benevolence have been made by exclusive religions, having incommunicable rights, inspiring intolerance, and representing unbelievers as infidels, the enemies of God.

In England, better than elsewhere, is understood the art of exciting beneficence by the publicity which is given to it. Is it wished to establish a charitable institution which requires many contributors?—a committee of the most active and distinguished benefactors is appointed; the amount of contributions is announced in the newspapers; and the names of the subscribers are printed from day to day. This publicity answers two ends. Its immediate object is, to guarantee the receipt and employment of the funds; but it is also a bait to vanity by which benevolence gains.

In charitable societies all the annual subscribers are named directors; the control they exercise, the little state they form, interest them in their office. They love to follow up the good they have done, and to enjoy the power which it confers. The benefactors being thus brought into contact with the unfortunate, misery being thus placed before their eyes, benevolence is strengthened and confirmed; it grows cool by the removal of the object, but warms again by its presence.

There are more of these benevolent societies in London than there ever were convents in Paris.

Many of these charities have particular objects: the blind, orphans, the maimed, widows, sailors, the children of clergymen. Each individual is more touched by one kind of misery than by another, and his sympathy almost always depends upon some personal circumstance. Of course, there is much art in diversifying charities, in separating them into many branches, in order that every kind of sensibility may be made available, and that none may be lost.

It is astonishing that more advantage has not been taken of the disposition of women, among whom the sentiment of pity is stronger than among men. Before the revolution, there were two institutions in France well adapted to this end: the *Daughters of Charity*, who devoted themselves to the service of the hospitals, and the *Society of Maternal Charity* at Paris, composed of married ladies, who visited poor women in their pregnancy, and aided them in the care of their infants.

2nd. The sentiment of benevolence is liable to deviate from the principle of general utility. It cannot be set right except by instruction. Command and force do not avail. Men must be persuaded, enlightened, taught little by little, to distinguish the different degrees of utility, and to proportion their benevolence to the extent of its object. The best model is traced by Fenelon in that sentence which paints his heart: "I prefer my family to myself, my country to my family, mankind to my country."

It should be the object of public instruction to direct the affections of the citizens towards the end of utility; to repress vagaries of benevolence; and to make each individual perceive how the general interest involves his own. Men should be taught to blush at that spirit of family, at that spirit of caste, at that spirit of party, sect or profession, which militates against the love of country; and at that unjust patriotism which glories in the hatred of other nations. They should be dissuaded from assuming, through a misplaced pity, the advocacy of deserters, smugglers, and other delinquents who sin against the state. They should be disabused of that false notion that there is any humanity in favouring the escape of a criminal, in lending impunity to crime, in encouraging mendicity to the prejudice of industry. The attempt should be made to give to all their sentiments of benevolence the most advantageous proportion, by pointing out the littleness and the danger of those caprices, antipathies, and momentary attachments, which incline the balance against general utility and permanent interest.

The more men become enlightened, the more they will contract a spirit of general benevolence, because the progress of enlightenment makes it evident that the interests of men are oftener harmonious than discordant. In commerce, nations not well informed treat each other as rivals, who cannot rise except upon each other's ruins. The work of Adam Smith is a treatise upon universal benevolence, because it shows that commerce is equally advantageous to all parties; that each party profits in its own way, according to its natural means; and that nations are partners, not rivals, in the great social enterprise.

CHAPTER XVII.

Employment of the Motive of Honour, or the Popular Sanction.

It should be the object of the legislator to increase the force of this motive, and to regulate its application.

The force of public opinion is in the compound ratio of its extent and its intensity. Its extent is measured by the number of suffrages; its intensity by the degree of blame or of approbation.

There are many means of increasing the power of opinion so far as concerns its extent: the principal are—liberty of the press, and publicity in all proceedings in which the nation is interested; publicity of the tribunals; publicity of accounts; publicity of state consultations when secrecy is not required for some particular reason. An enlightened public, the depository of the laws and of the archives of honour, and administrator of the moral sanction, forms a supreme tribunal, which decides upon all cases and all persons. By publicity in affairs, this tribunal is enabled to collect proofs and to form a judgment; by the liberty of the press it is enabled to pronounce its judgment, and to cause it to be executed.

There are also a number of means for increasing the intensity of the power of opinion ; such as punishments which bear some character of ignominy, or rewards of which the principal object is honour to those who receive them.

There is an art of guiding opinion, without the public suspecting how it is led. It consists in arranging things so that the act which you wish to prevent cannot be performed without first doing something else, which popular opinion condemns already. If it be desired, for example, to secure the payment of an impost, you may exact from him whose duty it is to pay, a certificate or an oath that he has paid.

To take a false oath, to fabricate a false certificate, under whatever pretence, are offences which the public is prepared beforehand to stamp with disapprobation. So that here we discover a sure means of rendering an offence infamous, which without this addition would not be so.

Sometimes a mere change in the name of a thing is enough to change the sentiments of a nation. The Romans abhorred the name of *king*, but they could put up with the titles of *dictator* and *emperor*. Cromwell did not succeed in seating himself upon the throne of England, but under the name of *protector*, he enjoyed more than kingly authority. Peter I. of Russia abdicated the title of *despot* for himself, and he ordered that the slaves of the nobles should henceforth be called only *subjects*.

If the people were philosophers, this expedient would not answer; but on this point philosophers are as weak as the people. What deception in the words *liberty* and *equality!* What contradictions between that *luxury* which all condemn, and that *public prosperity* which all admire!

The legislator ought to beware how he strengthens public opinion in cases where it is in opposition to the principle of utility. For this reason he ought to efface from the laws every vestige of those pretended offences of heresy and witchcraft, lest he give a legal foundation to superstitious notions. If he does not dare to attack errors, too generally diffused, at least he ought not to furnish them with a new sanction.

It is very difficult to employ the motive of honour as a means to aid the enforcement of the laws. Pecuniary rewards paid to informers, have failed of their object. The motive of gain has been opposed by that of shame; and the law, instead of increasing its power, has weakened itself by offering an inducement condemned by public opinion. Persons are afraid of the suspicion of acting from a mean motive. Rewards not well selected, repulse, instead of attracting, and deprive the law of much gratuitous assistance.

The most powerful means of producing an important revolution in public opinion, is, to strike the mind of the people by some great example. Thus Peter the Great himself, gradually passing through all the gradations of rank, taught his nobility, by his own example, to bear the yoke of military subordination. Thus Catherine II. surmounted the popular prejudice against inoculation, by trying it, not upon criminals, but on herself.

CHAPTER XVIII.

Employment of the Motive of Religion.

The culture of religion has two objects :—1st, To increase the power of that sanction; 2nd, To give that power a proper direction. If its direction be bad, it is plain that the less power that sanction has, the less evil it will do. With respect then to religion, the first thing to be examined is, its tendency; the search for means to augment its power, is but a secondary object.

Its tendency ought to be conformable to the plan of utility. As a sanction, it is composed of punishments and rewards. Its punishments ought to be attached to those acts which are injurious to society, and to such acts alone. Its rewards ought to be promised to acts the tendency of which is advantageous to society, and to no acts beside. This ought to be its fundamental dogma.

The only means to judge of its tendency is to consider it solely in its relation to the good of political society. Every other part of it is indifferent; and whatever is indifferent in religious belief is liable to become pernicious.

Every article of faith is of necessity injurious so soon as the legislator, in order to favour its adoption, resorts to coercive motives,—to motives derived from the fear of punishment. The persons whom he wishes to influence may be considered as forming three classes: those who are already of the same opinion with the legislator; those who reject that opinion; those who neither adopt nor reject it.

For those who conform voluntarily, a coercive law is not necessary; for nonconformists it is useless, as is proved by the very fact of their nonconformity; it does not fulfil its purpose.

When a man has formed his opinion, can punishments make him change it? The very question is an insult to common sense. Punishments have rather a contrary effect; they rather serve to confirm one's opinion than to shake it, partly because the employment of constraint is a tacit avowal that arguments are wanting; partly because recourse to violent means produces an aversion to opinions so sustained. Punishment never can oblige a man to believe, but only to pretend that he believes.

Those who, through conviction, or the pride of honour, refuse to pretend a belief they do not feel, are exposed to the evil of punishment,—that is, to persecution; for what is called *persecution* is an evil which is not compensated by any advantage; it is a pure loss; and though administered by the hand of the magistrate, it is precisely the same in nature, but much severer in degree, than if it had been the work of an ordinary malefactor.

Those persons, less strong-minded, and less noble, who escape by a false declaration, yield to threats, and to the immediate danger which presses them; but the momentary punishments thus avoided turn into a punishment of conscience, if they have any scruples, and into a punishment of contempt upon the part of society, which cannot endure the baseness of such hypocritical retractions.

In such a state of things, what happens? A portion of the citizens must accustom themselves to disregard the opinions of another part, in order to be at peace with themselves. There springs up an art of making subtle distinctions between innocent falsehoods and criminal falsehoods; there is established a class of privileged lies, permitted as a defence against tyranny,—a set of perjuries which are esteemed innocent, and false signatures considered as mere formalities. In the midst of these subtilties respect for truth disappears; the limits of good and evil are confounded; a train of less pardonable falsehoods is introduced under cover of those already described; the tribunal of opinion is divided; the judges who compose it do not follow the same law; they do not clearly know what degree of dissimulation they ought to condemn or what they ought to excuse. The votes are scattered and contradictory, and the moral sanction, having no longer a uniform regulator, grows weak, and loses its influence. Thus, the legislator who imposes religious tests becomes the corrupter of the nation. He sacrifices virtue to religion, though religion itself is a good only so far as it is the auxiliary of virtue.

The third class of the community, according to the division above stated, comprises those persons who, at the establishment of the penal law for the regulation of belief, had yet no settled opinion one way or the other. With respect to these, it is likely that the law may have an influence upon the formation of their opinions. Seeing danger upon one side, and security upon the other, it is natural that they should examine the arguments in favour of an opinion which the law condemns, with a degree of fear and aversion, that they will not feel for the arguments which support the favoured opinion. The arguments which we desire to find true, make a more lively impression than those which we hope to find false; and thus a man comes to believe, or rather not to reject, not to disbelieve a proposition which he would not have adopted had his inclinations been left free. In this last case, the evil, though not so great as in the two former, does not cease to be an evil. It may happen, but it does not always happen, that the judgment yields entirely to the affections; and even though it should so happen, though the belief should be as strong as it can be, if fear enters at all into the motives of that belief, the mind is never perfectly tranquil. There remains a secret dread that what is believed to-day may be disbelieved to-morrow. The conviction of a clear moral truth is never shaken; but belief in a mere dogma is always more or less wavering. Thence arises that impatience towards those who attack it. Examination and discussion are dreaded by men who feel the ground shaking under their feet. It will not do to allow any alterations in a building which lacks a foundation. The understanding is enfeebled; the mind seeks only for perfect repose in a sort of blind credulity; it collects together all the errors which have any affinity with its own; it fears to explain itself clearly as to the possible and impossible, and seeks to confound all their limits. It delights in all sorts of sophistries, in everything that shackles the human understanding, in everything which seems to show that no certain dependence can be placed upon reason. It acquires an inclination, an unhappy dexterity for rejecting evidence; for giving weight to half proofs; for hearing but one side; for evading the decisions of reason. In one word, according to this system, it is necessary to put a bandage about the eyes, lest we be wounded by the light of day.

Thus every penal means employed to augment the power of religion, acts as an indirect means against that essential part of morals, which consists in respect for truth, and respect for public opinion. All enlightened minds now hold this doctrine; but there are very few states which have yet adopted it. Violent persecutions have ceased, but moderate persecutions still exist, civil penalties, political incapacities, menacing laws, a precarious toleration;—a humiliating situation for large classes of men, who owe their tranquillity only to a tacit indulgence, to a continued pardon.

To form a clear idea of the advantage which the legislator may derive from augmenting the force of the religious sanction, it is necessary to distinguish three cases:—1st, That in which it is entirely under his control; 2nd, That in which other persons share the influence with him; 3rd, That in which it depends upon some foreign personage. In this last case, the sovereignty is really divided between two magistrates, the spiritual, as he is called, and the temporal. The temporal sovereign is in perpetual danger of seeing his authority disputed or snatched away by his rival, and everything he does for the augmentation of the religious sanction will produce a diminution of his own power. We find in history a picture of the effects which result from such a struggle. The temporal magistrate commands such or such an action; the spiritual magistrate forbids it. Whichsoever side the citizens take, they are punished by the one, or by the other; proscribed, or damned; they are placed between the fear of the gallows, and the dread of hell-fire.

In Protestant countries, the clergy are essentially subordinate to the political power. Dogmas do not depend upon the prince, but those do who interpret the dogmas. Now the right of interpretation is pretty much the same thing with the right of promulgation. Thus in Protestant countries, religion is easily modelled, according to the plans of political authority. Married priests are more like citizens; they do not form a phalanx which can become formidable; they have neither the power of the confessional, nor that of absolution.

But if we consider only facts, whether in Catholic or Protestant countries, religion, it must be admitted, has had too great a share in the misfortunes of mankind. It seems to have been oftener the enemy than the instrument of civil government. The moral sanction never has more power than when it agrees with utility; but unfortunately the religious sanction appears to have most power in the very cases where it is most opposite to utility. The inefficacy of religion, so far as relates to the promotion of political good, is the ceaseless subject of declamations on the part of those who have the greatest interest to exaggerate its good effects. Not powerful enough to produce good, its power of doing evil has always been too great. It was the moral sanction which animated Codrus, Regulus, the Russells, and the Sidneys. It was the religious sanction which made Philip II. the scourge of the Low Countries, Mary the tyrant of England, and Charles IX. the butcher of France.

The common solution of this difficulty is to attribute all the good to religion, and all the evil to superstition. But this distinction, in this sense, is purely verbal. The thing itself is not changed because a man chooses to describe it, in one case, by the word religion, and by the word superstition in another. The motive which acts upon the mind is precisely the same in both cases. It is always the fear of evil and the hope of good on the part of an all-powerful Being, of whom different ideas are entertained. In speaking of the conduct of the same man, upon the same occasion, some attribute to religion what others ascribe to superstition.

Another observation, as trivial as the first, and as weak as it is trivial, is the remark so often repeated, that it is not just to argue against the *use* of a thing from its *abuse*, and that the best instruments do the most harm when misemployed. The futility of this argument is obvious; it consists in calling the good effects of a thing its *use*, and in stigmatizing the bad effects as its abuse. To say that you ought not to argue from the abuse of a thing against its use, is to say that, in making a just appreciation of the tendency of a cause, you ought to consider only the good, and not the evil it produces. The instruments of good, wrongly employed, may often become instruments of evil; that is true; but the principal characteristic of perfection in an instrument is not to be liable to be so misemployed. The most efficacious ingredients in medicine may be converted into poisons; I admit it; but those which are dangerous are not so good, upon the whole, as those which answer the same purpose, if such there are, without being liable to the same abuses. Mercury and opium are very useful; bread and water are still more so.

I have spoken without evasion, and with perfect freedom. I have elsewhere explained the utility of religion, but I cannot here omit to observe that it tends more and more to disengage itself from futile and pernicious dogmas, and to reconcile itself to sound morals and to sound politics. Irreligion, on the other hand, has been manifested in our day under the most hideous forms of absurdity, of immorality, and of persecution. This experience is enough to show all well-disposed minds towards what end they ought to direct their efforts. But if the government should act too openly in favour of this salutary direction, it would fail of its end. It is freedom of inquiry which has corrected the errors of the ages of ignorance, and brought back religion towards its true object. Freedom of inquiry will complete the purification of religion, and its reconciliation with public utility.

This is not the place to examine all the services which religion may render, either as a consolation to the woes inseparable from humanity; or as moral instruction best adapted to the most numerous class of society; or finally as a means of exciting beneficence, and of producing acts of devoted virtue, which perhaps could hardly be obtained by the power of mere earthly motives.

The principal employment of religion, in civil and penal legislation, is to give a new degree of force to *oaths*, an additional support to confidence.

An oath includes two different ties, one religious, the other moral; one obligatory upon all, the other, obligatory upon those only who have a certain set of opinions. The same formula which, in case of perjury, purports to expose the offender to religious penalties, exposes him, at the same time, to legal punishments and to public contempt. The religious obligation is the striking part; but the main force of the oath depends upon the moral tie. The influence of the first is partial, that of the second is universal. It would be a great piece of imprudence to make use of the former and to neglect the latter.

There are cases in which oaths have a very great power; those, namely, in which they act in concert with public opinion, or have the support of the popular sanction. There are other cases in which their power is very small; those, namely, in which they are in opposition to public opinion, or are merely unsupported by it. Such are custom-house oaths, and those exacted from the pupils at certain universities.

It is the interest of a legislator, not less than of a military chief, to know the true state of the forces under his command. To avoid seeing the weak part, because the sight of that weak part gives little satisfaction, is pusillanimity. If the feebleness of oaths, so far as the religious obligation is concerned, has been fully made known, it is the fault of those who place the greatest reliance on this means. The abuse they have made of it, the prodigality with which they have employed it, has betrayed the little efficacy which it has in itself, distinct from the sanction of honour.

The power of oaths is necessarily enfeebled, when they are made to bear upon belief, upon opinions. Why? Because, in such cases, it is impossible to detect perjury, and because human reason, always afloat, always subject to variations, cannot bind itself for the future. Can I be certain that my belief to-day will be my belief ten years hence? These oaths are an advantage given to unscrupulous men over those who have a greater sensibility of conscience.

Oaths become degraded when they are used for puerile purposes; when they are employed for purposes as to which there is a general understanding to violate them; and still more when they are required in cases in which justice and humanity excuse, and perhaps applaud, their violation.

The human mind, almost always opposed to tyranny, perceives confusedly that the Deity, on account of his very perfections, cannot ratify unjust or frivolous laws. Man, in fact, by imposing an oath, wishes to exercise an authority over God himself; man decrees a punishment, and the Supreme Judge is called upon to execute it. Deny this supposition, and there is an end to the religious force of an oath.

It is very astonishing that in England, among a people otherwise prudent and religious, this powerful means has been almost ruined by the trivial and indecent use that has been made of it.

To show how far habit may deprave moral opinions upon some points, I shall cite a passage extracted from Lord Kaims, a judge of the Court of Session in Scotland, in a work upon education:—

"Custom-house oaths, at present, go for nothing; not because men are growing more immoral, but because no one attaches any importance to them. The duty upon French wines is the same in Scotland as in England; but, as we are not rich enough to pay it, a tacit permission to pay upon French wines the same duty as upon Spanish wines, is found more advantageous to the revenue than the rigour of the law. However, before the duty is paid, an oath must be taken that the French wines are Spanish wines. Such oaths in their origin were criminal, because they were a fraud upon the public; but at present the oath is only a matter of form, and does not imply any credit given or received; it is a mere manner of speaking, like the compliments of common civility, *your humble servant*, &c. And, in fact, we see merchants who gain a livelihood by these oaths, and who are trusted without scruple in the most important affairs."

What shall we think when a moralist and a judge holds language like this? The Quakers have raised a simple affirmation to the dignity of an oath; a magistrate degrades an oath into a mere formality; the oath implies no credit, given or received. Then why take it? Why exact it? For what does this farce serve? Is religion then the meanest of objects? If it is, why pay so dear for it? What an absurdity to maintain a clergy at so great an expense, to preach the sacredness of oaths, and to have judges and legislators who turn them into ridicule!

CHAPTER XIX.

Use to be made of the Power of Instruction.

INSTRUCTION does not form a separate subject; but this title will enable us to bring under one head a number of detached observations.

Government ought not to do everything by force; it is only the body which submits to that; nothing but wisdom can extend its empire over the mind. When a government orders, it but gives its subjects an artificial interest to obey; when it enlightens, it gives them an interior motive, the influence of which they cannot evade. The best method of instruction is the simple publication of facts, but sometimes it is advisable to aid the public in forming a judgment upon those facts.

When measures of government, excellent in themselves, are seen to fail through the opposition of an ignorant people, we feel an immediate irritation against the stupidity of the multitude, and a disinclination to trouble ourselves further with the promotion of the public good. But when we come to reflect, when we observe that this opposition was easy to be foreseen, and that government, with the habitual pride of authority, had taken no precautions to prepare the minds of the people, to dissipate prejudices, to conciliate confidence, our indignation ought to be transferred from a people ignorant and deceived, to its disdainful and despotic rulers.

Experience has proved, contrary to the general anticipation, that newspapers are one of the best means of directing opinion, of quieting its feverish movements, and of dissipating those falsehoods and concocted rumours by which the enemies of government aim to accomplish their evil designs. By means of these papers, instruction descends from the government to the people, and remounts from the people to the government; the more liberty the press enjoys the easier it is to ascertain the current of opinion, so as to act with certainty.

To form an adequate idea of their utility, it is necessary to go back to the times when newspapers did not exist, and to consider the scenes of imposture, political and religious, which were played off with success, in countries where the people could not read. The last of these personators of royalty was Pugatcheff. Would it have been possible in our times to play such a part in France or in England? Would not the imposture be unmasked as soon as it was announced? There are offences which are not even attempted among enlightened nations; the ease of detecting impostures prevents their existence.

There are many other snares from which the government can protect the people, by public instructions. How many frauds are practised in commerce, in the arts, in the price or quality of goods, which it would be easy to put an end to by exposing them! How many dangerous remedies, or rather true poisons, are impudently sold by empirics, as marvellous secrets, as to which it would be easy to disabuse the most credulous, by making known their composition! How many mischievous opinions, errors fatal or absurd, which might be extinguished at their birth, by enlightening public opinion! When the folly of animal magnetism, having seduced the idle coteries of Paris, began to spread throughout Europe, a report of the Academy of Sciences, by the mere force of truth, marked Mesmer as a charlatan, and left him no disciples except a few incurable fools, whose admiration completed his disgrace. If you wish to cure an ignorant and superstitious people, send as missionaries into the cities and the country, jugglers and wonder-workers, and let them begin with astonishing the people, by producing the most singular phenomena, and end by enlightening them. Those who are best acquainted with natural magic, are least likely to be duped by magicians. I could wish that the miracle of St. Januarius were repeated at Naples in all the public places, and were even made a plaything for children.

The principal sort of instruction which governments owe to the people, is knowledge of the laws. How can we require laws to be obeyed, when they are not even known? How can they be known, unless they are published under the simplest forms, so that each individual may read for himself, the enactments which are to regulate his conduct?

The legislator may exercise an influence over public opinion, by causing to be compiled a body of political morals, analogous to the body of laws, and divided in the same manner into a general and particular codes. The most delicate questions relative to each profession might be explained. It would not be necessary to confine the work to mere didactic lessons; by intermingling a judicious selection of historical anecdotes, it might be made a book of amusement for persons of all ages.

To compose such moral codes, would be dictating, as it were, the judgments of public opinion upon these different questions of politics and morals. In the same spirit, there might be added to these moral codes a list of popular prejudices, to which should be subjoined the considerations which prove their fallacy.

If sovereign power has ever appeared before men with dignity, it was in the *Instructions*, published by Catherine II., for a code of laws. Let us consider for a moment this unique example, distinct from the remembrance of an ambitious reign. It is impossible to see without admiration a woman descending from the car of victory to civilize so many semi-barbarous tribes, and to offer them the finest maxims of philosophy, sanctioned by the approval of an empress. Superior to the vanity of composing this work herself, she borrowed the best that could be found in the writings of the wise men of the age; but by adding the weight of her authority, she lent to those writers more than she borrowed. She seemed to say to her subjects, "You owe me the more confidence, since I have taken into my council the ablest men of the times; and I do not fear to call upon those masters of truth and virtue to hold me up to shame before the face of the world, if I dare to act unworthily." In the same spirit she divided among her courtiers the labours of legislation; and if she was often in contradiction with herself, like Tiberius, who was weary of the servitude of the senate, and yet would have punished an effort at liberty, still these solemn engagements, contracted in the face of the whole world, were like limits voluntarily put to her power, which she seldom dared to transcend.

CHAPTER XX.

Use to be made of the Power of Education.

Education may be considered as the government of a domestic magistrate.

The analogies between a family and a state are of a nature to strike at the first glance; but the *differences* are not less obvious, and are equally deserving of attention.

1st. Domestic government needs to be more active, more vigilant, more occupied with details, than civil government. Without an attention always vigilant families could not subsist.

Civil authority cannot do better than to trust the management of personal interests to the prudence of individuals who always understand them better than the magistrate; but the head of a family must be constantly aiding the inexperience of those submitted to his care.

Here it is that the censorship can be exercised,—a policy which we have condemned in civil government. The domestic governor may protect those subject to his authority from knowledge which may do them harm; he can watch over their social intercourse and their studies; he can accelerate or retard the progress of their enlightenment, according to circumstances.

2nd. This continual exercise of power, which would be liable to so many abuses in a state, is much less so in a family; for the father and mother have a natural affection for their children, far stronger than that of the civil magistrate for those whom he governs. On their part, indulgence is generally the prompting of nature, while severity is the effect of reflection.

3rd. Domestic government can employ punishments in many cases where the civil authority cannot; for the head of a family deals with individuals, while the legislator can only act upon classes. The one proceeds upon certainties, the other upon presumptions. A certain astronomer may be capable, perhaps, of resolving the problem of longitude, but can the civil magistrate know it? Can he command this discovery, and punish him for not making it? But a particular instructor will be likely to know whether a given problem of elementary geometry is level to the capacity of his pupil. Though idleness assume the mask of incapacity, the instructor will hardly be deceived; in such cases the magistrate is sure to be deceived.

It is the same with most of the vices. The public magistrate cannot repress them, because if he attempted it he must have spies in every family. The private magistrate, having under his eye and his immediate control those with whose conduct he is charged, can arrest the beginning of those vices, of which the laws can punish only the last excesses.

4th. It is especially as regards the power of rewarding, that these two governments differ. All the amusements, all the wants of the young, may be made to assume a remuneratory character by granting them on certain conditions, after certain performances. In the Isle of Minorca, the dinners of the boys depended upon their skill in shooting the bow; and the honour of eating at the public table was the price allotted at Lacedemon to the warlike virtues of the young. No civil government is rich enough to do much by rewards; no father is so poor as not to possess an inexhaustible fund of them.

The legislator ought nevertheless to pay particular attention to youth, that season of lively and durable impressions, in order to direct the course of the inclinations towards those tastes most conformable to the public interest.

In Russia, means as powerful, as they are well devised, have been employed to engage the young nobility to enter into the army. The good effects that have resulted in consequence, to the military service, are even less than those which have been felt in a civil point of view. The young nobles are accustomed to order, to vigilance, to subordination. They are obliged to quit their estates, where they exercise a corrupting dominion over slaves, and to show themselves on a greater theatre, where they have equals and superiors. The necessity of mingling with others produces the desire of pleasing; the mixture of men of different races diminishes reciprocal prejudice, and the pride of birth is compelled to bend before the gradations of the service. An unlimited domestic despotism such as that of Russia was, cannot but be improved by being changed into a military government, which has its limits. In the actual circumstances of that empire, it would have been difficult to find a general means of education which would have answered more useful purposes.

But when education is considered as an indirect means of preventing offences, an essential reform is evidently needed. The class most neglected ought to become the principal object of its cares. The less the parents are capable of discharging their duty in this respect, the more necessary it is that the government should make up for their deficiencies. Not only should attention be given to orphans left in indigence, but also to children whose parents are not of a character to be trusted; to those who have already committed some offence; and to those who, being destitute of protectors and resources, are a prey to all the seductions of want. These classes, so absolutely neglected in the greater number of states, become, in consequence, the pupils of crime.

A man of rare beneficence, the Chevalier Paulet, created at Paris an institution for more than two hundred children whom he took from among the very poorest class. His plan rested upon four principles: To offer the pupils many objects of study and of labour, and to leave them the greatest possible latitude of taste; to employ them in mutual instruction, by offering to the scholar, as the highest reward of proficiency, the honour of becoming in his turn a master; to employ them in all the domestic services of the establishment, for the double purpose of instruction and economy; to govern them by means of themselves, by putting each pupil under the inspection of an older one, in a way to render them securities for each other. In this establishment, everything breathed an appearance of freedom and gaiety; there was no punishment except compulsive idleness, and a change of dress.* The more advanced pupils were as much interested in the general success as the founder himself; and the whole was going on prosperously, when the revolution, amid the general overthrow, swallowed up also this little colony.

A greater extent might be given to institutions of this kind, and their expensiveness might be diminished, either by teaching a great number of trades, or by retaining the pupils till the age of eighteen or twenty, so that their labour might contribute to discharge the expense of their education, and to aid in that of the younger pupils. Schools upon this plan, instead of being an expense to the state, might become lucrative enterprises. But

* The common punishments were called, one the *little idleness*, and the other the *great idleness*. What could be more ingenious than to give to punishments the very name and character of a vice? It is obvious what a salutary association of ideas this was calculated to produce.

the pupils themselves should be interested in the labour, by allowing them a fair rate of wages, to be paid them at leaving the school.

CHAPTER XXI.

General Precautions against Abuses of Authority.

LET us consider some of the means which a government may employ to prevent abuses of authority on the part of those to whom it intrusts portions of its power.

Constitutional law has its direct and its indirect legislation. Its direct legislation consists in the establishment of certain magistracies, among which all the political power is divided. That subject is not included in this treatise. Its indirect legislation consists in general precautions, of which the object is to prevent misconduct, incapacity, or malversations among those who hold principal or subordinate stations in the administration.

A complete enumeration of these indirect means will not be attempted. It will be enough to direct attention towards this object, and thus to restrain the enthusiasm of certain political writers, who, from having got sight of one or two of these means, have flattered themselves that they have perfected a science, of which, in fact, they have hardly drawn the outlines.

I. *The Division of Power into different Branches.*—Every division of power is a refinement suggested by experience. The most natural plan, the first that presents itself, is to place the whole administration in the hands of a single person. Command upon one side and obedience upon the other is a kind of contract of which the terms are easily arranged, when he who is to govern has no associate. Among all the nations of the East, the fabric of government has continued to preserve its primitive structure. The monarchic power descends without division, stage by stage, from the highest to the lowest, from the great Mogul to the simple Havildar.

When the King of Siam heard the Dutch Ambassador speak

of an aristocratic government, he burst into laughter at the idea of such an absurdity.

It is enough merely to mention this principal means. To examine into how many branches the government ought to be divided, and which of all the possible divisions is the one that merits the preference, would be to compose a treatise upon constitutional law. I shall only remark that this division ought not to result in separate and independent powers; for that would bring on a state of anarchy. Some supreme authority, superior to all, must always be acknowledged, which does not receive law, but which gives it, and which has power over the very rules that regulate its own mode of action.

II. *The Distribution of particular Branches of Power among several Co-participators.*—In the provinces of Russia, previous to the regulations of Catherine II., all the different branches of power—military, fiscal, and judicial—were intrusted to a single body, a single council. So far, the constitution of these subordinate governments sufficiently resembled the form of Oriental despotism; but the power of the governor was somewhat limited by the powers of the council, and in this respect the form approached to that of an aristocracy. At present, the judicial power is separated into many branches, and each branch is divided among many judges, who exercise their functions conjointly. A law has been established of the nature of the English *Habeas Corpus*, for the protection of individuals against arbitrary imprisonment, and a governor has no more power of doing harm than a governor of Barbadoes or Jamaica.

The advantages of this division are principally these:—

1st. It diminishes the danger to be apprehended from precipitation.

2nd. It diminishes the danger to be apprehended from ignorance.

3rd. It diminishes the danger to be apprehended from want of probity.

This last advantage, however, can hardly be attained, except where the number of co-participators is very great,—so great that it will be difficult to separate the interests of the majority of them from the interests of the people at large.

The division of powers has also disadvantages, since it introduces delays and foments disputes which may produce the dissolution of the established government. The evil of delays may be obviated by graduating the division, according as the functions to which it is applied admit of more or less deliberation. In this point of view, the legislative power and the military power form the two extremes; the first admitting the greatest deliberation, the second demanding the greatest celerity. As to the dissolution of the government, that is an evil only upon one or the other of two suppositions:—1st, That the new government is worse than the old one; or 2nd, That the transition from one to the other is marked by calamities and civil wars.

The greatest danger arising from plurality, whether in a tribunal or an administrative council, is the diminution of responsibility. A numerous body can count upon a sort of deference on the part of the public, and allows itself to commit wrongs which an individual administrator would not dare to perpetrate. Where so many share in the act, the odium of it is shifted from one to another, and rests nowhere. All did it; no one avows it. If the censure of the public is excited, the more numerous the censured body is, the more it fortifies itself against external opinion, the more it tends to form a state within a state, a little community which has its own particular spirit, and which protects by its applauses those of its members who encounter the reproaches of the public.

Unity in all cases in which it is possible—that is, in all cases which do not demand a concentration of knowledge and a concurrence of wills, as in a legislative body—unity is advantageous, because it puts the whole responsibility, whether legal or moral, upon the head of an individual. He does not share the honour of his actions with anybody, and he bears the whole burden of the blame; he sees himself alone against all, having no other support but the integrity of his conduct, no other defence but the general esteem. Though he were not honest by inclination, he would become so, as it were, in spite of himself, by means of a position in which his interest is inseparable from his duty.

Besides, unity in subordinate employments is a certain means of discovering in a short time the real capacity of individuals. A narrow and unsound judgment may conceal itself a long while, amid a numerous company; but if it acts alone, and upon a public theatre, its insufficiency is soon unmasked. Men of moderate or small talents, always ready to solicit places where they can take refuge under the wing of some able assistant, would be afraid to expose themselves to a dangerous career, in which they would soon betray their want of ability.

But there are some cases in which it is possible to unite the advantages of a collective body with the responsibility of a single person.

In subordinate councils, there is always an individual who presides, and upon whom the principal confidence rests. Let him have associates, in order that he may profit by their advice, and that there may be witnesses against him, in case he abuses his trust. But these purposes do not require that his associates should be equal to him in authority, nor even that they should have the right of voting. It is only necessary that the chief should be obliged to communicate to them all that he intends to do, and that each councillor should make a declaration in writing touching each administrative act, expressing an approval of it or a disapproval. This communication ought generally to take place before the issue of orders for carrying his designs into execution; but in those cases which require an extraordinary despatch, it would be enough were it made immediately after. Would not such an arrangement obviate, in general, the danger of dissensions and delays?

III. *Putting the Power of Removal into different hands from the Power of Appointment.*—This idea is borrowed from an ingenious pamphlet published in America, in 1778,* by a member of the convention appointed to examine the form of government proposed for the state of Massachusetts.

Our pride is interested in not condemning a man of our own choice. Independently of affection, a superior will be less disposed to hear complaints against an officer of his own appointment, than against an indifferent person, and will have a pre-

* Reprinted in *Almon's Remembrancer*, No. 84, p. 223.

judice of self-love in his favour. This consideration will help to explain those abuses of power, so common in monarchies, where a subaltern is intrusted with great authority, of which he is not obliged to render any account, except to the very person who gave him his office.

In popular elections, the part which each individual has in the nomination of a magistrate, is so very trifling, that this kind of illusion does not exist.

In England, the choice of ministers belongs to the king; but the parliament has the actual right of dismission, whenever a majority votes against them. However, this is only an indirect application of the principle.

IV. *Not permitting Governors to remain a long time in the same Districts.*—This principle has a particular application to important commands in distant provinces, and especially those detached from the body of the empire.

A governor armed with great power, if he is allowed time for it, may attempt to establish his independence. The longer he remains in office, the more can he strengthen himself by creating a party of his own, or by uniting himself to one of the parties which existed before him. Thence originates oppression towards some, and partiality towards others. And though he has no party, he may be guilty of a thousand abuses of authority, without any one daring to complain to the sovereign. The duration of his power gives birth to fears or hopes, both of which equally favour him. He makes himself creatures, who look up to him as the sole distributor of favours; while those who suffer, fear to suffer more if they offend a ruler who is likely to retain his power for a long time.

The disadvantage of rapid changes consists in removing a man from his employment so soon as he has acquired the knowledge and experience of affairs. New men are liable to commit faults of ignorance. This inconvenience would be palliated by the establishment of a subordinate and permanent council, which should keep up the course and routine of affairs. What you gain is the diminution of a power, which may be turned against yourself; what you risk is a diminution in the skill with which the office is executed. There is no parity between these dangers, when revolt is the evil apprehended.

To avoid giving umbrage to individuals, this arrangement ought to be permanent. The change, at regular periods, should be regarded as fixed and necessary. If it were limited to particular cases, it might serve to provoke the evil which it is intended to prevent.

The danger of revolt on the part of provincial governors is unknown except in feeble and badly constituted governments. In the Roman empire, from Cæsar down to Augustulus, we see a constant succession of rebellious governors and generals. This was not owing to any neglect of the precaution here proposed, for new appointments were frequent; but because the application of it was not judicious, or because there was a want of vigilance and firmness, or to some other cause of a similar kind.

The want of a permanent arrangement of this sort, is plainly the cause of the continual revolutions to which the Turkish empire is subject; and nothing more evidently shows the stupidity of that barbarous court.

If there is any European government which ought to adopt this policy, it is Spain in her American, and England in her East Indian establishments.

In the more civilized states of Christendom, nothing is more uncommon than the revolt of a governor. That of Prince Gagarin, Governor of Siberia, under Peter I., is, I believe, the only example that can be cited in the two last centuries, and that happened in an empire which had not yet lost its Asiatic character. The revolutions which have broken out in Europe have originated from a more powerful and a more respectable principle, opinions, public feeling, the love of liberty.*

V. *Renewal of the Governing Bodies by Rotation.*—The reasons for not allowing a provincial governor to remain a long time in office, all apply with still more force to a council or a directory. Make them permanent, and if they agree among themselves with

* This principle has been judiciously adopted as respects the stipendiary magistrates in the British West Indies. They remain in one district only for a limited time.—*Translator.*

respect to the generality of their measures, it is probable that among those measures there will be many of which the object is to promote their own interest or that of their friends, at the expense of the community. If they disagree, and are afterwards reconciled, it is probable that the public will pay the cost of their reconciliation. On the other hand, if a certain number are dismissed at regular periods, if there are abuses, you have a chance to see them reformed by the new comers, before they have been long enough in office to be corrupted by their associates. A part should always be left, so that the course of affairs may go on without interruption. Ought the part reserved to be larger or smaller than the part renewed? If it is larger, there is reason to fear that the old system of corruption may be still kept up in full vigour; if it is smaller, there is reason to fear that a good system of administration may be embarrassed by capricious innovations. However this may be, it is plain that the mere right of renewal will hardly ever answer its purpose, especially if the power of filling vacancies belongs to the body itself. This right would never be exercised, except upon extraordinary occasions.

Ought those whose places are vacated to be ineligible for a time or for ever? If it is only for a time, it will presently happen that at the end of that time they will always be re-elected, and the council will become a close body. If they are never re-eligible, the community will be deprived of the talents and experience of its ablest servants. All things considered, this means seems to be only an imperfect substitute for others which will be presently mentioned, and especially for publicity in all proceedings and accounts.

The arrangement of rotation was long ago adopted in England by the great companies of commerce, and some years since it was introduced into the direction of the East India Company.

This political view is not the only one which rotation in office has been intended to answer. It has been often introduced for the mere object of producing a more equal distribution of the privileges which appertain to office.

Harrington's celebrated treatise on politics, entitled *Oceana*, depends almost entirely upon a system of rotation among the members of the government. Harrington was a man of talent, but one who did not grasp the whole science of government. Having seized a single idea he developed it, applied it to everything, and saw nothing beyond it. So it is in medicine: the less the extent of the art is perceived the more one is inclined to believe in an elixir of life, a universal remedy, a marvellous secret. Classification is useful in order to extend the attention successively to every means.

VI. *The Reception of Secret Informations.*—Everybody knows that at Venice secret informations were admitted. There were boxes placed here and there around the palace of St. Mark, the contents of which were regularly examined by the state inquisitors. It is pretended that in consequence of these anonymous accusations persons were seized, imprisoned, sent into exile, or even punished with death without any further proof If this be true, then there was nothing more salutary or more reasonable than the first part of the institution, nothing more pernicious and abominable than the second. The arbitrary tribunal of the inquisitors has cast a merited disgrace upon the Venetian government, which must have been wise in other respects, since it maintained itself for so long a time in a state of tranquillity and prosperity.

It is a great misfortune that a good institution should have been connected with a bad one; for all minds have not the prismatic power of disuniting good from evil. Where would be the harm of receiving secret informations, even though they were anonymous in the first instance? Certainly one hair of a single head ought not to be touched upon the mere ground of a secret information, nor should the slightest inquietude be given to a single individual; but, with this restriction, why forego the advantage of such informations? The magistrate can judge whether the object denounced merits his attention. If it does not merit it he need do nothing in the matter. But, if it seems to be of importance, let him give notice to the informer to present himself in person. After examining the facts, if the informer is found to be mistaken, he can be dismissed with praise for his good intentions, and his name may be kept secret. If the informer has brought a charge wilfully and maliciously false, his name and his accusation ought to be communicated to the party accused. If the denunciation is well founded, let a judicial prosecution be commenced, and let the informer be obliged to appear and give his evidence in public.

If it be asked upon what principle such an institution can be useful, the answer is, precisely on the principle of the vote by ballot. In the course of the prosecution the defendant ought certainly to be informed what witnesses will testify against him; but where is the necessity of his knowing it before the prosecution is begun? In that case a witness who may have something to fear on the part of the defendant, would not be willing to expose himself to a certain inconvenience for the chance of rendering a doubtful service to the public. Hence it is that offences so frequently remain unpunished, because no one is willing to make personal enemies without any certainty of serving the public.

I have enumerated this means under the head of abuses of authority, because it is against men in place that its efficacy is most marked; since, in that case, the supposed power of the delinquent is an additional weight in the balance of dissuasive motives.

The resolution to receive secret and even anonymous informations would be good for nothing, unless it were publicly known; but once known, the fear of these informations would soon render the occasions of them more rare, and would diminish their number. And upon whom would the fear fall? Only upon the guilty, and upon those who were plotting to become so; for with publicity of procedure, innocence could never be in danger; and the malice of false accusers would be confounded and punished.

VII. *The Right of Petitioning the Supreme Authority.*—Though informations reached only the minister, they would have their use; but to insure their utility, it is essential that they should come to the knowledge of the sovereign.

The great Frederic received letters, like a private individual, from the meanest of his subjects, and the answer was often written with his own hand. This fact would be incredible were it not perfectly well attested. But we are not to conclude from this example that the same thing is possible in all governments.

In England, every one has a right to present a petition to the king; but the fate of these petitions, handed the same moment to a gentlemen in waiting, has become proverbial; they serve the maids of honour for hair-papers. It may well be imagined, after this, that these petitions are not very frequent; but neither are they very necessary in a country where the subject is protected by laws which do not depend upon the sovereign. There are other means for a private man to obtain justice; there are other channels of information for the prince. It is in absolute monarchies that it is essential to maintain a communication, constantly open, between the subjects and the monarch; it is necessary that the subject may be sure of protection; it is necessary to assure the monarch against being duped by his ministers.

The people may be called *canaille*, *populace*, or what you will; but the prince who refuses to hear the lowest individual of that populace, so far from augmenting his power by doing so, in fact diminishes it. From that moment he loses the capacity of self-direction, and becomes an instrument in the hands of those who call themselves his servants. He may imagine that he does as he pleases, that he determines for himself; but in fact, it is they who determine for him; for to determine all the causes of a man's actions, is to determine all his actions. He who does not see and does not understand, except as it pleases those who surround him, is subject to all the impulses which they choose to give.

To put an unlimited confidence in his ministers, is to put an unlimited confidence in those who have the greatest interest to abuse it, and the greatest facility for doing so.

As to the minister himself, the more honest he is, the less will he need such a confidence; and it may be affirmed without paradox, that the more he deserves it, the less he will desire to possess it.

VIII. *Liberty of the Press.*—Hear advice from every quarter, and you may be the better for it; you cannot be the worse. Such is the decision of simple good sense. To establish the freedom of the press, is to admit the advice of everybody. It is true that upon most occasions the public judgment is heard, not before the measure is determined upon, but only after it is executed. Still, this judgment is always useful as regards all measures of legislation which can be rectified, and all executive acts which are of a nature to be repeated. The best advice given to a minister in a private manner may be thrown away; but good advice given to the public, if it does not avail at one time, may avail at another; if it does not avail to-day, it may avail to-morrow; if it is not presented in a becoming shape, it may receive from another hand ornaments that will make it attractive. Instruction is a seed which requires to be planted in a great variety of soils, and to be cultivated with patience, because its fruits are often a long time in ripening.

Freedom of the press is much more powerful than the right of petition in freeing the sovereign from the control of favourites. Whatever may be his discernment in the choice of his ministers, he can only select from a small number of candidates, whom the chances of birth and fortune present to his choice. It may be reasonably supposed that there are other men more enlightened than these; and the greater power he attains of knowing such men, the more he increases his power and his liberty of selection.

But opinions may be given with insolence and passion; instead of limiting itself to the examination of measures, criticism is extended to persons. And in fact, how much address is necessary to keep these two things distinct? How can a measure be censured without attacking, to a certain extent, the judgment or the probity of its author? This is the stumbling-block; this is the reason why the liberty of the press is as uncommon as its advantages are manifest. All the fears of self-love are against it. Yet Joseph II. and Frederic II. had the magnanimity to establish it. It exists in Sweden; it exists in England; it might exist everywhere, with such modifications as would prevent its greatest abuses.

If, according to the usages of the government, or owing to particular circumstances, the sovereign cannot admit a free examination of his administrative acts, he ought at least to permit the examination of the laws. Though he claims for himself the privilege of infallibility, he need not extend it to his predecessors. If he is so jealous of the supreme power as to extort respect for everything that has been touched by the royal sceptre, he might at least allow a free discussion of merely scientific subjects, such as principles of law, of procedure, and of subaltern administration.

Even granting that the liberty of the press may have inconveniences, as respects pamphlets and handbills which may be scattered among the people, and addressed to the ignorant part of a nation as well as to the enlightened, the same reason cannot apply to serious and lengthy works, to books which can have but a certain class of readers, and which, as they are unable to produce an immediate effect, always afford opportunity for preparing an antidote.

Under the old French regime, it was enough that a book of moral science was printed at Paris, to inspire a prejudice against it. The *Instructions* of the Empress of Russia to the Assembly of Deputies, respecting the compilation of a code of laws, were prohibited in France. The style and the sentiments of that performance appeared too popular to be tolerated in the French monarchy.

It is true that in France, as elsewhere, negligence and inconsistency palliated the evils of despotism. A foreign title served as a passport to genius. The rigour of the censorship only availed to transfer the trade in books to the bordering states, and to render more bitter the satire it was intended to suppress.

IX. *Publication of the Reasons and Facts on which the Laws and Administrative Acts are founded.*—This is a necessary part of a generous and magnanimous policy, and an indispensable attendant upon the liberty of the press. The freedom of the press is a debt which rulers owe to the people; to publish the reasons of their laws and acts is a debt they owe to themselves. If the government disdains to inform the nation of its motives upon important occasions, it thereby announces that it chooses to owe everything to force, and that it counts as nothing the opinions of its subjects.

The partisan of arbitrary power will not agree to this. He is unwilling to enlighten the people, while he despises them because they are not enlightened. You are not capable of judging, he says, because you are ignorant; and we will keep you ignorant, that you may not be capable of judging. This is the endless circle in which he moves. What is the consequence of this vulgar policy? Discontent spreads little by little, till at length it becomes general, founded sometimes upon false and exaggerated imputations, which gain credit because they are not examined and discussed. The minister complains of the injustice of the public, without remembering that he has not afforded to it the means to be just, and that a false interpretation of his conduct is a necessary consequence of the mystery with which it is covered. To be systematic and consistent, there are but two ways of acting with men,—absolute secrecy, or perfect frankness: the complete exclusion of the people from the knowledge of affairs, or making that knowledge as thorough as possible; preventing them from forming any judgment, or putting them into a condition to form the most enlightened judgment; to treat them like children, or to treat them like men. Between these two plans, a choice must be made.

The first of these plans was followed by the priests in ancient Egypt, by the Brahmins in Hindostan, by the Jesuits in Paraguay. The second is established by practice in England, and by law in the United States of America. The greater part of European governments float incessantly between one and the other, without daring to attach themselves exclusively to either; and they are constantly in contradiction with themselves, from a desire to have industrious and enlightened subjects, and from a fear of encouraging a spirit of examination and discussion.

In many branches of administration it would be useless, and it might be dangerous, to publish the reasons of measures beforehand. But those cases ought to be distinguished in which it is necessary to enlighten public opinion, to prevent it from being misled. In matters of legislation, this principle is always applicable. It may be laid down as a general rule that a law ought never to be made without some reason expressed or understood. For what is a good law but a law for which good reasons can be given? Of course, there must have been some reason, good or bad, for making it, since there is no effect without a cause. But oblige a minister to give his reasons, and he will be ashamed not to have good ones to give; he will be ashamed to offer you false coin if obliged to present a touch-stone along with it, by which it can be tried.

This is a means by which a sovereign may continue to reign after death. If there are good reasons for his laws, he gives them a support which cannot fail. His successors will be obliged to maintain them through a feeling of self-respect; and the more good he has done in his lifetime, the more will he contribute to the happiness of posterity.

X. *To forbid all Arbitrary Proceedings.*—"Clotaire made a law," says Montesquieu, "that no person accused of crime should be condemned without a hearing; a law which indicates a contrary practice in some particular case, or among some barbarous people."—*Spirit of Laws*, chap. xii.

Montesquieu did not dare to tell the whole. Did he write that passage without recollecting the *Lettres de Cachet*, and the administration of the police, such as it existed in his times? A *lettre de cachet* may be defined, an order to punish without proof for an act forbidden by no law.

It was in France and Venice that this abuse was carried to the highest pitch. These two governments, mild in other respects, gained themselves a very bad reputation by this piece of folly. They exposed themselves to imputations which were often unfounded, and to the re-action of alarm: for there are precautions which, by the terror they inspire, produce the very danger they aim to prevent. Behave well, it is said, and the government will not be your enemy. Perhaps so; but how can I be certain of it? I am hated by the minister, or by his valet, or by his valet's valet. If I am not to-day, I may be to-morrow, or somebody else may be, and I may be taken for that somebody else. It is not my conduct upon which my safety depends; it is the opinion of my conduct entertained by men more powerful than I. Under Louis XV., *lettres de cachet* were an article of trade, sold by ministers and mistresses to gratify private hatreds. If that could happen under a government which had the reputation of mildness, what fruits of such a law might we expect in less civilized countries? If justice and humanity have not influence enough, the pride of governments, at least, ought to induce them to abolish such remnants of barbarity.

Such expedients may be palmed off under the cover of maxims of state; but lately this pretext has lost its magic. The first thought they suggest is the idea of the incapacity and weakness of those who employ them. If you dared to hear what this prisoner has to say, you would not shut his mouth; if you compel him to be silent, it is a proof that you fear him.

XI. *The Exercise of Power according to certain Rules and Formalities.*—This is another regulation with respect to subordinate officers, not less applicable to absolute monarchies than to mixed governments. If the sovereign thinks it for his interest to be independent of the laws, there is no reason for extending the same independence to all his agents.

The laws which limit subordinate officers in the exercise of their power, may be divided into two classes: to the first class belong those laws which limit the cases in which the exercise of such or such a power is permitted; to the second, those which determine the formalities according to which its exercise is to be regulated. These cases and these formalities ought to be specifically enumerated in the law; and this being done, the citizens ought to be informed that these are the cases, and the only cases, in which their security, their liberty, their property, or their honour can be brought into danger. Thus, the first law at the very beginning of a code ought to be a general law in behalf of liberty, a law which restrains delegated powers, and limits their exercise to such or such particular occasions, for such or such specific causes.

Such was the intention of *Magna Charta*, and such would have been its effect, but for the unlucky want of precision in some of its expressions, as *lex terræ*, &c.; for all was made to depend upon an imaginary law, which restored all to uncertainty, since those in search of that law always referred back to the customs of ancient times, and sought examples and authorities among the very abuses which it was intended to prevent.

XII. *The Establishment of the Right of Association, that is, of Assemblies of the Citizens to express their sentiments and their wishes upon Public Measures.*—Among the rights which a people ought to reserve, when they establish a government, this is the chief, since it is the foundation of all the rest. Yet it is hardly necessary to mention it here, for to the people who possess it, it needs no recommendation, and those who possess it not, have but slight hope of obtaining it,—for what can induce their governments ever to grant it?

At the first view, this right of association seems incompatible with government; and it is admitted that to establish this right as a means of keeping the government under, would be absurd and contradictory. But the intention is very different. If the smallest act of violence is committed by one or more members of the association, punish it as if it had been committed by any other individual. If you perceive that you are not powerful enough to punish it, it is a proof that the association has made a progress it could not have made without a just cause; so that in fact it is either not an evil, or a necessary evil. It is taken for granted that you have a public force, an authority organized in all its parts; if, then, these associations have become strong enough to intimidate you, in the midst of all your regular means of power, if no associations have been formed upon your side, yours, who have so many means at your command to obtain a superiority in that respect,—is it not an infallible sign that the calm and considerate judgment of the nation is against you? This being granted, what reason can be given for keeping the government in the same state,—for not satisfying the public wish? I know of none. Doubtless, a nation, since it is composed of men, does not possess the privilege of infallibility; a nation may be deceived, as well as its rulers, as to its true interests; nothing is more certain; but if a great majority of the nation is seen upon one side, and its government upon the other, may it not be presumed, in the first instance, that the general discontent is well founded?

Far from being a cause of insurrection, I look upon these associations as one of the most powerful means of preventing that evil. Insurrections are the convulsions of weakness, finding strength in a momentary despair. They are the efforts of men who are not allowed to express their feelings, or whose projects could not succeed if they were known. Plots which are in opposition to the general sentiment of the people can only succeed by surprise and by violence. Those who plan them cannot hope for success, except by forcible means. But those who believe that the people are on their side, those who flatter themselves that the general opinion will secure their triumph, why should they use violence? Why expose themselves to manifest danger without advantage? I am persuaded that men who had a perfect liberty of association, and who could exercise it under protection of the laws, would never have recourse to insurrection, except in those rare and unfortunate cases in which rebellion has become necessary; and whether associations be permitted or forbidden, open and general rebellions never will take place until they are necessary.

The associations which were openly entered into in Ireland in 1780 did not produce any evil, and even served to maintain tranquillity and security, though that country, scarce semi-civilized, was distracted by all the possible causes of a civil war.

I even believe that associations might be permitted, and might become one of the principal means of government, in the most absolute monarchies. This kind of states are more troubled than others by risings and revolts. Everything is done by sudden movements. Associations would prevent these disorders. If the subjects of the Roman Empire had been in the habit of combining together, the empire and the lives of the emperors would not have been constantly put up at auction by the Prætorian Guards.

For the rest, I know very well that slaves cannot be allowed to assemble. Too much injustice has been done them not to have everything to fear from their ignorance or their resentment. It is not in the American islands, it is not in Mexico, that the people can be armed and allowed to form associations; but there are states in Europe in which this strong and generous policy might be safely adopted.

I admit that there is a degree of ignorance which renders associations dangerous. This proves that ignorance is a great evil; it does not prove that associations are not a great good. Besides, the measure itself may operate as an antidote against its own bad effects. In proportion as an association extends, the foundation on which it rests is examined, the public is enlightened, and the government may avail itself of all these means to spread the knowledge of facts and to dissipate errors. Liberty and instruction go hand in hand; liberty facilitates the progress of knowledge, and knowledge restrains the extravagancies of liberty.

I do not see why the establishment of this right need give disquiet to governments. There is no government which does not fear the people; which does not think it necessary to consult their will, and to accommodate itself to their opinions; and it would seem that the most despotic are the most timid. What sultan is so tranquil, so secure in the exercise of his power, as a British king? The janissaries and the populace inspire the same fear in the Seraglio that the Seraglio inspires among the janissaries and the populace. At London, the voice of the people makes itself be heard by lawful assemblages; at Constantinople, it bursts forth in outrage. At London, the people express their feelings in petitions; and at Constantinople by setting the city on fire.

Poland, perhaps, may be brought forward as an objection—a country in which associations seem to have produced so many evils. But that is a mistake. The Polish associations sprung from anarchy, they did not produce it. Besides, in speaking of this means as a restraint upon government, there is supposed to be a government established; it is offered as a remedy, not as an independent means.

It may even be added, that in states where this right exists, circumstances may occur in which it will be well,—not to suspend it entirely,—but to regulate its exercise. There is no need of an absolute and inflexible rule. We have seen the British Parliament, during the late war with France, restrain the right of assembling, and forbid meetings for a political object unless that object were publicly announced, and unless the meeting were held under the authority of a magistrate who had power to dissolve it; and these restrictions were imposed at the very time that the citizens were called upon to form military corps for the defence of the state, and whilst the government announced the most noble confidence in the general spirit of the nation.

Though these restraints have ceased, everything remains in the same condition; and it might be supposed that the restrictive law still existed. The reason is, that a people sure of its rights enjoys them with moderation and tranquillity. If they are ever abused, it is because they are thought to be in danger. The precipitation of the people is the effect of their fear.

CHAPTER XXII.

Means of Diminishing the Bad Effect of Offences. General Result and Conclusion.

The general result of the principles laid down in this treatise upon the subject of penal legislation, offers a happy perspective, and well-founded hopes of diminishing offences and of diminishing punishments. At first, this subject presents to the mind only sombre ideas, images of suffering and of terror. But while occupied with this class of evils, painful feelings soon give place to agreeable and consoling sentiments, when it is discovered that the human heart is not corrupted by any inherent and incurable perversity; that the multiplicity of offences is principally owing to errors of legislation easy to be reformed; and that even the evil that results from them is susceptible of being repaired in various ways.

This is the great problem of penal legislation:—1st, To reduce all the evil of offences, as far as possible, to that kind which can be cured by a pecuniary compensation. 2nd, To throw the expense of this cure upon the authors of the evil, or, in their default, upon the public. What can be done in this respect is much more than is generally imagined.

The word *cure* is employed in order to present the party injured, whether it be an individual or the community, under the character of a patient suffering from a disorder. The comparison is just, and it points out the procedure best adapted to the end in view, without the intermixture of popular passions, and of antipathies, which ideas of crime are but too apt to awaken, even in legislators themselves.

There are three principal sources of crime,—incontinence, hatred, and rapacity.

The offences which spring from *incontinence* are hardly of a nature to be cured by a pecuniary compensation. This remedy may apply to certain cases of seduction, and even of conjugal infidelity; but it does not cure that part of the evil which consists in dishonour and the disturbance of family peace.

The evil effects of other offences are more surely arrested in proportion as the offences themselves are more clearly proved; but it is to be observed as a remarkable and important singularity, that offences of incontinence only become hurtful in proportion as they become known. A good citizen should look upon it as his duty to make known an act of fraud; but he ought to be very much on his guard how he publishes to the world the secret faults of love. To conceal a fraud is to become a party to it; to betray to the public an unknown weakness is to do an evil without compensation; a wound is inflicted upon the sensibility of those who are exposed to shame, but the thing done is not repaired. I count among the establishments which do honour to the humanity of the present age, those secret asylums for accouchement, those foundling hospitals which have so often prevented the fatal effects of despair, by covering with the shade of mystery the consequences of a momentary error. The rigour which declares against this indulgence is founded upon the ascetic principle.

The offences which spring from *hatred* are often of such a kind that a pecuniary compensation can hardly be applied to them. Compensation, indeed, if in the case of such offences it can take place at all, is seldom complete; it cannot undo what is done; it cannot restore a lost limb; it cannot give back a son to his father, a father to his family; but it may act upon the condition of the party injured; it may furnish him a portion of good in consideration of a portion of evil; and, in regulating the account of his prosperity, it puts an item on the favourable side to balance an item on the other.

With respect to these offences, it is an essential observation that they diminish from day to day, by the progress of civilization. It is an admirable thing to observe, in the greater part of European states, how few crimes are produced by the irascible passions, so natural to man, and so violent in the infancy of society. What an object of emulation for those tardy governments which have not yet reached this degree of police, and among whom the sword of justice has not yet been able to banish the stilettoes of revenge!

Rapacity is an inexhaustible source of offences. This is the enemy, always active, always ready to seize every advantage, against which a continual war must be carried on; and this war demands a peculiar kind of tactics, the principles of which have not been well understood.

Be indulgent to this passion so long as it confines itself to the use of peaceable means; but be careful to deprive it of all its unlawful gains. Grow severe towards it in proportion as it breaks out in overt acts, and has recourse to menace and to violence. But still reserve means for further severity in case it is guilty of such atrocities as arson and murder. It is in the skilful gradation of these preventive means that the penal art consists.

Do not forget that all penal police is but a choice of evils. Let the wise administrator of punishments always keep the balance in his hand, and in his zeal to prevent trifling evils let him avoid the imprudence of himself producing great ones. Death is almost always a remedy which is unnecessary or inefficacious. It is not necessary as to those whom an inferior punishment might deter from crime, or whom imprisonment might restrain; it has no efficacy as to those who throw themselves, so to speak, in its way as a refuge against despair. The policy of a legislator who punishes every offence with death, is like the pusillanimous terror of a child who crushes the insect he does not dare to look at. But if the circumstances of society, if the frequency of a great offence demand this terrible means, be careful, without aggravating the torments of death, to give it an aspect more dreadful than nature gives it; surround it with mournful accessories, with emblems of crime, and the tragic pomp of ceremony.

But be slow to believe in this necessity for death. By disusing it as a punishment you will prevent it as a crime; for when men are placed between two offences it is desirable to give them a sensible interest not to commit the greater. It is desirable to convert the assassin into a thief; and to give him a reason for preferring a reparable to an irreparable offence.

That which can be repaired is comparatively trifling. Everything that can be made up for by a pecuniary indemnity, may soon become as if it had never been; for if the injured individual always receives an equivalent compensation, the alarm caused by the offence ceases altogether, or is reduced to its lowest term.

It is an object highly desirable that the fund of compensation due for offences should be amassed from among the delinquents themselves, either by being levied upon their property, or obtained from the profits of their compulsory labour. If this were so, security would be the inseparable companion of innocence; and grief and anguish would fall exclusively to the lot of the disturbers of social order. Such is the point of perfection to which we ought to aspire, though we can only expect to reach it slowly and by continuous efforts. It is enough for me to have pointed out the end. The happiness of attaining it will be the reward of persevering and enlightened governments.

This means failing, it is necessary to provide compensation either from the public treasury, or by means of *private insurances.*

The imperfections of our laws, in this behalf, are very flagrant. If an offence is committed, those who have suffered from it, either in their persons or their fortune, are abandoned to their fate. But society, which they have contributed to uphold, and which has undertaken to protect them, owes them an indemnity.

When an individual, even in his own case, prosecutes a criminal at his own expense, he is not less the defender of the state than he who fights its foreign enemies: the losses which he sustains in defending the public ought to be made up for at the public expense.

But when an innocent person has suffered by mistake of the courts, when he has been arrested, detained, subjected to suspicion, condemned to all the misery of a trial and a long confinement, it is not only for his sake, but for her own, that Justice should grant him compensation. Established to repair injuries, does she desire an exclusive privilege to injure?

Governments have made no provision for any of these indemnities. In England, some voluntary associations have been formed to supply this deficiency. If the institution of insurance is good in one case, it is good in all, with the precautions necessary to prevent negligence and fraud.*

The inconvenience of exposure to fraud is common to all funds, public and private. It may diminish the advantage of insurances without destroying it. Fruit-trees are still cultivated, though they are liable to perish by a thousand accidents. *Monts-de-piété* † have succeeded in many countries. An establishment of this kind, set up in London in the middle of the last century, failed at the beginning, through the dishonesty of the directors, and this theft left a prejudice which has prevented any subsequent attempt of the sort. According to the same logic, it might be concluded that vessels are bad instruments of war, because the *Royal George*, whose ports had been left open, sunk at her moorings.

Insurances against offences may have two objects:—1st, To create a fund to indemnify the parties injured, in case the delinquent is unknown or insolvent; 2nd, To defray, in the first

* Insurance is good, because the insurer has volunteered to sustain the loss, considering the premium he receives as equivalent to the danger he runs. But this remedy is imperfect in itself, because the premium, which is a certain loss, must always be paid, to guarantee one's self against a loss which is uncertain. In this point of view, it is desirable that all unforeseen losses, which may fall upon individuals without their fault, were made up at the public expense. The more numerous the contributors, the less sensibly do any of them feel the contribution. It is to be observed, on the other hand, that a public fund is more exposed to fraud, to peculation, and to loss, than a private fund. Losses which fall directly upon individuals give all possible force to motives of vigilance and economy.

† This was the name given to a kind of banks established in different parts of Europe, for the purpose of lending money to the poor upon pledges, without interest.—*Translator.*

instance, the expense of judicial prosecutions in favour of the poor. This payment might be extended to cases purely civil.

But the method of these indemnities would be foreign to the subject of this treatise; its principles have been explained elsewhere, and I must here confine myself to the announcement of the general result of this work. It is this: *That by good laws almost all offences may be reduced to acts which can be repaired by a simple pecuniary compensation, and thus the evil of offences may be almost wholly done away.*

At first, this result, simply announced, does not strike the imagination; it must be meditated upon before its importance can be perceived, and its weight be felt. It is not the brilliant society of fashion that can be interested by a formula almost arithmetic in expression. It is offered, statesmen, to you! It is yours to judge it!

The science of which the basis has been investigated in this work can be pleasing only to elevated souls who are warmed with a passion for the public good. It has no connection with that trickish and subversive kind of politics which prides itself upon clandestine projects, which acquires a glory composed wholly of human misery, which sees the prosperity of one nation in the abasement of another, and which mistakes convulsions of government for conceptions of genius. We are here employed upon the greatest interests of humanity; the art of forming the manners and the character of nations; of raising to its highest point the security of individuals; and of deriving results equally beneficial from different forms of government. Such is the object of this science; frank and generous; asking only for light; wishing nothing exclusive; and finding no means so sure to perpetuate the benefits it confers as to share them with the whole family of nations.

APPENDIX

'Preliminary Discourse. By M. Dumont'

From the second edition of *Traités de législation civile et pénale* (1820),
translated by John Neal, *Principles of Legislation* (1830), pp.175–93.

The works contained in these three volumes are only a part of those which I have collected from the manuscripts of Mr. Bentham, and which I announced five years ago, in the *Bibliothèque Britannique*. I have continued my labour, and the whole are now about to appear in succession.

If, in preparing these manuscripts, I had only to make a simple translation, I should have been more easy about the result. But I am not in a situation so fitted to inspire me with confidence. I owe it to the public not to conceal what is altogether my own in the compilation; and I owe it to the author to declare that he has yielded to the solicitations of friendship, and that he has often committed to me with regret, works that were unfinished, and sometimes materials that were not even arranged.

In giving a general idea of what more particularly concerns myself in this enterprise, I must begin with a declaration, which ought to protect me as well from unjust reproach, as from unmerited praise. I beg leave to say that I have neither part nor share in the composition of these different works: they belong to the author, and to him alone. The more lightly I prize them, the more eager I am to disavow an honor which would be a usurpation as contrary to the faith of friendship as to my own character. I am aware that this declaration, which I owe to myself, would be superfluous, if there were none but philosophical readers; such readers would recognize throughout all the diversity of these writings, the work of the same hand, the unity of plan, the original genius – as profound and analytical in the whole of the design, as in the execution of the parts.

My work, which is of a subordinate character, has only been applied to details. It was necessary to make a choice among a great number of various readings, to suppress repetitions, to clear up some obscurities, to bring together all that belong to the same subject, and to fill up the chasms which the author had left in the heat of the composition. I have had more to retrench than to add, more to abridge than to extend. The mass of manuscripts which have passed through my hands, and which I have had to decypher and compare, is considerable. I have had much to do for the uniformity of style and in the way of correction; little or nothing for the ideas. Nothing but good husbandry was required for the profusion of wealth that was committed to my care; and I have neglected no pains in my stewardship to make its value known and to put it in circulation.

The changes that I have had to make have varied according to the nature of the manuscript. When I have found several relating to the same subject, but composed at different periods and with different views, I have tried to reconcile them to each other, and so to unite them as to make but one whole. Where the author had discarded something that grew up out of the circumstances of the day, and which would not be interesting nor even intelligible now, I have not always been willing to have it utterly lost, but have rescued, as it were from the ruins, whatever was capable of being preserved. Where he had given himself up to abstractions that were too profound, or to metaphysics that were, I will not say too subtle, but too dry, I have tried to give more development to the ideas, and to render them more familiar by applications, by facts and by examples; and I have even permitted myself to scatter a few ornaments over the field of research as I proceeded. I have had to make up some entire chapters, but when I have done so, it has always been after the indications of the author and by the help of his notes; and the difficulty I have experienced when trying to supply his deficiencies would have led me back to a modest opinion of myself, even if I had been tempted astray.

His *Introduction of the Principles of Morals and Legislation*, which is regarded by a small number of enlightened judges as one of those extraordinary works that form an era and a revolution in science, in spite of its philosophical merit, or peradventure because of that merit, produced little or no sensation, and continued almost unknown to the public; although in England it is more common than elsewhere, to forgive a useful book for not being an easy and agreeable book. In making use of several chapters of that work for the *General Principles of Legislation*, I have tried to avoid what interfered with its success – forms that were too scientific, subdivisions that were too numerous, and an analysis that was too abstract. I have not translated the words; I have translated the ideas. I have made in some respects an abridgment, and in others a commentary; but in doing this, I have been guided by the counsels and indications of the author, in a preface, posterior by many years to the work itself; and I have found in his papers all the additions of any importance, that are assembled here.

In considering how that work, which I thought would be limited to two or three volumes extended itself by degrees, and what a vast field I have gone over, I regret that the undertaking should not have fallen into better hands; but notwithstanding this I venture to congratulate myself on my perseverance; being well convinced that these manuscripts would have remained a long while buried from the light,[1] and that the author, always pressing onward in his career, would never have had either the leisure or the courage to give himself up to the ungrateful task of a general revision.

That ardor to produce and that indifference about publishing, that perseverance in the greatest labors and that disposition to throw them aside at the moment of their completion, are phenomena which require to be explained.

From the time that Mr. Bentham had found the great divisions – the great leading classifications, or provinces of the law, he began to embrace the empire of legislation as a whole, and conceived the magnificent idea of treating it in all its parts. He considered it less as composed of detached fields than as forming one single field. He had before him a general chart of the science, and had formed upon this model the particular charts of the several departments. Thus, the most striking characteristic of his writings is their perfect

[1] Bentham himself says that they never would have seen the light, but for Dumont. See pages 64 and 153. See sketch of Dumont and the Familiar Anecdotes. [Neal's references to his edition of *Principles of Legislation: From the Ms. of Jeremy Bentham; Bencher of Lincoln's Inn. By M. Dumont, Member of the Representative and Sovereign Council of Geneva. Translated from the Second Corrected and Enlarged Edition [Paris 1802]; with Notes and a Biographical Notice of Jeremy Bentham and of M. Dumont. By John Neal.* (Boston: Wells and Lilly-Court-Street [etc.] 1830), pp.64, and 153; 'Sketch of the Life and Character of Stephen Dumont. – By J.C.L. De Sismondi', pp.157–72; and 'Familiar Anecdotes of Mr. Bentham', pp.27–40.]

concordance with each other. I found the earliest full of references to the treatises that were only planned at the time but of which the divisions, the forms, and the principle ideas were already marked out. It is thus that having arranged all his matters by a general plan; every branch of legislation occupies its own particular place, and none is found occupying more than one place in the system. Such order necessarily argues an author who has considered his subject for a long while, and under a variety of aspects, who comprehends it thoroughly, and who has no puerile impatience for renown.

I have seen him throw by a work that was nearly finished, and compose another, to assure himself of the truth of a single proposition, which appeared doubtful to him. A problem in finances has led him back over the whole field of political economy.[2] Some questions of procedure have made him feel the necessity of suspending a work till he had treated of the organization of a judiciary. All this preparatory labour – this labour in the mine, is immense. Without a view of the manuscripts themselves, the catalogues and the synoptical tables, no idea could be formed of it.

But I am not writing a panegyric; and I must acknowledge that the care of arranging and of polishing has few attractions for the peculiar genius of the author. So long as he is impelled by the energy that creates, he feels nothing but the pleasure of composition; but if he pauses to give shape and form, to re-digest, and to finish, he feels nothing but weariness. Let his work be interrupted, and the mischief is incurable; the charm disappears; it is succeeded by disgust; and he is only to be excited by a new object.

The same disposition has prevented him from contributing to the digest that I now offer to the public: it is but rarely that I have been able to obtain either the explanations or the aid that I have needed. It would have been too great a sacrifice to stop in the middle of his career and return upon the footsteps of a period long gone by.

But it is perhaps to this very difficulty that I owe my own perseverance. If I had only had to translate, I should have grown weary of the task; but being left to proceed as I thought proper with the manuscripts, I have been stimulated by an illusion that lasted as

2 See p. 27, where the anecdote is told of him about writing a book in reply to a note from the British minister. It originated in this fact. [Neal's reference to his edition of *Principles of Legislation*, p.27]

long as it could be of any use, and was only dissipated by the completion of the work.

I know not how to give a better general idea of this collection than by a naked enumeration of the treatises out of which it has been composed.

*1. General Principles of Legislation.

*2. Principles of Civil and Criminal Jurisprudence.

*3. Theory of Punishment.

*4. Penal Code.

*5. Theory of Reward.

6. Judiciary Organization.

7. Procedure Code.

1. Evidence; 2. Of the ends to be had in view; 3. Of the successive judicial steps from the commencement of an action to the execution of the sentence; 4. Examination of Jury trial.

*8. Manual of Political economy.

*9. Tactics of Deliberative Assemblies; that is to say, principles that are to be observed in the passing of a law, &c. in a political assembly; of proposing, of deliberating, of voting and of deciding.

Besides these principal works, there are others less considerable, some of which indeed are nothing but pamphlets.

*1. Critical Examination of the Declaration of the Rights of Man.

*2. Of the circumstances of time and place to be considered in the framing of laws.

3. Of offences against religion: offences committed by the abuse of the religious sanction.

4. Of invention in the matter of Legislation.

*5. Of the Panopticon; a house of central-inspection to supersede the common prisons.

*6. Of the promulgation of the laws, and of a promulgation separated from the rationale of the laws.[3]

[3] The works designated by an asterisk in this catalogue have all been published, some in three volumes, and others separately. The *Theory of Punishments and Rewards* appeared at London in two vols. in 1811,* and is now reprinting for Messrs. Bossange at Paris. The *Manual of Political Economy* is incorporated with the *Theory of Rewards*, of which it forms the fourth book, under the title of Encouragements (par rapport à) for industry and commerce. The *Tactics of*

It may appear extraordinary that in so vast an assemblage there is to be found no work upon political constitutions or forms of government.[4] Does the author regard the form as indifferent, or does he think that there is no arriving at certainty on the subject of political powers? Such an opinion would not be very likely to exist in the mind of an English Philosopher, and I may venture to say that it certainly does not in the mind of Mr. Bentham. But he is very far from attaching an exclusive preference to any form of government. He thinks the best constitution for a people is that to which they are accustomed;[5] that happiness is the only *end*, the only object of intrinsic worth, and that political liberty is but a relative good as one of the means to that end. He thinks that a people with good laws, even without any political power, may arrive at a high degree of happiness; and that, on the contrary, with the greatest political power, if they have bad laws, they will be necessarily unhappy.

Deliberative Assemblies and of Political Fallacies, appeared at Geneva in 1816, in two volumes; I have placed it as an appendix to the Critical Examination of the Declaration of the Rights of Man. D. [N indicates a note by Neal; D indicates a note by Dumont].

* In French – it has never been translated into English; nor should it be without the corrections of the author. N.

4 Here M. Dumont alludes only to the manuscripts he had collected. Mr. Bentham had not then come to the *political* division of his labour. His *Constitutional Code*, his letters on the subject of checks and balances have since appeared; and they go to the substance, not merely to the forms of liberty. N.

5 Mr. Bentham *did* think so; but his views are altered, and he is now altogether and most decidedly in favour of a republic. There was a time to be sure, when looking to the mischief that had been produced by change, overthrow and experiment, he was ready to say –

> 'For forms of Government let fools contest;
> That which is best administered is best.'

Of late however he appeals to the growth and history of our United-Republics, and has been most zealously and effectually employed in giving *Constitutional* governments to Europe and to America. Little do we know here, what he and his have done for the liberties of our age. His counsels have been heard throughout Europe, and the greatest statesmen of the day are among his disciples. It may be doubted however whether he is not going too far now. It does not appear very evident to me that a republican form of government would suit every people. They must be prepared for it, educated for it; and they must be surrounded with republican neighbors or separated from danger by impassable barriers; or how are they to carry through their experiments in safety? There is more distinctness and more energy in a despotism; and if the United States were transplanted to the centre of Europe, and surrounded as the

The fundamental vice of theories upon political constitutions is, that people begin by attacking those which exist, and alarming the jealousy of established power – a disposition not favourable to the improvement of the laws.

The only time for attempting with success, any great reform in legislation, is that when the public mind is calm, and the government enjoys the greatest degree of stability.

The object of Mr. Bentham in looking for the cause of our greatest evils in the laws themselves, has been to escape the greatest of all evils, the overthrow of authority, the revolution of property and power. The actual government is in fact the instrument wherewith he endeavours to work;[6] and in showing to all governments the way to self-improvement, he shows them how to prolong their own existence.

His results are applicable to monarchies as well as to Republics. He does not say to the people – Lay hold upon the supreme authority; change the form of the state: He says to the governments of the earth – Understand the maladies that weaken you; study the means of cure. Let your laws be conformable to the wants and the improvements of the age.

states of Europe are, by ambitious, quarrelsome and warlike neighbours, they would probably soon cease to be a republic. They would have to establish fortresses, to keep large armies afoot, to augment the power and stability of their executive, and gradually, as they would be exposed to the intrigue of every neighbouring power, they would be obliged, like Germany and Poland, either to withdraw the election from the hands of the many or to render it less frequent. In a word, the simplicity of a Republic would soon be lost: and our chief-magistrate would soon become, at the best, but a constitutional king. And so too, if Great Britain were transplanted to this New World, – there would soon be a great change in the form of her government. Her expenses would be diminished, her standing armies would disappear, and her fleets and courts, and sinecures would gradually drop off; and after a while, if Mexico did not become a bad neighbour, and if there were no separation of her own territory, she would become either a republic in form or in fact. Her king would be but a president for life (perhaps not even for life) – with some little additional power and prerogative. Would not there be the natural consequences of a change of territory? Let every man judge for himself, and then say whether any one form of government, even though it be *republican*, would be the best for every people. N.

6 Nothing was ever more true than this; and therefore should we look upon Mr. Bentham as a philosopher. He would strengthen the hands of every government on earth by making it just, and thereby giving it a hold upon the affections of the people. It were easier to reform that which they are accustomed to, so as to make it the best they could bear, than it would be to build up one altogether new. N.

Make good laws, civil and penal. Organize the tribunals of justice in such a manner as to inspire the public with confidence. Simplify procedure. Avoid constraint and waste in taxation. Encourage commerce by natural means. Have you not all the same interest in improving the several branches of administration? Appease the dangerous spirit that is spreading among the people, by promoting their happiness. You have the power of originating the laws, and this right alone, if judiciously employed, might be made the safe-guard of every other. It is by opening a career to legitimate hope, that you check the growth of profligate hope.

They who look in these writings for exclusive principles, unfavourable to this or that particular from of government will be disappointed; and they who need the stimulus of declamation or satire will find nothing here to satisfy them. To preserve while correcting, to study circumstances, to sooth the very prejudices of power; to prepare innovation at a distance, so that it may not appear to be innovation; to avoid violent changes, and the sudden shifting of property and power; to reform abuses without injury to actual interests, and without disturbing the natural course of habits and hopes – such are the objects and such the temper of the whole work.

The first part of this collection, entitled the *General Principles of Legislation* is the only one that is prepared partly from the manuscripts, and partly from a printed work of the author. It is a general introduction which includes the fundamental principles of all his writings. If one is master of that, all the others will appear but as natural consequences. The title that I should have chosen, but which I have forborne to give, in consequence of objections that perhaps were well founded, is that of *Logic of Legislation*. It contains the principles of reasoning; it teaches how to employ that principle; it furnishes new instruments of analysis and of moral calculation.

In the physical sciences, the discovery of a new mode of working is always the commencement of a new era. It is thus that the invention of the telescope, led to the science of astronomy. In general when the human mind stops long at the same point, it is because it has completely exhausted it's means of enquiry, and is obliged to wait until some new instrument be discovered for extending its researches and adding to it's power.

But what is properly an instrument in moral science? It is a means of bringing together and of comparing ideas; it is a new method of reasoning. Socrates had one which was suited to him and which was a sort of analysis. To this, Aristotle added a classification: he invented the structure of the syllogism, so ingenious and of so little use. These methods are instruments for the reason, as the rule is for the hand, or the microscope for the eyes. When Bacon gave to his great work the singular title of *Novum Organum*, he considered that philosophical method as a kind of intellectual machine, a logical tool which would improve the art of reasoning and assist in the structure of sciences.

Mr. Bentham has made for himself a system of logic which has its principles, its tables, its catalogues, its classes and its rules; by means of which he appears to me to have converted into a science, certain branches of Morals and of Legislation which till his time had been subject only to the speculations of learning, of eloquence, and of wit.[7]

The author himself is very far from thinking that he owes nothing to his predecessors.

All science is necessarily the work of time. We begin by vague conjectures. We observe a few scattered facts. We amass a great store of erudition in which the true and the false are jumbled together. When in the progress of events we have collected a great number of facts, we begin to perceive analogies; we try to reduce them to a system. The reign of imagination and wit precedes that of reason and science. It was for Descartes to prepare ingenious romances about general nature, before Newton could subject it to certain laws; for Leibnitz and Malebranche to conjure up their shadowy metaphysics, before Locke settled the first facts that now serve for a foundation to that science. Plato and Aristotle preceded Bodin, Grotius, Harrington, Hobbes and Puffendorf, all of whom were but preparatory to the Spirit of Laws: and the Spirit of Laws itself is but intermediate to the point where Legislation is to become a complete and simple system.

The author, in an interesting essay, has indicated the progress and the origin of his principal ideas.

'It is not,' says he, 'in the books of law that I have found the means of invention, or the models of method; it is rather in works on metaphysics, on physics, on natural history and on

[7] Here we have a sample of the rhetoric of the author. *Branches* are converted into a science. [Author of note not identified.]

medicine. In reading some modern treatises of the latter I was struck by the classification of mischiefs and remedies. Might we not carry the same order into legislation? Might not the body politic have its anatomy, its physiology, its nosology, its *materia medica*? What I have found in the Treboniuns, the Coccejiis, the Blackstones, the Vattels, the Pothiers, the Domats is very little: Hume, Helvetius, Linnaeus, Bergman, Cullen, have been more useful to me.'

In the very outset, it was necessary to find some one general principle which might be fixed, and to which the whole process of reasoning might refer. This fixed principle he denominated the *Principle of Utility*. But to do only this was to do nothing; for every body would give the name of *utility* to whatever pleased him; and nothing is ever done, nothing ever proposed by any body without a view to utility – either real or imaginary. It was necessary therefore to give to the term a precise signification; and that was a new task.

The author afterwards separated this true principle from two false principles which were associated with it, and which are the ground-work of all the erroneous systems of Morals and Legislation, that are known. By means of one single distinction, easy to be comprehended, we are enabled to separate truth from error with a degree of ease and certainty hitherto without example.

To get a precise knowledge of the principles of utility, it became necessary to exhibit *all the pleasures and all the pains, in a table;* for they are the first elements – the figures which are to be employed in a moral calculation. As in arithmetic, we proceed upon numbers, the value of which it is necessary to have exactly estimated.

After this, a method was to be contrived for measuring the value of a lot of pleasures or of pains for the purpose of comparing them together with accuracy. Here an error would be of the greatest consequence. The calculation goes back to the first operations in arithmetic. To know the worth of an action, we have only to add together all the pleasures or advantages which result from it; and then to add together all the pains or disadvantages; and to subtract the smaller sum from the larger.

But as the sensibility of mankind is not uniform, and as the same objects affect them more or less, and even differently, the calculation is to be qualified by a new element.

Age, education, rank, fortune, religion, climate, sex, and many other causes have a decided and constant influence. It was therefore necessary to frame an exact table of the *circumstances* which cause the sensibility of men to vary for the purpose of accommodating the means of legislation as far as possible to the diversity of their impressions.

By calculating the advantages and the disadvantages of an act, it was no difficult thing to find the true character of an offence; but the true character being had, the exact heinousness or gravity was to be estimated. And that is what the author has done by analyzing the progress or march of an evil – that is to say, by observing how it affects individuals, how it spreads from the first sufferer to others, and how it is lessened in some cases and aggravated in others by participation.

Having established these principles, whereby the gravity of offences might be weighed, he contrived a classification as new as it was abundant. By this classification we are enabled to see at a glance what they have in common, and in what they differ: we discover some general maxims which apply without exception to such and such kinds of crime. Chaos is no more; ... light spreads, and we get a glimpse of the plan of the Legislator. I might multiply such examples; but these are sufficient to explain what I understand by *logical instruments*, which, though necessary to legislation, have nevertheless been wanting till the present time. This analysis, these catalogues, these classifications, while they help us to work with certainty, are a check upon our oversights, a hindrance to our going astray from first principles, and serve to render the solution of the most difficult problems mechanical. It is in this way that in running over the table of chemical affinities, the physician preserves the connexion of his thoughts and saves time by the promptitude of his comparisons and recollections.

Uniformity of weights and measures might serve as an object of comparison for giving a better idea of Mr. Bentham's object. He felt the necessity of establishing an invariable principle, which might serve as the foundation for a common measure in morals, and which would give the uniformity required by the most important and most difficult problem in philosophy.

What I call the *Variety of weights and measures in morals* is the double diversity which exists, the one in the judgements of men upon actions reputed good or evil, the other in the principles themselves, upon which those judgements are founded. Hence it is that human actions have no fixed and authentic rate of value, and that the moral estimate varies with every people and with every class; and that having no common rule to refer to; those who happen to agree are always ready to disagree, while those who disagree have little chance of being reconciled; each having but his own authority to help him, cannot hope to prevail over his adversary, and a reciprocal accusation of obstinacy or bad faith, terminates almost always a controversy of opinion, by provoking mutual antipathy.

If there exists, as we cannot doubt there does, a common-interest among the community of nations, and throughout the whole human family; – to discover a uniform system of weights and measures in morals is to discover that common-interest; and the work of the legislator would consist in giving it effect by the sanction of penalties and rewards.

That common-interest will not be discovered but by the profound enquirer into the human heart. As we seek for physical truth among the phenomena of nature, so must we seek for moral truth among the opinions of men. An experimental search of this kind, methodically pursued, would give birth to two new sciences; one of which Mr. Bentham calls *Mental Pathology*, the other *Intellectual Dynamics*.

Mental pathology relates to the sensibility of man considered as a passive being, that is to say, as subject to the influence of various objects, which cause in him the various sensations either of pain or pleasure. The author has laid the foundations of the science in the catalogue of pleasures and pains, and in that of the circumstances that influence the sensibility of man.

Dynamics is the science of moving forces; and intellectual dynamics would therefore be the science that teaches the means of operating upon the *active* faculties of man. The object of the legislator being to guide the conduct of the people, he ought to understand all the springs of the will – he ought to study the simple and compound power of all the motives; he ought to know how to regulate them, to combine them, to counteract them, to augment and to lessen their power at pleasure. These are the levers, the powers, which he will have to make use of, in the execution of his plans.

In medicine, these two sciences have a marked correspondence. We are to study first the passive being, the physical state of man, and all the variations which occur in the living machine, from the influence either of external or internal causes. We are afterwards to understand the active principles, the powers which reside in organization, so as not to counteract them, to keep down such as are hurtful, and to stimulate such as are likely to lead to useful changes.

Considering the work as a whole, it appears to me to contain a necessary remedy for two kinds of political poison, one of which is distributed by the *Sceptical*, the other the *Dogmatical*.

I understand by the *Sceptical*, those who hold that there are no fixed and universal principles in legislation, that all is conjectural, that tradition is the only guide, that we must leave the laws as they are, and that, in a word, political writers are but a dangerous kind of romance writers, who are able to overthrow, but are not able to build up, – there being no foundation of moral certainty.

This discouraging doctrine, so flattering to egotism and to indolence, is only supported by vague ideas and badly-defined terms: for when we have stated the whole object of the laws in one single expression – the *prevention of evil* – it results, that as human nature is the same everywhere,[8] subject to the same ills and directed by the same motives, there ought to be some general principles which would serve for the ground-work of science. What has been done proves what may be done. Has not the empire of evil been subdued in part, and narrowed and weakened by the successful inroads of prudence and experience? Have we not seen legislation following, with slow steps, the progress of civilization, developing its powers, softening its aspects, acknowledging its mistakes – and meliorated by time? And why should errors in that career prove more numerous than in others?

All the arts, all the sciences have had the same gradations to go through. True philosophy is but lately born. Locke was the first who applied it to the study of man; Beccaria to some branches of legislation; and Mr. Bentham to a whole system. In the condition of the science now, provided with new instruments, with definitions, with nomenclatures, with classifications, and with methods, we must no longer compare it with what it was in the day of its

[8] See Chapter on Utility, p.139, where the Rev. Mr. Colton's discovery is mentioned. N. [Neal's reference to his edition of *Principles of Legislation*, p.139.]

feebleness, poverty, and uncertainty, when there was not even a general division, when the different parts were confounded together, and when offences, the first elements of law, were piled away under the most vague denominations.

As to the *Dogmatical*, they form a variety of sects, and consequently of hostile sects; but in politics they are all inspired. They believe, they command others to believe, and they do not vouchsafe to reason. They have their professions of faith and their magical words – such as equality, liberty, passive-obedience, divine right, rights-of-man, political-justice, natural-law, social-contracts. They have unlimited maxims, universal rules for government, which they apply without distinction, to the past and to the present – since from the elevated station they occupy, they are accustomed to look, not upon the individual but upon the species; and the happiness of one generation ought not to weigh against a sublime theory. Their impatience to act is in proportion to their incapability of doubting, and their intrepid vanity leads them to employ as much violence in what they do, as there is of despotism in what they think.

Nothing can be more opposite to such a dogmatical and peremptory mode of procedure than the system of Mr. Bentham. He was the first to arrange sympathies and antipathies among the false principles of reasoning, and teach a process of moral-arithmetic, whereby all the pains and all the pleasures, and all the circumstances that influence the sensibility are calculated; to tolerate no law which was unaccompanied with its rationale; to refute all the fallacies by which present and individual interests were to be sacrificed to distant and abstract interests. In fine he it is who would not suffer the smallest atom of evil to fall upon the head of the most abandoned malefactor, but on the ground of well-considered necessity. And he is so far from being arbitrary, so satisfied that we cannot hope to provide for everything, that in treating of the laws which are regarded by him as the best, and most indisputably good, he refuses to make them permanent for a fixed period – to encroach upon the rights of posterity. His system, which is always moderate and always accompanied by a *rationale*, wears a less imposing look therefore, and appears to be endowed with less energy than those of more dogmatical writers.[9]

[9] *Plus fecit qui judicium abstulit quam qui meruit. Sen.* D.

He does not flatter that slothful temper which would learn every thing by a formula or concentrate everything in a few brilliant phrases; he may be unattractive to such as love not the slow operation of the scales and dividers; and he will be sure to stir up the infallibles, by exposing the emptiness of their magisterial talk. '*How many things in a law?*' said he, on finishing his introduction. And assuredly we shall not have comprehended him, nor profited by his principles, if we do not also exclaim after going through his great work – *How many things in a law!*

However great may be the influence therefore to be expected from his writings, it is not probable that they will become popular. They teach a new science; but they teach also the difficulties of a new science. They give certainty to the labours of judgment; but they exact a studious reflection. To accomplish their purpose, disciples are needed; but unhappily for the great work, teachers only are to be met with in the science of legislation.

Fortunate are they, whom the study of this shall render more circumspect and slow in production. Their meditations being concentrated for a long time, will acquire substance and strength.

Facility is the snare of ordinary minds. No great thing is produced with ease. Meteors, that are lighted up in the sudden combustion of the atmosphere, may dazzle for a moment – but it is only for a moment – and they pass away forever, and leave no trace of their path. He who distrusts his first conceptions and does not evaporate too soon, fortifies his talent by all that he withholds from the indulgence of precipitate vanity; and the respect that he shows for the judgment of the enlightened is a sure guarantee of his own merit.[10]

[10] The passage from Dumont reads thus. I preserve it merely to show, out of his own mouth, how entirely he deserves what I have said of him in a previous note. He is aiming at a simile – and at a sort of antithesis at the same time – and he misses both.

'La facilité est le piège des hommes médiocres et ne produit jamais rien de grand. *Ces météors*, créations subites d'une atmosphère enflammée brillent un instant et s'éteignent sans laisser de trace. Mais *celui* qui se défie de ses premières conceptions, et qui ne *s'évapore* pas de bonne heure, donne à son talent tout ce qu'il refuse aux jouissances précoces de la vanité; et ce respect qu'il témoigne pour le jugement des hommes éclairés, est un garant sûr de celui qu'il méritera pour lui-même.' N. [Errors in Neal's French transcription corrected.]

INDEX TO TEXT

Heat Transfer — Minneapolis 1991

Elmer L. Gaden, series editor

Salim B. Yilmaz and Brian G. Volintine, volume editors

Maura Mullen, publications production manager

M. Aboye
Michael A. Adewumi
B. Adroguer
C.M. Allison
Samim Anghaie
B.N. Antar
Z.I. Antoniak
J.M. Bates
S. Bourdon
Neima Brauner
George Breber
B.J. Buescher
L. Catton
P. Chatelard
F.S. Chavez
John C. Chen
F.B. Cheung
Kenneth W. Childs
D. Chisholm
H.P. Chou
William Chu
R.D. Coffield
M.F. Cooper
M.L. Corradini
K.J. DeWitt
A.A. Debhi
Vijay K. Dhir
R.B. Dirling
P.E. Domagala
Suisheng Dou
Christine Doughty
M.J. Driscoll
D.M. France
J.T. Freire
G. Fu
G. Geoffroy
M.M. Golay
R. Gonzalez
R.O. Griffith
S. Hagen
Robert J. Hammersley
Mohammad Z. Hasan
G.L. Hawkes
Robert E. Henry
Blaine Herb
W. Hering
P. Hoffman
R.A. Holzl
M.L. Hou
Scott Huckerby
I. Huhtiniemi
Mamoru Ishii
P. Issacci
J.A. Jendrzejczyk
A.E. Kassem
M.S. Kazimi
George T. Klopp
P. Kuan
Tomoaki Kunigi
M. Kwaji
Sung Jin Lee
Gerard M. Ludtka
David Moalem Maron
Matl Merilo
Masaki Misawa
Darren Mitchell
Leksono Mucharam
K. Muller
Ralph A. Nelson
Hee Cheon No
J.E. O'Brien
N.T. Obot
Chan Y. Paik
C. Pan
G.C. Park
Hyunjae Park
James E. Park
Kemal O. Pasamehmetoglu
K.A. Pauley
B.S. Pei
A. Pernsteiner
Martin G. Plys
Michael Z. Podowski
A. Porracchia
Karsten Pruess
N. Rashidnia
J. Rempe
K.J. Renken
J. Rest
Kamiel Rezkallah
R.D. Rovang
N.A. Russell
G. Schanz
A. Schatz
J.E. Schmidt
G. Schumacher
F. Seibert
L. Sepold
Ariel Sharon
Chunkuan Shih
A.M. Silveria
D.Y. Sohn
Rusi P. Taleyarkhan
G.L. Thinnes
J.C. Thomeo
Marvin J. Thurgood
N.E. Todreas
Kemal Tuzla
Asim Ulke
P. Villalibre
M.W. Wambsganss
J.R. Wang
Taylor G. Wang
K.E. Washington
B.J. Webb
C.J. Westbye
Carl L. Wheeler
Lawrence E. Wiles
S. Yesilyurt
S.A. Zawadzki

Inquiries regarding the publication of Symposium Series Volumes should be directed to
Dr. Elmer L. Gaden, Jr., series editor,
University of Virginia, Department of Chemical Engineering,
Thornton Hall, Charlottesville, Virginia 22903-2442. FAX (804) 924-6270.

Number 283

AIChE Symposium Series
1991

Volume 87

Published by
American Institute of Chemical Engineers
345 East 47 Street
New York, New York 10017

American Institute of Chemical Engineers
345 East 47 Street, New York, N.Y. 10017

ISSN 0065-8812
ISBN 0-8169-0548-7